Cherokee

Verbs

The Four Stem Forms

JW WEBSTER

This work is licensed under a
Creative Commons Attribution 4.0
International License
https://creativecommons.org/licenses/by-nc-nd/4.0/

Copyright © 2023, JW Webster
ThinkCherokee LLC

NO PART OF THIS DOCUMENT IN WHOLE OR IN PART MAY BE COPIED, SOLD, OR REPRODUCED
WITHOUT THE EXPRESS WRITTEN CONCENT OF THE AUTHOR

1.0 LAYOUT

1.1 TONE MARKING

In Cherokee words, vowels carry length and tone—consonants do not. Therefore, in this guidebook--tone marking is placed above each vowel using my own adaptation of the number system that was presented in the Cherokee-English Dictionary, DF.

If the vowel is a short syllable—a single numeral representation of the tone is placed above that vowel.

E.g. na^{2}, 'that'

If the vowel is long syllable—the numeral tone representation is doubled and placed above that vowel.

E.g. tsi^{22}sdu^{2}, 'rabbit'

(The first syllable is long and the second is pronounced short)

Using the number system to mark tone and length, it is much easier to read the word more accurately by allowing tone and length to be presented together in the same area apart from the syllables themselves.

1.2 ASPIRATION

All aspirated consonants are marked by a preceding /h/.

E.g. hy, hl, etc.

Aspirated vowels (a, e, i, o, u, v) are represented by the syllabary characters ha, he, hi, ho, hu, and hv.

1.3 SILENT CHARACTERS

In this guidebook, all silent vowels are marked with a superscript 0 (^{0}).

E.g. go^{22}hwe^{22}li^{2} 'book' is frequently pronounced with the final vowel /i/ dropped and to show this vowel deletion—a superscript 0 is marked as shown below.

E.g. go^{22}hwe^{22}li^{0} ᎪᏪᎵ

2.0 CHEROKEE TONES

2.1 Level Tones:
- (1) low
- (2) mid or default
- (3) high
- (4) derivational tone or super-high

2.2 Contour Tones:
- (23) rising
- (32) falling
- (21) low-fall

Did you know that you already use Cherokee tones when you speak English? Below are isolated examples of the same tones used in English intonation.

2.3 Level Tone Cognates

(1)	u^{11}h... (when thinking)
(2)	I^{2}t's
(3)	Wha^{33}t??
(4)	No^{4}! (when aggrevated)

2.4 Contour Tone Cognates

(21)	Da^{21}ng! (unsympathetic/sarcastic)
(23)	Ri^{23}ght?
(32)	Ri^{32}ght!

2.5 English Sentences (With Tone Marking)

1) I^{2} ca^{22}n't be^{2}lie^{32}ve he^{2} di^{22}d tha^{2}t!
2) I^{2}s tha^{2}t fo^{2}r me^{23}?

2.6 Yes! You Already Use Cherokee Tones

Below are examples of single English words and by altering their tones (intonation) the expressed meanings are changed.

$Ye^{2}s$	neutral;uninterested
$Ye^{32}s$	positive response; 'I agree'
$Ye^{23}s$	question;eliciting a response
$Ye^{34}s$	disappointment;'Is it a yes??'
$Ye^{44}s$	aggravated; irritated response
$Ye^{3223}s$	carry on; 'I'm listening...'
$Ye^{2332}s$	reserved; indicating doubt

2.7 Frequency

Some tones occur more frequent than others.

(2) most common tone (default)

(3) very common ($-o^{33}$ʔi, $-e^{33}$ʔi)

(4) not very common (derivational tone)

$ga^{11}na^{3}$ʔli^{2}	'castrated animal'
$ga^{11}na^{44}li^{2}$	'lazy'
$ga^{2}du^{3}$	'on top'
$ga^{44}du^{3}$	'bread'

(21) not very common
($a^{21}gi^{2}$–, 'first person pronoun'/ $-sgo^{21}$, 'question suffix')

(23) very common (only occurs on long vowels)

(32) very common (only occurs on long vowels)

2.8 Derivational or Super-High Tone (4)

Rule: The super-high tone (4) is only found on the right-most long vowel of a word.

Examples:

1)	a^{4}ʔdv^{3},	'young animal' (litter/hatched)
2)	a^{2}ʔni^{44}dv^{3},	'young animals'
3)	e^{44}gwa^{3},	'large'
4)	wa^{2}hya^{2}ni^{44}dv^{0},	'Young Wolf'

In (1) and (3) above, another rule is governing over the rule that states the (4) tone can only be found on the right-most long vowel of a word. Since (1) and (3) above are both two syllable words consisting of short syllables--the (4) tone is placed on the first syllable of the word because the governing rule states that Cherokee words cannot end with long syllables.

2.9 Practicing Tone Application

The examples below have the same number of syllables in both Cherokee and English. Practice saying each English translation with the Cherokee tones that correspond with each syllable.

1) He^{3}llo^{2}! Ho^{22}w a^{33}re yo^{2}u
si^{3}yo^{2} to^{22}hi^{33}tsu^{2}

2) I^{22}t's ju^{23}st fi^{2}ne.
o^{22}si^{23}gwu^{2}

3) me^{22}di^{32}ci^{2}ne
nv^{22}wo^{32}ti^{2}

2.10 Examples of Cherokee Tone

(11) low-falling tone: (occurs only on long vowels)
sv^{11}gi^{2}, 'onion'   ko^{11}sdu^{2}, 'ashes'

(2) mid/default tone: (occurs on long or short vowels)
long vowel: yv^{22}gi^{2}, 'fork'   short vowel: a^{2}le^{3}, 'and'

(3) high tone: (occurs on long or short vowels)
long: ge^{33}ga^{2}, 'I'm going'   short: i^{2}tse^{3} 'new'

(4) derivational/super-high tone (occurs only on long vowels)
i^{2}yu^{44}sdi^{0}, 'like'   e^{33}gwa^{2}, 'large'

(23) rising: (occurs only on long vowels)
e^{23}ha^{2}, 'she/he's living'   ko^{23}la^{2}, 'bone'

(32) falling tone: (occurs only on long vowels)
ge^{23}do^{32}ʔa^{2},   'I'm going around'
a^{21}li^{0}sda^{32}yv^{22}hv^{3}sga^{2},   'She/he's eating a meal'

2.11 What? No Tone Markings

Cherokee is tonal and without a regular system of recording tone—students have no reference for pronunciation. Using the English tonal cognates given to you previously in this section—it is possible to isolate what your specific Cherokee tones would sound like.

If you are looking up a word in a dictionary other than The Cherokee-English Dictionary, DF, you have no idea how that word sounds. Remember! The tones are just as important as the vowels themselves. Learn the tones now and strive for accuracy because this is key to being understood.

If you are using a source that provides a voice recording of the pronunciation but does not supply the tone markings of a particular word, like many of the entries found at cherokeedictionary.net—listen to the word several times and listen for long and short vowels first. Then listen to tone patterns and mark them.

3.0 PRONUNCIATION GUIDE

3.1 VOWELS:	Ꭰ,	Ꭱ,	Ꭲ,	Ꭳ,	Ꭴ,	Ꭵ
Phonetic:	a,	e,	i,	o,	u,	v
Pronunciation	awe	ay	ee	oh	oo	uh

3.2 CONSONANTS

The consonants stem from the six vowels shown above. Presented below are the consonants and how they are pronounced with the vowels. For those sounds that have a corresponding English example, those words are presented with parentheses around the part of the word that contains the Cherokee sound. For other sounds that did not have a corresponding English equivalent, a simple "sounds like" example has been given.

Ꭶ (go)ne	Ꭸ (gue)ss	Ꭹ s(ki)	Ꭺ go	Ꭻ goo	Ꭼ (gu)
Ꭽ (ha)ll	Ꭾ (hea)vy	Ꭿ he	Ꮀ hoe	Ꮁ who	Ꮂ (hu)nt
Ꮃ law	Ꮄ (le)ver	Ꮅ lee	Ꮆ low	Ꮇ Lou	Ꮈ (lu)ck
Ꮉ (Mo)lly	Ꮊ (me)t	Ꮋ me	Ꮌ mow	Ꮍ moo	
Ꮎ (no)t Ꮏ hnaw	Ꮐ na Ꮑ (ne)t	Ꮒ knee	Ꮓ no	Ꮔ new	Ꮕ (nu)t
Ꮖ (qua)ntity	Ꮗ kweh	Ꮘ kwee	Ꮙ (quo)te	Ꮚ kwoo	Ꮛ kwuh
Ꮜ (sa)w	Ꮞ (se)t	Ꮟ see	Ꮠ sew	Ꮡ sue	Ꮢ (su)m
Ꮣ (do)ll	Ꮥ (de)bt	Ꮧ dee	Ꮩ doe	Ꮪ due	Ꮫ (du)ck
Ꮭ tlaw	Ꮮ tleh	Ꮯ Quie(tly)	Ꮰ tlow	Ꮱ tloo	Ꮲ tluh
Ꮳ jaw	Ꮴ jay	Ꮵ jee	Ꮶ (jo)ke	Ꮷ (Ju)ne	Ꮸ (ju)nk
Ꮹ (wa)ll	Ꮺ (we)st	Ꮻ we	Ꮼ (wo)'nt	Ꮽ wou)nd	Ꮾ (wha)t
Ꮿ (yo)nder	Ᏸ (ye)s	Ᏹ (yie)ld	Ᏺ (yol)k	Ᏻ you	Ᏼ (yu)ck

3.3 Special Sounds Due To Vowel Deletion

hw,	as (wh) in cool whip “Stewie Griffin”	
hy,	as (hu) in hue, huge, and human	
khk,	as in (ckg) in background	
	de^{33}ki^{0}gi^{22}lo^{33}ʔa^{2},	'he/she is washing (flexible items)'
ks,	as (x) in tax	
	tsu^{22}ka^{0}sv^{23}sdi^{2}	'smoke'
kd	as (ckd) in backdoor	
	kv^{0}di^{3}ha^{2}	'he/she is using it'
kt	as (ckt) in quick turn	
	sv^{22}ka^{0}ta^{2}	'apple'
skw,	as (squ) in squander and square	
	squu^{3}	’too/also’
dl	as (dl) in cold last night	
	a^{22}dla^{2}	'rubber'
ts	as (ts) in cuts and lights	
tskw	as (tsqu) in quit squawking	
ʔ	This symbol represents a (glottal stop). This is when you are speaking and the sound is abruptly cut off and then you continue speaking again.	

English example: Uh–oh!

The soundless space between (Uh) and (oh) is known as a glottal stop.

4.0 VERBS LAYOUT

The verbs listed in the next section are modeled after the layout of the CED (Cherokee-English Dictionary, DF 1975. Each entry given will be presented as shown below.

taking off flying (1)		
a^{21}hla^{2}wi^{23}di^{3}ha^{2} (2)	ᎠᏝᏫᏗᎭ	one is taking off flying
		(8) /h/ & /ʔ/ alternation
ga^{2}dla^{2}wi^{23}di^{3}ha^{2} (3)	ᎦᏜᏫᏗᎭ	
u^{21}hla^{2}wi^{22}dv^{22}hv^{23}ʔi^{2} (4)	ᎤᏝᏫᏛᎲᎢ	
a^{21}hla^{2}wi^{22}di^{23}sgo^{3}ʔi^{2} (5)	ᎠᏝᏫᏗᏍᎪᎢ	
ha^{2}hla^{2}wi^{23}da^{2} (6)	ᎭᏝᏫᏓ	
u^{22}hla^{2}wi^{22}di^{0}hdi^{2} (7)	ᎤᏝᏫᏗᏗ	

The English translation for the verb will given first in Bold, as shown in (1). The first entry directly under the English translation is the third person present tense form of the verb in Cherokee, as shown in (2). This will also be the form of the verb you will reference in order to determine whether the verb is Set A or Set B by default. Forms (3)-(8) are listed below.

(3) The first person present tense form of the verb
(4) The third person past tense form of the verb
(5) The incompletive form of the verb in the habitual tense
(6) The command form of the verb
(7) The infinitive form of the verb
(8) Any special information regarding the verb will be given in bold. In (8) above, the special information; /h/ & /ʔ/ alternation is telling you that there is a difference in pronunciation between first person and third person. Those differences are also shown in bold.

Classifying Pronouns

Set A (Shared Experience)

- **/a-/ verbs**

    - Highly frequent verbs that are performed anywhere and at various times.

ᎠᏑᎵᎠ	a^{33}su^{22}li^{23}ʔa^{2}	one is putting on pants
ᎠᏏᏁᎦ	a^{33}si^{22}ne^{33}ga^{2}	one is backing up
ᎠᏲᏢᏍᎦ	*a^{2}yo^{22}hlv^{3}sga^{2}	one is carving

* It is important to keep in mind that the determination of what is high or low frequency was and is (to some degree) governed by traditional Keetoowah Society. Historically, we would have seen our kin folks carving much more frequently than in today's assimilated society. Knowing that only a few speakers remaining today fully understand the distinction between /a-/ and /ga-/ verbs makes it very clear that assimilation has caused our own people to no longer classify (or think) in Cherokee. These types of "culturally" classified verbs should be updated to reflect the frequency of current society if we wish to bring back traditional thought processes to ensure the survival of our language. This is but one feature of our language that has been over lexicalized.

- **/ga-/ verbs**

    - Less frequent verbs that are rarely observed being performed.

ᎦᏕᎠ	ga^{2}de^{33}ʔa^{2}	one is removing it (from a hanging position)
ᎦᏕᏯᏍᏗᎭ	ga^{2}de^{23}ya^{0}sdi^{23}ha^{2}	one is turning it (car, bike, etc.)
ᎦᏚᎲᏍᎦ	ga^{33}du^{22}hv^{3}sga^{2}	one is baking it

In this verb the /g/ pronoun connects directly to the incorporated noun 'gadu' meaning, 'bread'.

Set B (Personal Experience)

- **/u(w)-/ verbs**

ᎤᏑᎳ u^{33}su^{22}la^{2} one is wearing pants

He or She is wearing a specific pair of pants that no one else can be wearing, and for that reason alone this verb is classified as Personal Experience.

ᎤᏲᏏᎭ u^{21}yo^{33}si^{3}ha^{3} one is hungry

He of She is experiencing hunger and there is no human way for anyone else to know exactly what he or she feels at that moment and he or she more than likely is craving something that another may or may not want to eat.

Vowel Length & Pronoun Attachment

[g(a)-] Verbs

If the first syllable of the stem is short, the pronoun /ga-/ will be long.

E.g. ga^{22}**sa^{2}**do^{32}ya^{0}sga^{2} one is pushing it
ga^{33}**sv^{2}**hntv^{3}sga^{2} one is piling it

If the first syllable of the stem is long, the pronoun /ga-/ will be short.

E.g. ga^{2}**we^{33}**hli^{23}ha^{2} one is joking or teasing
ga^{2}**tv^{23}**hv^{3}sga^{2} one is hanging it up

If the stem does have initial tone (which will be placed on the pronoun), you still follow the rules above regarding vowel length.

E.g. ga^{33}**sgwo^{2}**ʔi^{2}ha^{2} it is dripping

This rule applies for /g-/ verbs as well. The /g-/ verbs are still /ga-/ verbs but the stem vowel is any vowel other than /a/.

E.g. go^{32}**tsa^{2}**ne^{23}ʔa^{2} one is pulling a trigger

It is also necessary to realize how important morphology is to the study of Cherokee. It is important to know how to identify word boundaries in order to analyze tone. Look at the example below. According to the rule I just stated above, if the first syllable of the stem is long, the pronoun will be short; the verb below does not seem to follow the rule.

E.g. <u>gu</u>^{22}**hi**^{22}lo^{33}ʔa^{2}

Let's look at the morpheme boundaries of this word.

g-	Set A, third person
-u^{22}h(i^{2})-	into water
-i^{23}lo^{3}ʔa^{2}	repeatedly right now [repeatedly conditional suffix]

You can see that the syllable after the pronoun [/u/] is long and has a (^{22}) tone. This tone is lexical, meaning that it must stay in order to retain the meaning. Since the pronoun is a consonant alone it cannot carry tone. The third syllable is /h(i)/ and its vowel has been fused with the /i/ vowel of the conditional suffix.

In this case, the first vowel is pronounced and the reason the next syllable appears to not be short is because it fused with the conditional suffix. This understanding will become more clear as you work with the Root Word Method.

Stems & What They Express

The Keetoowah language expresses when an action happened by using tense suffixes. These are small word parts that are placed on the end of verb roots. These suffix endings are also connected to stems that are conditioned for these time frames as shown below.

Incompletive Stem: The action is happening, happens, was happening, or will be happening.

This stem is also the Present Tense and the Habitual Tense entries given in the CED (Cherokee-English Dictionary, DF 1975). The only difference between the two is that sometimes they use different root suffixes in order to alter the focus but the stem itself is still the same.

a^{21}ti^{2}yo^{23}hi^{3}ha^{2}	She's arguing
a^{21}ti^{2}yo^{23}hi^{3}ho^{33}ʔi^{2}	She argues
a^{21}ti^{2}yo^{23}hi^{3}hv^{23}ʔi^{2}	She was arguing
a^{21}ti^{2}yo^{23}hi^{3}he^{33}sdi^{2}	She will be arguing
a^{21}de^{33}yo^{2}ha^{2}	She's going around
a^{21}de^{33}yo^{2}ho^{33}ʔi^{2}	She goes around
a^{21}de^{33}yo^{2}hv^{23}ʔi^{2}	She was going around
a^{21}de^{33}yo^{2}he^{33}sdi^{2}	She will be going around

Incompletive Nouns:

a^{21}ti^{2}yo^{23}hi^{3}hv^{44}hi^{2}	quarrel
a^{21}de^{33}yo^{2}hv^{44}hi^{2}	a curve
na^{22}ti^{2}yo^{23}hi^{3}hv^{44}na^{2}	the one not arguing

Expressing While/When:

a^{21}ti^{2}yo^{23}hi^{3}hv^{44}ʔi^{2}	while/when she was arguing
a^{21}de^{33}yo^{2}hv^{44}ʔi^{2}	while/when she going around

Completive Stem: The action happened, the action will have happened, a future command, will happen, or was going to happen.

u^{21}ti^{2}yo^{23}hlv^{33}ʔi^{2}	She argued
u^{21}ti^{2}yo^{23}hle^{33}sdi^{2}	She will have argued
ha^{22}ti^{2}yo^{23}hlv^{33}ʔi^{2}	Argue later!
ta^{22}ti^{2}yo^{23}hli^{3}	You will argue
ta^{22}ti^{2}yo^{23}hlv^{33}ʔi^{2}	You were going to argue

Completive Nouns:

go^{22}tlv^{22}hnv^{44}hi^{2}	butter
u^{22}tv^{2}so^{2}hnv^{44}hi^{2}	fully grown (adult)
a^{21}ta^{2}le^{22}sv^{44}hi^{2}	a hole

Completive Adjectives:

u^{22}yo^{22}hu^{22}sv^{44}hi^{2}	dead
tsu^{21}di^{22}ga^{2}le^{23}yo^{32}tsv^{44}hi^{2}	scattered

The Completive Stem also takes most of the conditional suffixes (aspects).

a^{21}de^{23}yo^{32}hli^{23}lo^{3}ʔa^{2}	She's going around repeatedly
gi^{22}na^{0}ti^{2}yo^{23}hla^{32}ne^{22}lv^{23}ʔi^{2}	You and I argued for it

Immediate Stem: The action needs to happen now (as a command) or the action just now happened (the recent past)

ha^{2}ti^{2}yo^{23}ga^{2} Argue!
tsi^{2}ha^{2}ti^{2}yo^{22}ga^{2} You just now argued

ha^{2}de^{22}ya^{2}ga^{2} Go around it!
tsi^{2}ha^{2}de^{22}ya^{2}ga^{2} You just now went around it

Immediate Plurals:
Remember /di-/ if the action is unreal and /de-/ if the action is real.

di^{2}hi^{2}go^{22}li^{23}ya^{2} → ti^{2}go^{22}li^{23}ya^{2} Examine/Read them.
tsi^{2}de^{33}hi^{2}go^{22}li^{23}ya^{0} You just now read them

Immediate Stem Expresses Ability:

yi^{2}ha^{2}ti^{2}yo^{23}ga^{2} You can argue
yi^{2}ha^{2}de^{22}ya^{2}ga^{2} You can go around it

Other Expressions:

ga^{2}do^{23}hv^{3} tsi^{2}ga^{2}ga^{11}ta^{2}hv^{23}na^{2} Why did I turn around?
tle^{33}sdi^{2} tsi^{22}ha^{2}tse^{23}wi^{2} Don't spill it!

tla^{3} yi^{2}ga^{22}tsi^{2}lu^{11}ga^{2} I'm not able to kill it

Infinitive Stem: The infinitive form reflects someone's state of doing the action e.g. 'It's hard for him to sit still'. This is merely someone's belief or informed judgment about what they have observed about the subject performing the action. This stem is also used to reflect ability, obligation, and is also used for deriving nouns.

u^{22}ti^{2}yo^{23}sdi^{2} for her to argue
u^{22}de^{23}ya^{32}sdi^{2} for her to be going around it

Infinitive Obligation:

u^{22}ti^{2}yo^{23}sdi^{2} u^{21}du^{22}li^{23}ha^{2} She wants to argue

u^{22}ti^{2}yo^{44}sdi^{2} She has to argue

The (^{44}) tone change is always placed on the rightmost long vowel of the stem.

tsa^{22}ti^{2}yo^{44}sdi^{2} ge^{22}se^{33}sdi^{0} sa^{2}na^{33}le^{44}ʔi^{2}
You will have to argue tomorrow.

Infinitive Nouns:

u^{22}ti^{2}yo^{23}sdi^{2}, for her to argue → a^{2}ti^{2}yo^{23}sdi^{2}, argument

u^{22}de^{23}ya^{32}sdi^{2}, for her to go around it → a^{2}de^{23}ya^{0}sdi^{2}, detour

These nouns are known as having no tone change and the Set A pronoun is short instead of long. This is another tonal way of reflecting unreal action and change of word class.

Infinitive Ability:

ge^{22}tsa^{22}ti^{2}yo^{44}sdi^{2} yi^{22}gi^{2} — If you are able to argue

ge^{22}tsa^{2}de^{23}ya^{44}sdi^{2} — You are able to go around it

Infinitive Place Nouns:

tsu^{22}na^{0}de^{23}yo^{32}hli^{23}lo^{32}sdi^{44}yi^{2} — race track
(Literally, place where they go around repeatedly)

tsu^{22}na^{0}da^{22}ti^{2}yo^{23}sdi^{44}yi^{2} — Senate
(Literally, place where they argue amongst themselves)

Tone Importance:

Imagine you are in law school and you might say something like…

o^{44}sdv^{2} di^{2}gi^{22}ti^{2}yo^{23}sdi^{2}
My arguing is good.

This form does not require a tone change on the right-most long vowel. By adding the Set B first person pronoun it has been possessed and by adding the “unreal” plural prefix it now reflects the current and previous number of “arguings”.

You may also say something similar that does require a tone change...

> a^{22}se^{3} o^{44}sdv^{0} di^{2}gi^{22}ti^{2}yo^{44}sdi^{2}
> I have to argue good.

Here, a^{22}se^{3} 'must' is used to condition the meaning for "obligation". This conditioning is not required but many older speakers prefer this speech pattern to clarify exactly what they are wanting to say.

The (^{44}) tone is applied to right-most long vowel to give the infinitive verb the obligatory meaning.

Verb Conjugation

Let's conjugate the verb 'roping it'

What is our pronoun for third person present tense? a^{22}, a^{21}

Incompletive Stem **[-si^{23}la^{3}di^{23}ʔ-]**

happening: a^{21}si^{23}la^{3}di^{23}ʔa^{2}
happens: **unreal** **a^{22}si^{23}la^{3}di^{32}sgo^{33}ʔi^{2}**
was happening: a^{21}si^{23}la^{3}di^{32}sgv^{23}ʔi^{2}
will be happening: **unreal** **a^{22}si^{23}la^{3}di^{32}sge^{33}sdi^{2}**

Completive Stem **[-si^{23}la^{3}d--]**

happened: u^{21}si^{23}la^{3}dv^{23}ʔi^{2}
will have happened: **unreal** **dv^{22}si^{23}la^{3}di^{2}**
make it happen later: **unreal** **wa^{22}si^{23}la^{3}dv^{22}ʔi^{2}**
was going to happen: **unreal** **dv^{22}si^{23}la^{3}dv^{23}ʔi^{2}**

Immediate Stem **[-si^{23}la^{3}d-]**

needs to happen now (as a command): **unreal** **hi^{2}si^{22}la^{2}da^{2}**
just now happened (the recent past): tsi^{2}hi^{2}si^{22}la^{2}da^{2} chi^{2}si^{22}la^{2}da^{2}
no^{23}gwu^{3} tsi^{22}gi^{2}

Infinitive Stem **[-si^{23}la^{3}d]**

for it to happen: **unreal** **u^{22}si^{22}la^{2}di^{11}sdi^{2}**
it has to happen: **unreal** **a^{22}se^{3} u^{22}si^{22}la^{2}di^{44}sdi^{2}**
it is able to happen: **unreal** **gv^{22}wa^{2}si^{22}la^{2}di^{44}sdi^{2}**

Root Word Method

EXAMPLE VERB: 'WASHING'

ᎫᎯᎶᎠ gu^{22}hi^{22}lo^{33}ʔa^{2} he/she is washing it	ᎫᎢᎶᎠ gu^{2}ʔi^{22}lo^{33}ʔa^{2} I'm washing it

INCOMPLETIVE STEM

g-	SetA 3P	g-	SetA 1P
-u^{22}-	into water	-u^{2}-	into water
-h-	action focus	-ʔ-	stationary action focus
-i^{22}lo^{33}ʔ-	repeat condition (INC)	-i^{22}lo^{33}ʔ-	repeat condition (INC)
a^{2}	present tense	a^{2}	present tense

Note: The grayed out section in the table above shows the distinction between first and third person in the present tense. This process is known as */h/ & /ʔ/ Alternation.* **/h/ & /ʔ/ Alternation**, is a process where /h/ signifies that the action is being done by a single third person and /ʔ/ conveys that the action is being performed by first person. It is important to note that this only occurs between first person and third person and will not affect the pronouns of other persons.

ᎫᎯᎶᏍᎪᎢ
gu^{22}hi^{22}lo^{33}sgo^{33}ʔi^{2}
he/she washes it

g-	SetA 3P
-u^{22}-	into water
-h-	action focus
-i^{22}lo^{33}sg-	repeat condition (INC) + subject/object focus root suffix
-o^{33}ʔi^{2}	habitual tense

COMPLETIVE STEM

ᎤᏍᎯᎶᎥᎢ u^{21}wu^{22}hi^{22}lo^{33}ʔv^{23}ʔi^{2} he/she washed it		ᎠᏊᎯᎶᎥᎢ a^{21}gwu^{22}hi^{22}lo^{33}ʔv^{23}ʔi^{2} I washed it	
u^{21}w-	SetB 3P	a^{21}gw-	SetB 1P
-u^{22}-	into water	-u^{22}-	into water
-h-	action focus	-h-	action focus
-i^{22}lo^{33}ʔ-	repeat condition (CMP)	-i^{22}lo^{33}ʔ-	repeat condition (CMP)
-v^{23}ʔi^{2}	past tense (experienced)	-v^{23}ʔi^{2}	past tense (experienced)

IMMEDIATE STEM - COMMAND

ᎱᎯᎶᏣ hu^{22}hi^{22}lo^{23}tsa^{2} Wash it!	
h-	SetA 2P
-u^{22}-	into water
-h-	action focus
-i^{22}lo^{23}ts-	repeat condition (IMM)
-a^{2}	present tense

IMMEDIATE STEM - RECENT PAST

ᏥᎱᎯᎶᏣ tsi^{2}hu^{22}hi^{22}lo^{22}tsa^{2} You just washed it	
tsi^{2}-	famililar prefix (meaning familiar event in time)
-h-	SetA 2P
-u^{22}-	into water
-h-	action focus
-i^{22}lo^{22}ts-	repeat condition (IMM)
-a^{2}	present tense

INFINITIVE STEM

ᎤᏭᎯᎶᏍᏗ u^{22}wu^{22}hi^{22}lo^{11}sdi^{2} For him/her to wash it	
u^{22}w-	SetB 3P
-u^{22}-	into water
-h-	action focus
-i^{22}lo^{11}s-	repeat condition (INF)
-di^{2}	infinitive tense

thinkCHEROKEE www.thinkcherokee.com

INCOMPLETIVE STEM + CONDITIONS

ᎫᎯᎶᎢᏍᏏᎭ gu^{22}hi^{22}lo^{33}ʔi^{23}si^{3}ha^{2} he/she is washing it again	
g-	SetA 3P
-u-	into water
-h-	action focus
-iloʔ-	repeat condition (CMP)
-isih-	again condition (INC)
-a	present tense

ᎫᎯᎶᎢᎶᏍᎬᎢ gu^{22}hi^{22}lo^{33}ʔi^{23}lo^{32}sgv^{23}ʔi^{2} he/she was washing it repeatedly	
g-	SetA 3P
-u-	into water
-h-	action focus
-iloʔ-	repeat condition (CMP)
-ilosg-	repeat condition (INC)
-vʔi	past tense

ᎫᎯᎶᏍᏙᏗᎭᎢ gu^{22}hi^{22}lo^{33}ʔ(i^{3})s(di)do^{3}hdi^{3}ha^{2} he/she is washing it accidentally	
g-	SetA 3P
-u-	into water
-h-	action focus
-iloʔ-	repeat condition (CMP)
-is(di)-	causative infix
-dohdih-	accidental condition (INC)
-a	present tense

ᎫᎯᎶᎣᎲᏍᎦ gu^{22}hi^{22}lo^{33}ʔ(o^{3})hv^{3}sga^{2} he/she is finishing washing it	
g-	SetA 3P
-u-	into water
-h-	action focus
-iloʔ-	repeat condition (CMP)
-(o)hvsg-	finishing condition (INC)
-a	present tense

INCOMPLETIVE STEM + CONDITIONS

ᎫᎯᎶᎢᏍᏏᎭ gu²²hi²²lo³³ʔi²³si³ha² he/she is washing it again	
g-	SetA 3P
-u-	into water
-h-	action focus
-iloʔ-	repeat condition (CMP)
-isih-	again condition (INC)
-a	present tense

ᎫᎯᎶᎢᎶᏍᎬᎢ gu²²hi²²lo³³ʔi²³lo³²sgv²³ʔi² he/she was washing it repeatedly	
g-	SetA 3P
-u-	into water
-h-	action focus
-iloʔ-	repeat condition (CMP)
-ilosg-	repeat condition (INC)
-vʔi	past tense

ᎫᎯᎶᏍᏙᏗᎭ gu^{22}hi^{22}lo^{33}ʔ(i^{3})s(di)do^{3}hdi^{3}ha^{2} he/she is washing it accidentally	
g-	SetA 3P
-u-	into water
-h-	action focus
-iloʔ-	repeat condition (CMP)
-is(di)-	causative infix
-dohdih-	accidental condition (INC)
-a	present tense

ᎫᎯᎶᎣᎲᏍᎦ gu^{22}hi^{22}lo^{33}ʔ(o^{3})hv^{3}sga^{2} he/she is finishing washing it	
g-	SetA 3P
-u-	into water
-h-	action focus
-iloʔ-	repeat condition (CMP)
-(o)hvsg-	finishing condition (INC)
-a	present tense

ᎫᎯᏝᎢᏙᎲᎢ gu^{22}hi^{22}lo^{33}ʔi^{23}do^{32}hv^{23}ʔi^{2} he/she was going around washing it	
g-	SetA 3P
-u-	into water
-h-	action focus
-iloʔ-	repeat condition (CMP)
-idoh-	finishing condition (INC)
-vʔi	present tense

ᎫᎯᏝᎡᎦ gu^{22}hi^{22}lo^{33}ʔe^{33}ga^{2} he/she is washing it as he/she goes along	
g-	SetA 3P
-u-	into water
-h-	action focus
-iloʔ-	repeat condition (CMP)
-eg-	going condition (INC)
-a	present tense

ᎫᎭᎶᏟᎦ gu²²hi²²lo³³ʔ(i²³)hli³³ga² he/she is washing it as he/she goes along	
g-	SetA 3P
-u-	into water
-h-	action focus
-iloʔ-	repeat condition (CMP)
-(i)hl-	come to condition (CMP)
-ig-	come to condition (INC)
-a	present tense

ᎫᎭᎶᏦᏅᎲᏍᎦ gu²²hi²²lo³³ʔtso³hnv²³hv³sga² he/she is taking as long as it takes to finish washing it	
g-	SetA 3P
-u-	into water
-h-	action focus
-iloʔ-	repeat condition (CMP)
-ts-	completive infix
-ohn-	finishing condition (CMP)
-vhvsg-	taking time condition (INC)
-a	present tense

© www.thinkCHEROKEE.com

ᎫᎯᎶᎢᏲᎦ gu^{22}hi^{22}lo^{33}ʔi^{23}yo^{32}ga^{2} he/she/it is becoming washed	
g-	SetA 3P
-u-	into water
-h-	action focus
-iloʔ-	repeat condition (CMP)
-iy-	quantifier infix
-x^{3}o^{32}g-	becoming condition (INC)
-a	present tense

COMPLETIVE STEM + CONDITIONS

ᎠᏬᎯᎶᎢᏍᏌᏅᎢ a²¹gwu²²hi²²lo³³ʔi²³sa³hnv²³ʔi² I washed it again	
agw-	SetB 1P
-u-	into water
-h-	action focus
-iloʔ-	repeat condition (CMP)
-isahn-	again condition (CMP)
-vʔi	past tense

ᎤᏭᎯᎶᎢᎶᏨᎢ u²¹wu²²hi²²lo³³ʔi²³lo³²tsv²³ʔi² he/she washed it repeatedly	
uw-	SetB 3P
-u-	into water
-h-	action focus
-iloʔ-	repeat condition (CMP)
-ilots-	again condition (CMP)
-vʔi	past tense

© CWY thinkCHEROKEE www.thinkcherokee.com

ᎤᏬᎯᎶᎢᏍᏙᏔᏅᎢ u^{21}wu^{22}hi^{22}lo^{33}ʔ(i^{3})s(di)do^{3}hta^{3}nv^{23}ʔi^{2} he/she accidentally washed it	
uw-	SetB 3P
-u-	into water
-h-	action focus
-iloʔ-	repeat condition (CMP)
-is(di)-	causative infix (INF)
-dohtan-	accidental condition (CMP)
-vʔi	past tense

ᎤᏬᎯᎶᏦᏅᎢ u^{21}wu^{22}hi^{22}lo^{33}(ʔ)tso^{3}hnv^{23}ʔi^{2} he/she finished washing it	
uw-	SetB 3P
-u-	into water
-h-	action focus
-ilo(ʔ)-	repeat condition (CMP)
-ts-	completive infix
-ohn-	finishing condition (CMP)
-vʔi	past tense

ᎤᏭᎯᎶᏥᏙᎸᎢ u^{21}wu^{22}hi^{22}lo^{33}(ʔ)tsi^{23}do^{32}lv^{23}ʔi^{2} he/she washed it from place-to-place	
uw-	SetB 3P
-u-	into water
-h-	action focus
-ilo(ʔ)-	repeat condition (CMP)
-ts-	completive infix
-idol-	place-to-place condition (CMP)
-vʔi	past tense

ᎤᏭᎯᎶᏅᏍᏒᎢ u^{21}wu^{22}hi^{22}lo^{23}nv^{32}sv^{23}ʔi^{2} he/she had gone and washed it	
uw-	SetB 3P
-u-	into water
-h-	action focus
-ilo(ʔ)-	repeat condition (CMP)
-n-	characterizer infix
-vs-	going condition (CMP)
-vʔi	past tense

[u^{21}wu^{22}hi^{22}lo^{33}ʔv^{33}sv^{23}ʔi^{2}] > [u^{21}wu^{22}hi^{22}lo^{33}ʔ+n+v^{33}sv^{23}ʔi^{2}]

In order to simplify the two sets of (^{33}) tones right next to each other–they are distributed by converting them to a sequence of rising and falling tones. E.g. /lo^{33}ʔnv^{33}s/ becomes /lo^{23}nv^{32}s/.

ᎤᏭᎯᎶᎢᎸᎢ u²¹wu²²hi²²lo³³ʔi²³hlv³ʔi² he/she had come and washed it	
uw-	SetB 3P
-u-	into water
-h-	action focus
-ilo(ʔ)-	repeat condition (CMP)
-ihl-	come to condition (CMP)
-vʔi	past tense

ᎤᏭᎯᎶᎢᏗᏍᎡᎢ u²¹wu²²hi²²lo³³ʔi²³di³²sv²³ʔi² he/she was about to have washed it	
uw-	SetB 3P
-u-	into water
-h-	action focus
-ilo(ʔ)-	repeat condition (CMP)
-idis-	about to condition (CMP)
-vʔi	past tense

ᎤᏭᎯᎶᎢᏢᏅᎢ u^{21}wu^{22}hi^{22}lo^{33}ʔ(i)hlv^{22}hnv^{23}ʔi^{2} he/she has come and washed it over a period of time	
uw-	SetB 3P
-u-	into water
-h-	action focus
-ilo(ʔ)-	repeat condition (CMP)
-(i)hl-	come to condition (CMP) **AS AN ASPECT JOINER**
-vhn-	taking time condition (CMP)
-vʔi	past tense

© CWY think CHEROKEE www.thinkcherokee.com

bouncing/limping

a^{21}da^{2}de^{33}ga^{2}	ᎠᏓᏕᎦ	it's bouncing/one is limping
ga^{2}da^{2}de^{33}ga^{2}	ᎦᏓᏕᎦ	I'm bouncing/I'm limping
u^{21}da^{2}di^{23}nv^{32}sv^{23}ʔi^{2}	ᎤᏓᏗᏅᏍᏒᎢ	it bounced/one limped
a^{21}da^{2}de^{33}go^{33}ʔi^{2}	ᎠᏓᏕᎪᎢ	it bounces/one limps
ha^{2}da^{2}du^{11}ga^{2}	ᎭᏓᏚᎦ	bounce!/limp!
u^{22}da^{2}di^{23}nv^{32}di^{2}	ᎤᏓᏗᏅᏗ	for it to bounce/for one to limp

e^{22}la^{2}di^{2} wu^{22}di^{23}na^{4} sgwa^{22}hle^{44}sdi^{0} u^{21}da^{2}di^{23}nv^{32}sv^{23}ʔi^{2}
ᎡᎳᏗ ᏭᏗᎾ ᏍᏆᏞᏍᏗ ᎤᏓᏗᏅᏍᏒᎢ
When he or she threw the ball down, it bounced.

bouncing it

a^{21}da^{2}di^{23}nv^{32}di^{2}ha^{2}	ᎠᏓᏗᏅᏗᎭ	one is bouncing it
u^{21}da^{2}di^{23}nv^{32}ta^{2}nv^{23}ʔ^{2}i	ᎤᏓᏗᏅᏔᏅᎢ	one bounced it
a^{21}da^{2}di^{23}nv^{32}di^{22}sgo^{33}ʔi^{2}	ᎠᏓᏗᏅᏗᏍᎪᎢ	one bounces it
ha^{2}da^{2}di^{22}nv^{11}da^{2}	ᎭᏓᏗᏅᏓ	bounce it!
u^{22}da^{2}di^{23}nv^{32}do^{2}hdi^{2}	ᎤᏓᏗᏅᏙᏗ	for one to bounce it

putting on a belt

a^{21}da^{33}dlo^{22}hi^{3}ha^{2}	ᎠᏓᏠᎯᎭ	one is putting on a belt
ga^{2}da^{33}dlo^{22}hi^{3}ha^{2}	ᎦᏓᏠᎯᎭ	I'm putting on a belt
u^{21}da^{33}dlo^{22}hlv^{23}ʔi^{2}	ᎤᏓᏠᏢᎢ	one put on a belt
a^{21}da^{33}dlo^{22}hi^{2}ho^{33}ʔi^{2}	ᎠᏓᏠᎯᎰᎢ	one puts on a belt
ha^{2}da^{11}dlo^{23}ga^{2}	ᎭᏓᏠᎦ	put on a belt!
u^{22}da^{11}dlo^{23}sdi^{2}	ᎤᏓᏠᏍᏗ	for one to put on a belt

do^{23}yu^{3} o^{44}sdv^{0} a^{2}da^{11}dlo^{23}sdi^{2} tsa^{21}gwa^{2}da^{33}dlo^{22}hlv^{23}ʔi^{2} u^{2}sv^{4}(^{4}ʔi^{2}) tsi^{2}ge^{22}sv^{23}ʔi^{2}
ᏙᏳ ᎣᏍᏛ ᎠᏓᏠᏍᏗ ᏣᏆᏓᏠᏢᎢ ᎤᏍᏒᎢ ᏥᎨᏍᏒᎢ
I put on a really good belt last night.

praying

a^{21}da^{22}do^{23}li^{32}sdi^{2}ha^{2}	ᎠᏓᏙᎵᏍᏗᎭ	one is praying
ga^{2}da^{22}do^{23}li^{32}sdi^{2}ha^{2}	ᎦᏓᏙᎵᏍᏗᎭ	I'm praying
u^{21}da^{22}do^{23}li^{32}sta^{2}nv^{23}ʔi^{2}	ᎤᏓᏙᎵᏍᏔᏅᎢ	one prayed
a^{21}da^{22}do^{23}li^{32}sdi^{22}sgo^{33}ʔi^{2}	ᎠᏓᏙᎵᏍᏗᏍᎪᎢ	one prays
ha^{2}da^{22}do^{22}li^{11}sda^{2}	ᎭᏓᏙᎵᏍᏓ	pray!
u^{22}da^{22}do^{23}li^{32}sdo^{2}hdi^{2}	ᎤᏓᏙᎵᏍᏙᏗ	for one to pray

fanning oneself

a^{21}da^{2}hno^{33}ye^{2}ha^{2}	ᎠᏓᏃᏰᎭ	one is fanning oneself
ga^{2}da^{11}no^{33}ye^{2}ha^{2}	ᎦᏓᏃᏰᎭ	I'm fanning myself
u^{21}da^{2}hno^{33}ye^{22}hv^{23}ʔi^{2}	ᎤᏓᏃᏰᎲᎢ	one fanned oneself
a^{21}da^{2}hno^{33}ye^{22}sgo^{33}ʔi^{2}	ᎠᏓᏃᏰᏍᎪᎢ	one fans oneself
ha^{2}da^{2}hno^{22}hv^{23}la^{2}	ᎭᏓᏃᎲᎳ	fan yourself!
u^{22}da^{2}hno^{22}ye^{2}hdi^{23}ʔi^{2}	ᎤᏓᏃᏰᏗᎢ	for one to fan oneself

u^{21}lv^{23}gwo^{0}di^{2}dv^{33} u^{22}da^{2}hno^{22}ye^{2}hdi^{23}ʔi^{2}
ᎤᎸᏊᏗᏛ ᎤᏓᏃᏰᏗᎢ
He or She definitely likes to fan himself or herself.

visiting

a^{21}da^{22}hwa^{2}htv^{22}hi^{23}do^{32}ha^{2}	ᎠᏓᏩᏛᎯᏙᎭ	one is visiting
ga^{2}da^{11}wa^{2}htv^{22}hi^{23}do^{32}ha^{2}	ᎦᏓᏩᏛᎯᏙᎭ	I'm visiting
u^{21}da^{22}hwa^{2}htv^{22}hi^{23}do^{32}lv^{23}ʔi^{2}	ᎤᏓᏩᏛᎯᏙᎸᎢ	one visited
a^{21}da^{22}hwa^{2}htv^{22}hi^{23}do^{32}ho^{33}ʔi^{2}	ᎠᏓᏩᏛᎯᏙᎰᎢ	one visits
ha^{2}da^{22}hwa^{2}htv^{22}hi^{23}da^{2}	ᎭᏓᏩᏛᎯᏓ	visit
u^{22}da^{22}hwa^{2}htv^{22}hi^{23}da^{32}sdi^{2}	ᎤᏓᏩᏛᎯᏓᏍᏗ	for one to visit

wi^{2}ga^{2}da^{11}wa^{0}htv^{22}hi^{23}do^{32}he^{33}sdi^{0} sa^{2}na^{33}le^{44}ʔi^{2}
ᏫᎦᏓᏩᏛᎯᏙᎮᏍᏗ ᏌᎾᎴᎢ
I'll be visiting there tomorrow.

stretching

a^{21}da^{22}hya^{32}sdi^{2}ha^{2}	ᎠᏓᏯᏍᏗᎭ	one is stretching
ga^{2}da^{11}ya^{32}sdi^{2}ha^{2}	ᎦᏓᏯᏍᏗᎭ	I'm stretching
u^{21}da^{22}hya^{32}sta^{2}nv^{23}ʔi^{2}	ᎤᏓᏯᏍᏔᏅᎢ	one stretched
a^{21}da^{22}hya^{32}sdi^{22}sgo^{33}ʔi^{2}	ᎠᏓᏯᏍᏗᏍᎪᎢ	one stretches
ha^{2}da^{22}hya^{11}sda^{2}	ᎭᏓᏯᏍᏓ	stretch
u^{22}da^{22}hya^{11}sdo^{3}hdi^{2}	ᎤᏓᏯᏍᏙᏗ	for one to stretch

ripping

a^{21}da^{22}tsa^{2}ga^{2}li^{23}ha^{2}	ᎠᏓᏣᎦᎵᎭ	it's ripping
ga^{2}da^{22}tsa^{2}ga^{2}li^{23}ha^{2}	ᎦᏓᏣᎦᎵᎭ	I'm ripping
u^{21}da^{22}tsa^{2}ga^{2}lv^{22}hv^{23}ʔi^{2}	ᎤᏓᏣᎦᎸᎲᎢ	it ripped
a^{21}da^{22}tsa^{2}ga^{2}li^{23}sgo^{3}ʔi^{2}	ᎠᏓᏣᎦᎵᏍᎪᎢ	it rips
ha^{2}da^{22}tsa^{2}ga^{2}la^{2}	ᎭᏓᏣᎦᎳ	rip
u^{22}da^{22}tsa^{2}ga^{2}hlv^{0}hdi^{2}	ᎤᏓᏣᎦᎸᏗ	for it to rip

go^{22}hwe^{22}li^{0}dv^{33} do^{23}yu^{3} a^{2}hi^{44}di^{2} ge^{22}so^{3}(^{3}ʔi^{2}) u^{22}da^{22}tsa^{2}ga^{2}hlv^{0}hdi^{23}ʔi^{2}
ᎪᏪᎵᏛ ᏙᏳ ᎠᎯᏗ ᎨᏐᎢ ᎤᏓᏣᎦᎸᏗᎢ
Paper is really easy to rip.

looking at oneself via a mirror

a^{21}da^{22}ke^{23}ha^{2}	ᎠᏓᎨᎭ	one is looking at oneself in a mirror
ga^{2}da^{11}ke^{23}ha^{2}	ᎦᏓᎨᎭ	I looked at myself in a mirror
u^{21}da^{22}ke^{23}hv^{3}ʔi^{2}	ᎤᏓᎨᎲᎢ	one looked at oneself in a mirror
a^{21}da^{22}ke^{23}sgo^{3}ʔi^{2}	ᎠᏓᎨᏍᎪᎢ	one looks at oneself in a mirror
ha^{2}da^{22}kv^{23}la^{2}	ᎭᏓᎬᎳ	look at yourself in a mirror
u^{22}da^{22}ke^{3}hdi^{2}	ᎤᏓᎨᏗ	for one to look at oneself in a mirror

taking off running

a^{21}da^{2}na^{32}wa^{0}sdi^{23}ha^{2}	ᎠᏓᎾᏩᏍᏗᎭ	one is taking off running
ga^{2}da^{2}na^{32}wa^{0}sdi^{23}ha^{2}	ᎦᏓᎾᏩᏍᏗᎭ	I'm taking off running
u^{21}da^{2}na^{32}wa^{0}sta^{2}nv^{23}ʔi^{2}	ᎤᏓᎾᏩᏍᏔᏅᎢ	one took off running
a^{21}da^{2}na^{32}wa^{0}sdi^{23}sgo^{3}ʔi^{2}	ᎠᏓᎾᏩᏍᏗᏍᎪᎢ	one takes off running
ha^{2}da^{2}na^{11}wa^{0}sda^{2}	ᎭᏓᎾᏩᏍᏓ	take off running
u^{22}da^{2}na^{11}wa^{0}sdo^{3}hdi^{2}	ᎤᏓᎾᏩᏍᏙᏗ	for one to take off running

u^{22}sga^{32}lv^{23}ha^{4}, u^{21}da^{2}na^{32}wa^{0}sta^{2}nv^{23}ʔi^{2}
ᎤᏍᎦᎸᎭ, ᎤᏓᎾᏩᏍᏔᏅᎢ
When he or she was afraid, he or she took off running.

changing

a^{21}da^{2}ne^{22}dli^{33}yv^{23}ʔa^{2}	ᎠᏓᏁᏝᏴᎠ	one is changing
ga^{2}da^{2}ne^{22}dli^{33}yv^{23}ʔa^{2}	ᎦᏓᏁᏝᏴᎠ	I'm changing
u^{21}da^{2}ne^{22}dli^{33}yv^{11}sv^{23}ʔi^{2}	ᎤᏓᏁᏝᏴᏍᏒᎢ	one changed
a^{21}da^{2}ne^{22}dli^{33}yv^{11}sgo^{33}ʔi^{2}	ᎠᏓᏁᏝᏴᏍᎪᎢ	one changes
ha^{2}da^{2}ne^{22}dli^{22}yv^{23}na^{2}	ᎭᏓᏁᏝᏴᎾ	change
u^{22}da^{2}ne^{22}dli^{33}yv^{11}sdi^{2}	ᎤᏓᏁᏝᏴᏍᏗ	for one to change

tsa^{22}da^{2}ne^{22}dli^{33}yv^{11}se^{33}s tsa^{2}da^{33}nv^{0}tv^{2} sv^{22}hi^{4} tsi^{2}ge^{22}sv^{23}ʔi^{2}
ᏣᏓᏁᏝᏴᏍᏎᏍ ᏣᏓᏅᏛ ᏍᏒᎯ ᏥᎨᏍᏒᎢ
Did you change your mind last night?

taking turns

a^{21}da^{2}ne^{22}dli^{33}yv^{11}sdi^{23}ha^{2}	ᎠᏓᏁᏝᏴᏍᏗᎭ	one is taking turns with another
ga^{2}da^{2}ne^{22}dli^{33}yv^{11}sdi^{23}ha^{2}	ᎦᏓᏁᏝᏴᏍᏗᎭ	I'm taking turns with another
u^{21}da^{2}ne^{22}dli^{33}yv^{11}sta^{2}nv^{23}ʔi^{2}	ᎤᏓᏁᏝᏴᏍᏔᏅᎢ	one took turns with another
a^{21}da^{2}ne^{22}dli^{33}yv^{11}sdi^{22}sgo^{33}ʔi^{2}	ᎠᏓᏁᏝᏴᏍᏗᏍᎪᎢ	one takes turns with another
ha^{2}da^{2}ne^{22}dli^{22}yv^{11}sda^{2}	ᎭᏓᏁᏝᏴᏍᏓ	take turns with another
u^{22}da^{2}ne^{22}dli^{33}yv^{11}sdo^{2}hdi^{2}	ᎤᏓᏁᏝᏴᏍᏙᏗ	for one to take turns with another

thinking

a^{21}da^{22}nv^{0}hte^{23}ha^{2} ᎠᏓᏅᏖᎭ one is thinking
ga^{2}da^{22}nv^{11}te^{23}ha^{2} ᎦᏓᏅᏖᎭ I'm thinking
u^{21}da^{22}nv^{0}hte^{23}hlv^{3}ʔi^{2} ᎤᏓᏅᏖᎸᎢ one thought
a^{21}da^{22}nv^{0}hte^{23}sgo^{3}ʔi^{2} ᎠᏓᏅᏖᏍᎪᎢ one thinks
ha^{2}da^{22}nv^{0}htv^{23}la^{2} ᎭᏓᏅᏛᎳ think
u^{22}da^{22}nv^{0}hte^{2}hdi^{2} ᎤᏓᏅᏖᏗ for one to think

a^{21}na^{0}da^{22}nv^{0}hte^{23}ha^{2}dv^{33} ge^{23}li^{3}ʔa^{2}
ᎠᎾᏓᏅᏖᎭᏛ ᎨᎵᎠ
They are thinking. I think.

pondering

a^{21}da^{22}nv^{0}hte^{22}hi^{23}lo^{3}ʔa^{2} ᎠᏓᏅᏖᎯᎶᎠ one is pondering
ga^{2}da^{22}nv^{11}te^{22}hi^{23}lo^{3}ʔa^{2} ᎦᏓᏅᏖᎯᎶᎠ I'm pondering
u^{21}da^{22}nv^{0}hte^{22}hi^{23}lo^{3}ʔv^{23}ʔi^{2} ᎤᏓᏅᏖᎯᎶᎥᎢ one pondered
a^{21}da^{22}nv^{0}hte^{22}hi^{23}lo^{32}sgo^{33}ʔi^{2} ᎠᏓᏅᏖᎯᎶᏍᎪᎢ one ponders
ha^{2}da^{22}nv^{0}hte^{22}hi^{22}lo^{23}tsa^{2} ᎭᏓᏅᏖᎯᎶᏣ ponder
u^{22}da^{22}nv^{0}hte^{22}hi^{23}lo^{32}sdi^{2} ᎤᏓᏅᏖᎯᎶᏍᏗ for one to ponder

crawling

a^{21}da^{22}nv^{0}si^{23}ni^{3}ha^{2} ᎠᏓᏅᏍᏏᏂᎭ one is crawling
ga^{2}da^{2}nv^{11}si^{23}ni^{3}ha^{2} ᎦᏓᏅᏍᏏᏂᎭ I'm crawling
u^{21}da^{22}nv^{0}si^{23}nv^{32}sv^{23}ʔi^{2} ᎤᏓᏅᏍᏏᏅᏍᏒᎢ one crawled
a^{21}da^{22}nv^{0}h**si**^{23}**ne**^{32}go^{33}ʔi^{2} ᎠᏓᏅᏍᏏᏁᎪᎢ one crawls
(si^{23} make 'go' become lowfall (^{32}) tone)
ha^{2}da^{22}nv^{0}hsi^{22}nu^{11}ga^{2} ᎭᏓᏅᏍᏏᏄᎦ crawl
u^{22}da^{22}nv^{0}hsi^{23}nv^{32}sdi^{2} ᎤᏓᏅᏍᏏᏅᏍᏗ for one to crawl

u^{22}sdi^{4} tsa^{21}da^{22}nv^{0}si^{23}ni^{0}do^{32}hv^{23}ʔi^{2}
ᎤᏍᏗ ᏣᏓᏅᏍᏏᏂᏙᎲᎢ
The baby has been crawling around.

twisting

a^{21}da^{2}nu^{33}te^{23}yo^{3}ha^{2}	ᎠᏓᏄᏖᏲᎭ	it’s twisting
ga^{2}da^{2}nu^{33}te^{23}yo^{3}ha^{2}	ᎦᏓᏄᏖᏲᎭ	I’m twisting
u^{21}da^{2}nu^{33}te^{23}yo^{32}lv^{23}ʔi^{2}	ᎤᏓᏄᏖᏲᎸᎢ	it twisted
a^{21}da^{2}nu^{33}te^{23}yo^{3}ho^{33}ʔi^{2}	ᎠᏓᏄᏖᏲᎰᎢ	it twists
ha^{2}da^{2}nu^{11}te^{22}ya^{2}ga^{2}	ᎭᏓᏄᏖᏯᎦ	twist
u^{22}da^{2}nu^{11}te^{23}yo^{32}sdi^{2}	ᎤᏓᏄᏖᏲᏍᏗ	for it to twist

moving (from one place to another)

a^{21}da^{3}ʔnv^{23}ʔa^{2}	ᎠᏓᏅᎠ	it’s moving from one place to another
ga^{2}da^{3}ʔnv^{23}ʔa^{2}	ᎦᏓᏅᎠ	I’m moving from one place to another
u^{21}da^{3}ʔnv^{33}sv^{23}ʔi^{2}	ᎤᏓᏅᏍᏒᎢ	it moved from one place to another
a^{21}da^{3}ʔnv^{33}sgo^{33}ʔi^{2}	ᎠᏓᏅᏍᎪᎢ	it moves from one place to another
ha^{2}da^{2}nv^{23}na^{2}	ᎭᏓᏅᎾ	move from one place to another
u^{22}da^{2}nv^{11}sdi^{2}	ᎤᏓᏅᏍᏗ	for it to move from one place to another

u^{21}na^{2}da^{3}ʔnv^{33}sv^{23}ʔi^{2} su^{23}da^{3}li^{0} i^{2}tsu^{33}de^{22}ti^{2}yv^{33}dv^{0} tsi^{2}ge^{22}sv^{23}ʔi^{2}
ᎤᎾᏓᏅᏍᏒᎢ ᏍᏑᏓᎵ ᎢᏧᏕᏘᏴᏛ ᏥᎨᏍᏒᎢ
They moved six years ago.

ordering

a^{21}da^{2}nv^{33}sga^{2}	ᎠᏓᏅᏍᎦ	one is ordering it
ga^{2}da^{2}nv^{33}sga^{2}	ᎦᏓᏅᏍᎦ	
u^{21}da^{2}nv^{33}sv^{23}ʔi^{2}	ᎤᏓᏅᏍᏒᎢ	
a^{21}da^{2}nv^{33}sgo^{33}ʔi^{2}	ᎠᏓᏅᏍᎪᎢ	
ha^{2}da^{2}nv^{23}la^{2}	ᎭᏓᏅᎳ	
u^{22}da^{2}nv^{23}sdi^{2}	ᎤᏓᏅᏍᏗ	

cooking

a^{21}da^{22}sda^{32}yv^{0}hv^{3}sga^{2}	ᎠᏓᏍᏓᏴᎲᏍᎦ	done is cooking a meal
ga^{2}da^{11}sda^{32}yv^{0}hv^{3}sga^{2}	ᎦᏓᏍᏓᏴᎲᏍᎦ	
u^{21}da^{22}sda^{32}yv^{0}hnv^{23}ʔi^{2}	ᎤᏓᏍᏓᏴᏅᎢ	
a^{21}da^{22}sda^{32}yv^{0}hv^{3}sgo^{33}ʔi^{2}	ᎠᏓᏍᏓᏴᎲᏍᎪᎢ	
ha^{2}da^{22}sda^{11}yv^{0}hv^{11}ga^{2}	ᎭᏓᏍᏓᏴᎲᎦ	
u^{22}da^{22}sda^{11}yv^{0}hdi^{2}	ᎤᏓᏍᏓᏴᏗ	

tsa^{2}lv^{23}gwo^{0}di^{23}s tsa^{22}da^{22}sda^{11}yv^{0}hdi^{23}ʔi^{2}
ᏣᎸᏉᏗᏍ ᏣᏓᏍᏓᏴᏗᎢ
Do you like to cook?

burning

a^{21}da^{2}we^{23}la^{3}gi^{23}ʔa^{2}	ᎠᏓᏪᎳᎩᎠ	it's burning
ga^{2}da^{2}we^{23}la^{3}gi^{23}ʔa^{2}	ᎦᏓᏪᎳᎩᎠ	
u^{21}da^{2}we^{23}la^{3}gv^{23}ʔi^{2}	ᎤᏓᏪᎳᎬᎢ	
a^{21}da^{2}we^{23}la^{3}gi^{22}sgo^{33}ʔi^{2}	ᎠᏓᏪᎳᎩᏍᎪᎢ	
u^{22}da^{22}we^{23}la^{3}gi^{11}sdi^{2}	ᎤᏓᏪᎳᎩᏍᏗ	

resting

a^{21}da^{2}we^{33}so^{22}lv^{23}sdi^{3}ha^{2}	ᎠᏓᏪᏐᎸᏍᏗᎭ	one is resting
ga^{2}da^{2}we^{33}so^{22}lv^{23}sdi^{3}ha^{2}	ᎦᏓᏪᏐᎸᏍᏗᎭ	
u^{21}da^{2}we^{33}so^{22}l**v^{23}sta**^{3}nv^{23}ʔi^{2}	ᎤᏓᏪᏐᎸᏍᏓᏅᎢ	
(rising tone causes (^{3}) tone spread rightward)		
a^{21}da^{2}we^{33}so^{22}lv^{23}sdi^{32}sgo^{33}ʔi^{2}	ᎠᏓᏪᏐᎸᏍᏗᏍᎪᎢ	
ha^{2}da^{2}we^{11}so^{22}lv^{23}sda^{2}	ᎭᏓᏪᏐᎸᏍᏓ	
u^{22}da^{2}we^{11}so^{22}lv^{23}sdo^{3}hdi^{2}	ᎤᏓᏪᏐᎸᏍᏙᏗ	

ha^{2}da^{2}we^{33}so^{22}lv^{23}sta^{3}nv^{22}ʔi^{2}
ᎭᏓᏪᏐᎸᏍᏓᏅᎢ
Rest later on!

bathing/swimming

a^{21}da^{2}wo^{33}ʔa^{2} ᎠᏓᏬᎠ one is bathing/one is swimming

ga^{2}da^{2}wo^{33}ʔa^{2} ᎦᏓᏬᎠ
u^{21}da^{2}wo^{33}ʔv^{23}ʔi^{2} ᎤᏓᏬᎥᎢ
a^{21}da^{2}wo^{33}sgo^{33}ʔi^{2} ᎠᏓᏬᏍᎪᎢ
ha^{2}da^{2}wo^{23}tsa^{2} ᎭᏓᏬᏣ
u^{22}da^{2}wo^{11}sdi^{2} ᎤᏓᏬᏍᏗ

giving it to another (long object)

a^{21}de^{33}ha^{2} ᎠᏕᎭ one is giving it to another (a long object)

tsi^{22}de^{33}ha^{2} ᏥᏕᎭ
u^{21}de^{33}lv^{23}ʔi^{2} ᎤᏕᎸᎢ
a^{21}de^{33}ho^{33}ʔi^{2} ᎠᏕᎰᎢ
hi^{22}di^{11}si^{2} ᎯᏗᏏ
u^{22}de^{3}hdi^{2} ᎤᏕᏗ

ga^{22}li^{0}tsa^{2}ʔdi^{2} u^{21}de^{33}lv^{2} u^{22}we^{23}tsi^{0} a^{2}tsu^{23}tsa^{2}
ᎦᎵᏣᏗ ᎤᏕᎸ ᎤᏪᏥ ᎠᏧᏣ
He or She gave his or her (young) son a bow.

learning

a^{21}de^{22}hlo^{2}hgwa^{3}ʔa^{2} ᎠᏕᏝᏆᎠ one is learning

ga^{2}de^{11}lo^{2}hgwa^{3}ʔa^{2} ᎦᏕᎶᏆᎠ
u^{21}de^{22}hlo^{2}hgw**a**^{3}**ʔ**v^{23}ʔi^{2} (^{3}ʔ) ᎤᏕᏝᏆᎥᎢ
a^{21}de^{22}hlo^{2}hgw**a**^{32}**s**go^{33}ʔi^{2} (^{32}) ᎠᏕᏝᏆᏍᎪᎢ
ha^{2}de^{22}hlo^{2}hgwa^{2} ᎭᏕᏝᏆ
u^{22}de^{22}hlo^{2}hgwa^{11}sdi^{2} ᎤᏕᏝᏆᏍᏗ

embarrassing another

a^{21}de^{22}ho^{23}hi^{3}sdi^{23}ha^{2} ᎠᏕᎰᎯᏍᏗᎭ one is embarrassing another

tsi^{22}ya^{2}de^{22}ʔo^{23}hi^{3}sdi^{23}ha^{2} ᏥᏯᏕᎣᎯᏍᏗᎭ
u^{21}de^{22}ho^{23}hi^{3}sta^{2}nv^{23}ʔi^{2} ᎤᏕᎰᎯᏍᏔᏅᎢ
a^{21}de^{22}ho^{23}hi^{3}sdi^{22}sgo^{33}ʔi^{2} ᎠᏕᎰᎯᏍᏗᏍᎪᎢ
hi^{22}ya^{2}de^{22}ho^{22}hi^{2}sda^{2} ᎯᏯᏕᎰᎯᏍᏓ
u^{22}de^{22}ho^{23}hi^{3}sdo^{2}hdi^{2} ᎤᏕᎰᎯᏍᏙᏗ

being embarrassed

a^{21}de^{22}ho^{23}sga^{2} ᎠᏕᎰᏍᎦ one is embarrassed

ga^{2}de^{22}ʔo^{23}sga^{2} ᎦᏕᎣᏍᎦ

u^{21}de^{22}ho^{23}sv^{3}ʔi^{2} ᎤᏕᎰᏍᏒᎢ

a^{21}de^{22}ho^{23}sgo^{3}ʔi^{2} ᎠᏕᎰᏍᎪᎢ

ha^{2}de^{22}ho^{23}hi^{2} ᎭᏕᎰᎯ

u^{22}de^{22}ho^{23}hi^{3}sdi^{2} ᎤᏕᎰᎯᏍᏗ

being born

a^{21}de^{22}hv^{3}sga^{2} ᎠᏕᎲᏍᎦ one is being born

ga^{2}de^{22}ʔv^{3}sga^{2} ᎦᏕᎥᏍᎦ

u^{21}de^{22}hnv^{23}ʔi^{2} ᎤᏕᏅᎢ

a^{21}de^{22}hv^{3}sgo^{33}ʔi^{2} ᎠᏕᎲᏍᎪᎢ

ha^{2}de^{22}hv^{11}ga^{2} ᎭᏕᎲᎦ

u^{22}de^{2}hdi^{2} ᎤᏕᏗ

ga^{22}li^{0}kwo^{23}gi^{0} i^{2}yu^{33}wa^{22}hni^{2}lv^{4} u^{2}sv^{4} tsi^{2}ge^{22}sv^{2}, a^{2}gwe^{23}tsi^{0} a^{2}ge^{22}hyu^{23}tsa^{0} u^{21}de^{22}hnv^{23}ʔi^{2}

ᎦᎵᏉᎩ ᎢᏳᏩᏂᎸᎯ ᎤᏒ ᏥᎨᏍᏒᎢ, ᎠᏇᏥ ᎠᎨᏳᏣ ᎤᏕᏅᎢ

My daughter was born at 7:00 last night.

finding out something

a^{21}de^{22}lo^{2}ho^{22}sga^{2} ᎠᏕᎶᎰᏍᎦ one is finding it out

ga^{2}de^{22}lo^{2}ʔo^{23}sga^{2} ᎦᏕᎶᎣᏍᎦ

u^{21}de^{22}lo^{2}ho^{22}sv^{23}ʔi^{2} ᎤᏕᎶᎰᏍᏒᎢ

a^{21}de^{22}lo^{2}ho^{22}sgo^{33}ʔi^{2} ᎠᏕᎶᎰᏍᎪᎢ

ha^{2}de^{22}lo^{2}ho^{23}hi^{2} ᎭᏕᎶᎰᎯ

u^{22}de^{22}lo^{2}ho^{23}hi^{3}sdi^{2} ᎤᏕᎶᎰᎯᏍᏗ

tsa^{2}du^{22}li^{23}s tsa^{22}nv^{0}ta^{2}di^{11}sdi^{2} na^{22}gwa^{2}de^{22}lo^{2}ho^{22}sv^{44}hi^{2}

ᏣᏚᎵᏍ ᏣᏅᏔᏗᏍᏗ ᎾᏆᏕᎶᎰᏍᏒᎯ

Do you want to know what I found out?

diving

a^{21}de^{22}tv^{3}sga^{2} ᎠᏕᏛᏍᎦ one is diving

ga^{2}de^{11}dv^{3}sga^{2} ᎦᏕᏛᏍᎦ
u^{21}de^{22}ti^{3}nv^{33}ʔi^{2} ᎤᏕᏘᏅᎢ
a^{21}de^{22}tv^{3}sgo^{3}ʔi ᎠᏕᏛᏍᎪᎢ
ha^{2}de^{22}tv^{11}ga^{2} ᎭᏕᏛᎦ
u^{22}de^{22}tv^{0}hdi^{2} ᎤᏕᏛᏗ

going around a curve/circling it

a^{21}de^{33}yo^{2}ha^{2} ᎠᏕᏲᎭ one is going around a curve
one is circling it

ga^{22}de^{33}yo^{2}ha^{2} ᎦᏕᏲᎭ
u^{21}de^{23}yo^{32}lv^{23}ʔi^{2} ᎤᏕᏲᎸᎢ
a^{21}de^{33}yo^{2}ho^{33}ʔi^{2} ᎠᏕᏲᎰᎢ
ha^{22}de^{22}ya^{2}ga^{2} ᎭᏕᏯᎦ
u^{22}de^{23}ya^{0}sdi^{2} ᎤᏕᏯᏍᏗ

laying it down (a long object)

a^{21}di^{3}ʔa^{2} ᎠᏗᎠ one is laying it down (a long object)

tsi^{2}di^{3}ʔa^{2} ᏥᏗᎠ
u^{21}dv^{23}ʔi^{2} ᎤᏛᎢ
a^{21}di^{32}sgo^{33}ʔi^{2} ᎠᏗᏍᎪᎢ (minimal pair, *cf. 'says it'*)
hi^{2}da^{2} ᎯᏓ
u^{22}di^{11}sdi^{2} ᎤᏘᏍᏗ

e^{22}hi^{2}da^{2} na^{2} ga^{22}nv^{0}sda^{0} a^{3}ha^{2}ni^{2}
ᎡᎯᏓ Ꮎ ᎦᏅᏍᏓ ᎠᎭᏂ
Come and lay the stick right here.

getting up

a^{21}di^{23}di^{3}ha^{2} ᎠᏗᏗᎭ one is getting up

ga^{2}di^{23}di^{3}ʔa^{2} ᎦᏗᏗᎠ

u^{21}di^{22}dv^{22}hv^{23}ʔi^{2} ᎤᏗᏛᎲᎢ

a^{21}di^{22}di^{23}sgo^{3}ʔi^{2} ᎠᏗᏗᏍᎪᎢ

ha^{2}di^{23}da^{2} ᎭᏗᏓ

u^{22}di^{22}dv^{0}hdi^{2} ᎤᏗᏛᏗ

hi^{2}la^{4} (i)yu^{33}wa^{22}hni^{2}lv^{4} u^{21}di^{22}dv^{22}he^{33}ʔi^{2} sv^{22}hi^{0} sa^{2}na^{33}le^{44}ʔi^{2}

ᎯᎳ ᎢᏳᏩᏂᎸᎯ ᎤᏗᏛᎮᎢ ᏍᏒᎯ ᏍᏌᎾᎴᎢ

What time did he or she get up yesterday morning?

scattering it

a^{21}di^{22}ga^{2}le^{23}ya^{3}ʔa^{2} ᎠᏗᎦᎴᏯᎠ one is scattering it

ga^{2}di^{22}ga^{2}le^{23}ya^{3}ʔa^{2} ᎦᏗᎦᎴᏯᎠ

u^{21}di^{22}ga^{2}le^{22}yv^{23}ʔi^{2} ᎤᏗᎦᎴᏴᎢ

a^{21}di^{22}ga^{2}le^{23}ya^{32}sgo^{33}ʔi^{2} ᎠᏗᎦᎴᏯᏍᎪᎢ

ha^{2}di^{22}ga^{2}le^{23}ya^{2} ᎭᏗᎦᎴᏯ

u^{22}di^{22}ga^{2}le^{23}ya^{32}sdi^{2} ᎤᏗᎦᎴᏯᏍᏗ

it's scattered

a^{21}di^{22}ga^{2}le^{23}yo^{32}ga^{2} ᎠᏗᎦᎴᏲᎦ it's scattering

ga^{2}di^{22}ga^{2}le^{23}yo^{32}ga^{2} ᎦᏗᎦᎴᏲᎦ I'm scattering

u^{21}di^{22}ga^{2}le^{23}yo^{32}tsv^{23}ʔi^{2} ᎤᏗᎦᎴᏲᏨᎢ

a^{21}di^{22}ga^{2}le^{23}yo^{32}go^{33}ʔi^{2} ᎠᏗᎦᎴᏲᎪᎢ

ha^{2}di^{22}ga^{2}le^{22}yo^{11}gi^{2} ᎭᏗᎦᎴᏲᎩ Be scattered!

u^{22}di^{22}ga^{2}le^{23}yo^{32}sdi^{2} ᎤᏗᎦᎴᏲᏍᏗ

spinning/rotating

a^{21}di^{33}gwa^{2}lv^{22}de^{33}yo^{2}ha^{2} ᎠᏗᏆᎸᏕᏲᎭ it is spinning or rotating

ga^{22}di^{33}gwa^{2}lv^{22}de^{33}yo^{2}ha^{2} ᎦᏗᏆᎸᏕᏲᎭ

u^{21}di^{33}gwa^{2}lv^{22}de^{23}yo^{32}lv^{23}ʔi^{2} ᎤᏗᏆᎸᏕᏲᎸᎢ

a^{21}di^{33}gwa^{2}lv^{22}de^{33}yo^{2}ho^{33}ʔi^{2} ᎠᏗᏆᎸᏕᏲᎰᎢ

ha^{2}di^{11}gwa^{2}lv^{22}de^{22}ya^{2}ga^{2} ᎭᏗᏆᎸᏕᏯᎦ

u^{22}di^{11}gwa^{2}lv^{22}de^{23}ya(^{32})sdi^{2} ᎤᏗᏆᎸᏕᏯᏍᏗ

du^{21}di^{33}gwa^{2}lv^{22}de^{23}yo^{32}le^{33}s di^{2}ga^{33}gwa^{2}tv^{0}hdi^{2}
ᏚᏗᏆᎸᏕᏲᎴᏍ ᏗᎦᏆᏛᏗ
Did he or she spin the wheels?

saying

a^{21}di^{23}ha^{2} ᎠᏗᎭ one is saying it

ga^{2}di^{23}ʔa^{2} ᎦᏗᎠ

u^{21}dv^{22}hnv^{23}ʔi^{2} ᎤᏛᏅᎢ

a^{21}di^{23}sgo^{3}ʔi^{2} ᎠᏗᏍᎪᎢ (minimal pair, *cf. laying it down 'a long object'*)

ha^{2}da^{2} ᎭᏓ

u^{22}di^{0}hdi^{2} ᎤᏗᏗ

"a^{21}gi^{2}yo^{33}si^{23}ha^{2}", a^{21}di^{23}sgo^{3}(ʔi^{2}) ni^{2}go^{22}hi^{33}lv^{44}ʔi^{2}
"ᎠᎩᏲᏍᏏᎭ", ᎠᏗᏍᎪᎢ ᏂᎪᎯᎸᎢ
He or She is always saying "I'm hungry".

running over another

a^{21}ga^{2}di^{23}nv^{32}di^{23}ha^{2} ᎠᎦᏗᏅᏗᎭ one is running over another

tsi^{22}ya^{2}di^{23}nv^{32}di^{23}ha^{2} ᏥᏯᏗᏅᏗᎭ

u^{21}di^{23}nv^{32}ta^{2}nv^{23}ʔi^{2} ᎤᏗᏅᏔᏅᎢ

a^{21}ga^{2}di^{23}nv^{32}di^{22}sgo^{33}ʔi^{2} ᎠᎦᏗᏅᏗᏍᎪᎢ

hi^{22}ya^{2}di^{22}nv^{11}da^{2} ᎯᏯᏗᏅᏓ

u^{22}di^{23}nv^{32}do^{2}hdi^{2} ᎤᏗᏅᏙᏗ

a^{2}sga^{2}ya^{0} u^{21}di^{23}nv^{32}ta^{2}ne^{33}ʔi^{2} na^{2} gi^{22}hli^{0} ko^{22}hi^{0} sa^{2}na^{33}le^{33}ʔi^{2} a^{21}gwa^{0}tv^{23}ga^{32}nv^{23}ʔi^{2}
ᎠᏍᎦᏯ ᎤᏗᏅᏔᏁᎢ Ꮎ ᎩᎵ ᎪᎯ ᏌᎾᎴᎢ ᎠᏆᏛᎦᏅᎢ
I heard the man ran over the dog this morning.

hiding

a^{21}di^{22}sga^{2}hlv^{3}sga^{2} ᎠᏗᏍᎦᎸᏍᎦ one is hiding

ga^{2}di^{11}sga^{2}hlv^{3}sga^{2} ᎦᏗᏍᎦᎸᏍᎦ

(second syllable is (^{11}) tone to reflect [h/ʔ] alternation)

u^{21}di^{22}sga^{2}hla^{3}nv^{3}ʔi^{2} ᎤᏗᏍᎦᎳᏅᎢ

a^{21}di^{22}sga^{2}hlv^{3}sgo^{3}ʔi^{2} ᎠᏗᏍᎦᎸᏍᎪᎢ

ha^{2}di^{22}sga^{2}hlv^{11}ga^{2} ᎭᏗᏍᎦᎸᎦ

u^{22}di^{22}sga^{2}hlv^{0}hdi^{2} ᎤᏗᏍᎦᎸᏗ

leaving it behind (a long object)

a^{21}di^{32}si^{23}ya^{3}ʔa^{2} ᎠᏗᏏᏯᎠ one is leaving it behind (a long object)

tsi^{2}di^{32}si^{23}ya^{3}ʔa^{2} ᏥᏗᏏᏯᎠ

u^{21}di^{32}si^{23}ya^{3}ʔa^{2} ᎤᏗᏏᏯᎠ

a^{21}di^{32}si^{23}ya^{32}sgo^{33}ʔi^{2} ᎠᏗᏏᏯᏍᎪᎢ

hi^{2}di^{11}si^{23}ya^{2} ᎯᏗᏏᏯ

u^{22}di^{11}si^{23}ya^{32}sdi^{2} ᎤᏗᏏᏯᏍᏗ

drinking

a^{21}di^{23}ta^{3}sga^{2} ᎠᏗᏔᏍᎦ one is drinking it

ga^{2}di^{23}ta^{3}sga^{2} ᎦᏗᏔᏍᎦ

u^{21}di^{22}ta^{2}hv^{23}ʔi^{2} ᎤᏗᏔᎲᎢ

a^{21}di^{22}ta^{2}sgo^{33}ʔi^{2} ᎠᏗᏔᏍᎪᎢ

ha^{2}di^{23}ta^{2} ᎭᏗᏔ

u^{22}di^{22}ta^{2}sdi^{2} ᎤᏗᏔᏍᏗ

scratching

a^{21}dla^{2}go^{23}sga^{2} ᎠᏜᎪᏍᎦ one is scratching

ga^{2}dla^{2}go^{23}sga^{2} ᎦᏜᎪᏍᎦ

u^{21}dla^{2}go^{23}sv^{3}ʔi^{2} ᎤᏜᎪᏒᎢ

a^{21}dla^{2}go^{23}sgo^{3}ʔi^{2} ᎠᏜᎪᏍᎪᎢ

ha^{2}dla^{2}go^{23}la^{2} ᎭᏜᎪᎳ

u^{22}dla^{2}go^{23}sdi^{2} ᎤᏜᎪᏍᏗ

tle^{22}sdi^{2} tsi^{22}ha^{22}dla^{2}go^{23}sge^{33}sdi^{2}, u^{22}tsi^{2} u^{21}wo^{11}se^{23}le^{3}ʔi^{2}

ᏞᏍᏗ ᏥᎭᏜᎪᏍᎨᏍᏗ, ᎤᏥ ᎤᏬᏎᎴᎢ

"Don't be scratching!", his mom told him.

turning off

a^{21}dle^{33}ʔa^{2} ᎠᏞᎠ one is turning off the road
ga^{2}dle^{33}ʔa^{2} ᎦᏞᎠ
u^{21}dle^{33}sv^{23}ʔi^{2} ᎤᏞᏍᎡᎢ
a^{21}dle^{33}sgo^{33}ʔi^{2} ᎠᏞᏍᎪᎢ
ha^{2}dla^{2}gi^{2} ᎭᏜᎩ
u^{22}dle^{11}sdi^{2} ᎤᏞᏍᏗ

taking revenge

a^{21}dle^{33}che^{23}ha^{2} ᎠᏞᏤᎭ one is taking revenge against another
tsi^{22}ya^{2}dle^{33}che^{23}ha^{2} ᏥᏯᏞᏤᎭ
u^{21}dle^{33}che^{22}lv^{23}ʔi^{2} ᎤᏞᏤᎸᎢ
a^{21}dle^{33}che^{22}ho^{33}ʔi^{2} ᎠᏞᏤᎰᎢ
hi^{22}ya^{2}dle^{11}chi^{2}si^{2} ᎯᏯᏞᏥᏍᏏ
u^{22}dle^{11}che^{3}hdi^{2} ᎤᏞᏤᏗ

do^{23}yu^{3} u^{21}du^{22}lv^{22}hv^{2} u^{22}dle^{11}che^{2}hdi^{23}ʔi^{2}
ᏙᏳ ᎤᏚᎸᎲ ᎤᏞᏤᏗᎢ
He or She really wanted to take revenge against another.

pouring (into a container)

a^{21}dli^{3}ʔa^{2} ᎠᏟᎠ one is pouring **(pouring INTO something)**
tsi^{2}dli^{3}ʔa^{2} ᏥᏟᎠ
u^{21}dlv^{23}ʔi^{2} ᎤᏢᎢ
a^{21}dli^{32}sgo^{33}ʔi^{2} ᎠᏟᏍᎪᎢ
hi^{2}dli^{11}ga^{2} ᎯᏟᎦ
u^{22}dli^{11}sdi^{2} ᎤᏟᏍᏗ

sv^{23}ga^{0}ta^{2}s u^{22}wa^{22}gu^{23}sv^{44}hi^{0} tsu^{21}dle^{33}ʔi^{2}
ᏍᎡᎦᏔᏍ ᎤᏩᎫᏍᎡᎯ ᏧᏞᎢ
Was it apple juice that he or she poured?

pouring (from something)

a^{21}dli^{23}ha^{2}	ᎠᏟᎭ	one is drawing (a liquid) from a container
tsi^{2}dli^{3}ʔa^{2}	ᏥᏟᎠ	
u^{21}dlv^{22}hv^{23}ʔi^{2}	ᎤᏢᎲᎢ	
a^{21}dli^{23}sgo^{3}ʔi^{2}	ᎠᏟᏍᎪᎢ	
hi^{2}dla^{2}	ᎯᏜ	
u^{22}dlv^{2}hdi^{2}	ᎤᏢᏗ	

it is pouring

a^{21}dli^{32}ga^{2}	ᎠᏟᎦ	it is pouring into a container it is filling
ga^{2}dli^{32}ga^{2}	ᎦᏟᎦ	I'm filling
u^{21}dli^{32}tsv^{23}ʔi^{2}	ᎤᏟᏨᎢ	
a^{21}dli^{32}go^{33}ʔi^{2}	ᎠᏟᎪᎢ	
hi^{2}dli^{11}yo^{11}gi^{2}	ᎯᏟᏲᎩ	Be filling!
u^{22}dli^{11}y(o^{32})sdi^{2}	ᎤᏟᏲᏍᏗ	

making it pour

a^{21}dli^{32}sdi^{23}ha^{2}	ᎠᏟᏍᏗᎭ	one is making something pour **(causative suffix)**
tsi^{2}dli^{32}sdi^{23}ha^{2}	ᏥᏟᏍᏗᎭ	
u^{21}dli^{32}sta^{2}nv^{23}ʔi^{2}	ᎤᏟᏍᏔᏅᎢ	
a^{21}dli^{32}sdi^{22}sgo^{33}ʔi^{2}	ᎠᏟᏍᏗᏍᎪᎢ	
hi^{2}dli^{11}sda^{2}	ᎯᏟᏍᏓ	
u^{22}dli^{11}sdo^{2}hdi^{2}	ᎤᏟᏍᏙᏗ	

crying

a^{21}dlo^{22}y**i**^{0}**hi**^{3}**h**a^{2} ᎠᏠᏱᎯᎭ one is crying

'purpose' conditional suffix

ga^{2}dlo^{11}y**(i**^{0}**ʔ)i**^{3}**h**a^{2} ᎦᏠᏱᎢᎭ
u^{21}dlo^{22}yi^{0}**hi**^{2}**l**v^{23}ʔi^{2} ᎤᏠᏱᎯᎸᎢ
a^{21}dlo^{22}y**i**^{0}**hi**^{2}**h**o^{33}ʔi^{2} ᎠᏠᏱᎯᎰᎢ
ha^{2}dlo^{22}y(i^{2})h**(i**^{2}**)ga**^{2} ᎭᏠᏱᎯᎦ
u^{22}dlo^{22}y(i^{2})h**i**^{0}**sdi**^{2} ᎤᏠᏱᎯᏍᏗ

hi^{2}su^{22}la^{0}go^{2}ʔi^{2} tsi^{2}tsa^{2}dlo^{22}hyi^{2}hv^{23}ʔi^{2}
ᎯᏍᏑᏔᎪᎢ ᏥᏣᏠᏱᎯᎲᎢ
Quit your crying!

getting off

a^{21}dlo^{33}yi^{0}sga^{2} ᎠᏠᏱᏍᎦ one is getting off
one is getting down (off of something)

ga^{2}dlo^{33}yi^{0}sga^{2} ᎦᏠᏱᏍᎦ
u^{21}dlo^{33}yi^{0}sv^{23}ʔi^{2} ᎤᏠᏱᏍᎲᎢ
a^{21}dlo^{33}yi^{0}sgo^{33}ʔi^{2} ᎠᏠᏱᏍᎪᎢ
ha^{2}dlo^{11}hi^{2} ᎭᏠᎯ
u^{22}dlo^{11}hi^{2}sdi^{2} ᎤᏠᎯᏍᏗ

yi^{2}ha^{2}dlo^{11}hi^{2}
ᏱᎭᏠᎯ
You can get down.

bragging

a^{21}da^{0}lv^{23}gwo^{0}sga^{2} ᎠᏓᎸᏈᏍᎦ one is bragging
ga^{2}da^{0}lv^{23}gw(o^{32})sga^{2} ᎦᏓᎸᏈᏍᎦ
u^{21}da^{0}lv^{23}gwo^{0}sv^{23}ʔi^{2} ᎤᏓᎸᏈᏍᎲᎢ
a^{21}da^{0}lv^{23}gwo^{0}sgo^{3}ʔi^{2} ᎠᏓᎸᏈᏍᎪᎢ
ha^{2}da^{0}lv^{23}gwa^{2} ᎭᏓᎸᏆ
u^{22}da^{0}lv^{23}gwo^{0}sdi^{2} ᎤᏓᎸᏈᏍᏗ

catching up

a^{21}dlv^{22}ta^{3}sga^{2} ᎠᏢᏔᏍᎦ one is catching up with another

tsi^{22}ya^{2}dlv^{11}ta^{3}sga^{2} (animate) ᏥᏯᏢᏔᏍᎦ ga^{2}dlv^{11}ta^{3}sga^{2} ᎦᏢᏔᏍᎦ (inanimate)

u^{21}dlv^{22}ta^{2}hv^{23}ʔi^{2} ᎤᏢᏔᏂᎢ

a^{21}dlv^{22}ta^{2}sgo^{33}ʔi^{2} ᎠᏢᏔᏍᎪᎢ

hi^{22}ya^{2}dlv^{11}ta^{2} (animate) ᎯᏯᏢᏔ ha^{2}dlv^{23}ta^{2} ᎭᏢᏔ(inanimate)

u^{22}dlv^{22}ta^{2}sdi^{2} ᎤᏢᏔᏍᏗ

e^{22}li^{23}gwu^{3}dv^{33} yi^{2}ga^{2}tsi^{22}ya^{2}dlv^{11}ta^{2} ge^{23}li^{3}ʔa^{2}

ᎡᎵᏊᏛ ᏱᎦᏥᏯᏢᏔ ᎨᎵᎠ

I think I can catch up with him or her.

doing

a^{21}dv^{33}ne^{23}ha^{2} ᎠᏛᏁᎭ one is doing it

ga^{2}dv^{33}ne^{23}ha^{2} ᎦᏛᏁᎭ

u^{21}dv^{33}ne^{22}lv^{23}ʔi^{2} ᎤᏛᏁᎸᎢ

a^{21}dv^{33}ne^{22}ho^{33}ʔi^{2} ᎠᏛᏁᎰᎢ

ni^{0}ha^{2}dv^{11}ga^{2} ᏂᎭᏛᎦ

u^{22}dv^{11}ne^{0}hdi^{2} ᎤᏛᏁᏗ

ga^{2}do^{2} u^{44}sdi^{0} a^{22}na^{2}dv^{33}ne^{22}he^{33}sdi^{2} sa^{22}na^{33}le^{44}ʔi^{2}

ᎦᏙ ᎤᏍᏗ ᎠᎾᏛᏁᎮᏍᏗ ᏍᏌᎾᎴᎢ

What will they be doing tomorrow?

acting silly

a^{21}dv^{33}ne^{22}li^{23}ha^{2} ᎠᏛᏁᎵᎭ one is acting silly

ga^{2}dv^{33}ne^{22}li^{23}ha^{2} ᎦᏛᏁᎵᎭ

u^{21}dv^{33}ne^{22}lv^{22}hnv^{23}ʔi^{2} ᎤᏛᏁᎸᏅᎢ

a^{21}dv^{33}ne^{22}li^{23}sgo^{3}ʔi^{2} ᎠᏛᏁᎵᏍᎪᎢ

ha^{2}dv^{11}ne^{23}la^{2} ᎭᏛᏁᏔ

u^{22}dv^{22}ne^{23}hlv^{0}hdi^{2} ᎤᏛᏁᎸᏗ

preparing/getting ready

a^{21}dv^{22}nv^{33}ʔi^{0}sdi^{23}ha^{2} ᎠᏛᏁᎢᏍᏗᎭ one is preparing or getting ready

ga^{2}dv^{22}ne^{33}ʔi^{0}sdi^{23}ha^{2} ᎦᏛᏁᎢᏍᏗᎭ

u^{21}dv^{22}nv^{33}ʔi^{0}sta^{2}nv^{23}ʔi^{2} ᎤᏛᏅᎢᏍᏔᏅᎢ

a^{21}dv^{22}nv^{33}ʔi^{0}sdi^{23}sgo^{3}ʔi^{2} ᎠᏛᏅᎢᏍᏗᏍᎪᎢ

ha^{2}dv^{22}nv^{22}ʔi^{0}sda^{2} ᎭᏛᏅᎢᏍᏓ

u^{22}dv^{22}nv^{22}ʔi^{0}sdo^{3}hdi^{2} ᎤᏛᏅᎢᏍᏙᏗ

tsa^{2}dv^{22}nv^{33}ʔi^{0}sta^{2}no^{3}hnv^{23}tsu^{3}
ᏣᏛᏅᎢᏍᏔᏃᏅᏧ
Are you ready?

shining

a^{21}ga^{33}li^{23}ha^{2} ᎠᎦᎵᎭ the Sun is shining

A FIRST PERSON FROM CAN BE SAID BUT IS VERY DISRESPECTFUL

u^{21}ga^{22}li^{22}sv^{23}ʔi^{2} ᎤᎦᎵᏒᎢ

a^{21}ga^{33}li^{22}sgo^{33}ʔi^{2} ᎠᎦᎵᏍᎪᎢ

ha^{2}ga^{11}li^{2} ᎭᎦᎵ Be shining!

The command form of this verb would also be considered disrespectful because would not ever act as if we have the right to command the Sun.

u^{22}ga^{11}li^{23}hi^{3}sdi^{2} ᎤᎦᎵᎯᏍᏗ

breaking/cutting (a flexible object)

a^{21}ga^{32}la^{0}sga^{2} ᎠᎦᎳᏍᎦ one is breaking it/cutting it (a flexible object)

tsi^{2}ga^{32}la^{0}sga^{2} ᏥᎦᎳᏍᎦ

u^{21}ga^{32}la^{0}sv^{23}ʔi^{2} ᎤᎦᎳᏒᎢ

a^{21}ga^{32}la^{0}sgo^{33}ʔi^{2} ᎠᎦᎳᏍᎪᎢ

hi^{2}ga^{2}ʔla^{2} ᎯᎦᎳ

u^{22}ga^{11}la^{0}sdi^{2} ᎤᎦᎳᏍᏗ

ga^{2}nu^{23}lv^{2} tsi^{2}ga^{32}la^{0}sgv^{23}ʔi^{2} sv^{22}hi^{0} sv^{22}ye^{44}yi^{2} di^{33}tlv^{4} tsi^{2}ge^{22}sv^{23}ʔi^{2}
ᎦᏄᎸ ᏥᎦᎳᏍᎬᎢ ᏒᎯ ᏒᏰᏱ ᏗᏢ ᏥᎨᏒᎢ
I was cutting the grass yesterday afternoon.

licking

a^{21}ga^{2}na^{23}di^{3}ʔa^{2} (tone contraction) or a^{21}ga^{2}na^{33}di^{23}ʔa^{2} ᎠᎦᎾᏗᎠ one is licking it

tsi^{2}ga^{2}na^{23}di^{3}ʔa^{2} ᏥᎦᎾᏗᎠ

u^{21}ga^{2}na^{33}dv^{23}ʔi^{2} ᎤᎦᎾᏛᎢ

a^{21}ga^{2}na^{23}di^{32}sgo^{33}ʔi^{2} ᎠᎦᎾᏗᏍᎪᎢ

hi^{2}ga^{2}na^{23}da^{2} ᎯᎦᎾᏓ

u^{22}ga^{2}na^{23}di^{32}sdi^{2} ᎤᎦᎾᏗᏍᏗ

warming it

a^{21}ga^{22}na^{2}wo^{0}hdi^{23}ha^{2} ᎠᎦᎾᏬᏗᎭ one is warming it

tsi^{2}ga^{22}na^{2}wo^{11}di^{23}ha^{2} (inanimate) ᏥᎦᎾᏬᏗᎭ

tsi^{22}ga^{22}na^{2}wo^{11}di^{23}ha^{2} (animate) ᏥᎦᎾᏬᏗᎭ

u^{21}ga^{22}na^{2}wo^{0}hta^{2}nv^{23}ʔi^{2} ᎤᎦᎾᏬᏔᏅᎢ

a^{21}ga^{22}na^{2}wo^{0}hdi^{23}sgo^{3}ʔi^{2} ᎠᎦᎾᏬᏗᏍᎪᎢ

hi^{2}ga^{22}na^{2}wo^{0}hda^{2} (inanimate) ᎯᎦᎾᏬᏓ

hi^{22}ga^{22}na^{2}wo^{11}da^{2} (animate) ᎯᎦᎾᏬᏓ

u^{22}ga^{22}na^{2}wo^{0}hdo^{3}hdi^{2} ᎤᎦᎾᏬᏙᏗ

de^{33}tsi^{33}ye^{22}sa^{3}ʔdv^{4} de^{33}tsi^{2}ga^{22}na^{2}wo^{11}di^{23}ha^{2}
ᏕᏥᏰᏌᏛ ᏕᏥᎦᎾᏬᏗᎭ
I'm warming my fingers.

getting warm

a^{21}ga^{22}na^{2}wo^{22}sga^{2} ᎠᎦᎾᏬᏍᎦ one or it is getting warm

tsi^{2}ga^{22}na^{2}wo^{22}sga^{2} ᏥᎦᎾᏬᏍᎦ

u^{21}ga^{22}na^{2}wo^{22}sv^{23}ʔi^{2} ᎤᎦᎾᏬᏒᎢ

a^{21}ga^{22}na^{2}wo^{22}sgo^{33}ʔi^{2} ᎠᎦᎾᏬᏍᎪᎢ

hi^{2}ga^{22}na^{2}wo^{23}hi^{2} ᎯᎦᎾᏬᎯ

u^{22}ga^{22}na^{2}wo^{22}hi^{2}sdi^{2} ᎤᎦᎾᏬᎯᏍᏗ

raining

a^{21}ga^{22}sga^{2}	ᎠᎦᏍᎦ	it is raining
tsi^{22}ga^{22}sga^{2}	ᏥᎦᏍᎦ	I'm raining (as if I am the rain, figuratively)
u^{21}ga^{22}hna^{2}nv^{23}ʔi^{2}	ᎤᎦᏁᏅᎢ	
a^{21}ga^{22}sgo^{33}ʔi^{2}	ᎠᎦᏍᎪᎢ	
hi^{22}ga^{11}hna^{2}	ᎯᎦᏁ	Rain!

(we would not command the rain like this culturally)

a^{22}ga^{32}hna^{2}	ᎠᎦᏁ	It just now rained
hi^{22}ga^{22}sgi^{2}	ᎯᎦᏍᎩ	You are rain!

(as if you were speaking to the rain or calling someone 'the rain')

u^{22}ga^{22}nv^{0}hdi^{2}	ᎤᎦᏅᏗ	

eating (a solid)

a^{21}gi^{3}ʔa^{2}	ᎠᎩᎠ	one is eating it (something solid) **(minimal pair, *cf. 'one is picking up/getting'*)**
tsi^{2}gi^{3}ʔa^{2}	ᏥᎩᎠ	
u^{21}gv^{23}ʔi^{2}	ᎤᎬᎢ	
a^{21}gi^{32}sgo^{33}ʔi^{2}	ᎠᎩᏍᎪᎢ	
hi^{2}ga^{2}	ᎯᎦ	
u^{22}gi^{11}sdi^{2}	ᎤᎩᏍᏗ	

tsa^{2}du^{22}li^{23}s sv^{23}ga^{0}ta^{2} di^{22}tsa^{2}gi^{11}sdi^{23}ʔi^{2}
ᏣᏚᎵᏍ ᏍᏒᎦᏔ ᏗᏣᎩᏍᏗᎢ
Do you like to eat apples?

picking up/getting (a solid)

a^{21}gi^{33}ʔa^{2}	ᎠᎩᎠ	one is picking up/getting it **(minimal pair, *cf. 'one is eating it 'something solid'*)**
tsi^{2}gi^{33}ʔa^{2}	ᏥᎩᎠ	
u^{21}gi^{33}sv^{23}ʔi^{2}	ᎤᎩᏍᏒᎢ	
a^{21}gi^{33}sgo^{33}ʔi^{2}	ᎠᎩᏍᎪᎢ	
hi^{2}gi^{2}	ᎯᎩ	
u^{22}gi^{11}sdi^{2}	ᎤᎩᏍᏗ	

being in agony

a^{21}gi^{22}hli^{23}yo^{32}ga^{2}	ᎠᎩᏟᏲᎦ	one is in agony
tsi^{2}gi^{11}li^{23}yo^{32}ga^{2}	ᏥᎩᎵᏲᎦ	
u^{21}gi^{22}hli^{23}yo^{32}tsv^{23}ʔi^{2}	ᎤᎩᏟᏲᏨᎢ	
a^{21}gi^{22}hli^{23}yo^{32}go^{33}ʔi^{2}	ᎠᎩᏟᏲᎪᎢ	
hi^{2}gi^{22}hli^{22}yo^{11}gi^{2}	ᎯᎩᏟᏲᎩ	
u^{22}gi^{22}hli^{23}yo^{32}sdi^{2}	ᎤᎩᏟᏲᏍᏗ	

tso^{2}ʔi^{0} i^{23}ya^{3}nv^{44}dv^{0} i^{2}go^{33}hi^{44}dv^{2} tsa^{2}gi^{22}hli^{23}yo^{32}tsv^{23}ʔi^{2} do^{23}ka^{3}

ᏦᎢ ᎢᏯᏅᏛ ᎢᎪᎯᏛ ᏣᎩᏟᏲᏨᎢ ᏙᎧ

You were in agony for three months weren't you?

chewing

a^{21}gi^{32}sdo^{23}ʔa^{2}	ᎠᎩᏍᏙᎠ	one is chewing it
tsi^{2}gi^{32}sdo^{23}ʔa^{2}	ᏥᎩᏍᏙᎠ	
u^{21}gi^{32}sdo^{2}ʔv^{23}ʔi^{2}	ᎤᎩᏍᏙᎥᎢ	
a^{21}gi^{32}sdo^{2}ʔsgo^{33}ʔi^{2}	ᎠᎩᏍᏙᏍᎪᎢ	
hi^{2}gi^{11}sdo^{23}tsa^{2}	ᎯᎩᏍᏙᏣ	
u^{22}gi^{11}sdo^{11}sdi^{2}	ᎤᎩᏍᏙᏍᏗ	

burning another

a^{21}go^{3}hv^{2}sdi^{23}ha^{2}	ᎠᎪᎲᏍᏗᎭ	one is burning him or it
tsi^{22}ya^{3}go^{2}hv^{2}sdi^{23}ha^{2} (animate)	ᏥᏯᎪᎲᏍᏗᎭ	
ga^{3}go^{2}hv^{2}sdi^{23}ha^{2} (inanimate)	ᎦᎪᎲᏍᏗᎭ	
u^{21}go^{3}hv^{2}sta^{2}nv^{23}ʔi^{2}	ᎤᎪᎲᏍᏔᏅᎢ	
a^{21}go^{3}hv^{2}sdi^{23}sgo^{3}ʔi^{2}	ᎠᎪᎲᏍᏗᏍᎪᎢ	
hi^{22}ya^{2}go^{2}hv^{2}sda^{2} (animate)	ᎯᏯᎪᎲᏍᏓ	
ha^{2}go^{2}hv^{2}sda^{2} (inanimate)	ᎭᎪᎲᏍᏓ	
u^{22}go^{2}hv^{2}sdo^{2}hdi^{2}	ᎤᎪᎲᏍᏙᏗ	

it is burning

a^{21}go^{3}hv^{2}sga^{2} ᎠᎪᎲᏍᎦ one or it is burning

ga^{3}go^{2}hv^{2}sga^{2} ᎦᎪᎲᏍᎦ
u^{21}go^{3}hnv^{23}ʔi^{2} ᎤᎪᏅᎢ
a^{21}go^{3}hv^{2}sgo^{33}ʔi^{2} ᎠᎪᎲᏍᎪᎢ
ha^{2}go^{2}hna^{2} ᎭᎪᏏ
u^{22}go^{3}hv^{2}sdi^{2} ᎤᎪᎲᏍᏗ

reading/examining

a^{21}go^{22}li^{23}ye^{3}ʔa^{2} ᎠᎪᎵᏰᎠ one is reading or examining another or it

tsi^{22}go^{22}li^{23}ye^{3}ʔa^{2} (animate) ᏥᎪᎵᏰᎠ
tsi^{2}go^{22}li^{23}ye^{3}ʔa^{2} (inanimate) ᏥᎪᎵᏰᎠ
u^{21}go^{22}li^{23}ye^{3}ʔv^{23}ʔi^{2} ᎤᎪᎵᏰᎥᎢ
a^{21}go^{22}li^{23}ye^{32}sgo^{33}ʔi^{2} ᎠᎪᎵᏰᏍᎪᎢ
hi^{22}go^{22}li^{23}ya^{2} (animate) ᎯᎪᎵᏯ
hi^{2}go^{22}li^{23}ya^{2} (inanimate) ᎯᎪᎵᏯ
u^{22}go^{22}li^{23}ye^{32}di^{2} ᎤᎪᎵᏰᏗ

ga^{2}do^{2} u^{44}sdi^{0} a^{21}go^{22}li^{23}ye^{32}sgv^{23}ʔi^{2} na^{22}hi^{2}yu^{4} tsi^{2}ge^{22}sv^{23}ʔi^{2}
ᎦᏙ ᎤᏍᏗ ᎠᎪᎵᏰᏍᎬᎢ ᎾᎯᏳ ᏥᎨᏒᎢ
What was he or she reading back then?

target practicing

a^{33}go^{22}ni^{23}ha^{2} ᎠᎪᏂᎭ one is target practicing

ga^{33}go^{22}ni^{23}ha^{2} ᎦᎪᏂᎭ
u^{33}go^{22}nv^{22}hv^{23}ʔi^{2} ᎤᎪᏅᎲᎢ
a^{33}go^{22}ni^{23}sgo^{3}ʔi^{2} ᎠᎪᏂᏍᎪᎢ
ha^{11}go^{23}na^{2} ᎭᎪᎾ
u^{11}go^{23}nv^{0}hdi^{2} ᎤᎪᏅᏗ

seeing

a^{21}go^{22}hwa^{2}hti^{23}ha^{2} ᎠᎪᏩᏘᎭ one sees another or it

tsi^{22}go^{11}hwa^{0}hti^{23}ha^{2} (animate) ᏥᎪᏩᏘᎭ

tsi^{2}go^{11}hwa^{0}hti^{23}ha^{2} (inanimate) ᏥᎪᏩᏘᎭ

u^{21}go^{22}hv^{23}ʔi^{2} ᎤᎪᎲᎢ

a^{21}go^{22}hwa^{0}hti^{23}sgo^{3}ʔi^{2} ᎠᎪᏩᏘᏍᎪᎢ

hi^{22}go^{11}hwa^{2}hta^{2} (animate) ᎯᎪᏩᏔ

hi^{2}go^{11}hwa^{2}hta^{2} (inanimate) ᎯᎪᏩᏔ

(Rightmost long syllable receives the (^{11}) tone)

u^{22}go^{22}hwa^{0}htv^{3}hdi^{2} ᎤᎪᏩᏛᏗ

showing another

a^{21}go^{22}hwa^{0}htv^{2}hdi^{23}ha^{2} ᎠᎪᏩᏛᏗᎭ one is showing it to another

tsi^{22}go^{11}hwa^{0}htv^{2}hdi^{23}ha^{2} ᏥᎪᏩᏛᏗᎭ

u^{21}go^{22}hwa^{0}htv^{2}hta^{2}nv^{23}ʔi^{2} ᎤᎪᏩᏛᏔᏅᎢ

a^{21}go^{22}hwa^{0}htv^{2}hdi^{23}sgo^{3}ʔi^{2} ᎠᎪᏩᏛᏗᏍᎪᎢ

hi^{22}go^{11}hwa^{0}htv^{2}hda^{2} ᎯᎪᏩᏛᏓ

u^{22}go^{22}hwa^{0}htv^{2}hdo^{3}hdi^{2} ᎤᎪᏩᏛᏙᏗ

cutting/slicing

a^{21}gv^{22}ha^{2}li^{23}ha^{2} ᎠᎬᎭᎵᎭ one is cutting/slicing it

tsi^{2}gv^{2}ʔa^{2}li^{23}ha^{2} ᏥᎬᎠᎵᎭ

u^{21}gv^{22}ha^{2}lv^{22}hv^{23}ʔi^{2} ᎤᎬᎭᎸᎲᎢ

a^{21}gv^{22}ha^{2}li^{23}sgo^{3}ʔi^{2} ᎠᎬᎭᎵᏍᎪᎢ

hi^{2}gv^{22}ha^{2}la^{2} ᎯᎬᎭᎳ

u^{22}gv^{22}ha^{2}hlv^{0}hdi^{2} ᎤᎬᎭᎸᏗ

hi^{2}gv^{22}ha^{2}lv^{22}hv^{22}ʔi^{2} na^{2} ge^{22}li^{44}sdv^{0}gi^{2}

ᎯᎬᎭᎸᎲᎢ Ꮎ ᎨᎵᏍᏛᎩ

Slice the pie later!

chopping

$a^{21}gv^{22}ha^{3}lu^{32}hya^{0}sga^{2}$	ᎠᎬᎭᎷᏯᏍᎦ	one is chopping it
$tsi^{2}gv^{2}ʔa^{3}lu^{32}hya^{0}sga^{2}$	ᏥᎬᎠᎷᏯᏍᎦ	
$u^{21}gv^{22}ha^{3}lu^{32}hyv^{23}ʔi^{2}$	ᎤᎬᎭᎷᏴᎢ	
$a^{21}gv^{22}ha^{3}lu^{32}hya^{0}sgo^{33}ʔi^{2}$	ᎠᎬᎭᎷᏯᏍᎪᎢ	
$hi^{2}gv^{22}ha^{2}lu^{11}hya^{2}$	ᎯᎬᎭᎷᏯ	
$u^{22}gv^{22}ha^{2}lu^{11}hya^{0}sdi^{2}$	ᎤᎬᎭᎷᏯᏍᏗ	

$sv^{11}gi^{2}$ $de^{33}tsi^{2}gv^{2}ʔa^{2}lu^{32}hya^{0}sge^{33}sdi$ $ko^{22}hi^{32}yv^{4}$ $a^{2}da^{22}sda^{11}yv^{0}hdi^{44}yi^{2}$
ᏍᏒᎩ ᏕᏥᎬᎠᎷᏯᏍᎨᏍᏗ ᎪᎯᏴᎢ ᎠᏓᏍᏓᏴᏗᏱ
I’ll be chopping onions in the kitchen in a while.

scolding

$a^{21}gv^{22}sgo^{23}lv^{32}sga^{2}$	ᎠᎬᏍᎪᎸᏍᎦ	one is scolding another
$tsi^{22}gv^{11}sgo^{23}lv^{32}sga^{2}$	ᏥᎬᏍᎪᎸᏍᎦ	
$u^{21}gv^{22}sgo^{23}lv^{32}nv^{23}ʔi^{2}$	ᎤᎬᏍᎪᎸᏅᎢ	
$a^{21}gv^{22}sgo^{23}lv^{32}sgo^{33}ʔi^{2}$	ᎠᎬᏍᎪᎸᏍᎪᎢ	
$hi^{22}gv^{22}sgo^{23}lv^{3}ʔv^{11}ga^{2}$	ᎯᎬᏍᎪᎸᎥᎦ	
$u^{22}gv^{22}sgo^{23}lv^{32}sdi^{2}$	ᎤᎬᏍᎪᎸᏍᏗ	

$a^{22}gv^{11}sgo^{22}lv^{2}ʔv^{22}ga^{2}sgo^{0}$ $di^{22}de^{23}hlo^{0}gwa^{11}sgi^{4}$
ᎠᎬᏍᎪᎸᎥᎥᎦᏍᎪ ᏗᏕᏠᏆᏍᎩ
Did he or she just now scold the student?

washing one’s face

$a^{21}gv^{22}sgwo^{33}ʔa^{2}$	ᎠᎬᏍᏉᎠ	one is washing one’s face
$ga^{2}gv^{11}sgwo^{33}ʔa^{2}$	ᎦᎬᏍᏉᎠ	
$u^{21}gv^{22}sgwo^{33}ʔv^{23}ʔi^{2}$	ᎤᎬᏍᏉᎥᎢ	
$a^{21}gv^{22}sgwo^{33}sgo^{33}ʔi^{2}$	ᎠᎬᏍᏉᏍᎪᎢ	
$ha^{2}gv^{22}sgwo^{23}tsa^{2}$	ᎭᎬᏍᎪᏣ	
$u^{22}gv^{22}sgwo^{11}sdi^{2}$	ᎤᎬᏍᏉᏍᏗ	

diverting/flagging down

a^{21}ha^{2}lu^{23}gi^{3}ʔa^{2} ᎠᎭᎷᎩᎠ one is diverting/flagging down another

tsi^{2}ʔa^{2}lu^{23}gi^{3}ʔa^{2} ᏥᎠᎷᎩᎠ

u^{21}ha^{2}lu^{23}gi^{32}sv^{23}ʔi^{2} ᎤᎭᎷᎩᏍᏒᎢ

a^{21}ha^{2}lu^{23}gi^{32}sgo^{33}ʔi^{2} ᎠᎭᎷᎩᏍᎪᎢ

hi^{2}ʔa^{2}lu^{23}gi^{2} ᎯᎠᎷᎩ

u^{22}ha^{2}lu^{23}gi^{32}sdi^{2} ᎤᎭᎷᎩᏍᏗ

smothering/suffocating

a^{21}ha^{2}wo^{33}sdi^{23}ha^{2} ᎠᎭᏬᏍᏗᎭ one is smothering another

tsi^{2}ʔa^{2}wo^{33}sdi^{23}ha^{2} ᏥᎠᏬᏍᏗᎭ

u^{21}ha^{2}wo^{33}sta^{2}nv^{23}ʔi^{2} ᎤᎭᏬᏍᏔᏅᎢ

a^{21}ha^{2}wo^{33}sdi^{22}sgo^{33}ʔi^{2} ᎠᎭᏬᏍᏗᏍᎪᎢ

hi^{2}ha^{2}wo^{11}sda^{2} ᎯᎭᏬᏍᏓ

u^{22}ha^{2}wo^{11}sdo^{2}hdi^{2} ᎤᎭᏬᏍᏙᏗ

a^{2}tsi^{23}lv^{0} u^{21}ha^{2}wo^{33}sta^{2}nv^{23}ʔi^{2}
ᎠᏥᎸ ᎤᎭᏬᏍᏔᏅᎢ
He or She smothered the fire.

carrying in hand

a^{21}hi^{23}do^{32}ha^{2} ᎠᎯᏙᎭ one is handling it/has in hand

tsi^{2}ʔi^{23}do^{32}ha^{2} ᏥᎢᏙᎭ

u^{21}hi^{23}do^{32}lv^{23}ʔi^{2} ᎤᎯᏙᎸᎢ

a^{21}hi^{23}do^{32}ho^{33}ʔi^{2} ᎠᎯᏙᎰᎢ

hi^{2}hi^{23}da^{2} ᎯᎯᏓ

u^{22}hi^{23}da^{32}sdi^{2} ᎤᎯᏓᏍᏗ

tsa^{22}nv^{0}ta^{2}s i^{0}yu^{44}sdi^{0} ge^{22}hv^{4} tsi^{2}ʔi^{23}do^{32}hv^{23}ʔi^{2}
ᏣᏅᏔᏍ ᎢᏳᏍᏗ ᎨᎲ ᏥᎢᏙᎲᎢ
Do you know what I have been carrying around in my hand?

killing

a^{21}hi^{3}ha^{2} ᎠᎯᎭ one is killing another

tsi^{2}ʔi^{3}ha^{2} ᏥᎢᎭ

u^{21}hlv^{23}ʔi^{2} ᎤᏢᎢ

a^{21}hi^{3}ho^{33}ʔi^{2} ᎠᎯᎰᎢ

hi^{22}lu^{11}ga^{2} ᎯᎷᎦ

u^{22}hi^{2}sdi^{2} ᎤᎯᏍᏗ

driving

a^{21}hi^{3}ʔle^{23}ha^{2} ᎠᎯᎴᎭ one is driving

tsi^{2}ʔi^{3}le^{23}ha^{2} ᏥᎢᎴᎭ

u^{21}hi^{3}ʔle^{22}hv^{23}ʔi^{2} ᎤᎯᎴᎲᎢ one had drove

a^{21}hi^{3}ʔle^{22}ho^{33}ʔi^{2} ᎠᎯᎴᎰᎢ

ha^{2}hi^{2}ʔlv^{23}la^{2} ᎭᎯᎸᎳ

u^{22}hi^{2}ʔlv^{11}sdi^{2} ᎤᎯᎸᏍᏗ

leaving behind

a^{21}hi^{23}ya^{3}ʔa^{2} ᎠᎯᏯᎠ one is leaving it behind

tsi^{2}ʔi^{23}ya^{3}ʔa^{2} ᏥᎢᏯᎠ

u^{21}hi^{33}yv^{23}ʔi^{2} ᎤᎯᏴᎢ

a^{21}hi^{23}ya^{32}sgo^{33}ʔi^{2} ᎠᎯᏯᏍᎪᎢ

hi^{2}hi^{23}ya^{3} ᎯᎯᏯ

u^{22}hi^{23}ya^{32}sdi^{2} ᎤᎯᏯᏍᏗ

ka^{2}no^{22}he^{33}dv^{2} hi^{2}hi^{23}ya^{2} yi^{2}tsa^{2}du^{22}li^{23}ha^{2}
ᎧᏃᎮᏛ ᎯᎯᏯ ᏱᏣᏚᎵᎭ
Leave a message if you want.

placing something elevated

a^{21}hla^{2}hv^{3}sga^{2} ᎠᏝᎲᏍᎦ one is putting it up on something (like a table)

tsi^{22}ʔla^{2}hv^{3}sga^{2} ᏥᎳᎲᏍᎦ

u^{21}hla^{2}hnv^{23}ʔi^{2} ᎤᏝᏅᎢ

a^{21}hla^{2}hv^{3}sgo^{3}ʔi^{2} ᎠᏝᎲᏍᎪᎢ

hi^{2}hla^{2}hv^{11}ga^{2} ᎯᏝᎲᎦ

u^{22}hlo^{2}hdi^{2} ᎤᏠᏗ

taking off flying

a^{21}**hla**^{2}wi^{23}di^{3}ha^{2} ᎠᏝᏫᏗᎭ one is taking off flying

/h/ & /ʔ/ alternation

ga^{2}**dla**^{2}wi^{23}di^{3}ha^{2} ᎦᏜᏫᏗᎭ

u^{21}hla^{2}wi^{22}dv^{22}hv^{23}ʔi^{2} ᎤᏝᏫᏛᎲᎢ

a^{21}hla^{2}wi^{22}di^{23}sgo^{3}ʔi^{2} ᎠᏝᏫᏗᏍᎪᎢ

ha^{2}hla^{2}wi^{23}da^{2} ᎭᏝᏫᏓ

u^{22}hla^{2}wi^{22}di^{0}hdi^{2} ᎤᏝᏫᏗᏗ

making another fly

a^{21}hla^{2}wi^{22}di^{0}hdi^{23}ha^{2} ᎠᏝᏫᏗᏗᎭ one is making another fly

tsi^{22}ya^{2}dla^{2}wi^{22}di^{0}hdi^{23}ha^{2} ᏥᏯᏜᏫᏗᏗᎭ

u^{21}hla^{2}wi^{22}di^{0}hd(i^{0})**a^{3}<hn**v^{23}ʔi^{2} **(< means, the /h/ fuzed leftward and a^{3}<hn, is the populative infix which is sometimes required to form a completive past on some verbs)**

ᎤᏝᏫᏗᏓᏅᎢ

a^{21}hla^{2}wi^{22}di^{0}hdi^{23}sgo^{3}ʔi^{2} ᎠᏝᏫᏗᏗᏍᎪᎢ

hi^{22}ya^{2}hla^{2}wi^{22}di^{0}hda^{2} (animate) ᎯᏯᏝᏫᏗᏓ

ha^{2}hla^{2}wi^{22}di^{0}hda^{2} (inanimate) ᎭᏝᏫᏗᏓ

u^{22}hla^{2}wi^{22}di^{0}hdo^{3}hdi^{2} ᎤᏝᏫᏗᏙᏗ

do^{22}gwa^{2}le^{33}lu^{0} u^{22}hla^{2}wi^{22}di^{0}h^{3}di^{2} u^{22}du^{22}li^{23}ha^{2}

ᏙᏆᎴᎷ ᎤᏝᏫᏗᏗ ᎤᏚᎵᎭ

He or She wants to make the car fly.

having a nightmare

a^{21}**hli**^{2}gi^{23}ʔa^{2} ᎠᏟᎩᎠ one is having a nightmare

ga^{2}**dli**^{2}gi^{23}ʔa^{2} ᎦᏟᎩᎠ

u^{21}hli^{2}gi^{33}sv^{23}ʔi^{2} ᎤᏟᎩᏍᏒᎢ

a^{21}hli^{2}gi^{33}sgo^{33}ʔi^{2} ᎠᏟᎩᏍᎪᎢ

ha^{2}hli^{2}gi^{2} ᎭᏟᎩ

u^{22}hli^{2}gi^{11}sdi^{2} ᎤᏟᎩᏍᏗ

taking time

a^{21}**hli**^{3}ʔi^{2}li^{23}do^{32}ha^{2}	ᎠᏟᎢᎵᏙᎭ	it is taking time
		/h/ & /ʔ/ alternation
ga^{2}**dli**^{3}ʔi^{2}li^{23}do^{32}ha^{2}	ᎦᏟᎢᎵᏙᎭ	I am taking time
u^{21}hli^{3}ʔi^{2}li^{23}do^{32}lv^{23}ʔi^{2}	ᎤᏟᎢᎵᏙᎸᎢ	
a^{21}hli^{3}ʔi^{2}li^{23}do^{32}ho^{33}ʔi^{2}	ᎠᏟᎢᎵᏙᎰᎢ	
ha^{2}hli^{2}ʔi^{2}li^{23}da^{2}	ᎭᏟᎢᎵᏓ	take time
u^{22}hli^{2}ʔi^{2}li^{23}da^{32}sdi^{2}	ᎤᏟᎢᎵᏓᏍᏗ	

hi^{2}la^{32}ga^{4} dv^{22}hli^{3}ʔi^{2}li^{23}do^{32}li^{2} he^{23}li^{3}ʔa^{2}
ᎯᎳᎢᎦ ᏛᏟᎢᎵᏙᎵ ᎮᎵᎠ
How much time will it take, do you think?

measuring

a^{21}hli^{22}lo^{33}ʔa^{2}	ᎠᏟᎶᎠ	one is measuring it
ga^{2}dli^{22}lo^{33}ʔa^{2}	ᎦᏟᎶᎠ	
u^{22}hli^{22}lo^{33}ʔv^{23}ʔi^{2}	ᎤᏟᎶᎥᎢ	
a^{21}hli^{22}lo^{33}sgo^{33}ʔi^{2}	ᎠᏟᎶᏍᎪᎢ	
ha^{2}hli^{22}lo^{23}tsa^{2}	ᎭᏟᎶᏣ	
u^{22}hli^{22}lo^{11}sdi^{2}	ᎤᏟᎶᏍᏗ	

it's bending

a^{21}hli^{2}yv^{22}gwi^{3}dv^{32}sga^{2}	ᎠᏟᏴᏇᏛᎥᏍᎦ	it is bending
tsi^{2}dli^{22}yv^{22}gwi^{3}dv^{32}sga^{2}	ᏥᏟᏴᏇᏛᎥᏍᎦ	
u^{21}hli^{2}yv^{22}gwi^{3}dv^{32}nv^{23}ʔi^{2}	ᎤᏟᏴᏇᏛᏅᎢ	
a^{21}hli^{2}yv^{22}gwi^{3}dv^{32}sgo^{33}ʔi^{2}	ᎠᏟᏴᏇᏛᎥᏍᎪᎢ	
ha^{22}hli^{2}yv^{22}gwi^{2}dv^{11}gi^{2}	ᎭᏟᏴᏇᏛᎩ	Be bending!
u^{22}hli^{2}yv^{22}gwi^{2}dv^{11}di^{2}	ᎤᏟᏴᏇᏛᏗ	

snorting

a^{21}hli^{2}yv^{23}s**a^{3}na^{11}wa^{0}sdi^{23}**ha^{2} ᎠᏟᏴᏍᏌᎾᏩᏍᏗᎭ one is snorting

(**a^{3}na^{11}wa^{0}sdi**, suffix meaning 'making it perform its duty')

ga^{2}li^{11}yv^{23}sa^{3}na^{11}wa^{0}sdi^{23}ha^{2} ᎦᏟᏴᏍᏌᎾᏩᏍᏗᎭ

u^{21}hli^{2}yv^{23}sa^{3}na^{11}wa^{0}sta^{2}nv^{23}ʔi^{2} ᎤᏟᏴᏍᏌᎾᏩᏍᏔᏅᎢ

a^{21}hli^{2}yv^{23}sa^{3}na^{11}wa^{0}sdi^{23}sgo^{3}ʔi^{2} ᎠᏟᏴᏍᏌᎾᏩᏍᏗᏍᎪᎢ

ha^{2}hli^{2}yv^{22}sa^{2}na^{11}wa^{0}sda^{2} ᎭᏟᏴᏍᏌᎾᏩᏍᏓ

u^{22}hli^{2}yv^{23}sa^{3}na^{11}wa^{0}sdo^{3}hdi^{2} ᎤᏟᏴᏍᏌᎾᏩᏍᏙᏗ

si^{2}hgwa^{0} u^{22}we^{23}li^{32}sdi^{0} a^{21}hli^{2}yv^{23}sa^{3}na^{11}wa^{0}sdi^{22}sgv^{23}ʔi^{2}

ᏍᏏᏆ ᎤᏪᏟᏍᏗ ᎠᏟᏴᏍᏌᎾᏩᏍᏗᏍᎨᎢ

He or She was snorting like a pig.

it's shattering

a^{21}hli^{0}ko^{22}dv^{22}sga^{2} ᎠᏟᎪᏛᏍᎦ it is shattering

ga^{2}li^{11}ko^{22}dv^{22}sga^{2} ᎦᏟᎪᏛᏍᎦ I'm shattering

u^{21}hli^{0}ko^{22}dv^{22}hnv^{23}ʔi^{2} ᎤᏟᎪᏛᏅᎢ

a^{21}hli^{2}ko^{22}dv^{22}sgo^{33}ʔi^{2} ᎠᏟᎪᏛᏍᎪᎢ

ha^{22}hli^{0}ko^{22}dv^{23}na^{2} ᎭᏟᎪᏛᎾ

u^{22}hli^{0}ko^{22}dv^{2}hdi^{2} ᎤᏟᎪᏛᏗ

making it shatter

a^{21}hli^{0}ko^{22}dv^{0}hdi^{23}ha^{2} ᎠᏟᎪᏛᏗᎭ one is shattering it

ga^{2}li^{11}ko^{22}dv^{0}hdi^{23}ha^{2} ᎦᏟᎪᏛᏗᎭ

u^{21}hli^{0}ko^{22}dv^{0}hta^{2}nv^{23}ʔi^{2} ᎤᏟᎪᏛᏔᏅᎢ

a^{21}hli^{0}ko^{22}dv^{0}hdi^{23}sgo^{3}ʔi^{2} ᎠᏟᎪᏛᏗᏍᎪᎢ

ha^{2}hli^{0}ko^{22}dv^{0}hda^{2} ᎭᏟᎪᏛᏓ

u^{22}hli^{0}ko^{22}dv^{0}hdo^{3}hdi^{2} ᎤᏟᎪᏛᏙᏗ

beating another

a^{21}hlo^{22}sga^{2} ᎠᏰᏍᎦ one is beating another at a game

tsi^{22}hlo^{22}sga^{2} ᏥᏰᏍᎦ

u^{21}hlo^{22}sv^{23}ʔi^{2} ᎤᏰᏍᏒᎢ

a^{21}hlo^{22}sgo^{33}ʔi^{2} ᎠᏰᏍᎪᎢ

hi^{22}hlo^{23}hi^{2} ᎯᏰᎯ

u^{22}hlo^{22}hi^{2}sdi^{2} ᎤᏰᎯᏍᏗ

winning

a^{21}da^{22}hlo^{22}sga^{2} ᎠᏓᏰᏍᎦ one is winning

ga^{2}da^{22}hlo^{22}sga^{2} ᎦᏓᏰᏍᎦ

u^{21}da^{22}hlo^{22}sv^{23}ʔi^{2} ᎤᏓᏰᏍᏒᎢ

a^{21}da^{22}hlo^{22}sgo^{33}ʔi^{2} ᎠᏓᏰᏍᎪᎢ

ha^{2}da^{22}hlo^{23}hi^{2} ᎭᏓᏰᎯ

u^{22}da^{22}hlo^{22}hi^{2}sdi^{2} ᎤᏓᏰᎯᏍᏗ

combing

a^{21}hli^{0}ta^{2}wo^{33}ʔa^{2} ᎠᎵᏔᏬᎠ one is combing

ga^{2}li^{11}ta^{2}wo^{33}ʔa^{2} ᎦᎵᏔᏬᎠ

u^{21}hli^{0}ta^{2}wo^{33}ʔa^{2} ᎤᎵᏔᏬᎠ

a^{21}hli^{0}ta^{2}wo^{33}sgo^{33}ʔi^{2} ᎠᎵᏔᏬᏍᎪᎢ

ha^{22}hli^{0}ta^{2}wo^{23}tsa^{2} ᎭᎵᏔᏬᏣ

u^{22}hli^{0}ta^{2}wo^{11}sdi^{2} ᎤᎵᏔᏬᏍᏗ

moving

a^{21}hli^{0}te^{33}lv^{23}hv^{3}sga^{2} ᎠᎵᏖᎸᎲᏍᎦ one is moving

ga^{2}li^{11}te^{33}lv^{23}hv^{3}sga^{2} ᎦᎵᏖᎸᎲᏍᎦ

u^{21}hli^{0}te^{33}lv^{23}hnv^{33}ʔi^{2} ᎤᎵᏖᎸᏅᎢ

a^{21}hli^{0}te^{33}lv^{23}hv^{3}sgo^{33}ʔi^{2} ᎠᎵᏖᎸᎲᏍᎪᎢ

ha^{22}hli^{0}te^{11}lv^{22}hv^{11}ga^{2} ᎭᎵᏖᎸᎲᎦ

u^{22}hli^{0}te^{11}hlv^{0}hdi^{2} ᎤᎵᏖᎸᏗ

changing one's shirt

a^{21}hna^{2}wa^{3}ʔi^{22}yv^{33}ʔa^{2}	ᎠᏏᏩᎢᏴᎠ	one is changing one's shirt
ga^{2}na^{11}wa^{3}ʔi^{22}yv^{33}ʔa^{2}	ᎦᏀᎢᏴᎠ	
u^{21}hna^{2}wa^{3}ʔi^{22}yv^{33}sv^{23}ʔi^{2}	ᎤᏏᏩᎢᏴᏍᏒᎢ	
a^{21}hna^{2}wa^{3}ʔi^{22}yv^{33}sgo^{33}ʔi^{2}	ᎠᏏᏩᎢᏴᏍᎪᎢ	
ha^{2}hna^{2}wa^{2}ʔi^{22}yv^{23}na^{2}	ᎭᏏᏩᎢᏴᎾ	
u^{22}hna^{2}wa^{2}ʔi^{23}yv^{32}sdi^{2}	ᎤᏏᏩᎢᏴᏍᏗ	

taking off a coat/shirt

a^{21}hna^{2}we^{33}ʔa^{2}	ᎠᏏᏪᎠ	one is taking off one's shirt or coat
ga^{2}na^{11}we^{33}ʔa^{2}	ᎦᏀᏪᎠ	
u^{21}hna^{2}we^{33}sv^{23}ʔi^{2}	ᎤᏏᏪᏍᏒᎢ	
a^{21}hna^{2}we^{33}sgo^{33}ʔi^{2}	ᎠᏏᏪᏍᎪᎢ	
ha^{2}hna^{2}wa^{2}gi^{2}	ᎭᏏᏩᎩ	
u^{22}hna^{2}we^{11}sdi^{2}	ᎤᏏᏪᏍᏗ	

putting on a coat/shirt

a^{21}hna^{2}wo^{33}ʔa^{2}	ᎠᏏᏬᎠ	one is putting on a shirt or coat
ga^{2}na^{11}wo^{33}ʔa^{2}	ᎦᏀᏬᎠ	
u^{21}hna^{2}wo^{33}ʔv^{23}ʔi^{2}	ᎤᏏᏬᎥᎢ	
a^{21}hna^{2}wo^{33}sgo^{33}ʔi^{2}	ᎠᏏᏬᏍᎪᎢ	
ha^{2}hna^{2}wo^{23}tsa^{2}	ᎭᏏᏬᏣ	
u^{22}hna^{2}wo^{11}sdi^{2}	ᎤᏏᏬᏍᏗ	

giving it to another

a^{21}hne^{23}ha^{2}	ᎠᏁᎭ	one is giving it to another
tsi^{22}ne^{23}ha^{2}	ᏥᏁᎭ	
u^{21}hne^{22}lv^{23}ʔi^{2}	ᎤᏁᎸᎢ	
a^{21}hne^{23}ho^{3}ʔi^{2}	ᎠᏁᎰᎢ	
hi^{2}ʔv^{2}si^{2}	ᎯᎥᏍᏏ	
u^{22}hne^{3}hdi^{2}	ᎤᏁᏗ	

wrestling

a^{33}hn**e^{23}hi^{3}h**a^{2} ᎠᏁᎯᎭ one is wrestling (now is said, a^{33}hne^{23}hi^{3}ha^{2})

(This is the -(i)^{23}hi^{3}h-, 'come for the purpose of' conditional suffix, incompletive stem and the leading (i) vowel of this morpheme can drop and take the final vowel of the root.)

ga^{33}hn**e^{23}hi^{3}h**a^{2} ᎦᏁᎯᎭ
u^{33}hn**e^{33}hl**v^{23}ʔi^{2} ᎤᏁᏢᎢ
a^{33}hn**e^{23}hi^{3}ho**^{33}ʔi^{2} ᎠᏁᎯᎰᎢ
ha^{11}hn**e^{23}g**a^{2} ᎭᏁᎦ
u^{11}hn**e^{23}sd**i^{2} ᎤᏁᏍᏗ

translating

a^{21}hne^{33}hlv^{0}hdi^{23}ha^{2} ᎠᏁᎲᏗᎭ one is translating it

ga^{21}ne^{33}hlv^{0}hdi^{23}ha^{2} ᎦᏁᎲᏗᎭ
u^{21}hne^{33}hlv^{0}hta^{2}nv^{23}ʔi^{2} ᎤᏁᎲᏔᏅᎢ
a^{21}hne^{33}hlv^{0}hdi^{22}sgo^{33}ʔi^{2} ᎠᏁᎲᏗᏍᎪᎢ
ha^{22}hne^{22}hlv^{0}hda^{2} ᎭᏁᎲᏓ
u^{22}hne^{33}hlv^{0}hdo^{2}hdi^{2} ᎤᏁᎲᏙᏗ

ki^{2}lo^{44}wu^{0}ke^{3} hi^{22}yo^{23}li^{32}gi^{0} a^{22}hne^{33}hlv^{0}hdi^{44}sgi^{2}
ᎩᎶᏭᎨ ᎯᏲᎵᎩ ᎠᏁᎲᏗᏍᎩ
Do you know anyone who is a translator or interpreter?

frolicking

a^{21}hne^{22}tso^{3}sga^{2} ᎠᏁᏦᏍᎦ one is frolicking

ga^{2}ʔne^{23}tso^{3}sga^{2} ᎦᏁᏦᏍᎦ
u^{21}hne^{23}tso^{3}hnv^{23}ʔi^{2} ᎤᏁᏦᏅᎢ
a^{21}hne^{23}tso^{3}sgo^{33}ʔi^{2} ᎠᏁᏦᏍᎪᎢ
ha^{22}hne^{22}tso^{2}ʔv^{11}ga^{2} ᎭᏁᏦᎥᎦ
u^{22}hne^{22}tso^{11}hdi^{2} ᎤᏁᏦᏗ

building a house

a^{21}hne^{33}sge^{23}ha^{2}	ᎠᏁᏍᎨᎭ	one is building a house
ga^{21}ne^{33}sge^{23}ha^{2}	ᎦᏁᏍᎨᎭ	
u^{21}hne^{33}sge^{22}hv^{23}ʔi^{2}	ᎤᏁᏍᎨᎲᎢ	
a^{21}hne^{33}sge^{22}sgo^{33}ʔi^{2}	ᎠᏁᏍᎨᏍᎪᎢ	
ha^{22}hne^{11}sgv^{23}la^{2}	ᎭᏁᏍᎬᎳ	
u^{22}hne^{11}sge^{2}hdi^{2}	ᎤᏁᏍᎨᏗ	

starting/leaving

a^{21}hni^{3}gi^{3}ʔa^{2}	ᎠᏂᎩᎠ	one is starting or leaving

Morphemes:
a^{21}- 3P, Set A
a^{3}h(a^{2})ni^{2} 'here'
-gi^{33}- 'reversive' suffix
ʔ 'stationary focus (no one has actually left yet)
-a^{2} present tense suffix

Literally, 'someone is in the process of reversing their being here'

ga^{21}ni^{3}gi^{3}**ʔ**a^{2}	ᎦᏂᎩᎠ
u^{21}hni^{3}g**i**^{32}sv^{23}ʔi^{2}	ᎤᏂᎩᏍᎥᎢ
a^{21}hni^{3}gi^{32}sgo^{33}ʔi^{2}	ᎠᏂᎩᏍᎪᎢ
ha^{22}hni^{2}gi^{2}	ᎭᏂᎩ
u^{22}hni^{2}gi^{11}sdi^{2}	ᎤᏂᎩᏍᏗ

hi^{2}la^{32}yv^{4} ta^{2}hni^{3}gi^{32}si^{2}
ᎯᎳᎢᏴ ᏔᏂᎩᏍᏏ
When will you leave?

making it start

a^{21}hni^{3}gi^{32}sdi^{23}ha^{2} ᎠᏂᎩᏍᏗᎭ one is starting it

The (^{3}) tone of the root causes a (^{3}) spread rightward one mora which creates a falling (^{32}) tone.

ga^{21}ni^{3}gi^{32}sdi^{23}ha^{2} ᎦᏂᎩᏍᏗᎭ

u^{21}hni^{3}gi^{32}sta^{2}nv^{23}ʔi^{2} ᎤᏂᎩᏍᏔᏅᎢ

a^{21}hni^{3}gi^{32}sdi^{22}sgo^{33}ʔi^{2} ᎠᏂᎩᏍᏗᏍᎪᎢ

ha^{22}hni^{2}gi^{11}sda^{2} ᎭᏂᎩᏍᏓ

(A (^{33}) tone becomes (^{11}) on unrealistic stems and a (^{3}) tone becomes a (^{2}) tone on unrealistic stems)

u^{22}hni^{2}gi^{11}sdo^{2}hdi^{2} ᎤᏂᎩᏍᏙᏗ

carrying by shoulder

a^{21}no^{23}ha^{3}li^{23}ne^{32}ga^{2} ᎠᏃᎭᎵᏁᎦ

one is carrying it on one's shoulder (a long object)

(Now is said, a^{21}hno^{22}h(a)li^{23}ne^{32}ga^{2}. This contraction also makes it much more difficult to see that both this verb root and the verb for 'hunting' have the exact same meaning.)

Morphemes:	**a^{21},**	**3P, Set A**
	no^{22}h,	**shoulder**
	a^{3}l,	**affixed upon**
	i^{23}n,	**along *(going along)***
	e^{33}g,	**going**
		If a preceding syllable has a (^{23}) rising tone, it will call this morpheme to become a (^{32}) falling.
	a^{2},	**present tense suffix**

ga^{21}no^{23}ha^{3}li^{23}ne^{32}ga^{2} ᎦᏃᎭᎵᏁᎦ
u^{21}no^{23}ha^{3}li^{23}nv^{32}sv^{23}ʔi^{2} ᎤᏃᎭᎵᏅᏍᏒᎢ
a^{21}no^{23}ha^{3}li^{23}ne^{32}go^{33}ʔi^{2} ᎠᏃᎭᎵᏁᎪᎢ
ha^{22}no^{22}ha^{2}li^{22}nu^{11}ga^{2} ᎭᏃᎭᎵᏄᎦ
u^{22}no^{22}ha^{2}li^{23}nv^{32}sdi^{2} ᎤᏃᎭᎵᏅᏍᏗ

di^{22}do^{22}la^{2}nv^{33}sdi^{2} du^{21}hno^{22}h(a)li^{23}nv^{32}sv^{23}ʔi^{2}
ᏗᏙᎳᏅᏍᏗ ᏚᏃᎭᎵᏅᏍᏒᎢ
He or She carried the crutches on his or her shoulder.

putting into a liquid (a long object)

a^{21}hu^{33}di^{23}ʔa^{2} ᎠᎱᏗᎠ one is putting (a long object) into a liquid

tsi^{2}ʔu^{33}di^{23}ʔa^{2} ᏥᎤᏗᎠ

u^{21}hu^{33}dv^{23}ʔi^{2} ᎤᎱᏛᎢ

a^{21}hu^{33}di^{22}sgo^{33}ʔi^{2} ᎠᎱᏗᏍᎪᎢ

hi^{2}hu^{23}da^{2} ᎯᎱᏓ

u^{22}hu^{23}di^{32}sdi^{2} ᎤᎱᏗᏍᏗ

hitting another's mouth

a^{21}hu^{22}lv^{33}ni^{23}ha^{2} ᎠᎱᎸᏂᎭ one is hitting another in the mouth

tsi^{2}ʔu^{22}lv^{33}ni^{23}ha^{2} ᏥᎤᎸᏂᎭ

u^{21}hu^{22}lv^{23}ni^{3}lv^{23}ʔi^{2} ᎤᎱᎸᏂᎸᎢ

a^{21}hu^{22}lv^{23}ni^{3}ho^{33}ʔi^{2} ᎠᎱᎸᏂᎰᎢ

hi^{22}hu^{22}lv^{22}ni^{11}ga^{2} ᎯᎱᎸᏂᎦ

u^{22}hu^{22}lv^{23}n(i^{32})sdi^{2} ᎤᎱᎸᏂᏍᏗ

moving it (from one place to another)

a^{21}hv^{33}ʔa^{2} ᎠᎲᎠ one is moving it from one place to another

tsi^{2}ʔv^{33}ʔa^{2} ᏥᎥᎠ

u^{21}hv^{33}sv^{23}ʔi^{2} ᎤᎲᏍᏒᎢ

a^{21}hv^{33}sgo^{33}ʔi^{2} ᎠᎲᏍᎪᎢ

hi^{2}hv^{23}na^{2} ᎯᎲᎾ

u^{22}hv^{11}sdi^{2} ᎤᎲᏍᏗ

sitting down

a^{21}hv^{3}sga^{2} ᎠᎲᏍᎦ one is setting it down

tsi^{2}ʔv^{3}sga^{2} ᏥᎥᏍᎦ

u^{21}hnv^{23}ʔi^{2} ᎤᏅᎢ

a^{21}hv^{3}sgo^{33}ʔi^{2} ᎠᎲᏍᎪᎢ

hi^{2}hv^{11}ga^{2} ᎯᎲᎦ

u^{22}hv^{0}hdi^{2} ᎤᎲᏗ

finding it

a^{21}hwa^{2}hti^{23}ha^{2} ᎠᏩᏘᎭ one is finding another or it

tsi^{22}hwa^{2}hti^{23}ha^{2} ᏥᏩᏘᎭ

u^{21}hwa^{2}htv^{22}hv^{23}ʔi^{2} ᎤᏩᏛᎲᎢ

a^{21}hwa^{2}hti^{23}sgo^{3}ʔi^{2} ᎠᏩᏘᏍᎪᎢ

hi^{22}hwa^{2}hta^{2} (animate) ᎯᏩᏔ

hi^{2}hwa^{2}hta^{2} (inanimate) ᎯᏩᏔ

u^{22}hwa^{2}htv^{2}hdi^{2} ᎤᏩᏛᏗ

visiting

a^{21}hwa^{2}htv^{22}hi^{23}do^{32}ha^{2} ᎠᏩᏛᎯᏙᎭ one is visiting another

tsi^{22}wa^{2}htv^{22}hi^{23}do^{32}ha^{2} ᏥᏩᏛᎯᏙᎭ

u^{21}hwa^{2}htv^{22}hi^{23}do^{32}lv^{23}ʔi^{2} ᎤᏩᏛᎯᏙᎸᎢ

a^{21}hwa^{2}htv^{22}hi^{23}do^{32}ho^{33}ʔi^{2} ᎠᏩᏛᎯᏙᎰᎢ

hi^{22}hwa^{2}htv^{22}hi^{23}da^{2} ᎯᏩᏛᎯᏓ

u^{22}hwa^{2}htv^{22}hi^{23}da^{32}sdi^{2} ᎤᏩᏛᎯᏓᏍᏗ

taking it somewhere

a^{21}hwi^{22}di^{3}ha^{2} ᎠᏫᏗᎭ one is take it somewhere

tsi^{22}wi^{22}di^{3}ha^{2} ᏥᏫᏗᎭ

u^{21}hwi^{22}dv^{22}hv^{23}ʔi^{2} ᎤᏫᏛᎲᎢ

a^{21}hwi^{22}di^{23}sgo^{3}ʔi^{2} ᎠᏫᏗᏍᎪᎢ

hi^{2}hwi^{23}da^{2} ᎯᏫᏓ

u^{22}hwi^{22}dv^{0}hdi^{2} ᎤᏫᏛᏗ

planting

a^{21}hwi^{2}sga^{2} ᎠᏫᏍᎦ one is planting

tsi^{22}wi^{2}sga^{2} ᏥᏫᏍᎦ

u^{21}hwi^{2}sv^{23}ʔi^{2} ᎤᏫᏍᏒᎢ

a^{21}hwi^{2}sgo^{33}ʔi^{2} ᎠᏫᏍᎪᎢ

hi^{2}hwi^{2} ᎯᏫ

u^{22}hwi^{2}sdi^{2} ᎤᏫᏍᏗ

becoming frosty

a^{21}hya^{2}htv^{23}hv^{3}sga^{2}	ᎠᏯᏛᎲᏍᎦ	it is becoming frosty
tsi^{22}ya^{2}htv^{23}hv^{3}sga^{2}	ᏥᏯᏛᎲᏍᎦ	I'm becoming frosty
u^{21}hya^{2}htv^{23}hnv^{3}ʔi^{2}	ᎤᏯᏛᏅᎢ	
a^{21}hya^{2}htv^{23}hv^{3}sgo^{33}ʔi^{2}	ᎠᏯᏛᎲᏍᎪᎢ	
ha^{22}hli^{22}hya^{2}htv^{22}hv^{11}ga^{2}	ᎭᏟᏯᏛᎲᎦ	
u^{22}hya^{2}htv^{2}hdi^{2}	ᎤᏯᏛᏗ	

calling/inviting

a^{21}hya^{2}ni^{23}ha^{2}	ᎠᏯᏂᎭ	one is calling, getting, inviting, or receiving another
tsi^{22}ya^{2}ni^{23}ha^{2}	ᏥᏯᏂᎭ	
u^{21}hya^{2}nv^{22}hv^{23}ʔi^{2}	ᎤᏯᏅᎲᎢ	
a^{21}hya^{2}ni^{23}sgo^{3}ʔi^{2}	ᎠᏯᏂᏍᎪᎢ	
hi^{22}ya^{2}na^{2}	ᎯᏯᎾ	
u^{22}hya^{22}nv^{0}hdi^{2}	ᎤᏯᏅᏗ	

da^{22}tsi^{22}hya^{2}nv^{22}hi^{2} ki^{2}la^{3}wu^{0} i^{2}yu^{44}sdi^{2}
ᏓᏥᏯᏅᎯ ᎩᎳᏭ ᎢᏳᏍᏗ
He or She will call him or her in a little bit.

taking somewhere by hand

a^{21}hye^{33}ga^{2}	ᎠᏰᎦ	one is taking it somewhere by hand
tsi^{22}ye^{33}ga^{2}	ᏥᏰᎦ	
u^{21}hyv^{33}sv^{23}ʔi^{2}	ᎤᏴᏍᏒᎢ	
a^{21}hye^{33}go^{33}ʔi^{2}	ᎠᏰᎪᎢ	
hi^{2}hyu^{11}ga^{2}	ᎯᏳᎦ	
u^{22}hyv^{11}sdi^{2}	ᎤᏴᏍᏗ	

having in hand

a^{21}hye^{23}ha^{2}	ᎠᏰᎭ	one has in it one's hand
tsi^{22}ye^{23}ha^{2}	ᏥᏰᎭ	
u^{21}hye^{22}hv^{23}ʔi^{2}	ᎤᏰᎲᎢ	
a^{21}hye^{22}ho^{33}ʔi^{2}	ᎠᏰᎰᎢ	
hi^{22}hye^{22}hv^{11}ga^{2}	ᎯᏰᎲᎦ	Have it in your hand!
u^{22}hye^{3}hdi^{2}	ᎤᏰᏗ	

quilting

a^{21}hye^{22}ga^{2}hlv^{3}sga^{2} ᎠᏰᎦᏢᏍᎦ one is quilting

tsi^{22}ye^{22}ga^{2}hlv^{3}sga^{2} ᏥᏰᎦᏢᏍᎦ

u^{21}hye^{22}ga^{2}hla^{3}nv^{23}ʔi^{2} ᎤᏰᎦᏝᏅᎢ

a^{21}hye^{22}ga^{2}hlv^{3}sgo^{3}ʔi^{2} ᎠᏰᎦᏢᏍᎪᎢ

hi^{2}hye^{22}ga^{2}hlv^{11}ga^{2} ᎯᏰᎦᏢᎦ

u^{22}hye^{22}ga^{2}hlv^{0}hdi^{2} ᎤᏰᎦᏢᏗ

cutting/operating

a^{21}hye^{23}hlo^{3}ha^{2} ᎠᏰᏠᎭ

one is making a cut or operating on another

tsi^{22}ye^{23}hlo^{3}ha^{2} ᏥᏰᏠᎭ

u^{21}hye^{23}hla^{3}lv^{23}ʔi^{2} ᎤᏰᏝᎸᎢ

a^{21}hye^{23}hlo^{3}ho^{33}ʔi^{2} ᎠᏰᏠᎰᎢ

hi^{22}hye^{22}la^{2}ga^{2} (animate) ᎯᏰᎳᎦ

hi^{2}hye^{22}la^{2}ga^{2} (inanimate) ᎯᏰᎳᎦ

u^{22}hye^{23}la^{0}sdi^{2} ᎤᏰᎳᏍᏗ

imitating/mocking

a^{21}hye^{22}li^{33}ʔa^{2} ᎠᏰᎵᎠ one is imitating or mocking another

tsi^{22}ye^{22}li^{33}ʔa^{2} ᏥᏰᎵᎠ

u^{21}hye^{22}li^{33}sv^{23}ʔi^{2} ᎤᏰᎵᏍᏒᎢ

a^{21}hye^{22}li^{33}sgo^{33}ʔi^{2} ᎠᏰᎵᏍᎪᎢ

hi^{22}hye^{23}la^{2} ᎯᏰᎳ

u^{22}hye^{22}li^{11}sdi^{2} ᎤᏰᎵᏍᏗ

looking for another

a^{21}hyo^{3}ha^{2} ᎠᏲᎭ one is looking for another

tsi^{22}yo^{3}ha^{2} ᏥᏲᎭ

u^{21}hya^{2}lv^{23}ʔi^{2} ᎤᏯᎸᎢ

a^{21}hyo^{2}ho^{33}ʔi^{2} ᎠᏲᎰᎢ

hi^{22}hyo^{0}ga^{2} ᎯᏲᎦ

u^{22}hyo^{0}sdi^{2} ᎤᏲᏍᏗ

swimming

a^{21}hyu^{3}ʔi^{22}ne^{33}ga^{2} ᎠᏳᎢᏁᎦ one is swimming

ga^{21}yu^{3}ʔi^{22}ne^{33}ga^{2} ᎦᏳᎢᏁᎦ

u^{21}hyu^{3}ʔi^{22}nv^{33}sv^{23}ʔi^{2} ᎤᏳᎢᏅᏍᏒᎢ

a^{21}hyu^{3}ʔi^{22}ne^{33}go^{33}ʔi^{2} ᎠᏳᎢᏁᎪᎢ

ha^{22}hyu^{2}ʔi^{22}nu^{11}ga^{2} ᎭᏳᎢᏄᎦ

u^{22}hyu^{2}ʔi^{23}nv^{32}sdi^{2} ᎤᏳᎢᏅᏍᏗ

Thundering

a^{21}hyv^{22}da^{2}gwa^{2}lo^{33}ʔa^{2} ᎠᏴᏓᏆᎶᎠ it is thundering

WE DON'T SAY THE FIRST PERSON FORM TO REMAIN RESPECTFUL

u^{21}hyv^{22}da^{2}gwa^{2}lo^{33}ʔv^{23}ʔi^{2} ᎤᏴᏓᏆᎶᎥᎢ

a^{21}hyv^{22}da^{2}gwa^{3}lo^{32}sgo^{33}ʔi^{2} ᎠᏴᏓᏆᎶᏍᎪᎢ

WE DON'T SAY THE COMMAND FORM TO REMAIN RESPECTFUL

u^{22}hyv^{22}da^{2}gwa^{2}lo^{11}sdi^{2} ᎤᏴᏓᏆᎶᏍᏗ

bending/hemming

a^{21}hyv^{2}hgwi^{3}dv^{32}sga^{2} ᎠᏴᏘᏛᎥᏍᎦ one is bending or hemming it

tsi^{22}yv^{2}hgwi^{3}dv^{32}sga^{2} ᏥᏴᏘᏛᎥᏍᎦ

u^{21}hyv^{2}hgwi^{3}dv^{32}nv^{23}ʔi^{2} ᎤᏴᏘᏛᏅᎢ

a^{21}hyv^{2}gwi^{3}dv^{32}sgo^{33}ʔi^{2} ᎠᏴᏘᏛᎥᏍᎪᎢ

hi^{2}hyv^{2}hgwi^{2}dv^{2}ʔv^{11}ga^{2} ᎯᏴᏘᏛᎥᎦ

u^{22}hyv^{2}hgwi^{2}dv^{11}di^{2} ᎤᏴᏘᏛᏗ

kicking

a^{21}hyv^{2}hte^{33}ʔa^{2} ᎠᏴᏖᎠ one is kicking another or it

tsi^{22}ya^{11}yv^{2}hte^{33}ʔa^{2} (animate) ᏥᏯᏴᏖᎠ

ga^{22}yv^{2}hte^{33}ʔa^{2} (inanimate) ᎦᏴᏖᎠ

u^{21}hyv^{2}hte^{33}sv^{23}ʔi^{2} ᎤᏴᏖᏍᏒᎢ

a^{21}hyv^{2}hte^{33}sgo^{33}ʔi^{2} ᎠᏴᏖᏍᎪᎢ

hi^{22}hyv^{2}hta^{2}gi^{2} (animate) ᎯᏴᏔᎩ

ha^{2}hyv^{2}hta^{2}gi^{2} (inanimate) ᎭᏴᏔᎩ

u^{22}hyv^{2}hte^{11}sdi^{2} ᎤᏴᏖᏍᏗ

capturing

a^{21}hyv^{22}ki^{33}di^{23}ʔa^{2} ᎠᏴᎩᏗᎠ one is capturing another

tsi^{22}yv^{22}ki^{33}di^{23}ʔa^{2} ᏥᏴᎩᏗᎠ

u^{21}hyv^{22}ki^{33}dv^{23}ʔi^{2} ᎤᏴᎩᏛᎢ

a^{21}hyv^{22}ki^{33}di^{22}sgo^{33}ʔi^{2} ᎠᏴᎩᏗᏍᎪᎢ

hi^{22}hyv^{22}ki^{23}da^{2} ᎯᏴᎩᏓ

u^{22}hyv^{22}ki^{23}di^{32}sdi^{2} ᎤᏴᎩᏗᏍᏗ

hitting one's nose

a^{21}hyv^{22}sde^{33}lu^{23}hv^{3}sga^{2} ᎠᏴᏍᏕᎷᎲᏍᎦ

one is hitting another in the nose

tsi^{22}yv^{22}sde^{33}lu^{23}hv^{3}sga^{2} ᏥᏴᏍᏕᎷᎲᏍᎦ

u^{21}hyv^{22}sde^{33}lu^{22}hnv^{23}ʔi^{2} ᎤᏴᏍᏕᎷᏅᎢ

a^{21}hyv^{22}sde^{33}lu^{23}hv^{3}sgo^{33}ʔi^{2} ᎠᏴᏍᏕᎷᎲᏍᎪᎢ

hi^{22}hyv^{22}sde^{11}lu^{22}hv^{11}ga^{2} ᎯᏴᏍᏕᎷᎲᎦ

u^{22}hyv^{22}sde^{33}lu^{2}hdi^{2} ᎤᏴᏍᏕᎷᏗ

tsa^{2}do^{22}da^{2}s tsa^{22}hyv^{22}sde^{33}lu^{22}hne^{33}ʔi^{2}

ᏣᏙᏓᏍ ᏣᏴᏍᏕᎷᏁᎢ

Did your father hit you in the nose?

choking

a^{21}hyv^{2}sgi^{23}yi^{3}ha^{2} ᎠᏴᏍᎩᏱᎭ one is choking another

tsi^{22}yv^{2}sgi^{23}yi^{3}ha^{2} ᏥᏴᏍᎩᏱᎭ

u^{21}hyv^{2}sgi^{23}yv^{32}hv^{23}ʔi^{2} ᎤᏴᏍᎩᏴᎲᎢ

a^{21}hyv^{2}sgi^{23}yi^{32}sgo^{33}ʔi^{2} ᎠᏴᏍᎩᏱᏍᎪᎢ

hi^{22}hyv^{2}sgi^{23}ya^{2} ᎯᏴᏍᎩᏯ

u^{22}hyv^{2}sgi^{23}yv^{0}hdi^{2} ᎤᏴᏍᎩᏴᏗ

hatching

a^{21}tsa^{3}ʔi^{3}ʔa^{2} ᎠᏣᎢᎠ it is hatching

ga^{2}tsa^{3}ʔi^{3}ʔa^{2} ᎦᏣᎢᎠ
u^{21}tsa^{3}ʔi^{32}sv^{23}ʔi^{2} ᎤᏣᎢᏍᎡᎢ
a^{21}tsa^{3}ʔi^{32}sgo^{33}ʔi^{2} ᎠᏣᎢᏍᎪᎢ
ha^{2}tsa^{2}ʔi^{2} ᎭᏣᎢ
u^{22}tsa^{2}ʔi^{11}sdi^{2} ᎤᏣᎢᏍᏗ

ga^{33}yu^{22}la^{2}s u^{22}na^{0}tsa^{3}ʔi^{22}se^{33}ʔi^{2} na^{2} tsu^{22}we^{23}tsi^{2}
ᎦᏳᎳᏍ ᎤᎾᏣᎢᏍᏎᎢ Ꮎ ᏧᏪᏥ
Did the eggs hatch already?

dressing up

a^{21}tsa^{2}nv^{22}sga^{2} ᎠᏣᏅᏍᎦ
one is dressing up (in really nice clothes)

ga^{2}tsa^{2}nv^{22}sga^{2} ᎦᏣᏅᏍᎦ
u^{21}tsa^{2}nv^{22}hnv^{23}ʔi^{2} ᎤᏣᏅᏅᎢ
a^{21}tsa^{2}nv^{22}sgo^{33}ʔi^{2} ᎠᏣᏅᏍᎪᎢ
ha^{2}tsa^{2}nv^{23}na^{2} ᎭᏣᏅᎾ
u^{21}tsa^{2}nv^{2}hdi^{2} ᎤᏣᏅᏗ

lv^{23}hi^{3}yu^{44}sgo^{0} ha^{22}tsa^{2}nv^{22}sgo^{33}ʔi^{2}
ᏙᎯᏳᏍᎪ ᎭᏣᏅᏍᎪᎢ
Do you ever dress up?

getting inside (confined space)

a^{21}tsa^{3}ʔv^{2}sga^{2} ᎠᏣᎥᏍᎦ

one is getting inside it (a confined/tighter space)

ga^{2}tsa^{3}ʔv^{2}sga^{2} ᎦᏣᎥᏍᎦ

u^{21}ts**a**^{32}**n**v^{23}ʔi^{2} ᎤᏣᏅᎢ (**a**^{32}**n**, populative infix)

a^{21}tsa^{3}ʔv^{2}sgo^{33}ʔi^{2} ᎠᏣᎥᏍᎪᎢ

ha^{2}tsa^{2}ʔv^{11}ga^{2} ᎭᏣᎥᎦ

u^{22}tso^{11}di^{2} ᎤᏦᏗ

do^{22}gwa^{2}le^{33}lu^{0} wi^{2}sda^{22}tsa^{2}ʔv^{11}ga^{2}

ᏙᏆᎴᎷ ᏫᏍᏓᏣᎥᎦ

You two go get in the car!

acting like another

a^{21}tse^{22}lv^{22}sga^{2} ᎠᏤᎸᏍᎦ one is acting like another

ga^{2}tse^{22}lv^{22}sga^{2} ᎦᏤᎸᏍᎦ

u^{21}tse^{22}lv^{22}hnv^{23}ʔi^{2} ᎤᏤᎸᏅᎢ

a^{21}tse^{22}lv^{22}sgo^{33}ʔi^{2} ᎠᏤᎸᏍᎪᎢ

ha^{2}tse^{22}lv^{23}na^{2} ᎭᏤᎸᎾ

u^{22}tse^{22}hlv^{0}hdi^{2} ᎤᏤᎸᏗ

u^{22}do^{22}da^{2}dv^{33} a^{21}tse^{22}lv^{22}sgo^{33}ʔi^{2}

ᎤᏙᏓᏛ ᎠᏤᎸᏍᎪᎢ

He or She definitely usually acts like his or her father.

perceives/discern/conceptualizing/feel about (it)

a^{21}ye^{22}lv^{22}sga^{2} ᎠᏰᎸᏍᎦ

tsi^{2}ye^{22}lv^{22}sga^{2} ᏥᏰᎸᏍᎦ

u^{21}ye^{22}lv^{22}sv^{23}ʔi^{2} ᎤᏰᎸᏍᏒᎢ

a^{21}ye^{22}lv^{22}sgv^{23}ʔi^{2} ᎠᏰᎸᏍᎬᎢ

hi^{2}ye^{22}lv^{23}na^{2} ᎯᏰᎸᎾ

u^{22}ye^{22}hlv^{0}hdi^{2} ᎤᏰᎸᏗ

spilling/wasting

a^{21}tse^{23}wi^{3}ʔa^{2} ᎠᏤᏫᎠ one is spilling/wasting it

ga^{2}tse^{23}wi^{3}ʔa^{2} ᎦᏤᏫᎠ

u^{21}tse^{33}wv^{23}ʔi^{2} ᎤᏤᏮᎢ

a^{21}tse^{23}wi^{32}sgo^{33}ʔi^{2} ᎠᏤᏫᏍᎪᎢ

ha^{2}tse^{23}wa^{2} ᎭᏤᏩ

u^{22}tse^{23}wa^{32}sdi^{2} ᎤᏤᏩᏍᏗ

blooming

a^{21}tsi^{22}lv^{22}sga^{2} ᎠᏥᎸᏍᎦ it is blooming

ga^{2}tsi^{22}lv^{22}sga^{2} ᎦᏥᎸᏍᎦ I'm blooming

u^{21}tsi^{22}lv^{22}hnv^{23}ʔi^{2} ᎤᏥᎸᏅᎢ

a^{21}tsi^{22}lv^{22}sgo^{33}ʔi^{2} ᎠᏥᎸᏍᎪᎢ

ha^{2}tsi^{22}lv^{23}na^{2} ᎭᏥᎸᎾ

u^{22}tsi^{22}hlv^{0}hdi^{2} ᎤᏥᎸᏗ

tla^{3} ya^{22}ni^{22}tsi^{22}lv^{22}sgv^{23}ʔi^{2} hi^{2}ʔa^{2} a^{2}ni^{22}tsi^{22}lv^{44}sgi^{2}

Ꮭ ᏯᏂᏥᎸᏍᎬᎢ ᎯᎠ ᎠᏂᏥᎸᏍᎩ

These flowers haven't been blooming.

lighting a fire

a^{21}tsi^{33}shlv^{2}sga^{2} ᎠᏥᏍᎸᏍᎦ one is lighting a fire or match

tsi^{2}tsi^{33}shlv^{2}sga^{2} ᏥᏥᏍᎸᏍᎦ

u^{21}tsi^{33}shla^{2}nv^{23}ʔi^{2} ᎤᏥᏍᎳᏅᎢ

a^{21}tsi^{33}shlv^{2}sgo^{33}ʔi^{2} ᎠᏥᏍᎸᏍᎪᎢ

hi^{2}tsi^{11}shlv^{11}ga^{2} ᎯᏥᏍᎸᎦ

u^{22}tsi^{11}shlv^{2}sdi^{2} ᎤᏥᏍᎸᏍᏗ

a^{2}tsi^{23}lv^{0}-go^{33}hlv^{2}hdo^{2}hdi^{2} u^{21}tsi^{11}slv^{3}sta^{3}nv^{23}ʔi^{2} na^{2} a^{2}tsi^{23}lv^{2}

ᎠᏥᎸ-ᎪᏢᏙᏗ ᎤᏥᏍᎸᏍᏔᏅᎢ ᎠᏥᎳ

He or She lit the fire with a match.

blowing

a^{21}tso^{33}ta^{2}sga^{2}	ᎠᏦᏔᏍᎦ	one is blowing or blowing on it
ga^{2}tso^{33}ta^{2}sga^{2}	ᎦᏦᏔᏍᎦ	
u^{21}tso^{33}ta^{2}hv^{23}ʔi^{2}	ᎤᏦᏔᏂᎢ	
a^{21}tso^{33}ta^{2}sgo^{33}ʔi^{2}	ᎠᏦᏔᏍᎪᎢ	
ha^{2}tso^{11}ta^{2}	ᎭᏦᏔ	
u^{22}tso^{11}ta^{2}sdi^{2}	ᎤᏦᏔᏍᏗ	

turning on a light

a^{21}tsv^{22}stv^{3}(hv)sga^{2}	ᎠᏨᏍᏛᏂᏍᎦ	one is turning on a light
tsi^{2}tsv^{11}stv^{3}(hv)sga^{2}	ᏥᏨᏍᏛᏂᏍᎦ	
u^{21}tsv^{22}st**a**^{3}**n**v^{33}ʔi^{2}	ᎤᏨᏍᏔᏅᎢ	(**a**^{3}**n**, populative suffix)
a^{21}tsv^{22}stv^{3}(hv)sgo^{3}ʔi^{2}	ᎠᏨᏍᏛᏂᏍᎪᎢ	
hi^{2}tsv^{22}stv^{11}ga^{2}	ᎯᏨᏍᏛᎥᎦ	
u^{22}tsv^{22}stv^{3}(hv)sdi^{2}	ᎤᏨᏍᏛᏂᏍᏗ	

chasing

a^{21}ke^{23}he^{32}ga^{2}	ᎠᎨᎮᎦ	one is chasing another or it
tsi^{22}ke^{23}he^{32}ga^{2}	ᏥᎨᎮᎦ	
u^{21}ke^{23}hv^{32}sv^{23}ʔi^{2}	ᎤᎨᏂᏍᏒᎢ	
a^{21}ke^{23}he^{32}go^{33}ʔi^{2}	ᎠᎨᎮᎪᎢ	
hi^{22}ke^{22}hu^{11}ga^{2} (animate)	ᎯᎨᎱᎦ	
hi^{2}ke^{22}hu^{11}ga^{2} (inanimate)	ᎯᎨᎱᎦ	
u^{22}ke^{23}hv^{32}sdi^{2}	ᎤᎨᏂᏍᏗ	

riding

a^{21}ki^{2}lv^{32}sdi^{23}ha^{2}	ᎠᎩᎸᏍᏗᎭ	one is riding it (something that is straddled)
tsi^{22}ya^{11}ki^{2}lv^{32}di^{23}ha^{2} (animate)	ᏥᏯᎩᎸᏗᎭ	
ga^{22}ki^{2}lv^{32}di^{23}ha^{2} (inanimate)	ᎦᎩᎸᏗᎭ	
u^{21}ki^{2}lv^{32}ta^{2}nv^{23}ʔi^{2}	ᎤᎩᎸᏔᏅᎢ	
a^{21}ki^{2}lv^{32}di^{22}sgo^{33}ʔi^{2}	ᎠᎩᎸᏗᏍᎪᎢ	
hi^{22}ya^{11}ki^{2}lv^{11}da^{2} (animate)	ᎯᏯᎩᎸᏓ	
ha^{22}ki^{2}lv^{11}da^{2} (inanimate)	ᎭᎩᎸᏓ	
u^{22}ki^{2}lv^{11}do^{2}hdi^{2}	ᎤᎩᎸᏙᏗ	

swallowing

a^{21}ki^{2}sga^{2} ᎠᎩᏍᎦ one is swallowing

tsi^{2}ʔki^{2}sga^{2} ᏥᎩᏍᎦ

u^{21}ki^{2}sv^{23}ʔi^{2} ᎤᎩᏍᏒᎢ

a^{21}ki^{2}sgo^{33}ʔi^{2} ᎠᎩᏍᎪᎢ

hi^{2}ki^{2}hi^{2} ᎯᎩᎯ

u^{22}ki^{2}hi^{2}sdi^{2} ᎤᎩᎯᏍᏗ

tle^{22}sdi^{2} yi^{2}hi^{22}ki^{2}sge^{33}sdi^{2} hi^{22}hnv^{0}go^{33}ʔi^{2}

ᏞᏍᏗ ᏱᎯᎩᏍᎨᏍᏗ ᎯᏅᎪᎢ

Don’t swallow your tongue!

shoveling

a^{21}ko^{33}de^{23}ʔa^{2} ᎠᎪᏕᎠ one is shoveling it

tsi^{22}ko^{33}de^{23}ʔa^{2} ᏥᎪᏕᎠ

u^{21}ko^{23}de^{32}sv^{23}ʔi^{2} ᎤᎪᏕᏍᏒᎢ

a^{21}ko^{23}de^{32}sgo^{33}ʔi^{2} ᎠᎪᏕᏍᎪᎢ

hi^{2}ko^{22}de^{2}gi^{2} ᎯᎪᏕᎩ

u^{22}ko^{23}de^{32}sdi^{2} ᎤᎪᏕᏍᏗ

chi^{2}no^{22}sga^{2}s hi^{2}ko^{33}de^{23}ʔa^{2}

ᏥᏃᏍᎦᏍ ᎯᎪᏕᎠ

Are you shoveling coal?

going down hill

a^{21}ga^{0}so^{3}sga^{2} ᎠᎦᏍᏐᏍᎦ one is going down hill

tsi^{2}ga^{11}so^{3}sga^{2} ᏥᎦᏍᏐᏍᎦ

u^{21}ga^{0}so^{3}sv^{23}ʔi^{2} ᎤᎦᏍᏐᏍᏒᎢ

a^{21}ga^{0}so^{3}sgo^{33}ʔi^{2} ᎠᎦᏍᏐᏍᎪᎢ

hi^{2}ga^{0}so^{11}hi^{2} ᎯᎦᏍᏐᎯ

u^{22}ga^{0}so^{11}hi^{2}sdi^{2} ᎤᎦᏍᏐᎯᏍᏗ

knows how

a^{21}ga^{0}ta^{2}ha^{2}	ᎠᎦᏔᎭ	one knows how
tsi^{2}ga^{11}ta^{2}ha^{2}	ᏥᎦᏔᎭ	
u^{21}wa^{22}ga^{0}ta^{2}hv^{23}ʔi^{2}	ᎤᏩᎦᏔᎲᎢ	
a^{21}ga^{0}ta^{2}ho^{33}ʔi^{2}	ᎠᎦᏔᎰᎢ	
hi^{22}ga^{0}ta^{2}he^{33}sdi^{2}	ᎯᎦᏔᎮᏍᏗ	
or hi^{22}ga^{0}ta^{2}hi^{2}	ᎯᎦᏔᎯ	
u^{22}wa^{22}ga^{0}tv^{22}ni^{23}da^{32}sdi^{2}	ᎤᏩᎦᏛᏂᏓᏍᏗ	

hi^{22}ga^{0}ta^{2}ha^{2}sgo^{0} tsa^{2}hyu^{2}ʔi^{23}nv^{32}sdi^{23}ʔi^{2}
ᎯᎦᏔᎭᏍᎪ ᏣᏳᎢᏅᏍᏗᎢ
Do you know how to swim?

turning back

a^{21}ga^{0}ta^{2}hv^{33}ʔa^{2}	ᎠᎦᏔᎲᎠ	one is turning back
ga^{2}ga^{11}ta^{2}hv^{33}ʔa^{2}	ᎦᎦᏔᎲᎠ	
u^{21}ga^{0}ta^{2}hv^{33}sv^{23}ʔi^{2}	ᎤᎦᏔᎲᏍᏒᎢ	
a^{21}ga^{0}ta^{2}hv^{33}sgo^{33}ʔi^{2}	ᎠᎦᏔᎲᏍᎪᎢ	
ha^{2}ga^{0}ta^{2}hv^{23}na^{2}	ᎭᎦᏔᎲᎾ	
u^{22}ga^{0}ta^{2}hv^{11}sdi^{2}	ᎤᎦᏔᎲᏍᏗ	

winking

a^{21}ga^{0}ta^{32}sdi^{23}ha^{2}	ᎠᎦᏔᏍᏗᎭ	one is winking
ga^{2}ga^{11}ta^{32}sdi^{23}ha^{2}	ᎦᎦᏔᏍᏗᎭ	
u^{21}ga^{0}ta^{32}sta^{2}nv^{23}ʔi^{2}	ᎤᎦᏔᏍᏔᏅᎢ	
a^{21}ga^{0}ta^{32}sdi^{22}sgo^{33}ʔi^{2}	ᎠᎦᏔᏍᏗᏍᎪᎢ	
ha^{2}ga^{0}ta^{11}sda^{2}	ᎭᎦᏔᏍᏓ	
u^{22}ga^{0}ta^{11}sdo^{2}hdi^{2}	ᎤᎦᏔᏍᏙᏗ	

hitting another's eye

a^{21}ga^{0}te^{22}lu^{22}(v)hv^{3}sga^{2} ᎠᎦᏖᎷᎲᏍᎦ
one is hitting another in the eye

tsi^{22}ga^{11}te^{22}lu^{22}(v)hv^{3}sga^{2} ᏥᎦᏖᎷᎲᏍᎦ
u^{21}ga^{0}te^{22}lu^{22}(v)h(v)nv^{23}ʔi^{2} ᎤᎦᏖᎷᏅᎢ
a^{21}ga^{0}te^{22}lu^{22}(v)hv^{2}sgo^{33}ʔi^{2} ᎠᎦᏖᎷᎲᏍᎪᎢ
hi^{22}ga^{11}te^{22}lu^{22}hv^{11}ga^{2} ᎯᎦᏖᎷᎲᎦ
u^{22}ga^{0}te^{22}lu^{2}hdi^{2} ᎤᎦᏖᎷᏗ

looking around

a^{21}ga^{0}te^{33}no^{23}ha^{2} ᎠᎦᏖᏃᎭ one is looking around
tsi^{2}ga^{11}te^{33}no^{23}ha^{2} ᏥᎦᏖᏃᎭ
u^{21}ga^{0}te^{23}no^{32}lv^{23}ʔi^{2} ᎤᎦᏖᏃᎸᎢ
a^{21}ga^{0}te^{33}no^{2}ho^{33}ʔi^{2} ᎠᎦᏖᏃᎰᎢ
hi^{2}ga^{0}te^{22}na^{2}ga^{2} ᎯᎦᏖᎾᎦ
u^{22}ga^{0}te^{23}na^{32}sdi^{2} ᎤᎦᏖᎾᏍᏗ

peeking through

a^{2}ga^{0}ti^{23}ha^{2} ᎠᎦᏘᎭ one is peeking through it
ga^{2}ga^{11}ti^{23}ha^{2} ᎦᎦᏘᎭ
u^{21}ga^{0}t**a^{2}hn**v^{23}ʔi^{2} ᎤᎦᏔᏅᎢ (**a^{2}n**, populative suffix)
a^{21}ga^{0}ti^{23}sgo^{3}ʔi^{2} ᎠᎦᏘᏍᎪᎢ
ha^{2}ga^{0}ta^{2} ᎭᎦᏔ
u^{22}ga^{0}to^{2}hdi^{2} ᎤᎦᏙᏗ

ha^{2}ga^{0}ta^{2}s no^{23}gwu^{3} tsi^{2}gi^{2}
ᎯᎦᏔᏍ ᏃᏊ ᏥᎩ
Do you take a peek just now?

waiting

a^{21}ga^{0}ti^{23}ya^{2} ᎠᎦᏘᏯ one is waiting for another or it

tsi^{2}ga^{11}ti^{23}ya^{2} ᏥᎦᏘᏯ

u^{21}ga^{0}ti^{33}dv^{23}ʔi^{2} ᎤᎦᏘᏛᎢ

a^{21}ga^{0}ti^{23}yo^{3}ʔi^{2} ᎠᎦᏘᏲᎢ

hi^{22}ga^{0}ti^{23}da^{2} ᎯᎦᏘᏓ

u^{22}ga^{0}ti^{23}di^{32}sdi^{2} ᎤᎦᏘᏗᏍᏗ

becoming wise

a^{21}ga^{0}to^{32}hv^{2}sga^{2} ᎠᎦᏙᎲᏍᎦ one is becoming wise

tsi^{2}ga^{11}to^{32}hv^{2}sga^{2} ᏥᎦᏙᎲᏍᎦ

u^{21}ga^{0}to^{32}hv^{2}sv^{23}ʔi^{2} ᎤᎦᏙᎲᏍᏒᎢ

a^{21}ga^{0}to^{32}hv^{2}sgo^{33}ʔi^{2} ᎠᎦᏙᎲᏍᎪᎢ

hi^{2}ga^{0}to^{2}ʔv^{2}hi^{2} ᎯᎦᏙᎥᎯ

u^{22}ga^{0}to^{2}ʔv^{2}hi^{3}sdi^{2} ᎤᎦᏙᎥᎯᏍᏗ

looking at another

a^{21}ga^{0}to^{23}sdi^{3}ha^{2} ᎠᎦᏙᏍᏗᎭ one is looking at another or it

tsi^{22}ya^{2}ga^{11}to^{23}sdi^{3}ha^{2} (animate) ᏥᏯᎦᏙᏍᏗᎭ

ga^{2}ga^{11}to^{23}sdi^{3}ha^{2} (inanimate) ᎦᎦᏙᏍᏗᎭ

u^{21}ga^{0}to^{23}sta^{3}nv^{23}ʔi^{2} ᎤᎦᏙᏍᏔᏅᎢ

a^{21}ga^{0}to^{23}di^{32}sgo^{33}ʔi^{2} ᎠᎦᏙᏗᏍᎪᎢ

hi^{22}ya^{2}ga^{0}to^{23}sda^{2} (animate) ᎯᏯᎦᏙᏍᏓ

ha^{2}ga^{0}to^{23}sda^{2} (inanimate) ᎭᎦᏙᏍᏓ

u^{22}ga^{0}to^{23}sdo^{3}hdi^{2} ᎤᎦᏙᏍᏙᏗ

going through

a^{21}ga^{0}tv^{33}le^{22}sga^{2} ᎠᎦᏛᎴᏍᎦ one is going through it

tsi^{2}ga^{11}tv^{33}le^{22}sga^{2} ᏥᎦᏛᎴᏍᎦ

u^{21}ga^{0}tv^{33}le^{22}sv^{23}ʔi^{2} ᎤᎦᏛᎴᏍᏒᎢ

a^{21}ga^{0}tv^{33}le^{22}sgo^{33}ʔi^{2} ᎠᎦᏛᎴᏍᎪᎢ

hi^{2}ga^{0}tv^{22}le^{23}hi^{2} ᎯᎦᏛᎴᎯ

u^{22}ga^{0}tv^{22}le^{23}hi^{3}sdi^{2} ᎤᎦᏛᎴᎯᏍᏗ

a^{21}gwo^{22}hi^{2}yu^{33}dv^{33} yi^{2}hi^{2}ga^{0}tv^{22}le^{23}hi^{2}

ᎠᏉᎯᏳᏛ ᏱᎯᎦᏛᎴᎯ

I believe you can get through it.

dipping

a^{21}ku^{23}gi^{3}ʔa^{2} ᎠᎫᎩᎠ one is dipping (a liquid)

tsi^{2}ʔgu^{23}gi^{3}ʔa^{2} ᏥᎫᎩᎠ

u^{21}ku^{23}gi^{32}sv^{23}ʔi^{2} ᎤᎫᎩᏍᏒᎢ

a^{21}ku^{23}gi^{32}sgo^{33}ʔi^{2} ᎠᎫᎩᏍᎪᎢ

hi^{2}ku^{23}gi^{2} ᎯᎫᎩ

u^{22}ku^{23}gi^{32}sdi^{2} ᎤᎫᎩᏍᏗ

paying

a^{21}gwi^{2}yi^{23}ha^{2} ᎠᏘᏱᎭ one is paying

ga^{2}gwi^{2}yi^{23}ha^{2} ᎦᏘᏱᎭ

u^{21}gwi^{2}yv^{22}hv^{23}ʔi^{2} ᎤᏘᏴᎲᎢ

a^{21}gwi^{2}yi^{23}sgo^{3}ʔi^{2} ᎠᏘᏱᏍᎪᎢ

ha^{2}gwi^{2}ya^{2} ᎭᏘᏯ

u^{22}gwi^{2}yv^{0}hdi^{2} ᎤᏘᏴᏗ

hi^{2}la^{32}ga^{4} ha^{2}gwi^{2}yi^{23}ha^{2} si^{22}nv^{44}dv^{2} ge^{22}hv^{4}

ᎯᎳᎢᎦ ᎭᏘᏱᎭ ᏍᏏᏅᏮ ᎨᎲᎢ

How much are you paying each month?

paying another

a^{21}gwi^{2}yv^{33}ʔe^{23}ha^{2} ᎠᏈᏴᎡᎭ one is paying another

tsi^{22}ya^{2}gwi^{2}yv^{33}ʔe^{23}ha^{2} ᏥᏯᏈᏴᎡᎭ

u^{21}gwi^{2}yv^{33}ʔe^{22}lv^{23}ʔi^{2} ᎤᏈᏴᎡᎸᎢ

a^{21}gwi^{2}yv^{33}ʔe^{22}ho^{33}ʔi^{2} ᎠᏈᏴᎡᎰᎢ

hi^{22}ya^{2}gwi^{2}yv^{11}si^{2} ᎯᏯᏈᏴᏏ

u^{22}kwi^{2}yv^{22}ʔe^{3}hdi^{2} ᎤᏈᏴᎡᏗ

hi^{2}la^{32}yv^{4} da^{2}sgwa^{2}gwi^{2}yv^{33}ʔe^{22}li^{0}

ᎯᎳᎢᏴ ᏓᏍᏆᏈᏴᎡᎵ

When are you going to pay me?

stomping

a^{21}la^{32}sda^{2}ʔe^{23}ha^{2} ᎠᎳᏍᏓᎡᎭ one is stomping on another (literal)

one is speaking badly of someone (figurative)

tsi^{22}ya^{2}la^{32}sda^{2}ʔe^{23}ha^{2} ᏥᏯᎳᏍᏓᎡᎭ

u^{21}la^{32}sda^{2}ʔe^{22}hlv^{23}ʔi^{2} ᎤᎳᏍᏓᎡᎸᎢ

a^{21}la^{32}sda^{2}ʔe^{22}sgo^{33}ʔi^{2} ᎠᎳᏍᏓᎡᏍᎪᎢ

hi^{22}ya^{2}la^{11}sda^{2}ʔv^{23}la^{2} (animate) ᎯᏯᎳᏍᏓᎥᎳ

ha^{2}la^{11}sda^{2}ʔv^{23}la^{2} (inanimate) ᎭᎳᏍᏓᎥᎳ

u^{22}la^{11}sda^{2}ʔe^{3}hdi^{2} ᎤᎳᏍᏓᎡᏗ

stepping

a^{21}la^{32}sdv^{2}sga^{2} ᎠᎳᏍᏛᏍᎦ one is stepping on another or it

tsi^{22}ya^{2}la^{32}sdv^{2}sga^{2} (animate) ᏥᏯᎳᏍᏛᏍᎦ

ga^{2}la^{32}sdv^{2}sga^{2} (inanimate) ᎦᎳᏍᏛᏍᎦ

u^{21}la^{32}sdv^{22}hnv^{23}ʔi^{2} ᎤᎳᏍᏛᏅᎢ

a^{21}la^{32}sdv^{2}sgo^{33}ʔi^{2} ᎠᎳᏍᏛᏍᎪᎢ

hi^{22}ya^{2}la^{11}sdv^{2}ʔv^{11}ga^{2} (animate) ᎯᏯᎳᏍᏛᎥᎦ

ha^{2}la^{11}sdv^{2}ʔv^{11}ga^{2} (inanimate) ᎭᎳᏍᏓᎥᎦ

u^{22}la^{11}sdv^{11}di^{2} ᎤᎳᏍᏛᏗ

playing ball

a^{21}la^{32}sga^{2}li^{23}ha^{2} ᎠᎳᏍᎦᎵᎭ one is playing ball

ga^{2}la^{32}sga^{2}li^{23}ha^{2} ᎦᎳᏍᎦᎵᎭ

u^{21}la^{32}sga^{2}lv^{22}hv^{23}ʔi^{2} ᎤᎳᏍᎦᎸᎲᎢ

a^{21}la^{32}sga^{2}li^{23}sgo^{3}ʔi^{2} ᎠᎳᏍᎦᎵᏍᎪᎢ

ha^{2}la^{11}sga^{2}la^{2} ᎭᎳᏍᎦᎳ

u^{22}la^{11}sga^{2}hlo^{0}hdi^{2} ᎤᎳᏍᎦᏠᏗ

taking a step

a^{21}la^{32}sgv^{23}ʔa^{2} ᎠᎳᏍᎬᎠ one is taking a step

ga^{2}la^{32}sgv^{23}ʔa^{2} ᎦᎳᏍᎬᎠ

u^{21}la^{32}sgv^{22}sv^{23}ʔi^{2} ᎤᎳᏍᎬᏍᏒᎢ

a^{21}la^{32}sgv^{22}sgo^{33}ʔi^{2} ᎠᎳᏍᎬᏍᎪᎢ

ha^{2}la^{11}sgv^{23}na^{2} ᎭᎳᏍᎬᎾ

u^{22}la^{11}sgv^{22}sdi^{2} ᎤᎳᏍᎬᏍᏗ

standing it up (a long object)

a^{21}le^{2}hdi^{23}ha^{2} ᎠᎴᏗᎭ one is standing it up (a long object)

ga^{2}le^{11}di^{23}ha^{2} ᎦᎴᏗᎭ

u^{21}le^{2}hta^{2}nv^{23}ʔi^{2} ᎤᎴᏔᏅᎢ

a^{21}le^{2}hdi^{23}sgo^{3}ʔi^{2} ᎠᎴᏗᏍᎪᎢ

ha^{2}le^{2}hda^{2} ᎭᎴᏓ

u^{22}le^{2}hdo^{3}hdi^{2} ᎤᎴᏙᏗ

ha^{11}ne^{22}hlv^{0}da^{2} tsa^{2}le^{2}hdo^{3}hdi^{2} hi^{2}ʔa^{2}nv^{3} ge^{33}tv^{2}sdi^{23}ʔi^{2}

ᎭᏁᎸᏓ ᏣᎴᏙᏗ ᎯᎠᏅ ᎨᏛᏍᏗᎢ

Try to stand this post up!

standing

a^{21}le^{22}hv^{3}sga^{2} ᎠᎴᎲᏍᎦ one is standing (in a certain spot)

ga^{2}le^{2}ʔv^{3}sga^{2} ᎦᎴᎥᏍᎦ

u^{21}le^{22}hnv^{23}ʔi^{2} ᎤᎴᏅᎢ

a^{21}le^{22}hv^{2}(hv^{3})sgo^{33}ʔi^{2} ᎠᎴᎲᏍᎪᎢ

ha^{2}le^{22}hv^{11}ga^{2} ᎭᎴᎲᎦ

u^{22}le^{2}hdi^{2} ᎤᎴᏗ

stopping

a^{21}le^{22}hwi^{2}sdi^{23}ha^{2} ᎠᎴᏫᏍᏗᎭ one is stopping

ga^{2}le^{11}wi^{2}sdi^{23}ha^{2} ᎦᎴᏫᏍᏗᎭ

u^{21}le^{22}hwi^{2}sta^{2}nv^{23}ʔi^{2} ᎤᎴᏫᏍᏔᏅᎢ

a^{21}le^{22}hwi^{2}sdi^{23}sgo^{3}ʔi^{2} ᎠᎴᏫᏍᏗᏍᎪᎢ

ha^{2}le^{22}hwi^{2}sda^{2} ᎭᎴᏫᏍᏓ

u^{22}le^{22}hwi^{2}sdo^{3}hdi^{2} ᎤᎴᏫᏍᏙᏗ

tla^{3}dv^{33} yi^{2}dv^{22}le^{22}hwi^{2}sta^{2}ni^{2} ge^{22}li^{3}ʔa^{2}

ᏝᏛ ᏱᏛᎴᏫᏍᏔᏂ ᎨᎵᎠ

I don’t think he or she is going to stop.

stopping another

a^{21}le^{22}hwi^{2}sdo^{2}hdi^{23}ha^{2} ᎠᎴᏫᏍᏙᏗᎭ one is stopping another or it

tsi^{22}ya^{2}le^{11}wi^{22}sdo^{2}hdi^{23}ha^{2} (animate) ᏥᏯᎴᏫᏍᏙᏗᎭ

ga^{2}le^{11}wi^{2}sdo^{2}hdi^{23}ha^{2} (inanimate) ᎦᎴᏫᏍᏙᏗᎭ

u^{21}le^{22}hwi^{2}sdo^{2}hta^{2}nv^{23}ʔi^{2} ᎤᎴᏫᏍᏙᏔᏅᎢ

a^{21}le^{22}hwi^{2}sdo^{2}hdi^{22}sgo^{33}ʔi^{2} ᎠᎴᏫᏍᏙᏗᏍᎪᎢ

hi^{22}ya^{2}le^{11}wi^{2}sdo^{2}hda^{2} (animate) ᎯᏯᎴᏫᏍᏙᏓ

ha^{2}le^{22}hwi^{2}sdo^{2}hda^{2} (inanimate) ᎭᎴᏫᏍᏙᏓ

u^{22}le^{22}hwi^{2}sdo^{2}hdo^{3}hdi^{2} ᎤᎴᏫᏍᏙᏗ

starting/beginning

a^{21}le^{22}ni^{23}ha^{2} ᎠᎴᏂᎭ one is starting or beginning

ga^{2}le^{22}ni^{23}ʔa^{2} ᎦᎴᏂᎠ

u^{21}le^{22}nv^{22}hv^{23}ʔi^{2} ᎤᎴᏅᎲᎢ

a^{21}le^{22}ni^{23}sgo^{3}ʔi^{2} ᎠᎴᏂᏍᎪᎢ

ha^{2}le^{23}na^{2} ᎭᎴᎾ

u^{22}le^{22}nv^{0}hdi^{2} ᎤᎴᏅᏗ

thanking

a^{21}li^{22}he^{23}li^{32}che^{23}ha^{2} ᎠᎵᎮᎵᏤᎭ one is thanking another

tsi^{22}ya^{2}li^{2}ʔe^{23}li^{32}che^{23}ha^{2} ᏥᏯᎵᎡᎵᏤᎭ

u^{21}li^{22}he^{23}li^{32}che^{22}lv^{23}ʔi^{2} ᎤᎵᎮᎵᏤᎸᎢ

a^{21}li^{22}he^{23}li^{32}che^{22}ho^{33}ʔi^{2} ᎠᎵᎮᎵᏤᎰᎢ

hi^{22}ya^{2}li^{2}ʔe^{22}li^{11}chi^{2}si^{2} ᎯᏯᎵᎡᎵᏥᏍᏏ

u^{22}li^{22}he^{23}li^{32}che^{2}hdi^{2} ᎤᎵᎮᎵᏤᏗ

a^{21}gwa^{2}li^{22}he^{23}li^{32}che^{22}ho^{33}ʔi^{2} ni^{2}go^{33}lv^{4}

ᎠᏆᎵᎮᎵᏤᎰᎢ ᏂᎪᎯᎸ

He or She always thanks me.

happy/thankful

a^{21}li^{22}he^{23}li^{32}ga^{2} ᎠᎵᎮᎵᎦ one is happy or thankful

ga^{2}li^{2}ʔe^{23}li^{32}ga^{2} ᎦᎵᎡᎵᎦ

u^{22}li^{22}he^{23}li^{32}tsv^{23}ʔi^{2} ᎤᎵᎮᎵᏨᎢ

a^{21}li^{22}he^{23}li^{32}go^{33}ʔi^{2} ᎠᎵᎮᎵᎪᎢ

ha^{2}li^{22}he^{22}li^{11}gi^{2} ᎭᎵᎮᎵᎩ

u^{22}li^{22}he^{23}li^{3}sdi^{2} ᎤᎵᎮᎵᏍᏗ

exchanging/trading

a^{21}li^{3}ʔi^{23}di^{3}ʔa^{2} ᎠᎵᎢᏗᎠ one is exchanging or trading it

ga^{2}li^{3}ʔi^{23}di^{3}ʔa^{2} ᎦᎵᎢᏗᎠ

u^{21}li^{3}ʔi^{22}dv^{23}ʔi^{2} ᎤᎵᎢᏛᎢ

a^{21}li^{3}ʔi^{23}di^{32}sgo^{33}ʔi^{2} ᎠᎵᎢᏗᏍᎪᎢ

ha^{22}li^{2}ʔi^{23}da^{2} ᎭᎵᎢᏓ

u^{22}li^{2}ʔi^{23}di^{32}sdi^{2} ᎤᎵᎢᏗᏍᏗ

running away/escaping

a^{21}li^{2}ti^{33}ʔa^{2} ᎠᎵᏘᎠ one is running away
one is escaping

ga^{2}li^{11}ti^{33}ʔa^{2} ᎦᎵᏘᎠ
u^{21}li^{2}ti^{33}sv^{23}ʔi^{2} ᎤᎵᏘᏍᏒᎢ
a^{21}li^{2}ti^{33}sgo^{33}ʔi^{2} ᎠᎵᏘᏍᎪᎢ
ha^{2}li^{2}ti^{2} ᎭᎵᏘ
u^{22}li^{2}ti^{11}sdi^{2} ᎤᎵᏘᏍᏗ

u^{21}li^{0}ti^{3}ʔe^{22}le^{33}ʔi^{2} a^{21}gwa^{0}tv^{23}ga^{32}hnv^{23}ʔi^{2}
ᎤᎵᏘᎡᎴᎢ ᎠᏆᏛᎦᏅᎢ
I heard it got aways from him, her, or it.

taking off a ring

a^{21}li^{2}ye^{32}su^{22}sdv^{0}gi^{33}ʔa^{2} ᎠᎵᏰᏍᏑᏍᏛᎩᎠ one is taking off a ring

ga^{2}li^{2}ye^{32}su^{22}sdv^{0}gi^{33}ʔa^{2} ᎦᎵᏰᏍᏑᏍᏛᎩᎠ
u^{22}li^{2}ye^{32}su^{22}sdv^{0}gi^{33}sv^{23}ʔi^{2} ᎤᎵᏰᏍᏑᏍᏛᎩᏍᏒᎢ
a^{21}li^{2}ye^{32}su^{22}sdv^{0}gi^{33}sgo^{33}ʔi^{2} ᎠᎵᏰᏍᏑᏛᎩᏍᎪᎢ
ha^{2}li^{2}ye^{11}su^{22}sdv^{0}gi^{2} ᎭᎵᏰᏍᏑᏍᏛᎩ
u^{22}li^{2}ye^{11}su^{22}sdv^{0}gi^{33}sdi^{2} ᎤᎵᏰᏍᏑᏍᏛᎩᏍᏗ

putting on a ring

a^{21}li^{2}ye^{32}su^{22}sdv^{3}sga^{2} ᎠᎵᏰᏍᏑᏍᏛᏍᎦ one is putting on a (finger) ring

ga^{2}li^{2}ye^{32}su^{23}sdv^{3}sga^{2} ᎦᎵᏰᏍᏑᏍᏛᏍᎦ
u^{22}li^{2}ye^{32}su^{22}sta^{2}nv^{23}ʔi^{2} ᎤᎵᏰᏍᏑᏍᏔᏅᎢ
a^{21}li^{2}ye^{32}su^{23}sdv^{3}sgo^{3}ʔi^{2} ᎠᎵᏰᏍᏑᏍᏛᏍᎪᎢ
ha^{2}li^{2}ye^{11}su^{22}sdv^{11}ga^{2} ᎭᎵᏰᏍᏑᏍᏛᎦ
u^{22}li^{2}ye^{11}su^{23}sdv^{32}sdi^{2} ᎤᎵᏰᏍᏑᏍᏛᏍᏗ

spitting

a^{21}li^{0}tsi^{33}gwi^{0}sga^{2} ᎠᎵᏥᏈᏍᎦ one is spitting

ga^{22}li^{0}tsi^{33}gwi^{0}sga^{2} ᎦᎵᏥᏈᏍᎦ

u^{21}li^{0}tsi^{33}gwi^{0}sv^{23}ʔi^{2} ᎤᎵᏥᏈᏒᎢ

a^{21}li^{0}tsi^{33}kwi^{0}sgo^{33}ʔi^{2} ᎠᎵᏥᏈᏍᎪᎢ

ha^{22}li^{0}tsi^{11}sgwa^{2} ᎭᎵᏥᏍᏆ

u^{22}li^{0}tsi^{11}gwi^{0}sdi^{2} ᎤᎵᏥᏈᏍᏗ

ascending/raising

a^{21}li^{0}sa^{2}la^{2}di^{23}ʔa^{2} ᎠᎵᏌᎳᏗᎠ one is ascending or raising

ga^{2}li^{11}sa^{2}la^{2}di^{23}ʔa^{2} ᎦᎵᏌᎳᏗᎠ

u^{21}li^{0}sa^{2}la^{0}da^{32}nv^{23}ʔi^{2} ᎤᎵᏌᎳᏓᏅᎢ

a^{21}li^{0}sa^{2}la^{0}di^{32}sgo^{33}ʔi^{2} ᎠᎵᏌᎳᏗᏍᎪᎢ

ha^{22}li^{0}sa^{2}la^{0}dv^{11}ga^{2} ᎭᎵᏌᎳᏛᎦ

u^{22}li^{0}sa^{2}la^{0}do^{11}di^{2} ᎤᎵᏌᎳᏙᏗ

eating a meal

a^{21}li^{0}sda^{32}yv^{23}hv^{3}sga^{2} ᎠᎵᏍᏓᏴᎲᏍᎦ one is eating a meal

ga^{2}li^{11}sda^{32}yv^{23}hv^{3}sga^{2} ᎦᎵᏍᏓᏴᎲᏍᎦ

u^{21}li^{0}sda^{32}yv^{22}hnv^{23}ʔi^{2} ᎤᎵᏍᏓᏴᏅᎢ

a^{21}li^{0}sda^{32}yv^{23}hv^{3}sgo^{33}ʔi^{2} ᎠᎵᏍᏓᏴᎲᏍᎪᎢ

ha^{22}li^{0}sda^{11}yv^{0}hv^{11}ga^{2} ᎭᎵᏍᏓᏴᎲᎦ

u^{22}li^{0}sda^{11}yv^{0}hdi^{2} ᎤᎵᏍᏓᏴᏗ

helping

a^{21}li^{0}sde^{22}li^{23}ha^{2} ᎠᎵᏍᏕᎵᎭ one is helping

ga^{2}li^{11}sde^{22}li^{23}ha^{2} ᎦᎵᏍᏕᎵᎭ

u^{21}li^{0}sde^{22}lv^{22}hv^{23}ʔi^{2} ᎤᎵᏍᏕᎸᎲᎢ

a^{21}li^{0}sde^{22}li^{23}sgo^{3}ʔi^{2} ᎠᎵᏍᏕᎵᏍᎪᎢ

ha^{22}li^{0}sde^{23}la^{2} ᎭᎵᏍᏕᎳ

u^{22}li^{0}sde^{22}hlv^{0}hdi^{2} ᎤᎵᏍᏕᎸᏗ

taking off a cap

a^{21}li^{0}sdu^{33}le^{23}ʔa^{2} ᎠᎵᏍᏚᎴᎠ one is taking off a cap (from their head)
ga^{2}li^{11}sdu^{33}le^{23}ʔa^{2} ᎦᎵᏍᏚᎴᎠ
u^{21}li^{0}sdu^{23}le^{32}sv^{23}ʔi^{2} ᎤᎵᏍᏚᎴᏍᎡᎢ
a^{21}li^{0}sdu^{23}le^{32}sgo^{33}ʔi^{2} ᎠᎵᏍᏚᎴᏍᎪᎢ
ha^{22}li^{0}sdu^{22}le^{2}gi^{2} ᎭᎵᏍᏚᎴᎩ
u^{22}li^{0}sdu^{23}le^{32}sdi^{2} ᎤᎵᏍᏚᎴᏍᏗ

washing one's hair

a^{21}li^{0}sdu^{22}le^{33}ha^{2} ᎠᎵᏍᏚᎴᎭ one is washing one's hair
ga^{2}li^{11}sdu^{22}le^{33}ha^{2} ᎦᎵᏍᏚᎴᎭ
u^{21}li^{0}sdu^{22}le^{33}hv^{23}ʔi^{2} ᎤᎵᏍᏚᎴᎲᎢ
a^{21}li^{0}sdu^{22}le^{33}sgo^{33}ʔi^{2} ᎠᎵᏍᏚᎴᏍᎪᎢ
ha^{22}li^{0}sdu^{23}la^{2} ᎭᎵᏍᏚᎳ
u^{22}li^{0}sdu^{23}hle^{0}hdi^{2} ᎤᎵᏍᏚᎴᏗ

putting on a cap

a^{21}li^{0}sdu^{23}li^{3}ʔa^{2} ᎠᎵᏍᏚᎵᎠ one is putting a cap on (their head)
ga^{2}li^{11}sdu^{23}li^{3}ʔa^{2} ᎦᎵᏍᏚᎵᎠ
u^{21}li^{0}sdu^{23}l**a^{32}n**v^{23}ʔi^{2} ᎤᎵᏍᏚᎳᏅᎢ (a^{32}n, populative suffix)
a^{21}li^{0}sdu^{23}li^{32}sgo^{33}ʔi^{2} ᎠᎵᏍᏚᎵᏍᎪᎢ
ha^{22}li^{0}sdu^{22}lv^{11}ga^{2} ᎭᎵᏍᏚᎸᎦ
u^{22}li^{0}sdu^{23}lo^{32}di^{2} ᎤᎵᏍᏚᎶᏗ

taking a seat

a^{21}li^{0}sdv^{22}hlu^{3}sga^{2} ᎠᎵᏍᏛᏡᏍᎦ one is taking a seat
ga^{2}li^{11}sdv^{22}hlu^{3}sga^{2} ᎦᎵᏍᏛᏡᏍᎦ
u^{21}li^{0}sdv^{23}hlu^{3}nv^{23}ʔi^{2} ᎤᎵᏍᏛᏡᏅᎢ
a^{21}li^{0}sdv^{23}hlu^{3}sgo^{33}ʔi^{2} ᎠᎵᏍᏛᏡᏍᎪᎢ
ha^{22}li^{0}sdv^{22}hlu^{11}ga^{2} ᎭᎵᏍᏛᏡᎦ
u^{22}li^{0}sdv^{23}hlu^{3}sdi^{2} ᎤᎵᏍᏛᏡᏍᏗ

shaking one's head

a^{21}li^{0}sdv^{23}hni^{3}ha^{2}	ᎠᎵᏍᏛᏂᎭ	one is shaking one's head
ga^{2}li^{11}**sdv^{23}hni^{3}**ha^{2}	ᎦᎵᏍᏛᏂᎭ	
u^{21}li^{0}sdv^{22}**hni^{2}lv^{23}**ʔi^{2}	ᎤᎵᏍᏛᏂᎸᎢ	
a^{21}li^{0}s**dv^{23}hni^{3}ho^{33}**ʔi^{2}	ᎠᎵᏍᏛᏂᎰᎢ	
ha^{22}li^{0}sdv^{22}hni^{0}ga^{2}	ᎭᎵᏍᏛᏂᎦ	
u^{22}li^{0}sdv^{22}hni^{0}hdi^{2}	ᎤᎵᏍᏛᏂᏗ	

*By default Cherokee requires a rising tone on the penultimate syllable (the rightmost long vowel). It is because of this requirement that you can see the tones shifting as shown in the bolded segments above.

dancing

a^{21}li^{0}sgi^{33}ʔa^{2}	ᎠᎵᏍᎩᎠ	one is dancing
ga^{2}li^{11}sgi^{33}ʔa^{2}	ᎦᎵᏍᎩᎠ	
u^{21}li^{0}sgi^{33}sv^{23}ʔi^{2}	ᎤᎵᏍᎩᏍᎡᎢ	
a^{21}li^{0}sgi^{33}sgo^{33}ʔi^{2}	ᎠᎵᏍᎩᏍᎪᎢ	
ha^{22}li^{0}sgi^{2}	ᎭᎵᏍᎩ	
u^{22}li^{0}sgi^{11}sdi^{2}	ᎤᎵᏍᎩᏍᏗ	

permitting/allowing

a^{21}li^{0}sgo^{22}hlv^{0}da^{32}ne^{23}ha^{2}	ᎠᎵᏍᎪᎸᏓᏁᎭ	one is permitting another
tsi^{22}ya^{2}li^{11}sgo^{22}hlv^{0}da^{32}ne^{23}ha^{2}	ᏥᏯᎵᏍᎪᎸᏓᏁᎭ	
u^{21}li^{0}sgo^{22}hlv^{0}da^{32}ne^{22}lv^{23}ʔi^{2}	ᎤᎵᏍᎪᎸᏓᏁᎸᎢ	
a^{21}li^{0}sgo^{22}hlv^{0}da^{32}ne^{22}ho^{33}ʔi^{2}	ᎠᎵᏍᎪᎸᏓᏁᎰᎢ	
hi^{22}ya^{2}li^{11}sgo^{22}hlv^{0}da^{11}si^{2}	ᎯᏯᎵᏍᎪᎸᏓᏍᏏ	
u^{22}li^{0}sgo^{22}hlv^{0}da^{11}ne^{2}hdi^{2}	ᎤᎵᏍᎪᎸᏓᏁᏗ	

wi^{2}hi^{22}ya^{2}li^{0}sgo^{22}hlv^{0}da^{11}si^{2} tsu^{22}hno^{22}gi^{11}sdi^{23}ʔi^{2}
ᏫᎯᏯᎵᏍᎪᎸᏓᏍᏏ ᏧᏃᎩᏍᏗᎢ
Permit/Allow him or her to sing!

nodding

a^{21}li^{0}sgu^{32}sga^{2} ᎠᎵᏍᎫᏍᎦ one is nodding one's head

ga^{2}li^{11}(u^{2})sg(i^{33})u^{32}sga^{2} ᎦᎵᏍᎫᏍᎦ (the **reversive morpheme** is phonologically hidden due to contraction by speakers)

u^{21}li^{0}sgu^{32}hyv^{23}ʔi^{2} ᎤᎵᏍᎫᏴᎢ

a^{21}li^{0}sgu^{32}sgo^{33}ʔi^{2} ᎠᎵᏍᎫᏍᎪᎢ

ha^{22}li^{0}sgu^{11}hya^{2} ᎭᎵᏍᎫᏯ

u^{22}li^{0}sgu^{11}sdi^{2} ᎤᎵᏍᎫᏍᏗ

ending

a^{21}li^{0}sgwa^{2}di^{23}ʔa^{2} ᎠᎵᏍᏆᏗᎠ it is ending

ga^{2}li^{11}sgwa^{2}di^{23}ʔa^{2} ᎦᎵᏍᏆᏗᎠ I'm ending

u^{21}li^{0}sgwa^{3}dv^{23}ʔi^{2} ᎤᎵᏍᏆᏛᎢ

a^{21}li^{0}sgwa^{2}di^{32}sgo^{33}ʔi^{2} ᎠᎵᏍᏆᏗᏍᎪᎢ

ha^{22}li^{0}sgwa^{2}da^{2} ᎭᎵᏍᏆᏓ Be ending!

u^{22}li^{0}sgwa^{2}di^{11}sdi^{2} ᎤᎵᏍᏆᏗᏍᏗ

sticking one's head out

a^{21}li^{0}sgwa^{2}lu^{23}di^{3}ʔa^{2} ᎠᎵᏍᏆᎷᏗᎠ one is sticking one's head out

ga^{2}li^{11}sgwa^{2}lu^{23}di^{3}ʔa^{2} ᎦᎵᏍᏆᎷᏗᎠ

u^{21}li^{0}sgwa^{2}lu^{23}da^{32}nv^{23}ʔi^{2} ᎤᎵᏍᏆᎷᏓᏅᎢ

a^{21}li^{0}sgwa^{2}lu^{23}di^{32}sgo^{33}ʔi^{2} ᎠᎵᏍᏆᎷᏗᏍᎪᎢ

ha^{22}li^{0}sgwa^{2}lu^{22}dv^{11}ga^{2} ᎭᎵᏍᏆᎷᏛᎦ

u^{22}li^{0}sgwa^{2}lu^{23}do^{32}di^{2}ᎤᎵᏍᏆᎷᏙᏗ

taking one's hat off

a^{21}li^{0}sgwe^{33}tu^{2}hgi^{33}ʔa^{2}	ᎠᎵᏍᏇᏚᎩᎠ	one is taking off one's hat
ga^{2}li^{11}sgwe^{33}tu^{2}hgi^{33}ʔa^{2}	ᎦᎵᏍᏇᏚᎩᎠ	
u^{21}li^{0}sgwe^{33}tu^{2}hgi^{33}sv^{23}ʔi^{2}	ᎤᎵᏍᏇᏚᎩᏍᏒᎢ	
a^{21}li^{0}sgwe^{33}tu^{2}hgi^{33}sgo^{33}ʔi^{2}	ᎠᎵᏍᏇᏚᎩᏍᎪᎢ	
ha^{22}li^{0}sgwe^{11}tu^{2}hgi^{2}	ᎭᎵᏍᏇᏚᎩ	
u^{21}li^{0}sgwe^{11}tu^{2}hgi^{11}sdi^{2}	ᎤᎵᏍᏇᏚᎩᏍᏗ	

ha^{22}li^{0}sgwe^{33}tu^{2}hgi^{2}. tsi^{2}go^{22}li^{23}ya^{2}.
ᎭᎵᏍᏇᏚᎩ. ᏥᎪᎵᏯ.
Take your hat off. Let me look at it.

putting a hat on

a^{21}li^{0}sgwe^{33}tu^{2}hv^{3}sga^{2}	ᎠᎵᏍᏇᏚᎲᏍᎦ	one is putting a hat on
ga^{2}li^{11}sgwe^{33}tu^{2}hv^{3}sga^{2}	ᎦᎵᏍᏇᏚᎲᏍᎦ	
u^{21}li^{0}sgwe^{33}tu^{2}hnv^{23}ʔi^{2}	ᎤᎵᏍᏇᏚᏅᎢ	
a^{21}li^{0}sgwe^{33}tu^{3}hv^{3}sgo^{33}ʔi^{2}	ᎠᎵᏍᏇᏚᎲᏍᎪᎢ	
ha^{22}li^{0}sgwe^{11}tu^{2}hv^{11}ga^{2}	ᎭᎵᏍᏇᏚᎲᎦ	
u^{22}li^{0}sgwe^{11}tu^{2}(hv)sdi^{2}	ᎤᎵᏍᏇᏚᎲᏍᏗ	

di^{2}ga^{22}du^{33}hv^{4} yu^{22}we^{23}na^{4} tsu^{22}da^{2}nv^{22}ga^{2}lv^{44}dv^{0} da^{21}hna^{2}wo^{33}sgo^{33}ʔi^{2} o^{44}sdv^{2}hno^{33} a^{22}li^{0}sgwe^{11}tu^{2}wo^{3} a^{21}li^{0}sgwe^{33}tu^{3}hv^{3}sgo^{33}ʔi^{2}
ᏗᎦᏚᎲ ᏳᏪᎾ ᏧᏓᏅᎦᎸᏛ ᏓᎿᏬᏍᎪᎢ ᎣᏍᏛᏃ ᎠᎵᏍᏇᏚᏬ ᎠᎵᏍᏇᏚᎲᏍᎪᎢ
When she goes to town, she wears clean clothes and she puts on a good hat.

setting a goal/aiming

a^{21}li^{0}so^{23}sdi^{3}ha^{2} ᎠᎵᏍᏐᏍᏗᎭ one is setting a goal
one is aiming

ga^{2}li^{11}so^{23}sdi^{3}ha^{2} ᎦᎵᏍᏐᏍᏗᎭ
u^{21}li^{0}so^{23}sta^{3}nv^{23}ʔi^{2} ᎤᎵᏍᏐᏍᏔᏅᎢ
a^{21}li^{0}so^{23}sdi^{32}sgo^{33}ʔi^{2} ᎠᎵᏍᏐᏍᏗᏍᎪᎢ
ha^{22}li^{0}so^{23}sda^{2} ᎭᎵᏍᏐᏍᏓ
u^{22}li^{0}so^{23}sdo^{3}hdi^{2} ᎤᎵᏍᏐᏍᏙᏗ

ga^{2}do^{2} u^{22}dv^{11}ne^{2}hdi^{2} a^{21}li^{0}so^{23}sdi^{3}ha^{2}
ᎦᏙ ᎤᏛᏁᏗ ᎠᎵᏍᏐᏍᏗᎭ
What is she aiming to do?

smelling it

a^{21}li^{0}sv^{32}sdi^{23}ha^{2} ᎠᎵᏍᏒᏍᏗᎭ one is smelling it

ga^{2}li^{11}sv^{32}sdi^{23}ha^{2} ᎦᎵᏍᏒᏍᏗᎭ
u^{21}li^{0}sv^{32}sta^{2}nv^{23}ʔi^{2} ᎤᎵᏍᏒᏍᏔᏅᎢ
a^{21}li^{0}sv^{32}sdi^{22}sgo^{33}ʔi^{2} ᎠᎵᏍᏒᏍᏗᏍᎪᎢ
ha^{22}li^{0}sv^{11}sda^{2} ᎭᎵᏍᏒᏍᏓ
u^{22}li^{0}sv^{11}sdo^{2}hdi^{2} ᎤᎵᏍᏒᏍᏙᏗ

do^{23}yu^{3} u^{22}lv^{23}gwo^{0}di^{2} a^{22}ni^{22}tsi^{22}lv^{44}sgi^{2} tsu^{22}li^{0}sv^{11}sdo^{2}hdi^{2}
ᏙᏳ ᎤᎸᏚᏗ ᎠᏂᏥᎸᏍᎩ ᏧᎵᏍᏒᏍᏙᏗ
She really likes to smell flowers.

gathering

a^{21}na^{2}da^{33}hl**i^{23}si^{3}h**a^{2} ᎠᎾᏓᏟᏍᏏᎭ they are gathering

'customary' conditional suffix

o^{21}tsa^{2}da^{33}hl**i^{23}si^{3}h**a^{2} ᎣᏣᏓᏟᏍᏏᎭ We (not you) are gathering

u^{21}na^{2}da^{33}hl**i^{23}sa^{3}hn**v^{23}ʔi^{2} ᎤᎾᏓᏟᏍᏌᏅᎢ

a^{21}na^{2}da^{33}hl**i^{23}si^{32}sg**o^{33}ʔi^{2} ᎠᎾᏓᏟᏍᏏᏍᎪᎢ

i^{22}tsa^{2}da^{11}hl**i^{23}sa^{3}** ᎢᏣᏓᏟᏍᏌ You all gather

u^{22}na^{2}da^{11}hl**i^{23}so^{3}hdi^{2}** ᎤᎾᏓᏟᏍᏐᏗ

do^{23}yu^{3} tsu^{0}gwi^{44}sdi^{2} yv^{22}wi^{2} a^{21}na^{2}da^{33}hli^{23}si^{3}ha^{2} di^{2}ga^{22}du^{33}hv^{44}ʔi^{2} ko^{22}hi^{0} i^{22}ga^{2}

ᏙᏳ ᏧᏘᏍᏗ ᏴᏫ ᎠᎾᏓᏟᏍᏏᎭ ᏗᎦᏚᎲᎢ ᎪᎯ ᎢᎦ

Really a lot of people are gathering in town today.

getting together

a^{21}na^{2}li^{33}go^{23}h**(v^{23})hv^{3}sg**a^{2} ᎠᎾᎵᎪᎲᏍᎦ they are getting together

'reduplicative' conditional suffix

o^{21}tsa^{2}li^{33}go^{23}**(v^{23})hv^{3}sg**a^{2} ᎣᏣᎵᎪᎲᏍᎦ

u^{21}na^{2}li^{33}go^{22}**(v^{23}hv^{3}n)**hnv^{23}ʔi^{2} ᎤᎾᎵᎪᏅᎢ

a^{21}na^{2}li^{33}go^{23}**(v^{23})hv^{3}sg**o^{33}ʔi^{2} ᎠᎾᎵᎪᎲᏍᎪᎢ

i^{21}tsa^{2}li^{11}go^{22}**(v^{22})hv^{11}g**a^{2} ᎢᏣᎵᎪᎲᎦ

u^{22}na^{2}li^{11}go^{0}**(v^{22}hv^{2})hdi** ᎤᎾᎵᎪᎲᏗ

hi^{2}ʔa^{2} a^{2}ge^{22}hyu^{23}tsa^{0} a^{2}tsu^{23}tsa^{2}hno^{3} u^{22}na^{2}li^{11}go^{0}hdi^{2} u^{21}na^{0}du^{22}li^{33}ha^{2}

ᎯᎠ ᎠᎨᏳᏣ ᎠᏧᏣᏃ ᎤᎾᎵᎪᎲᏗ ᎤᎾᏚᎵᎭ

This boy and girl want to get together (they want to be a couple).

asleep

a^{21}ni^{22}hli^{3}ʔna^{2}	ᎠᏂᏟᎾ	they are asleep
o^{21}tsi^{22}hli^{3}ʔna^{2}	ᎣᏥᏟᎾ	they and I are asleep
tsa^{21}ni^{22}hli^{3}ʔnv^{23}ʔi^{2}	ᏣᏂᏟᏅᎢ	they were asleep
a^{21}ni^{22}hli^{3}ʔno^{33}ʔi^{2}	ᎠᏂᏟᏃᎢ	they are usually asleep
i^{22}tsi^{22}hli^{3}ʔnv^{11}gi^{2}	ᎢᏥᏟᏅᎩ	you all be asleep
u^{22}ni^{22}hli^{3}ʔnv^{22}ʔi^{3}sdi^{23}ʔi^{2}	ᎤᏂᏟᏅᎢᏍᏗᎢ	for them to be asleep

sa^{3}ʔdu^{2} i^{2}yu^{33}wa^{22}hni^{2}lv^{4} u^{2}sv^{4} tsi^{2}ge^{22}sv^{23}ʔi^{2}, ga^{33}yu^{22}la^{0} tsa^{21}ni^{22}hli^{3}ʔnv^{23}ʔi^{2}
ᏍᏌᏚ ᎢᏳᏩᏂᏞ ᎤᏍᏒᎢ ᏥᎨᏍᏒᎢ, ᎦᏳᎳ ᏣᏂᏟᏅᎢ
They were already asleep at 11:00 last night.

setting a trap

a^{21}sa^{2}dv^{3}ʔv^{2}sga^{2} or a^{21}sa^{2}dv^{32}sga^{2} (contraction) ᎠᏍᏌᏛᎥᏍᎦ
one is setting a trap

tsi^{22}sa^{2}dv^{3}ʔv^{2}sga^{2} or tsi^{22}sa^{2}dv^{32}sga^{2}	ᏥᏍᏌᏛᎥᏍᎦ
u^{21}sa^{2}dv^{3}ʔv^{2}hnv^{23}ʔi^{2} or u^{21}sa^{2}dv^{32}hnv^{23}ʔi^{2}	ᎤᏍᏌᏛᏅᎢ
a^{21}sa^{2}dv^{3}ʔv^{2}sgo^{33}ʔi^{2} or a^{21}sa^{2}dv^{32}sgo^{33}ʔi^{2}	ᎠᏍᏌᏛᎥᏍᎪᎢ
hi^{2}sa^{2}dv^{2}ʔv^{11}ga^{2}	ᎯᏍᏌᏛᎥᎦ
u^{22}sa^{2}dv^{11}di^{2}	ᎤᏍᏌᏛᏗ

u^{21}sa^{2}dv^{3}ʔv^{2}hnv^{23}ʔi^{2} a^{22}se^{33}hnv^{3} tla^{2} go^{22}hu^{44}sdi^{2} yu^{22}ni^{33}yv^{22}he^{33}ʔi^{2}
ᎤᏍᏌᏛᏅᎢ ᎠᏍᏎᏅ Ꮭ ᎪᎱᏍᏗ ᏳᏂᏴᎮᎢ
She had set a trap but she didn't catch anything.

lifting/raising

a^{21}sa^{2}la^{0}di^{23}ʔa^{2} ᎠᏍᏌᏓᏗᎠ one is lifting or raising another or it

tsi^{22}sa^{2}la^{0}di^{23}ʔa^{2} (animate) ᏥᏍᏌᏓᏗᎠ

tsi^{2}sa^{2}la^{0}di^{23}ʔa^{2} (inanimate) ᏥᏍᏌᏓᏗᎠ

u^{21}sa^{2}la^{0}d**a^{32}n**v^{23}ʔi^{2} ᎤᏍᏌᏓᏓᏅᎢ (a^{32}n, populative suffix)

a^{21}sa^{2}la^{0}di^{32}sgo^{33}ʔi^{2} ᎠᏍᏌᏓᏗᏍᎪᎢ

hi^{22}sa^{2}la^{0}dv^{11}ga^{2} (animate) ᎯᏍᏌᏓᏛᎦ

hi^{2}sa^{2}la^{0}dv^{11}ga^{2} (inanimate) ᎯᏍᏌᏓᏛᎦ

u^{22}sa^{2}la^{0}do^{11}di^{2} ᎤᏍᏌᏓᏙᏗ

hi^{2}sa^{2}la^{0}dv^{11}ga^{0} tsa^{33}su^{22}lv^{2}
ᎯᏍᏌᏓᏛᎦ ᏣᏍᏑᎸ
Pull your pants up!

making crisp/starching

a^{21}sda^{2}ga^{22}y**(v^{23}hv^{3})**hdi^{23}ha^{2} ᎠᏍᏓᎦᏴᏂᏗᎭ one is making it crisp
one is starching it

'reduplicative' conditional suffix

tsi^{22}sda^{2}ga^{22}y**(v^{23}hv^{3})**hdi^{23}ha^{2} ᏥᏍᏓᎦᏴᏂᏗᎭ

u^{21}sda^{2}ga^{22}y**(v^{23}hv^{3})**hta^{2}nv^{23}ʔi^{2} ᎤᏍᏓᎦᏴᏂᏔᏅᎢ

a^{21}sda^{2}ga^{22}y**(v^{23}hv^{3})**hdi^{22}sgo^{33}ʔi^{2} ᎠᏍᏓᎦᏴᏂᏗᏍᎪᎢ

hi^{2}sda^{2}ga^{22}y**(v^{23}hv^{3})**hda^{2} ᎯᏍᏓᎦᏴᏂᏓ

u^{22}sda^{2}ga^{22}y**(v^{23}hv^{3})**hdo^{2}hdi^{2} ᎤᏍᏓᎦᏴᏂᏙᏗ

This is an incorporated infinitive and that is why the 'reduplicative' conditional suffix remains the same throughout the stem forms. In this instance, the 'reduplicative' suffix is frozen within the incorporated infinitive stem.

attempting/trying

a^{33}ne^{22}hlv^{0}hdi^{23}ha^{2} ᎠᏁᏈᏗᎭ one is attempting or trying

ga^{33}ne^{22}hlv^{0}hdi^{23}ha^{2} ᎦᏁᏈᏗᎭ

u^{33}ne^{22}hlv^{0}hta^{2}nv^{23}ʔi^{2} ᎤᏁᏈᏔᏅᎢ

a^{33}ne^{22}hlv^{0}hd**i^{22}sgo^{33}**ʔi^{2} ᎠᏁᏈᏗᏍᎪᎢ

Alternatively, you can choose to contract the penultimate (^{33}) tone by shift the tone leftward onto the previous syllable as in: a^{33}ne^{22}hlv^{0}hd**i^{23}sgo^{3}**ʔi^{2}. This is speaker choice, (not grammar).

ha^{11}ne^{22}hlv^{0}hda^{2} ᎭᏁᏈᏓ

u^{11}ne^{22}hlv^{0}hdo^{2}hdi^{2} ᎤᏁᏈᏙᏗ

do^{22}gwa^{2}le^{33}lu^{0} u^{23}hni^{3}gi^{11}sdo^{2}hdi^{2} a^{33}ne^{22}hlv^{0}hdi^{23}ha^{2}

ᏙᏆᏞᎷ ᎤᏂᎩᏍᏙᏗ ᎠᏁᏈᏗᎭ

One is trying to start the car.

getting married

a^{21}ne^{23}la^{3}di^{23}ʔa^{2} ᎠᏁᎳᏗᎠ one is getting married

ga^{22}ne^{23}la^{3}di^{23}ʔa^{2} ᎦᏁᎳᏗᎠ

u^{21}ne^{23}la^{3}dv^{23}ʔi^{2} ᎤᏁᎳᏛᎢ

a^{21}ne^{23}la^{3}di^{11}sgo^{33}ʔi^{2} ᎠᏁᎳᏗᏍᎪᎢ

ha^{22}ne^{22}la^{2}da^{2} ᎭᏁᎳᏓ

u^{22}ne^{23}la^{3}di^{11}sdi^{2} ᎤᏁᎳᏗᏍᏗ

ne^{23}la^{32}du^{23}gwu^{3} nu^{22}de^{22}ti^{2}yv^{23}ha^{4} u^{21}ne^{23}la^{3}dv^{23}ʔi^{2} o^{22}gi^{2}na^{22}li^{44}ʔi^{2}

ᏁᎳᏚᏇ ᏄᏕᏘᏴᎭ ᎤᏁᎳᏛᎢ ᎣᎩᎾᎵᎢ

My friend got married when he or she was just eighteen years old.

remembering

a^{21}nv^{0}hda^{2}di^{23}ʔa^{2} ᎠᏅᏓᏗᎠ one is remembering another or it

tsi^{22}ya^{22}nv^{11}da^{2}di^{23}ʔa^{2} (animate) ᏥᏯᏅᏓᏗᎠ

ga^{22}nv^{11}da^{2}di^{23}ʔa^{2} (inanimate) ᎦᏅᏓᏗᎠ

u^{21}nv^{0}hda^{2}di^{32}sv^{23}ʔi^{2} ᎤᏅᏓᏗᏍᏒᎢ

a^{21}nv^{0}hda^{2}di^{32}sgo^{33}ʔi^{2} ᎠᏅᏓᏗᏍᎪᎢ

hi^{22}ya^{22}nv^{11}da^{2}da^{2} (animate) ᎯᏯᏅᏓᏓ

ha^{22}nv^{0}hda^{2}da^{2} (inanimate) ᎭᏅᏓᏓ

u^{22}nv^{0}hda^{2}di^{11}sdi^{2} ᎤᏅᏓᏗᏍᏗ

ha^{22}nv^{0}hda^{2}di^{23}ʔa^{2}s na^{22}gi^{2}we^{11}sv^{4} ko^{22}hi^{44}gi^{2}yv^{4} tsi^{2}ge^{22}sv^{23}ʔi^{2}

ᎭᏅᏓᏗᎠᏍ ᎾᎩᏪᏍᏒ ᎪᎯᎩᏴᎢ ᏥᎨᏍᏒᎢ

Do you remember what I said a long time ago?

becoming crisp

a^{21}sda^{2}ga^{2}yv**(i)^{23}hi^{3}h**a^{2} ᎠᏍᏓᎦᏴᎯᎭ it is becoming crisp

'came for purpose' conditional suffix

tsi^{22}sda^{2}ga^{2}yv**(i)^{23}hi^{3}h**a^{2} ᏥᏍᏓᎦᏴᎯᎭ I'm becoming crisp

u^{21}sda^{2}ga^{2}yv**(i)^{22}hl**v^{23}ʔi^{2} ᎤᏍᏓᎦᏴᎸᎢ

a^{21}sda^{2}ga^{2}yv**(i)^{23}hi^{3}h**o^{33}ʔi^{2} ᎠᏍᏓᎦᏴᎯᎰᎢ

hi^{22}sda^{2}ga^{2}yv^{23}ha^{2} ᎯᏍᏓᎦᏴᎭ

u^{22}sda^{2}ga^{2}yv^{22}di^{23}ʔi^{2} ᎤᏍᏓᎦᏴᏗᎢ

a^{2}ga^{33}li^{22}sgv^{4} wu^{22}nv^{23}na^{4} i^{22}na^{2}dv^{2} ga^{2}ne^{11}ga^{2} u^{21}sda^{2}ga^{2}yv^{22}hlv^{23}ʔi^{2}

ᎠᎦᎵᏍᎬ ᏭᏅᎾ ᎢᎾᏛ ᎦᏁᎦ ᎤᏍᏓᎦᏴᎸᎢ

When she layed (flexible) the snake skin down in the Sunshine, it became crisp.

drawing a line

a^{21}sda^{2}nv^{22}hn**(v^{23}h)v^{3}**sga^{2} ᎠᏍᏓᏅᏅᏂᏍᎦ one is drawing a line

'reduplicative' conditional suffix

tsi^{22}sda^{2}nv^{22}hnv^{3}sga^{2} ᏥᏍᏓᏅᏅᏍᎦ

u^{21}sda^{2}nv^{23}**h**n**o^{3}n**v^{23}ʔi^{2} ᎤᏍᏓᏅᏃᏅᎢ one had drawn a line

'completive' conditional suffix

a^{21}sda^{2}nv^{22}hnv^{3}sgo^{33}ʔ^{2} ᎠᏍᏓᏅᏅᏍᎪᎢ

hi^{2}sda^{2}nv^{22}hnv^{11}ga^{2} ᎯᏍᏓᏅᏅᎦ

u^{22}sda^{2}nv^{22}hnv^{0}hdi^{2} ᎤᏍᏓᏅᏅᏗ

u^{21}sda^{2}nv^{23}hno^{3}nv^{23}ʔi^{2} gv^{23}na^{3}ge^{4} di^{2}go^{22}hwe^{23}lo^{32}di^{2} gv^{4}hdi^{2}

ᎤᏍᏓᏅᏃᏅᎢ ᎬᎾᎨᎢ ᏗᎪᏪᎶᏗ ᎬᏗ

She drew a line with a black writing utensil.

following

a^{21}sd**a^{32}wa^{2}de^{33}g**a^{2} ᎠᏍᏓᏩᏕᎦ one is following another or it

'going along' conditional suffix

tsi^{22}sd**a^{32}wa^{2}de^{33}g**a^{2} ᏥᏍᏓᏩᏕᎦ

u^{21}sd**a^{32}wa^{2}dv^{33}s**v^{23}ʔi^{2} ᎤᏍᏓᏩᏛᏒᎢ

a^{21}sd**a^{32}wa^{2}de^{33}g**o^{33}ʔi^{2} ᎠᏍᏓᏩᏕᎪᎢ

hi^{22}sd**a^{11}wa^{2}du^{11}g**a^{2} (animate) ᎯᏍᏓᏩᏚᎦ

hi^{2}sda^{11}wa^{2}du^{11}ga^{2} (inanimate) ᎯᏍᏓᏩᏚᎦ

u^{22}sd**a^{11}wa^{2}dv^{11}sdi^{2}** ᎤᏍᏓᏩᏛᏍᏗ

u^{2}sdi^{4} a^{2}tsu^{23}tsa^{2} u^{22}do^{22}dv^{2} a^{21}sda^{32}wa^{2}de^{33}ga^{2}

ᎤᏍᏗ ᎠᏧᏣ ᎤᏙᏛ ᎠᏍᏓᏩᏕᎦ

The little boy is following his dad.

helping another

a^{21}sde^{22}li^{23}ha^{2} ᎠᏍᏕᎵᎭ one is helping another

tsi^{22}sde^{22}li^{23}ha^{2} ᏥᏍᏕᎵᎭ
u^{21}sde^{22}lv^{22}hv^{23}ʔi^{2} ᎤᏍᏕᎸᎲᎢ
a^{21}sde^{22}li^{22}sgo^{33}ʔi^{2} ᎠᏍᏕᎵᏍᎪᎢ
or a^{21}sde^{22}li^{23}sgo^{3}ʔi^{2} (tone contraction)
hi^{22}sde^{23}la^{2} ᎯᏍᏕᎳ
u^{22}sde^{22}hlv^{0}hdi^{2} ᎤᏍᏕᎸᏗ

ga^{22}li^{0}tso^{23}de^{2} a^{21}hne^{33}sge^{22}sgv^{2} tsi^{22}sde^{22}li^{23}ha^{2}
ᎦᎵᏦᏕ ᎠᏁᏍᎨᏍᎬ ᏥᏍᏕᎵᎭ
I'm helping him or her build the house.
Literally, the house he or she has been building, I'm helping him or her.

braiding

a^{21}sde^{33}yo^{2}ha^{2} ᎠᏍᏕᏲᎭ one is braiding it

tsi^{22}sde^{33}yo^{2}ha^{2} ᏥᏍᏕᏲᎭ
u^{21}sde^{23}yo^{32}lv^{23}ʔi^{2} ᎤᏍᏕᏲᎸᎢ
a^{21}sde^{33}yo^{2}ho^{33}ʔi^{2} ᎠᏍᏕᏲᎰᎢ
hi^{2}sde^{22}ya^{2}ga^{2} ᎯᏍᏕᏯᎦ
u^{22}sde^{23}yo^{32}di^{2} ᎤᏍᏕᏲᏗ

a^{2}ge^{22}hyu^{23}tsa^{2} u^{22}sti^{23}ye^{0}hgv^{4} a^{21}sde^{33}yo^{2}ha^{2}
ᎠᎨᏳᏣ ᎤᏍᏘᏰᎬ ᎠᏍᏕᏲᎭ
The girl is braiding her hair.

eating (a long object)

a^{21}sdi^{23}gi^{3}ʔa^{2} or a^{21}sdi^{33}gi^{23}ʔa^{2} ᎠᏍᏗᎩᎠ one is eating it (a long object)

tsi^{22}sdi^{23}gi^{3}ʔa^{2} or tsi^{22}sdi^{33}gi^{23}ʔa^{2} ᏥᏍᏗᎩᎠ

u^{21}sdi^{33}gv^{23}ʔi^{2} ᎤᏍᏗᎬᎢ

a^{21}sdi^{23}gi^{32}sgo^{33}ʔi^{2} or a^{21}sdi^{33}gi^{22}sgo^{33}ʔi^{2} ᎠᏍᏗᎩᏍᎪᎢ

hi^{2}sdi^{23}ga^{2} ᎯᏍᏗᎦ

u^{22}sdi^{23}gi^{32}sdi^{2} ᎤᏍᏗᎩᏍᏗ

do^{23}yu^{3}dv^{33} u^{22}lv^{23}gwo^{0}di^{2} tsu^{22}sdi^{23}gi^{32}sdi^{2} ga^{23}ga^{3}ma^{0}

ᏙᏳᏛ ᎤᎸᏉᏗ ᏧᏍᏗᎩᏍᏗ ᎦᎦᎹ

He or She really likes to eat (long things) cucumbers.

crushing/grinding

a^{21}sdo^{33}ʔa^{2} ᎠᏍᏙᎠ one is crushing or grinding it

tsi^{22}sdo^{33}ʔa^{2} ᏥᏍᏙᎠ

u^{21}sdo^{33}ʔv^{23}ʔi^{2} ᎤᏍᏙᎥᎢ

a^{21}sdo^{33}sgo^{33}ʔi^{2} ᎠᏍᏙᏍᎪᎢ

hi^{2}sdo^{23}tsa^{2} ᎯᏍᏙᏣ

u^{22}sdo^{11}sdi^{2} ᎤᏍᏙᏍᏗ

so^{2}hi^{23}tsu^{3} tsu^{22}sdo^{11}sdi^{2} tsa^{22}du^{22}li^{33}ha^{2}

ᏐᎯᏧ ᏧᏍᏙᏍᏗ ᏣᏚᎵᎭ

Do you want him or her to crush/grind some hickory nuts?

trimming (hair/grass)

a^{21}sdo^{22}ye^{23}ha^{2} ᎠᏍᏙᏰᎭ one is trimming (hair, grass, and the like)

tsi^{22}sdo^{22}ye^{23}ha^{2} ᏥᏍᏙᏰᎭ

u^{21}sdo^{22}ye^{22}hv^{23}ʔi^{2} ᎤᏍᏙᏰᎲᎢ

a^{21}sdo^{22}ye^{22}sgo^{33}ʔi^{2} ᎠᏍᏙᏰᏍᎪᎢ

or a^{21}sdo^{22}ye^{23}sgo^{3}ʔi^{2} (tone contraction)

hi^{22}sdo^{23}ya^{2} (animate) ᎯᏍᏙᏯ

hi^{2}sdo^{23}ya^{2} (inanimate) ᎯᏍᏙᏯ

u^{22}sdo^{22}ye^{0}hdi^{2} ᎤᏍᏙᏰᏗ

di^{22}da^{22}sdo^{22}ye^{44}sgi^{2} na^{2} a^{2}sga^{2}ya^{2} a^{21}do^{22}ye^{22}sgo^{33}ʔi^{2} ni^{2}go^{23}hi^{3}lv^{44}ʔi^{2}

ᏗᏓᏍᏙᏰᏍᎩ Ꮎ ᎠᏍᎦᏯ ᎠᏙᏰᏍᎪᎢ ᏂᎪᎯᎸᎢ

The barber always cuts the man's hair.

closing

a^{21}sdu^{32}**(v)hv^{2}sg**a^{2} ᎠᏍᏚᎲᏍᎦ one is closing it

one is putting another in jail

'reduplicative' conditional suffix

tsi^{22}sdu^{32}**(v)hv^{2}sg**a^{2} ᏥᏍᏚᎲᏍᎦ

u^{21}sdu^{32}**(v)hn**v^{23}ʔi^{2} ᎤᏍᏛᏅᎢ

a^{21}sdu^{32}**(v)hv^{2}sg**o^{33}ʔi^{2} ᎠᏍᏚᎲᏍᎪᎢ

hi^{22}sdu^{11}**(v)hv^{11}g**a^{2} (animate) ᎯᏍᏚᎲᎦ

hi^{2}sdu^{11}hv^{11}ga^{2} (inanimate) ᎯᏍᏚᎲᎦ

u^{22}sdu^{11}**(vhv)hdi^{2}** ᎤᏍᏚᎲᏗ

na^{2} ga^{2}lo^{22}hi^{2}sdi^{4} tsi^{2}sdu^{32}hv^{22}ga^{2} no^{23}gwu^{3} tsi^{2}gi^{2}

Ꮎ ᎦᎶᎯᏍᏗ ᏥᏍᏚᎲᎦ ᏃᏊ ᏥᎩ

I just now closed the door.

opening

a^{21}sdu^{3}ʔi^{2}ha^{2} ᎠᏍᏚᎢᎭ one is opening it

tsi^{22}sdu^{3}ʔi^{2}ha^{2} ᏥᏍᏚᎢᎭ

u^{21}sdu^{3}ʔi^{22}sv^{23}ʔi^{2} ᎤᏍᏚᎢᏒᎢ

a^{21}sdu^{3}ʔi^{22}sgo^{33}ʔi^{2} ᎠᏍᏚᎢᏍᎪᎢ

hi^{2}sdu^{2}ʔi^{2} ᎯᏍᏚᎢ

u^{22}sdu^{2}ʔi^{22}sdi^{2} ᎤᏍᏚᎢᏍᏗ

hi^{2}la^{32}yv^{4} dv^{22}ni^{22}sdu^{3}ʔi^{22}si^{2} di^{22}da^{22}na^{3}ʔnv^{44}ʔi^{2}.

ᎯᎳᏴ ᏛᏂᏍᏚᎢᏍᏏ ᏗᏓᎾᏅᎢ

When will the store open?

sandwiching

a^{21}sdv^{23}ha^{3}hl**v^{2}(hv)sg**a^{2} ᎠᏍᏛᎭᎵᏍᎦ one is sandwiching it

'reduplicative' conditional suffix

tsi^{22}sdv^{23}ha^{3}hl**v^{2}(hv)sg**a^{2} ᏥᏍᏛᎭᎵᏍᎦ

u^{21}sdv^{23}ha^{3}hl**v^{2}(hv)n**v^{23}ʔi^{2} ᎤᏍᏛᎭᎵᏅᎢ

a^{21}sdv^{23}ha^{3}hl**v^{2}(hv)sg**o^{33}ʔi^{2} ᎠᏍᏛᎭᎵᏍᎪᎢ

hi^{2}sdv^{22}ha^{2}hl**(v^{0}ʔ)v**^{11}**g**a^{2} ᎯᏍᏛᎭᎵᎦ

u^{22}sdv^{23}ha^{3}hl**v^{0}(hv)hdi**^{2} ᎤᏍᏛᎭᎵᎲᏗ

a^{2}sdv^{23}ha^{3}hli^{2} u^{21}du^{22}lv^{22}hv^{2}, u^{22}dv^{23}hnv^{3}ʔi^{2}

ᎠᏍᏛᎭᏟ ᎤᏚᎸᎲ, ᎤᏛᏅᎢ

He or She said he or she wanted a sandwich.

showing

a^{21}se^{2}he^{23}ha^{2} ᎠᏍᏎᎮᎭ one is showing another

tsi^{22}ya^{11}se^{2}he^{23}ha^{2} ᏥᏯᏍᏎᎮᎭ
u^{21}se^{2}he^{22}lv^{23}ʔi^{2} ᎤᏍᏎᎮᎸᎢ
a^{21}se^{2}he^{22}ho^{33}ʔi^{2} ᎠᏍᏎᎮᎰᎢ
hi^{22}ya^{11}se^{2}hi^{2}si^{2} ᎯᏯᏍᏎᎯᏍᏏ
u^{22}se^{2}he^{2}hdi^{2} ᎤᏍᏎᎮᏗ

wi^{2}hi^{22}ya^{11}se^{22}he^{22}lv^{2} i^{2}tse^{4} do^{22}gwa^{2}le^{33}lu^{0} tsa^{2}tse^{22}li^{44}ʔi^{2}
ᏫᎯᏯᏍᏎᎮᎸ ᎢᏤᎢ ᏙᏆᎴᎷ ᏣᏤᎵᎢ
Show him or her your new car later!

counting another

a^{21}se^{2}sdi^{23}ha^{2} or a^{21}se^{2}sdi^{3}ha^{2} (tone contraction) ᎠᏍᏎᏍᏗᎭ
one is counting another

tsi^{22}ya^{11}se^{2}sdi^{23}ha^{2} ᏥᏯᏍᏎᏍᏗᎭ
u^{21}se^{2}sta^{2}nv^{23}ʔi^{2} ᎤᏍᏎᏍᏔᏅᎢ
a^{21}se^{2}sdi^{22}sgo^{33}ʔi^{2} ᎠᏍᏎᏍᏗᏍᎪᎢ
hi^{22}ya^{11}se^{2}sda^{2} (animate) ᎯᏯᏍᏎᏍᏓ
ha^{2}se^{2}sda^{2} (inanimate) ᎭᏍᏎᏍᏓ
u^{22}se^{2}sdo^{2}hdi^{2} ᎤᏍᏎᏍᏙᏗ

u^{21}wa^{22}ke^{22}wa^{0}sv^{2} u^{22}se^{2}sdo^{2}hdi^{2} o^{22}gi^{2}na^{22}li^{44}ʔi^{2}
ᎤᏩᎨᏩᏍᎥ ᎤᏍᏎᏍᏙᏗ ᎣᎩᎾᎵᎢ
He or She forgot to count or include my friend.

drawing in/pulling out/withdrawing

a^{33}se^{22}si^{23}ha^{2} or a^{33}se^{22}si^{3}ha^{2} (tone contraction) ᎠᏍᏎᏍᏏᎭ
one is drawing it in
one is withdrawing
one is pulling it out

ga^{33}se^{22}si^{23}ha^{2} ᎦᏍᏎᏍᏏᎭ
u^{33}se^{22}sv^{22}hv^{23}ʔi^{2} ᎤᏍᏎᏍᏒᎲᎢ
a^{33}se^{22}si^{22}sgo^{33}ʔi^{2} ᎠᏍᏎᏍᏏᏍᎪᎢ
or a^{33}se^{22}si^{23}sgo^{3}ʔi^{2} (tone contraction)
ha^{11}se^{23}sa^{2} ᎭᏍᏎᏍᏌ
u^{11}se^{22}sv^{2}hdi^{2} ᎤᏍᏎᏍᏒᏗ

u^{22}gv^{22}wi^{2}yu^{22}hi^{2} yi^{2}ga^{22}li^{0}sdi^{44}sgi^{2} ge^{22}sv^{4} u^{33}se^{22}sv^{22}hv^{23}ʔi^{2}
ᎤᎬᏫᏳᎯ ᏱᎦᎵᏍᏗᏍᎩ ᎨᏍᏒ ᎤᏍᏎᏍᏒᎲᎢ
He pulled out from becoming President.

reprimanding

a^{21}sga^{32}ga^{2} ᎠᏍᎦᎦ one is reprimanding another

tsi^{22}sga^{32}ga^{2} ᏥᏍᎦᎦ
u^{21}sga^{32}tsv^{23}ʔi^{2} ᎤᏍᎦᏨᎢ
a^{21}sga^{32}go^{33}ʔi^{2} ᎠᏍᎦᎪᎢ
hi^{22}sga^{11}ga^{2} (animate) ᎯᏍᎦᎦ
hi^{2}sga^{11}ga^{2} (inanimate) ᎯᏍᎦᎦ
u^{22}sga^{11}go^{23}ʔi^{3}sdi^{2} ᎤᏍᎦᎪᎢᏍᏗ

u^{22}do^{22}dv^{2} u^{21}sga^{32}tsv^{23}i^{2}
ᎤᏙᏛ ᎤᏍᎦᏨᎢ
His or Her dad reprimanded him or her.

afraid

a^{21}sga^{32}ʔi^{2}ha^{2} or a^{21}sga^{32}ha^{2} (tone contraction) ᎠᏍᎦᎢᎭ
one is afraid

tsi^{22}sga^{32}ʔi^{2}ha^{2} ᏥᏍᎦᎢᎭ
u^{22}sga^{32}ʔ(i^{2})lv^{23}ʔi^{2} ᎤᏍᎦᎢᎸᎢ
a^{21}sga^{32}ʔ(i^{2})ho^{33}ʔi^{2} ᎠᏍᎦᎢᎰᎢ
hi^{2}sga^{11}ʔi^{2}hi^{2} ᎯᏍᎦᎢᎯ Be afraid!
u^{22}sga^{11}ʔi^{2}sdi^{2} ᎤᏍᎦᎢᏍᏗ

na^{2} gi^{22}hli^{2} a^{21}sga^{32}ʔi^{2}ho^{33}ʔi^{2}
Ꮎ ᎩᎵ ᎠᏍᎦᎢᎰᎢ
He or She is usually afraid of that dog.

biting

a^{21}sga^{22}hlo^{0}hga^{2} ᎠᏍᎦᎶᎦ one is biting another or it
tsi^{22}sga^{22}hlo^{0}hga^{2} ᏥᏍᎦᎶᎦ
u^{21}sga^{22}hlo^{0}htsv^{23}ʔi^{2} ᎤᏍᎦᎶᏨᎢ
a^{21}sga^{22}hlo^{0}hgo^{33}ʔi^{2} ᎠᏍᎦᎶᎪᎢ
hi^{22}sga^{2}la^{2} (animate) ᎯᏍᎦᎳ
hi^{2}sga^{2}la^{2} (inanimate) ᎯᏍᎦᎳ
u^{22}sga^{22}hl(o^{0}ʔi^{2})sdi^{2} ᎤᏍᎦᎶᎢᏍᏗ

gi^{22}hli^{2} u^{33}ne^{22}hlv^{0}hta^{2}nv^{2} u^{22}sga^{22}hl(o^{0}ʔi^{2})sdi^{2} na^{2} a^{2}sga^{2}ya^{2}
ᎩᎵ ᎤᏁᎸᏔᏅ ᎤᏍᎦᎶᎢᏍᏗ Ꮎ ᎠᏍᎦᏯ
The dog tried to bite the man.

committing a crime

a^{21}sga^{2}nv^{3}ʔv^{22}ga^{2} or a^{21}sga^{2}nv^{32}ga^{2} (tone contraction) ᎠᏍᎦᏅᎥᎦ

one is committing a crime

tsi^{22}sga^{2}nv^{3}ʔv^{22}ga^{2} or tsi^{22}sga^{2}nv^{32}ga^{2} ᏥᏍᎦᏅᎥᎦ
u^{21}sga^{2}nv^{3}ʔv^{22}tsv^{23}ʔi^{2} or u^{21}sga^{2}nv^{32}tsv^{23}ʔi^{2} ᎤᏍᎦᏅᏨᎢ
a^{21}sga^{2}nv^{3}ʔv^{22}go^{33}ʔi^{2} or a^{21}sga^{2}nv^{32}go^{33}ʔi^{2} ᎠᏍᎦᏅᎥᎪᎢ
hi^{2}sga^{2}nv^{2}ʔv^{11}ga^{2} or hi^{2}sga^{2}nv^{11}ga^{2} ᎯᏍᎦᏅᎥᎦ
u^{22}sga^{2}nv^{2}ʔv^{11}sdi^{2} or u^{22}sga^{2}nv^{11}sdi^{2} ᎤᏍᎦᏅᏍᏗ

tla^{3}dv^{33} yu^{21}sga^{2}nv^{32}tsv^{23}ʔi^{2}
ᏝᏛ ᏳᏍᎦᏅᏨᎢ
He or She didn’t commit a crime.

dreaming

a^{21}sgi^{33}d(v)sga^{2} ᎠᏍᎩᏛᏍᎦ one is dreaming about another or it

(Literally, one is spirited over time regarding it)

’reduplicative’ conditional suffix

Morephemes:

a-,	3P (Set A)
-(v)sg(a)-,	hide
-gi-	reversive
-iʔid(v)-	past participle suffix
-vhv-	reduplicative conditional suffix (over a period of time)
-sg-	subject/object focus
-a,	present tense suffix

(Literally, one is revealing what is hidden (within them) over a period of time)

tsi^{22}ya^{11}sgi^{33}d(v)sga^{2} (animate) ᏥᏯᏍᎩᏛᏍᎦ
ga^{22}sgi^{33}d(v)sga^{2} (inanimate) ᎦᏍᎩᏛᏍᎦ
u^{21}sgi^{33}d(v)sv^{23}ʔi^{2} ᎤᏍᎩᏛᏍᏒᎢ
a^{21}sgi^{33}d(v)sgo^{33}ʔi^{2} ᎠᏍᎩᏛᏍᎪᎢ

hi^{22}ya^{11}sgi^{11}d(v)sa^{2} ᎯᏯᏍᎩᏛᏍᏌ
u^{22}sgi^{11}d(v)sdi^{2} ᎤᏍᎩᏛᏍᏗ

gnawing

a^{21}sgo^{33}gi^{23}ʔa^{2} ᎠᏍᎪᎩᎠ one is gnawing it
tsi^{22}sgo^{33}gi^{23}ʔa^{2} ᏥᏍᎪᎩᎠ
u^{21}sgo^{33}gv^{23}ʔi^{2} ᎤᏍᎪᎬᎢ
a^{21}sgo^{33}gi^{22}sgo^{33}ʔi^{2} ᎠᏍᎪᎩᏍᎪᎢ
hi^{2}sgo^{23}ga^{2} ᎯᏍᎪᎦ
u^{22}sgo^{23}gi^{32}sdi^{2} ᎤᏍᎪᎩᏍᏗ

do^{22}ya^{2} a^{2}da^{0} a^{21}sgo^{33}gi^{23}ʔa^{2} tsi^{22}go^{11}wa^{0}hti^{23}ha^{2}
ᏙᏯ ᎠᏓ ᎠᏍᎪᎩᎠ ᏥᎪᏩᏘᎭ
I see a beaver gnawing wood.

mourning

a^{21}sgo^{23}hni^{3}ha^{2} ᎠᏍᎪᏂᎭ one is mourning for another or it
'with purpose' conditional suffix
tsi^{22}sgo^{23}hni^{3}ha^{2} ᏥᏍᎪᏂᎭ
u^{21}sgo^{23}hni^{3}lv^{23}ʔi^{2} ᎤᏍᎪᏂᎸᎢ
a^{21}sgo^{23}hni^{3}ho^{33}ʔi^{2} ᎠᏍᎪᏂᎰᎢ
hi^{22}sgo^{23}hni^{0}ga^{2} (animate) ᎯᏍᎪᏂᎦ
hi^{2}sgo^{23}hni^{0}ga^{2} (inanimate) ᎯᏍᎪᏂᎦ
u^{22}sgo^{11}hni^{0}sdi^{2} ᎤᏍᎪᏂᏍᏗ

rubbing

a^{21}sgo^{22}li^{23}ye^{3}ʔa^{2} ᎠᏍᎪᎵᏰᎠ one is rubbing another or it
tsi^{22}ya^{11}sgo^{22}li^{23}ye^{3}ʔa^{2} (animate) ᏥᏯᏍᎪᎵᏰᎠ
ga^{21}sgo^{22}li^{23}ye^{3}ʔa^{2} (inanimate) ᎦᏍᎪᎵᏰᎠ
u^{21}sgo^{22}li^{23}ye^{3}ʔv^{23}ʔi^{2} ᎤᏍᎪᎵᏰᎥᎢ
a^{21}sgo^{22}li^{23}ye^{32}sgo^{33}ʔi^{2} ᎠᏍᎪᎵᏰᏍᎪᎢ
hi^{22}ya^{11}sgo^{22}li^{23}ya^{2} (animate) ᎯᏯᏍᎪᎵᏯ
ha^{2}sgo^{22}li^{23}ya^{2} (inanimate) ᎭᏍᎪᎵᏯ
u^{22}sgo^{22}li^{23}ye^{32}di^{2} ᎤᏍᎪᎵᏰᏗ

erasing

a^{21}sgo^{22}lv^{33}di^{23}ʔa^{2} ᎠᏍᎪᎸᏗᎠ one is erasing it

tsi^{22}sgo^{22}lv^{33}di^{23}ʔa^{2} ᏥᏍᎪᎸᏗᎠ

u^{21}sgo^{22}lv^{33}dv^{23}ʔi^{2} ᎤᏍᎪᎸᏛᎢ

a^{21}sgo^{22}lv^{33}di^{22}sgo^{33}ʔi^{2} ᎠᏍᎪᎸᏗᏍᎪᎢ

hi^{2}sgo^{22}lv^{23}da^{2} ᎯᏍᎪᎸᏓ

u^{22}sgo^{22}lv^{23}di^{32}sdi^{2} ᎤᏍᎪᎸᏗᏍᏗ

digging

a^{21}sgo^{33}sga^{2} ᎠᏍᎪᏍᎦ one is digging it

ga^{21}sgo^{33}sga^{2} ᎦᏍᎪᎦ

u^{21}sgo^{33}sv^{23}ʔi^{2} ᎤᏍᎪᏍᏒᎢ

a^{21}sgo^{33}sgo^{33}ʔi^{2} ᎠᏍᎪᏍᎪᎢ

ha^{2}sgo^{23}la^{2} ᎭᏍᎪᎳ

u^{22}sgo^{11}sdi^{2} ᎤᏍᎪᏍᏗ

finishing

a^{21}sgwa^{2}di^{23}ʔa^{2} ᎠᏍᏆᏗᎠ one is finishing it

tsi^{22}sgwa^{2}di^{23}ʔa^{2} ᏥᏍᏆᏗᎠ

u^{21}sgwa^{2}dv^{23}ʔi^{2} ᎤᏍᏆᏛᎢ

a^{21}sgwa^{2}di^{22}sgo^{33}ʔi^{2} ᎠᏍᏆᏗᏍᎪᎢ

hi^{22}sgwa^{2}da^{2} ᎯᏍᏆᏓ

u^{22}sgwa^{2}di^{11}sdi^{2} ᎤᏍᏆᏗᏍᏗ

catching it falling

a^{21}sgwa^{22}hle^{33}ʔa^{2} ᎠᏍᏆᎴᎠ one is catching another or it falling

tsi^{22}sgwa^{22}hle^{33}ʔa^{2} ᏥᏍᏆᎴᎠ

u^{21}sgwa^{22}hle^{33}sv^{23}ʔi^{2} ᎤᏍᏆᎴᏍᏒᎢ

a^{21}sgwa^{22}hle^{33}sgo^{33}ʔi^{2} ᎠᏍᏆᎴᏍᎪᎢ

hi^{22}sgwa^{22}hle^{2}gi^{2} (animate) ᎯᏍᏆᎴᎩ

hi^{2}sgwa^{22}hle^{2}gi^{2} (inanimate) ᎯᏍᏆᎴᎩ

u^{22}sgwa^{22}hle^{11}sdi^{2} ᎤᏍᏆᏞᏍᏗ

getting shorter

a^{21}sgwa^{2}l**o**^{32}**g**a^{2} ᎠᏍᏆᎶᎦ one is getting shorter

'transformative' conditional suffix

tsi^{22}sgwa^{2}l**o**^{32}**g**a^{2} ᏥᏍᏆᎶᎦ

u^{21}sgwa^{2}l**o**^{32}**ts**v^{23}ʔi^{2} ᎤᏍᏆᎶᏨᎢ

a^{21}sgwa^{2}l**o**^{32}**g**o^{33}ʔi^{2} ᎠᏍᏆᎶᎪᎢ

hi^{2}sgwa^{2}l**o**^{11}**g**i^{2} ᎯᏍᏆᎶᎩ

u^{22}sgwa^{2}l**o**^{11}**sd**i^{2} ᎤᏍᏆᎶᏍᏗ

di^{2}go^{22}hwe^{23}lo^{32}di^{0} a^{21}sgwa^{2}lo^{32}ga^{2}

ᏗᎪᏪᎶᏗ ᎠᏍᏆᎶᎦ

The pencil is getting shorter.

breaking (a long object)

a^{21}sgwa^{32}la^{0}sga^{2} ᎠᏍᏆᎳᏍᎦ one is breaking a long object

tsi^{22}sgwa^{32}la^{0}sga^{2} ᏥᏍᏆᎳᏍᎦ

u^{21}sgwa^{32}la^{0}sv^{23}ʔi^{2} ᎤᏍᏆᎳᏍᎥᎢ

a^{21}sgwa^{32}la^{0}sgo^{33}ʔi^{2} ᎠᏍᏆᎳᏍᎪᎢ

hi^{2}sgwa^{2}la^{2} ᎯᏍᏆᎳ

u^{22}sgwa^{11}la^{0}sdi^{2} ᎤᏍᏆᎳᏍᏗ

ka^{2}no^{22}ge^{44}ni^{0} u^{21}li^{0}sgwa^{32}la^{2}se^{33}ʔi^{2}

ᎧᏃᎨᏂ ᎤᎵᏍᏆᎳᏍᏎᎢ

He or She broke his or her arm.

hitting on the head with it (a long object)

a^{21}sgwa^{2}lv^{33}ni^{23}ha^{2} ᎠᏍᏆᎸᏂᎭ

one is hitting another in the head (with a long object)

tsi^{22}sgwa^{2}lv^{33}ni^{23}ha^{2} ᏥᏍᏆᎸᏂᎭ

u^{21}sgwa^{2}lv^{23}ni^{32}lv^{23}ʔi^{2} ᎤᏍᏆᎸᏂᎸᎢ

a^{21}sgwa^{2}lv^{33}ni^{2}ho^{33}ʔi^{2} ᎠᏍᏆᎸᏂᎰᎢ

hi^{22}sgwa^{2}lv^{22}ni^{11}ga^{2} ᎯᏍᏆᎸᏂᎦ

u^{22}sgwa^{2}lv^{23}ni^{32}sdi^{2} ᎤᏍᎦᎸᏂᏍᏗ

amazed

a^{21}sgwa^{2}ni^{2}go^{23}sga^{2} ᎠᏍᏆᏂᎪᏍᎦ one is amazed

tsi^{22}sgwa^{2}ni^{2}go^{23}sga^{2} ᏥᏍᏆᏂᎪᏍᎦ

u^{21}sgwa^{2}ni^{2}go^{33}sv^{23}ʔi^{2} ᎤᏍᏆᏂᎪᏍᏒᎢ

a^{21}sgwa^{2}ni^{2}go^{33}sgo^{33}ʔi^{2} ᎠᏍᏆᏂᎪᏍᎪᎢ

hi^{2}sgwa^{2}ni^{2}go^{23}hi^{2} ᎯᏍᏆᏂᎪᎯ

u^{22}sgwa^{2}ni^{2}go^{23}hi^{3}sdi^{2} ᎤᏍᏆᏂᎪᎯᏍᏗ

u^{21}sgwa^{2}ni^{0}go^{33}se^{33}sgo^{0} sv^{22}hi^{0} sa^{2}na^{33}le^{44}ʔi^{2}

ᎤᏍᏆᏂᎪᏍᏎᏍᎪ ᏍᏒᎯ ᏍᏌᎾᎴᎢ

Was she or he amazed yesterday morning?

sucking

a^{21}sgwa^{2}nu^{32}ti^{0}sga^{2} ᎠᏍᏆᏄᏘᏍᎦ one is sucking it

tsi^{22}sgwa^{2}nu^{32}ti^{0}sga^{2} ᏥᏍᏆᏄᏘᏍᎦ

u^{21}sgwa^{2}nu^{32}ti^{0}sv^{23}ʔi^{2} ᎤᏍᏆᏄᏘᏍᏒᎢ

a^{21}sgwa^{2}nu^{32}ti^{0}sgo^{33}ʔi^{2} ᎠᏍᏆᏄᏘᏍᎪᎢ

hi^{2}sgwa^{2}nu^{11}ti^{0}sa^{2} ᎯᏍᏆᏄᏘᏍᏌ

u^{22}sgwa^{2}nu^{11}ti^{0}sdi^{2} ᎤᏍᏆᏄᏘᏍᏗ

hitting in the stomach with it (a long object)

a^{21}sgwo^{22}ha^{2}lv^{33}ni^{23}ha^{2} ᎠᏍᏉᎭᎸᏂᎭ

one is hitting another in the stomach (with a long object)

tsi^{22}sgwo^{22}ha^{2}lv^{33}ni^{23}ha^{2} ᏥᏍᏉᎭᎸᏂᎭ

u^{21}sgwo^{22}ha^{2}lv^{23}ni^{32}lv^{23}ʔi^{2} ᎤᏍᏉᎭᎸᏂᎸᎢ

a^{21}sgwo^{22}ha^{2}lv^{23}ni^{32}ho^{33}ʔi^{2} ᎠᏍᏉᎭᎸᏂᎰᎢ

hi^{22}sgwo^{22}ha^{2}lv^{22}ni^{11}ga^{2} ᎯᏍᏉᎭᎸᏂᎦ

u^{22}sgwo^{22}ha^{2}lv^{23}ni^{32}sdi^{2} ᎤᏍᏉᎭᎸᏂᏍᏗ

placing a hand on it

a^{21}si^{2}hta^{2}di^{23}ʔa^{2} ᎠᏍᏏᏔᏗᎠ one is placing one's hand on another or it

tsi^{22}ya^{11}si^{2}hta^{2}di^{23}ʔa^{2} (animate) ᏥᏯᏍᏏᏔᏗᎠ

ga^{21}si^{2}hta^{2}di^{23}ʔa^{2} (inanimate) ᎦᏍᏏᏔᏗᎠ

u^{21}si^{2}hta^{2}dv^{23}ʔi^{2} ᎤᏍᏏᏔᏛᎢ

a^{21}si^{2}hta^{3}di^{32}sgo^{33}ʔi^{2} ᎠᏍᏏᏔᏗᏍᎪᎢ

hi^{22}ya^{11}si^{2}hta^{2}da^{2} (animate) ᎯᏯᏍᏏᏔᏓ

ha^{2}si^{2}hta^{2}da^{2} (inanimate) ᎭᏍᏏᏔᏓ

u^{22}si^{2}hta^{2}sdi^{11}sdi^{2} ᎤᏍᏏᏔᏗᏍᏗ

slapping

a^{21}si^{2}htv^{33}ni^{2}ha^{2} ᎠᏍᏏᏛᏂᎭ one is slapping another or it

tsi^{22}ya^{11}si^{2}htv^{33}ni^{2}ha^{2} (animate) ᏥᏯᏍᏏᏛᏂᎭ

ga^{21}si^{2}htv^{33}ni^{2}ha^{2} (inanimate) ᎦᏍᏏᏛᏂᎭ

u^{21}si^{2}htv^{23}ni^{32}lv^{23}ʔi^{2} ᎤᏍᏏᏛᏂᎸᎢ

a^{21}si^{2}htv^{33}ni^{2}ho^{33}ʔi^{2} ᎠᏍᏏᏛᏂᎰᎢ

hi^{22}ya^{11}si^{2}htv^{22}ni^{11}ga^{2} (animate) ᎯᏯᏍᏏᏛᏂᎦ

ha^{2}si^{2}htv^{22}ni^{11}ga^{2} (animate) ᎭᏍᏏᏛᏂᎦ

u^{22}si^{2}htv^{23}ni^{32}sdi^{2} ᎤᏍᏏᏛᏂᏍᏗ

backing up

a^{33}si^{22}ne^{33}ga^{2} ᎠᏍᏏᏁᎦ one is backing up

ga^{33}si^{22}ne^{33}ga^{2} ᎦᏍᏏᏁᎦ

u^{33}si^{22}nv^{33}sv^{23}ʔi^{2} ᎤᏍᏏᏅᏍᏒᎢ

a^{33}si^{22}ne^{33}go^{33}ʔi^{2} ᎠᏍᏏᏁᎪᎢ

ha^{11}si^{22}nu^{11}ga^{2} ᎭᏍᏏᏄᎦ

u^{11}si^{23}nv^{32}sdi^{2} ᎤᏍᏏᏅᏍᏗ

roping

a^{21}s(i^{23})la^{3}di^{23}ʔa^{2} ᎠᏍᏏᎳᏗᎠ one is roping another or it

tsi^{22}s(i^{23})la^{3}di^{23}ʔa^{2} ᏥᏍᏏᎳᏗᎠ

u^{21}s(i^{23})la^{3}dv^{23}ʔi^{2} ᎤᏍᏏᎳᏛᎢ

a^{21}s(i^{23})la^{3}di^{32}sgo^{33}ʔi^{2} ᎠᏍᏏᎳᏗᏍᎪᎢ

hi^{22}s(i^{23})la^{3}da^{2} (animate) ᎯᏍᏏᎳᏓ

hi^{2}s(i^{23})la^{2}da^{2} (inanimate) ᎯᏍᏏᎳᏓ

u^{22}s(i^{22})la^{2}di^{11}sdi^{2} ᎤᏍᏏᎳᏗᏍᏗ

building a fence

a^{21}so^{23}hyo^{3}ha^{2} ᎠᏍᏐᏲᎭ one is building a fence

ga^{21}so^{23}hyo^{3}ha^{2} ᎦᏍᏐᏲᎭ

u^{21}so^{23}hya^{3}lv^{23}ʔi^{2} ᎤᏍᏐᏯᎸᎢ

a^{21}so^{23}hyo^{3}ho^{33}ʔi^{2} ᎠᏍᏐᏲᎰᎢ

ha^{2}so^{23}hya^{0}ga^{2} ᎭᏍᏐᏯᎦ

u^{22}so^{23}hya^{32}sdi^{2} ᎤᏍᏐᏯᏍᏗ

waving (with one's hand)

a^{21}so^{22}lv^{22}da^{2}gi^{33}ʔa^{2} ᎠᏍᏐᎸᏓᎩᎠ one is waving one's hand

ga^{21}so^{22}lv^{22}da^{2}gi^{33}ʔa^{2} ᎦᏍᏐᎸᏓᎩᎠ

u^{21}so^{22}lv^{22}da^{2}gi^{33}sv^{23}ʔi^{2} ᎤᏍᏐᎸᏓᎩᏍᏒᎢ

a^{21}so^{22}lv^{22}da^{2}gi^{33}sgo^{33}ʔi^{2} ᎠᏍᏐᎸᏓᎩᏍᎪᎢ

ha^{2}so^{22}lv^{22}da^{2}gi^{2} ᎭᏍᏐᎸᏓᎩ

u^{22}so^{22}lv^{22}da^{2}gi^{11}sdi^{2} ᎤᏍᏐᎸᏓᎩᏍᏗ

pressing down

a^{21}so^{32}nv^{0}sdi^{23}ha^{2} ᎠᏍᏐᏅᏍᏗᎭ one is pressing down on another or it

tsi^{22}ya^{11}so^{32}nv^{0}sdi^{23}ha^{2} (animate) ᏥᏯᏍᏐᏅᏍᏗᎭ

ga^{21}so^{32}nv^{0}sdi^{23}ha^{2} (inanimate) ᎦᏍᏐᏅᏍᏗᎭ

u^{21}so^{32}nv^{0}sta^{2}nv^{23}ʔi^{2} ᎤᏍᏐᏅᏍᏔᏅᎢ

a^{21}so^{32}nv^{0}sdi^{22}sgo^{33}ʔi^{2} ᎠᏍᏐᏅᏍᏗᏍᎪᎢ

hi^{22}ya^{11}so^{11}nv^{0}sda^{2} (animate) ᎯᏯᏍᏐᏅᏍᏓ

ha^{2}so^{11}nv^{0}sda^{2} (inanimate) ᎭᏐᏅᏍᏓ
u^{22}so^{11}nv^{0}sdo^{2}hdi^{2} ᎤᏐᏅᏍᏙᏗ

wounding

a^{21}so^{22}nv^{22}sga^{2}	ᎠᏐᏅᏍᎦ	one is wounding another or it
tsi^{22}so^{22}nv^{22}sga^{2}	ᏥᏐᏅᏍᎦ	
u^{21}so^{22}nv^{22}hnv^{23}ʔi^{2}	ᎤᏐᏅᏅᎢ	
a^{21}so^{22}nv^{22}sgo^{33}ʔi^{2}	ᎠᏐᏅᏍᎪᎢ	
hi^{22}so^{22}nv^{23}na^{2}	ᎯᏐᏅᎾ	
u^{22}so^{22}nv^{22}sdi^{2}	ᎤᏐᏅᏍᏗ	

sopping

a^{21}su^{33}ʔa^{2}	ᎠᏑᎠ	one is sopping it up
ga^{22}su^{33}ʔa^{2}	ᎦᏑᎠ	
u^{21}su^{33}sv^{23}ʔi^{2}	ᎤᏑᏍᎡᎢ	
a^{21}su^{33}sgo^{33}ʔi^{2}	ᎠᏑᏍᎪᎢ	
ha^{2}su^{23}tsa^{2}	ᎭᏑᏣ	
u^{22}su^{11}sdi^{2}	ᎤᏑᏍᏗ	

fishing

a^{21}su^{23}hv^{3}sga^{2}	ᎠᏑᎲᏍᎦ one is fishing	
	'reduplicative' conditional suffix	
ga^{22}su^{23}hv^{3}sga^{2}	ᎦᏑᎲᏍᎦ	
u^{21}su^{33}hnv^{23}ʔi^{2}	ᎤᏑᏅᎢ	
a^{21}su^{23}hv^{3}sgo^{33}ʔi^{2}	ᎠᏑᎲᏍᎪᎢ	
ha^{2}su^{22}hv^{11}ga^{2}	ᎭᏑᎲᎦ	
u^{22}su^{2}hdi^{2}	ᎤᏑᎲᏗ	

painting

a^{21}su^{23}hwi^{3}sga^{2}	ᎠᏑᏫᏍᎦ	one is painting it
tsi^{22}su^{23}hwi^{3}sga^{2}	ᏥᏑᏫᏍᎦ	
u^{21}su^{23}hwi^{3}sv^{23}ʔi^{2}	ᎤᏑᏫᏍᎡᎢ	
a^{21}su^{23}hwi^{3}sgo^{33}ʔi^{2}	ᎠᏑᏫᏍᎪᎢ	
hi^{2}su^{23}hwa^{2}	ᎯᏑᏩ	
u^{22}su^{23}hwi^{3}sdi^{2}	ᎤᏑᏫᏍᏗ	

changing pants

a^{33}su^{22}la^{3}ʔi^{22}yv^{33}ʔa^{2} ᎠᏍᏑᎳᎢᏴᎠ one is changing one's pants

ga^{33}su^{22}la^{3}ʔi^{22}yv^{33}ʔa^{2} ᎦᏍᏑᎳᎢᏴᎠ

u^{33}su^{22}la^{3}ʔi^{22}yv^{33}sv^{23}ʔi^{2} ᎤᏍᏑᎳᎢᏴᏍᏒᎢ

a^{33}su^{22}la^{3}ʔi^{22}yv^{33}sgo^{33}ʔi ᎠᏍᏑᎳᎢᏴᏍᎪᎢ

ha^{11}su^{22}la^{2}ʔi^{22}yv^{23}na^{2} ᎭᏍᏑᎳᎢᏴᎾ

u^{11}su^{23}la^{3}ʔi^{22}yv^{11}sdi^{2} ᎤᏍᏑᎳᎢᏴᏍᏗ

taking pants off

a^{33}su^{22}le^{33}ʔa^{2} ᎠᏍᏑᎴᎠ one is taking one's pants off

'reversive' infix

ga^{33}su^{22}le^{33}ʔa^{2} ᎦᏍᏑᎴᎠ

u^{33}su^{22}le^{33}sv^{23}ʔi^{2} ᎤᏍᏑᎴᏍᏒᎢ

a^{33}su^{22}le^{33}sgo^{33}ʔi^{2} ᎠᏍᏑᎴᏍᎪᎢ

ha^{11}su^{22}le^{2}gi^{2} ᎭᏍᏑᎴᎩ

u^{22}su^{23}le^{32}sdi^{2} ᎤᏍᏑᎴᏍᏗ

putting pants on

a^{33}su^{23}li^{3}ʔa ᎠᏍᏑᎵᎠ one is putting on pants

ga^{33}su^{23}li^{3}ʔa^{2} ᎦᏍᏑᎵᎠ

u^{33}su^{23}l**a^{32}n**v^{23}ʔi^{2} ᎤᏍᏑᎳᏅᎢ **(populative infix)**

a^{33}su^{23}li^{32}sgo^{33}ʔi^{2} ᎠᏍᏑᎵᏍᎪᎢ

ha^{11}su^{22}lv^{11}ga^{2} ᎭᏍᏑᎸᎦ

u^{22}su^{23}lo^{32}di^{2} ᎤᏍᏑᎶᏗ

quitting

a^{21}su^{22}li^{2}go^{33}ga^{2} ᎠᏍᏑᎵᎪᎦ one is quitting

tsi^{22}su^{22}li^{2}go^{33}ga^{2} ᏥᏍᏑᎵᎪᎦ

u^{21}su^{22}li^{2}go^{33}tsv^{23}ʔi^{2} ᎤᏍᏑᎵᎪᏨᎢ

a^{21}su^{22}li^{2}go^{33}go^{33}ʔi^{2} ᎠᏍᏑᎵᎪᎪᎢ

hi^{2}su^{22}li^{2}go^{2}ʔi^{2} ᎯᏍᏑᎵᎪᎢ

u^{22}su^{22}li^{2}go^{11}sdi^{2} ᎤᏍᏑᎵᎪᏍᏗ

choosing

a^{21}su^{22}ye^{33}ʔa^{2} ᎠᏍᏑᏰᎠ one is choosing another or it

- tsi^{22}ya^{11}su^{22}ye^{33}ʔa^{2} (animate) ᏥᏯᏍᏑᏰᎠ
- ga^{22}su^{22}ye^{33}ʔa^{2} (inanimate) ᎦᏍᏑᏰᎠ
- u^{21}su^{22}ye^{33}sv^{23}ʔi^{2} ᎤᏍᏑᏰᏍᏒᎢ
- a^{21}su^{22}ye^{33}sgo^{33}ʔi^{2} ᎠᏍᏑᏰᏍᎪᎢ
- hi^{22}ya^{11}su^{22}ya^{2}gi^{2} (animate) ᎯᏯᏍᏑᏯᎩ
- ha^{2}su^{22}ya^{2}gi^{2} (inanimate) ᎭᏍᏑᏯᎩ
- u^{22}su^{22}ye^{11}sdi^{2} ᎤᏍᏑᏰᏍᏗ

stirring

a^{21}su^{33}ye^{23}ha^{2} ᎠᏍᏑᏰᎭ one is stirring it

- ga^{22}su^{33}ye^{23}ha^{2} ᎦᏍᏑᏰᎭ
- u^{21}su^{33}ye^{22}hv^{23}ʔi^{2} ᎤᏍᏑᏰᎲᎢ
- a^{21}su^{33}ye^{22}sgo^{33}ʔi^{2} ᎠᏍᏑᏰᏍᎪᎢ
- hi^{22}ya^{11}su^{22}ye^{2}gi^{2} (animate) ᎯᏯᏍᏑᏰᎩ
- ha^{2}su^{22}ye^{2}gi^{2} (inanimate) ᎭᏍᏑᏰᎩ
- u^{22}su^{22}ye^{2}hdi^{2} ᎤᏍᏑᏰᏗ

mixing

a^{21}su^{22}yv^{3}sga^{2} ᎠᏍᏑᏴᏍᎦ one is mixing it in

- ga^{22}su^{22}yv^{3}sga^{2} ᎦᏍᏑᏴᏍᎦ
- u^{21}su^{22}yv^{33}nv^{23}ʔi^{2} ᎤᏍᏑᏴᏅᎢ
- a^{21}su^{22}yv^{33}sgo^{33}ʔi^{2} ᎠᏍᏑᏴᏍᎪᎢ
- ha^{2}su^{22}yv^{2}ʔv^{11}ga^{2} ᎭᏍᏑᏴᎥᎦ
- u^{22}su^{22}yv^{11}di^{2} ᎤᏍᏑᏴᏗ

touching

a^{21}sv^{22}hni^{3}ha^{2} ᎠᏍᏒᏂᎭ one is touching another or it

tsi^{22}ya^{11}sv^{22}hni^{3}ha^{2} (animate) ᏥᏯᏍᏒᏂᎭ
ga^{22}sv^{22}hni^{3}ha^{2} (inanimate) ᎦᏍᏒᏂᎭ
u^{21}sv^{23}hni^{3}lv^{23}ʔi^{2} ᎤᏍᏒᏂᏢᎢ
a^{21}sv^{23}hni^{3}ho^{33}ʔi^{2} ᎠᏍᏒᏂᎰᎢ
hi^{22}ya^{11}sv^{22}hni^{0}ga^{2} (animate) ᎯᏯᏍᏒᏂᎦ
ha^{2}sv^{22}hni^{0}ga^{2} (inanimate) ᎭᏍᏒᏂᎦ
u^{22}sv^{22}hni^{0}sdi^{2} ᎤᏍᏒᏂᏍᏗ

using up

a^{21}sv^{3}hv^{3}sga^{2} ᎠᏍᏒᎲᏍᎦ one is using, drinking, or eating it up
'completely' conditional suffix i.e. -o^{3}hv^{3}sg-

tsi^{22}sv^{3}hv^{3}sgo^{33}ʔi^{2} ᏥᏍᏒᎲᏍᎪᎢ
u^{21}sv^{3}hnv^{23}ʔi^{2} ᎤᏍᏒᏅᎢ
a^{21}sv^{3}hv^{3}sgo^{33}ʔi^{2} ᎠᏍᏒᎲᏍᎪᎢ
hi^{2}sv^{2}hna^{2} ᎯᏍᏒᎿ
u^{22}sv^{3}hv^{3}sdi^{2} ᎤᏍᏒᎲᏍᏗ

holding one's breath

a^{21}ta^{2}hwo^{33}sdi^{2}ha^{2} ᎠᏔᏬᏍᏗᎭ one is holding one's breath

ga^{2}ʔda^{2}hwo^{33}sdi^{2}ha^{2} ᎦᏓᏬᏍᏗᎭ
u^{21}ta^{2}hwo^{33}sta^{2}nv^{23}ʔi^{2} ᎤᏔᏬᏍᏔᏅᎢ
a^{21}ta^{2}hwo^{33}sdi^{22}sgo^{33}ʔi^{2} ᎠᏔᏬᏍᏗᏍᎪᎢ
ha^{2}ta^{2}hwo^{11}sda^{2} ᎭᏔᏬᏍᏓ
u^{22}ta^{2}hwo^{11}sdo^{2}hdi^{2} ᎤᏔᏬᏍᏙᏗ

mooring

a^{21}ta^{2}la^{2}di^{23}ʔa^{2} ᎠᏔᎳᏗᎠ one is mooring a boat

tsi^{22}ta^{2}la^{2}di^{23}ʔa^{2} ᏥᏔᎳᏗᎠ
u^{21}ta^{2}la^{2}dv^{23}ʔi^{2} ᎤᏔᎳᏛᎢ
a^{21}ta^{2}la^{2}di^{22}sgo^{33}ʔi^{2} ᎠᏔᎳᏗᏍᎪᎢ

hi^{2}ta^{2}la^{2}da^{2} ᎯᏔᎳᏓ

u^{22}ta^{2}la^{2}di^{11}sdi^{2} ᎤᏔᎳᏗᏍᏗ

drilling

a^{21}ta^{2}le^{22}sga^{2} ᎠᏔᎴᏍᎦ one is drilling a hole

tsi^{22}ta^{2}le^{22}sga^{2} ᏥᏔᎴᏍᎦ

u^{21}ta^{2}le^{22}sv^{23}ʔi^{2} ᎤᏔᎴᏍᏒᎢ

a^{21}ta^{2}le^{22}sgo^{33}ʔi^{2} ᎠᏔᎴᏍᎪᎢ

hi^{2}ta^{2}la^{2}ga^{2} ᎯᏔᎳᎦ

u^{22}ta^{2}le^{22}sdi^{2} ᎤᏔᎴᏍᏗ

exploding

a^{21}ta^{2}sgi^{33}sdi^{2}ha^{2} ᎠᏔᏍᎩᏍᏗᎭ one is exploding it

tsi^{22}ta^{2}sgi^{33}sdi^{2}ha^{2} ᏥᏔᏍᎩᏍᏗᎭ

u^{21}ta^{2}sgi^{33}sta^{2}nv^{23}ʔi^{2} ᎤᏔᏍᎩᏍᏔᏅᎢ

a^{21}ta^{2}sgi^{33}sdi^{22}sgo^{33}ʔi^{2} ᎠᏔᏍᎩᏍᏗᏍᎪᎢ

ha^{2}ta^{2}sgi^{11}sda^{2} ᎭᏔᏍᎩᏍᏓ

u^{22}ta^{2}sgi^{11}sdo^{2}hdi^{2} ᎤᏔᏍᎩᏍᏙᏗ

kissing

a^{21}ta^{2}we^{23}do^{3}ʔv^{2}sga^{2} ᎠᏔᏪᏙᎥᏍᎦ one is kissing another

'completive' conditional suffix

tsi^{22}da^{2}we^{23}do^{3}ʔv^{2}sga^{2} ᏥᏓᏪᏙᎥᏍᎦ

u^{21}ta^{2}we^{23}d**o^{3}hn**v^{23}ʔi^{2} ᎤᏔᏪᏙᏅᎢ

a^{21}ta^{2}we^{23}do^{3}ʔv^{2}sgo^{33}ʔi^{2} ᎠᏔᏪᏙᎥᏍᎪᎢ

hi^{22}ta^{2}we^{22}do^{2}ʔv^{11}ga^{2} ᎯᏔᏪᏙᎥᎦ

u^{22}ta^{2}we^{23}do^{32}sdi^{2} ᎤᏔᏪᏙᏍᏗ

combing hair

a^{21}ta^{2}wo^{33}ʔa^{2} ᎠᏔᏬᎠ one is combing another's hair

tsi^{22}ta^{2}wo^{33}ʔa^{2} ᏥᏔᏬᎠ

u^{21}ta^{2}wo^{33}ʔv^{2}ʔi^{2} ᎤᏔᏬᎥᎢ

a^{21}ta^{2}wo^{33}sgo^{33}ʔi^{2} ᎠᏔᏬᏍᎪᎢ

hi^{22}ta^{2}wo^{23}tsa^{2} ᎯᏔᏬᏣ

u^{22}ta^{2}wo^{11}sdi^{2} ᎤᏔᏬᏍᏗ

asking

a^{21}ta^{2}yo^{23}hi^{3}ha^{2} ᎠᏔᏲᎯᎭ one is asking for it

tsi^{22}ta^{2}yo^{23}hi^{3}ha^{2} ᏥᏔᏲᎯᎭ

u^{21}ta^{2}yo^{22}hlv^{23}ʔi^{2} ᎤᏔᏲᎵᎢ

a^{21}ta^{2}yo^{22}hi^{2}ho^{33}ʔi^{2} ᎠᏔᏲᎯᎰᎢ

hi^{2}ta^{2}yo^{23}ha^{2} ᎯᏔᏲᎭ

u^{22}ta^{2}yo^{22}sdi^{2} ᎤᏔᏲᏍᏗ

joining a group

a^{21}te^{22}la^{2}di^{23}ʔa^{2} ᎠᏖᎳᏗᎠ one is joining (a group, membership, etc.)

ga^{2}de^{2}ʔla^{3}di^{33}ʔa^{2} ᎦᏕᎳᏗᎠ

u^{21}te^{22}la^{3}dv^{33}ʔi^{2} ᎤᏖᎳᏛᎢ

a^{21}te^{22}la^{3}di^{32}sgo^{33}ʔi^{2} ᎠᏖᎳᏗᏍᎪᎢ

ha^{2}te^{22}la^{2}da^{2} ᎭᏖᎳᏓ

u^{22}te^{22}la^{2}di^{11}sdi^{2} ᎤᏖᎳᏗᏍᏗ

shaking

a^{21}te^{33}lv^{23}hv^{3}sga^{2} ᎠᏖᎸᎲᏍᎦ one is shaking another or it

tsi^{22}te^{33}lv^{23}hv^{3}sga^{2} ᏥᏖᎸᎲᏍᎦ

u^{21}te^{33}lv^{22}hnv^{23}ʔi^{2} ᎤᏖᎸᏅᎢ

a^{21}te^{33}lv^{23}hv^{3}sgo^{33}ʔi^{2} ᎠᏖᎸᎲᏍᎪᎢ

hi^{22}te^{11}lv^{23}na^{2} (animate) ᎯᏖᎸᎾ

hi^{2}te^{11}lv^{23}na^{2} (inanimate) ᎯᏖᎸᎾ

u^{22}te^{11}hlv^{0}hdi^{2} ᎤᏖᎸᏗ

leading

a^{21}ti^{3}hni^{2} **(a^{21}ti^{2}hne^{33}ga^{2})** ᎠᏘᏁᎦ one is leading another

The bolded version reflects the 'going' conditional suffix that is used on the rest of the entries.

'going' conditional suffix

tsi^{22}ya^{11}ti^{3}hni^{2} **(tsi^{22}ya^{11}ti^{2}hne^{33}ga^{2})** ᏥᏯᏘᏁᎦ
u^{21}ti^{2}hn**v^{33}s**v^{23}ʔi^{2} ᎤᏘᏅᏍᏒᎢ
a^{21}ti^{2}hn**e^{33}g**o^{33}ʔi^{2} ᎠᏘᏁᎪᎢ
hi^{22}ya^{11}ti^{2}hn**u^{11}g**a^{2} ᎯᏯᏘᏄᎦ
u^{22}ti^{2}hn**v^{11}sdi^{2}** ᎤᏘᏅᏍᏗ

arguing

a^{21}ti^{2}yo**^{23}hi^{3}h**a^{2} ᎠᏘᏲᎯᎭ one is arguing

'with purpose' conditional suffix

ga^{2}ʔdi^{2}yo**^{23}hi^{3}h**a^{2} ᎦᏗᏲᎯᎭ
u^{21}ti^{2}yo**^{23}hl**v^{33}ʔi^{2} ᎤᏘᏲᏢᎢ
a^{21}ti^{2}yo**^{23}hi^{3}h**o^{33}ʔi^{2} ᎠᏘᏲᎯᎰᎢ
ha^{2}ti^{2}yo**^{23}g**a^{2} ᎭᏘᏲᎦ
u^{22}ti^{2}yo**^{23}sdi^{2}** ᎤᏘᏲᏍᏗ

racing/running for office

a^{21}to^{2}hgi^{23}ya^{3}ʔa^{2} ᎠᏙᎩᏯᎠ one is racing
one is running for office

ga^{21}to^{2}hgi^{23}ya^{3}ʔa^{2} ᎦᏙᎩᏯᎠ
u^{21}to^{2}hgi^{33}yv^{23}ʔi^{2} ᎤᏙᎩᏴᎢ
a^{21}to^{2}hgi^{23}ya^{32}sgo^{33}ʔi^{2} ᎠᏙᎩᏯᏍᎪᎢ
ha^{2}to^{2}hgi^{23}ya^{2} ᎭᏙᎩᏯ
u^{22}to^{2}hgi^{23}ya^{32}sdi^{2} ᎤᏙᎩᏯᏍᏗ

loaning

a^{21}to^{22}li^{0}sdi^{23}ha^{2} ᎠᏙᎵᏍᏗᎭ one is loaning it to another

tsi^{22}ya^{11}to^{22}li^{0}sdi^{23}ha^{2} ᏥᏯᏙᎵᏍᏗᎭ
u^{21}to^{22}li^{0}sta^{2}nv^{23}ʔi^{2} ᎤᏙᎵᏍᏔᏅᎢ
a^{21}to^{22}li^{0}sdi^{22}sgo^{33}ʔi^{2} ᎠᏙᎵᏍᏗᏍᎪᎢ
hi^{22}ya^{11}to^{22}li^{0}sda^{2} ᎯᏯᏙᎵᏍᏓ
u^{22}to^{22}li^{0}sdo^{2}hdi^{2} ᎤᏙᎵᏍᏙᏗ

borrowing

a^{21}to^{22}li^{0}sga^{2} ᎠᏙᎵᏍᎦ one is borrowing another or it

tsi^{22}ya^{11}to^{22}li^{0}sga^{2} (animate) ᏥᏯᏙᎵᏍᎦ
ga^{21}to^{22}li^{0}sga^{2} (inanimate) ᎦᏙᎵᏍᎦ
u^{21}to^{22}li^{0}sv^{23}ʔi^{2} ᎤᏙᎵᏍᎥᎢ
a^{21}to^{22}li^{0}sgo^{33}ʔi^{2} ᎠᏙᎵᏍᎪᎢ
hi^{22}ya^{11}to^{23}la^{2} (animate) ᎯᏯᏙᎳ
ha^{2}to^{23}la^{2} (inanimate) ᎭᏙᎳ
u^{22}to^{22}hli^{2}sdi^{2} ᎤᏙᎵᎯᏍᏗ

flashing

a^{21}to^{23}y**a**^{32}**wa**^{0}**sg**a^{2} ᎠᏙᏯᏩᏍᎦ it is flashing (a light)

'performing a duty' conditional suffix

tsi^{22}to^{23}y**a**^{32}**wa**^{0}**sg**a^{2} ᏥᏙᏯᏩᏍᎦ I'm flashing
u^{21}to^{23}y**a**^{32}**wa**^{0}**s**v^{23}ʔi^{2} ᎤᏙᏯᏩᏍᎥᎢ
a^{21}to^{23}y**a**^{32}**wa**^{0}**sg**o^{33}ʔi^{2} ᎠᏙᏯᏩᏍᎪᎢ
ha^{2}to^{23}y**a**^{32}**w**a^{2} ᎭᏙᏯᏩ
u^{22}to^{23}y**a**^{32}**wa**^{0}**sdi**^{2} ᎤᏙᏯᏩᏍᏗ

taking a bite

a^{21}tsi^{0}sde^{33}ʔa^{2} ᎠᏥᏍᏕᎠ one is taking a bite

- ga^{2}tsi^{11}sde^{33}ʔa^{2} ᎦᏥᏍᏕᎠ
- u^{21}tsi^{0}sde^{33}sv^{23}ʔi^{2} ᎤᏥᏍᏕᏍᎥᎢ
- a^{21}tsi^{0}sde^{33}sgo^{33}ʔi^{2} ᎠᏥᏍᏕᏍᎪᎢ
- ha^{2}tsi^{0}sda^{2}gi^{2} ᎭᏥᏍᏓᎩ
- u^{22}tsi^{0}sde^{11}sdi^{2} ᎤᏥᏍᏕᏍᏗ

telling a lie

a^{21}tsi^{0}sgo^{3}ʔv^{2}sga^{2} or a^{21}tsi^{0}sgo^{33}(ʔv^{2})sga^{2} ᎠᏥᏍᎪᎥᏍᎦ
one is telling a lie (lying)

- ga^{2}tsi^{11}sgo^{3}ʔv^{2}sga^{2} ᎦᏥᏍᎪᎥᏍᎦ
  or ga^{2}tsi^{11}sgo^{33}(ʔv^{2})sga^{2}
- u^{21}tsi^{0}sgo^{33}nv^{23}ʔi ᎤᏥᏍᎪᏅᎢ
- a^{21}tsi^{0}sgo^{3}ʔv^{2}sgo^{33}ʔi^{2} ᎠᏥᏍᎪᎥᏍᎪᎢ
  or a^{21}tsi^{0}sgo^{33}(ʔv^{2})sgo^{33}ʔi^{2}
- ha^{2}tsi^{0}sgo^{2}ʔv^{11}ga^{2} ᎭᏥᏍᎪᎥᎦ
- u^{22}tsi^{0}sgo^{11}di^{2} ᎤᏥᏍᎪᏗ

drinking alcohol

a^{21}tu^{23}gi^{3}ʔa^{2} ᎠᏚᎩᎠ one is taking a drink (of alcohol)

- ga^{2}ʔdu^{23}gi^{3}ʔa^{2} ᎦᏚᎩᎠ
- u^{21}tu^{23}gi^{32}sv^{23}ʔi^{2} ᎤᏚᎩᏍᎥᎢ
- a^{21}tu^{23}gi^{32}sgo^{33}ʔi^{2} ᎠᏚᎩᏍᎪᎢ
- ha^{2}tu^{23}gi^{2} ᎭᏚᎩ
- u^{22}tu^{23}gi^{32}sdi^{2} ᎤᏚᎩᏍᏗ

promising

a^{21}tu^{3}ʔi^{2}sdi^{23}ha^{2} ᎠᏚᎢᏍᏗᎭ one is promising

tsi^{21}tu^{3}ʔi^{2}sdi^{23}ha^{2} ᏥᏚᎢᏍᏗᎭ

u^{21}tu^{3}ʔi^{2}sta^{2}nv^{23}ʔi^{2} ᎤᏚᎢᏍᏔᏅᎢ

a^{21}tu^{3}ʔi^{2}sdi^{22}sgo^{33}ʔi^{2} ᎠᏚᎢᏍᏗᏍᎪᎢ

hi^{2}tu^{2}ʔi^{2}sda^{2} ᎯᏚᎢᏍᏓ

u^{22}tu^{2}ʔi^{2}ʔsdo^{2}hdi^{2} ᎤᏚᎢᏍᏙᏗ

listening

a^{21}tv^{23}da^{32}sdi^{23}ha^{2} ᎠᏛᏓᏍᏗᎭ one is listening to another or it

tsi^{22}ya^{11}tv^{23}da^{32}sdi^{23}ha^{2} (animate) ᏥᏯᏛᏓᏍᏗᎭ

ga^{21}tv^{23}da^{32}sdi^{23}ha^{2} (inanimate) ᎦᏛᏓᏍᏗᎭ

u^{21}tv^{23}da^{32}sta^{2}nv^{23}ʔi^{2} ᎤᏛᏓᏍᏔᏅᎢ

a^{21}tv^{23}da^{32}sdi^{22}sgo^{33}ʔi^{2} ᎠᏛᏓᏍᏗᏍᎪᎢ

hi^{22}ya^{11}tv^{22}da^{11}sda^{2} (animate) ᎯᏯᏛᏓᏍᏓ

ha^{2}tv^{22}da^{11}sda^{2} (inanimate) ᎭᏛᏓᏍᏓ

u^{22}tv^{22}da^{11}sdo^{2}hdi^{2} ᎤᏛᏓᏍᏙᏗ

questioning

a^{21}tv^{22}dv^{33}hv^{2}sga^{2} ᎠᏛᏛᏂᏍᎦ one is asking another a question
one is asking a question

tsi^{22}ya^{11}tv^{22}dv^{33}hv^{2}sga^{2} (animate) ᏥᏯᏛᏛᏂᏍᎦ

ga^{21}tv^{22}dv^{33}hv^{2}sga^{2} (inanimate) ᎦᏛᏛᏂᏍᎦ

u^{21}tv^{22}dv^{33}hnv^{23}ʔi^{2} ᎤᏛᏛᏅᎢ

a^{21}tv^{22}dv^{33}hv^{2}sgo^{33}ʔi^{2} ᎠᏛᏛᏂᏍᎪᎢ

hi^{22}ya^{11}tv^{22}dv^{22}hv^{11}ga^{2} (animate) ᎯᏯᏛᏛᏂᎦ

ha^{2}tv^{22}dv^{22}hv^{11}ga^{2} (inanimate) ᎭᏛᏛᏂᎦ

u^{22}tv^{22}d(v)hdi^{2} ᎤᏛᏛᏗ

hearing

a^{21}tv^{22}gi^{33}ʔa^{2}	ᎠᏛᎩᎠ	one hears another or it
tsi^{22}ya^{11}tv^{22}gi^{33}ʔa^{2} (animate)	ᏥᏯᏛᎩᎠ	
ga^{21}tv^{22}gi^{33}ʔa^{2} (inanimate)	ᎦᏛᎩᎠ	
u^{21}tv^{23}ga^{32}nv^{23}ʔi^{2}	ᎤᏛᎦᏅᎢ	
a^{21}tv^{22}gi^{33}sgo^{33}ʔi^{2}	ᎠᏛᎩᏍᎪᎢ	
hi^{22}ya^{11}tv^{22}gv^{11}ga^{2} (animate)	ᎯᏯᏛᎬᎦ	
ha^{2}tv^{22}gv^{11}ga^{2} (inanimate)	ᎭᏛᎬᎦ	
u^{22}tv^{23}go^{32}di^{2}	ᎤᏛᎪᏗ	

raising

a^{21}tv^{2}hi^{2}sdi^{23}ha^{2}	ᎠᏛᎯᏍᏗᎭ	one is raising another one is growing it
tsi^{22}ya^{2}ʔdv^{2}hi^{2}sdi^{23}ha^{2} (animate)	ᏥᏯᏛᎯᏍᏗᎭ	
ga^{2}ʔdv^{2}hi^{2}sdi^{23}ha^{2} (inanimate)	ᎦᏛᎯᏍᏗᎭ	
u^{21}tv^{2}hi^{2}sta^{2}nv^{23}ʔi^{2}	ᎤᏛᎯᏍᏔᏅᎢ	
a^{21}tv^{2}hi^{2}sdi^{22}sgo^{33}ʔi	ᎠᏛᎯᏍᏗᏍᎪᎢ	
hi^{22}ya^{2}tv^{2}hi^{2}sda^{2} (animate)	ᎯᏯᏛᎯᏍᏓ	
ha^{2}tv^{2}hi^{2}sda^{2} (inanimate)	ᎭᏛᎯᏍᏓ	
u^{22}tv^{2}hi^{2}sdo^{2}hdi^{2}	ᎤᏛᎯᏍᏙᏗ	

growing

a^{21}tv^{2}sga^{2}	ᎠᏛᏍᎦ	one is growing
ga^{2}ʔdv^{2}sga^{2}	ᎦᏛᏍᎦ	
u^{21}tv^{2}sv^{23}ʔi^{2}	ᎤᏛᏍᏒᎢ	
a^{21}tv^{2}sgo^{33}ʔi^{2}	ᎠᏛᏍᎪᎢ	
ha^{2}tv^{2}hi^{2}	ᎭᏛᎯ	
u^{22}tv^{2}hi^{2}sdi^{2}	ᎤᏛᎯᏍᏗ	

inside

a^{21}ya^{3}ʔa^{2} ᎠᏯᎠ one is inside

tsi^{22}ya^{3}ʔa^{2} ᏥᏯᎠ

u^{21}ya^{3}ʔv^{23}ʔi^{2} ᎤᏯᎥᎢ

a^{21}ya^{3}ʔo^{33}ʔi^{2} ᎠᏯᎣᎢ

hi^{22}ya^{2}hi^{2} ᎯᏯᎯ

u^{22}yv^{0}hdi^{2} ᎤᏴᏗ

distributing

a^{21}ya^{32}to^{2}hi^{3}ha^{2} ᎠᏯᏙᎯᎭ one is distributing it

tsi^{2}ya^{32}to^{2}hi^{3}ha^{2} ᏥᏯᏙᎯᎭ

u^{21}ya^{32}to^{2}hlv^{23}ʔi^{2} ᎤᏯᏙᏢᎢ

a^{21}ya^{32}to^{2}hi^{2}ho^{33}ʔi^{2} ᎠᏯᏙᎯᎰᎢ

hi^{2}ya^{11}to^{2}hi^{2} ᎯᏯᏙᎯ

u^{22}ya^{11}to^{2}hi^{3}sdi^{2} ᎤᏯᏙᎯᏍᏗ

waking up

a^{21}ye^{33}ga^{2} ᎠᏰᎦ one is waking up

tsi^{2}ye^{33}ga^{2} ᏥᏰᎦ

u^{21}ye^{33}tsv^{23}ʔi^{2} ᎤᏰᏨᎢ

a^{21}ye^{33}go^{33}ʔi^{2} ᎠᏰᎪᎢ

hi^{2}ye^{11}gi^{2} ᎯᏰᎩ

u^{22}ye^{2}ʔi^{2}sdi^{2} ᎤᏰᎢᏍᏗ

waking up another

a^{21}ye^{33}ʔi^{2}sdi^{23}ha^{2} ᎠᏰᎢᏍᏗᎭ one is waking up another

tsi^{22}ye^{33}ʔi^{2}sdi^{23}ha^{2} ᏥᏰᎢᏍᏗᎭ

u^{21}ye^{33}ʔi^{2}sta^{2}nv^{23}ʔi^{2} ᎤᏰᎢᏍᏔᏅᎢ

a^{21}ye^{33}ʔi^{2}sdi^{22}sgo^{33}ʔi^{2} ᎠᏰᎢᏍᏗᏍᎪᎢ

hi^{22}ye^{2}ʔi^{2}sda^{2} ᎯᏰᎢᏍᏓ

u^{22}ye^{2}ʔi^{2}sdo^{3}hdi^{2} ᎤᏰᎢᏍᏙᏗ

putting it inside (a confined space)

a^{21}yv^{0}hdi^{23}ha^{2} ᎠᏴᏗᎭ

one is putting another inside it (an unconfined space)

tsi^{22}yv^{11}di^{23}ha^{2} ᏥᏴᏗᎭ
u^{21}yv^{0}ta^{2}nv^{23}ʔi^{2} ᎤᏴᏔᏅᎢ
a^{21}yv^{0}hdi^{22}sgo^{33}ʔi^{2} ᎠᏴᏗᏍᎪᎢ
hi^{22}yv^{11}da^{2} ᎯᏴᏓ
u^{22}yv^{0}hdo^{3}hdi^{2} ᎤᏴᏙᏗ

crowing

a^{33}yv^{0}hga^{2} ᎠᏴᎦ one is crowing (as the sound a rooster makes)

ga^{33}yv^{0}hga^{2} ᎦᏴᎦ
u^{33}yv^{22}hli^{0}sv^{23}ʔi^{2} ᎤᏴᏟᏍᏒᎢ
a^{33}yv^{0}hgo^{33}ʔi^{2} ᎠᏴᎪᎢ
ha^{11}yv^{23}la^{2} ᎭᏴᎳ
u^{21}yv^{23}hli^{3}sdi^{2} ᎤᏴᏟᏍᏗ

getting/picking up (a long object)

a^{21}yi^{3}ha^{2} ᎠᏱᎭ one is getting it or picking it up (a long object)

tsi^{2}yi^{33}ʔa^{2} ᏥᏱᎠ
u^{21}yv^{22}hv^{23}ʔi^{2} ᎤᏴᎲᎢ
a^{21}yi^{22}sgo^{33}ʔi^{2} ᎠᏱᏍᎪᎢ
hi^{2}ya^{2} ᎯᏯ
u^{22}yv^{0}hdi^{2} ᎤᏴᏗ

breaking/becoming spoiled

a^{21}yo^{33}ga^{2} ᎠᏲᎦ it is breaking or it is becoming spoiled

tsi^{2}yo^{33}ga^{2} ᏥᏲᎦ
u^{21}yo^{33}tsv^{23}ʔi^{2} ᎤᏲᏨᎢ
a^{21}yo^{33}go^{33}ʔi^{2} ᎠᏲᎪᎢ
hi^{2}yo^{11}gi^{2} ᎯᏲᎩ
u^{22}yo^{11}sdi^{2} ᎤᏲᏍᏗ

shooting

a^{21}yo^{23}hi^{3}ha^{2} ᎠᏲᎯᎭ one is shooting another or it

tsi^{22}yo^{2}ʔi^{3}ha^{2} (animate) ᏥᏲᎢᎭ

tsi^{2}yo^{2}ʔi^{3}ha^{2} (inanimate) ᏥᏲᎢᎭ

u^{21}yo^{22}hlv^{23}ʔi^{2} ᎤᏲᎸᎢ

a^{21}yo^{22}hi^{2}ho^{33}ʔi^{2} ᎠᏲᎯᎰᎢ

hi^{22}yo^{2}ha^{2} (animate) hi^{2}yo^{23}ha^{2} (inanimate) ᎯᏲᎭ

or ***hi^{22}yo^{2}ha^{2} (animate) hi^{3}yo^{2}ha^{2} (inanimate)*** ᎯᏲᎭ

This is the only immediate stem form I have found that has an entirely different pronunciation pattern to distinguish animacy. This is because this verb begins and ends with /h/ sounds which make the inanimate form somewhat difficult to pronounce (as compared to other stem forms). Raising the tone of the penultimate syllable of the inanimate form allows it to still be distinguished from the animate form and decreases the vocal harshness of shorter form. I give above in italics the version that is consistent with the other animate and inanimate forms found in our language.

taking a break

a^{21}yo^{3}hi^{2}sdi^{23}ha^{2} ᎠᏲᎯᏍᏗᎭ one is taking a break

tsi^{2}ʔyo^{3}hi^{2}sdi^{23}ha^{2} ᏥᏲᎯᏍᏗᎭ

u^{22}yo^{3}hi^{2}sta^{2}nv^{23}ʔi^{2} ᎤᏲᎯᏍᏔᏅᎢ

a^{21}yo^{3}hi^{2}sdi^{22}sgo^{33}ʔi^{2} ᎠᏲᎯᏍᏗᏍᎪᎢ

hi^{2}yo^{2}hi^{2}sda^{2} ᎯᏲᎯᏍᏓ

u^{22}yo^{2}hi^{2}sdo^{2}hdi^{2} ᎤᏲᎯᏍᏙᏗ

carving/whittling

a^{21}yo^{22}hlv^{3}h(v)sga^{2} ᎠᏲᎸᎲᏍᎦ one is whittling, carving, hewing, etc.

tsi^{2}yo^{11}lv^{3}h(v)sga^{2} ᏥᏲᎸᎲᏍᎦ

u^{21}yo^{22}hl**a**^{3}**nv**^{33}ʔi^{2} ᎤᏲᎳᏅᎢ

This is an example of the populative suffix causing the (^{3}) tone to spread rightward onto the tense suffix. (See the bolded portion above). This could be remedied by the following pronunciation; u^{21}yo^{23}hla^{32}nv^{23}ʔi^{2}. I say "remedied" because this alternate pronunciation is the form that is consistent with the populative suffix tone pattern. The form with rightward tone spread is the contracted form. Contracted forms are made by speakers and are a process of condensing tone down to smaller units to make pronunciation shorter and easier. You may choose which pronunciation you would like to use because they are both correct. I felt it was necessary to both include the original form, and explain the contracted form. The original form however, allows for much easier understanding of Cherokee via the Root Word Method.

Secondly, the use of the populative infix here is not consistent with the other forms listed. The other forms use the 'reduplicative' conditional suffix, meaning 'the verb is being performed over a period of time'. If we adjust the completive stem form to reflect the reduplicative in its completive form, we have u^{21}yo^{22}hl**v**^{3}**h(v)n**v^{23}ʔi^{2}. This form is consistent with the other forms and also a tone contraction is not needed.

a^{21}yo^{22}hlv^{3}h(v)sgo^{33}ʔi^{2} ᎠᏲᎸᎲᏍᎪᎢ

hi^{2}yo^{22}hlv^{11}ga^{2} ᎯᏲᎸᎦ

u^{22}yo^{22}hlv^{11}sdi^{2} ᎤᏲᎸᏍᏗ

dying (a human dying)

a^{21}yo^{22}hu^{22}sga^{2} ᎠᏲᎱᏍᎦ one is dying (a human is dying)

tsi^{2}yo^{2}ʔu^{22}sga ᏥᏲᎤᏍᎦ

u^{21}yo^{22}hu^{22}sv^{23}ʔi^{2} ᎤᏲᎱᏍᏒᎢ

a^{21}yo^{22}hu^{22}sgo^{33}ʔi^{2} ᎠᏲᎱᏍᎪᎢ

hi^{2}yo^{22}hu^{23}hi^{2} ᎯᏲᎱᎯ

u^{22}yo^{22}hu^{22}hi^{2}sdi^{2} ᎤᏲᎱᎯᏍᏗ

greeting

a^{21}yo^{33}li^{23}ha^{2} ᎠᏲᎵᎭ one is greeting another

tsi^{22}yo^{33}li^{23}ha^{2} ᏥᏲᎵᎭ

u^{21}yo^{23}li^{32}lv^{23}ʔi^{2} ᎤᏲᎵᎸᎢ

a^{21}yo^{33}li^{2}ho^{33}ʔi^{2} ᎠᏲᎵᎰᎢ

hi^{22}yo^{22}li^{2}ga^{2} ᎯᏲᎵᎦ

u^{22}yo^{23}li^{32}sdi^{2} ᎤᏲᎵᏍᏗ

breaking it up (i.e. a fight)

a^{21}yo^{3}ʔi^{22}sdi^{23}ha^{2} ᎠᏲᎢᏍᏗᎭ
one is breaking it up (a fight or breaking something)

tsi^{2}yo^{3}ʔi^{22}sdi^{23}ha^{2} ᏥᏲᎢᏍᏗᎭ

u^{21}yo^{3}ʔi^{22}sta^{2}nv^{23}ʔi^{2} ᎤᏲᎢᏍᏔᏅᎢ

a^{21}yo^{3}ʔi^{22}sdi^{22}sgo^{33}ʔi^{2} ᎠᏲᎢᏍᏗᏍᎪᎢ

hi^{2}yo^{2}ʔi^{22}sda^{2} ᎯᏲᎢᏍᏓ

u^{22}yo^{2}ʔi^{22}sdo^{2}hdi^{2} ᎤᏲᎢᏍᏙᏗ

spoiling

a^{21}yo^{33}sdi^{23}ha^{2} ᎠᏲᏍᏗᎭ one is spoiling another
one is breaking it

tsi^{22}yo^{33}sdi^{23}ha^{2} ᏥᏲᏍᏗᎭ

u^{21}yo^{33}sta^{2}nv^{23}ʔi^{2} ᎤᏲᏍᏔᏅᎢ

a^{21}yo^{33}sdi^{22}sgo^{33}ʔi^{2} ᎠᏲᏍᏗᏍᎪᎢ

hi^{22}yo^{11}sda^{2} (animate) ᎯᏲᏍᏓ

hi^{2}yo^{11}sda^{2} (inanimate) ᎯᏲᏍᏓ

u^{22}yo^{11}sdo^{2}hdi^{2} ᎤᏲᏍᏙᏗ

destroying

a^{21}yo^{33}sta^{2}no^{3}hv^{3}sga^{2} ᎠᏲᏍᏔᏃᎲᏍᎦ one is destroying it

'completely' conditional suffix

tsi^{2}yo^{33}sta^{2}no^{3}hv^{3}sga^{2} ᏥᏲᏍᏔᏃᎲᏍᎦ

u^{22}yo^{33}sta^{2}no^{3}hnv^{23}ʔi^{2} ᎤᏲᏍᏔᏃᏅᎢ

a^{21}yo^{33}sta^{2}no^{3}hv^{3}sgo^{33}ʔi^{2} ᎠᏲᏣᏃᎲᏍᎪᎢ

hi^{2}yo^{11}sta^{2}no^{2}hna^{2} ᎯᏲᏍᏔᏃᏏ

u^{22}yo^{11}sta^{2}no^{3}hv^{3}sdi^{2} ᎤᏲᏍᏔᏃᎲᏍᏗ

entering

a^{21}yv^{22}hi^{3}ha^{2} ᎠᏴᎯᎭ one is entering it

tsi^{2}yv^{2}ʔi^{3}ha^{2} ᏥᏴᎢᎭ

u^{21}yv^{22}hlv^{23}ʔi^{2} ᎤᏴᎵᎢ

a^{21}yv^{22}hi^{3}ho^{33}ʔi^{2} ᎠᏴᎯᎰᎢ

hi^{2}yv^{23}ha^{2} ᎯᏴᎭ

u^{22}yv^{22}sdi^{2} ᎤᏴᏍᏗ

finding it (a long object)

a^{21}yv^{22}hwa^{2}hti^{23}ha^{2} ᎠᏴᏩᏘᎭ one is finding it (a long object)

tsi^{22}yv^{11}wa^{2}hti^{23}ha^{2} ᏥᏴᏩᏘᎭ

u^{21}yv^{22}hwa^{2}htv^{22}hv^{23}ʔi^{2} ᎤᏴᏩᏛᎲᎢ

a^{21}yv^{22}hwa^{2}hti^{22}sgo^{33}ʔi^{2} ᎠᏴᏩᏘᏍᎪᎢ

hi^{2}yv^{22}hwa^{2}hta^{2} ᎯᏴᏩᏔ

u^{22}yv^{22}hwa^{2}htv^{2}hdi^{2} ᎤᏴᏩᏛᏗ

taking it somewhere (a long object)

a^{21}yv^{22}hwi^{22}di^{23}ha^{2} ᎠᏴᏫᏗᎭ one is taking it somewhere (a long object)

tsi^{2}yv^{11}wi^{22}di^{23}ha^{2} ᏥᏴᏫᏗᎭ

u^{21}yv^{22}hwi^{22}dv^{22}hv^{23}ʔi^{2} ᎤᏴᏫᏛᎲᎢ

a^{21}yv^{22}hwi^{22}di^{22}sgo^{33}ʔi^{2} ᎠᏴᏫᏗᏍᎪᎢ

hi^{2}yv^{22}hwi^{23}da^{2} ᎯᏴᏫᏓ

u^{22}yv^{22}hwi^{22}dv^{0}hdi^{2} ᎤᏴᏫᏛᏗ

making an 'X'

da^{21}da^{22}hna^{32}wa^{0}sdi^{23}ha^{2} ᏓᏓᏏᏍ one is making an X

de^{33}ga^{2}da^{11}na^{32}wa^{0}sdi^{23}ha^{2} ᏕᎦᏓᏀᏩᏍᏗᎭ

du^{21}da^{22}hna^{32}wa^{0}sta^{2}nv^{23}ʔi^{2} ᏚᏓᎿᏩᏍᏔᏅᎢ

da^{21}da^{22}hna^{32}wa^{0}sdi^{22}sgo^{33}ʔi^{2} ᏓᏓᎿᏩᏍᏗᏍᎪᎢ

ta^{2}da^{22}hna^{11}wa^{0}sda^{2} ᏔᏓᎿᏩᏍᏓ

tsu^{22}da^{22}hna^{11}wa^{0}sdo^{2}hdi^{2} ᏧᏓᎿᏩᏍᏙᏗ

or di^{22}ʔu^{22}da^{22}hna^{11}wa^{0}sdo^{2}hdi^{2} ᏗᎤᏓᎿᏩᏍᏙᏗ

conjuring

da^{21}da^{22}hne^{22}se^{33}ʔa^{2} ᏓᏓᏁᏍᏎᎠ one is conjuring

de^{33}ga^{2}da^{11}ne^{22}se^{33}ʔa^{2} ᏕᎦᏓᏁᏍᏎᎠ

du^{21}da^{22}hne^{22}sa^{3}ʔv^{23}ʔi^{2} ᏚᏓᏁᏍᏌᎥᎢ

da^{21}da^{22}hne^{22}se^{33}sgo^{33}ʔi^{2} ᏓᏓᏁᏍᏎᏍᎪᎢ

ta^{2}da^{22}hne^{22}sa^{2}ga^{2} ᏔᏓᏁᏍᏌᎦ (this is odd to say)

tsu^{22}da^{22}hne^{22}se^{11}sdi^{2} ᏧᏓᏁᏍᏎᏍᏗ

or di^{22}ʔu^{22}da^{22}hne^{22}se^{11}sdi^{2} ᏗᎤᏓᏁᏍᏎᏍᏗ

accepting/welcoming

da^{21}da^{2}ni^{22}lv^{33}ga^{2} ᏓᏓᏂᎸᎦ one is accepting or welcoming another

one is accepting or welcoming it

de^{22}tsi^{33}ya^{2}da^{2}ni^{22}lv^{33}ga^{2} (animate) ᏕᏥᏯᏓᏂᎸᎦ

de^{33}ga^{2}da^{2}ni^{22}lv^{33}ga^{2} (inanimate) ᏕᎦᏓᏂᎸᎦ

du^{21}da^{2}ni^{22}lv^{33}tsv^{23}ʔi^{2} ᏚᏓᏂᎸᏨᎢ

da^{21}da^{2}ni^{22}lv^{33}go^{33}ʔi^{2} ᏓᏓᏂᎸᎪᎢ

ti^{22}ya^{2}da^{2}ni^{22}lv^{11}gi^{2} (animate) ᏘᏯᏓᏂᎸᎩ

ta^{2}da^{2}ni^{22}lv^{11}gi^{2} (inanimate) ᏔᏓᏂᎸᎩ

tsu^{22}da^{2}ni^{22}lv^{22}sdi^{2} (contracted form) ᏧᏓᏂᎸᏍᏗ

or di^{22}ʔu^{22}da^{2}ni^{22}lv^{22}sdi^{2} ᏗᎤᏓᏂᎸᏍᏗ

dodging

da^{21}da^{2}nv^{23}di^{32}sdi^{23}ha^{2} ᏓᏓᏅᏗᏍᏗᎭ one is dodging it

de^{33}ga^{2}da^{2}nv^{23}di^{32}sdi^{23}ha^{2} ᏕᎦᏓᏅᏗᏍᏗᎭ

du^{21}da^{2}nv^{23}di^{32}sta^{2}nv^{23}ʔi^{2} ᏚᏓᏅᏗᏍᏔᏅᎢ

da^{21}da^{2}nv^{23}di^{32}sgo^{33}ʔi^{2} ᏓᏓᏅᏗᏍᎪᎢ

ta^{2}da^{2}nv^{22}di^{11}sda^{2} ᏔᏓᏅᏗᏍᏓ

tsu^{22}da^{2}nv^{23}di^{32}sdo^{2}hdi^{2} (contracted form) ᏧᏓᏅᏗᏍᏙᏗ

or di^{22}ʔu^{22}da^{2}nv^{23}di^{32}sdo^{2}hdi^{2} ᏗᎤᏓᏅᏗᏍᏙᏗ

submerging (in water)

da^{21}da^{22}wo^{33}ʔa^{2} ᏓᏓᏬᎠ one is submerging themselves in water

de^{33}ga^{2}da^{22}wo^{33}ʔa^{2} ᏕᎦᏓᏬᎠ

du^{21}da^{22}wo^{33}ʔv^{23}ʔi^{2} ᏚᏓᏬᎥᎢ

da^{21}da^{22}wo^{33}sgo^{33}ʔi^{2} ᏓᏓᏬᏍᎪᎢ

ta^{2}da^{22}wo^{23}tsa^{2} ᏔᏓᏬᏣ

tsu^{22}da^{22}wo^{11}sdi^{2} (contracted form) ᏧᏓᏬᏍᏗ

or di^{22}ʔu^{22}da^{22}wo^{22}sdi^{2} ᏧᎤᏓᏬᏍᏗ

giving up/surrendering

da^{21}da^{22}yo^{3}sga^{2} ᏓᏓᏲᏍᎦ one is giving up or surrendering

de^{33}ga^{2}da^{23}yo^{3}sga^{2} ᏕᎦᏓᏲᏍᎦ

du^{21}da^{23}yo^{3}sv^{23}ʔi^{2} ᏚᏓᏲᏍᎡᎢ

da^{21}da^{23}yo^{3}sgo^{33}ʔi^{2} ᏓᏓᏲᏍᎪᎢ

ta^{2}da^{22}yo^{2}hi^{2} ᏔᏓᏲᎯ

tsu^{22}da^{22}yo^{3}hi^{3}sdi^{2} (contracted form) ᏧᏓᏲᎯᏍᏗ

or di^{22}ʔu^{22}da^{22}yo^{3}hi^{3}sdi^{2} ᏗᎤᏓᏲᎯᏍᏗ

teaching

da^{21}de^{22}**h**yo^{23}hv^{3}sga^{2} ᏓᏕᏲᎲᏍᎦ one is teaching

(3rd Person /h/ & /ʔ/ alternation pattern)

de^{33}ga^{2}de^{11}yo^{23}hv^{3}sga^{2} ᏕᎦᏕᏲᎲᏍᎦ

(1st Person /h/ & /ʔ/ alternation pattern)

The reason the 1st Person from does not have a /ʔ/ in place of the /h/ is because when 3rd Person transitive verb stems begin with /h/, the /h/ will simply delete in the 1st Person form.

du^{21}de^{22}hyo^{23}hnv^{33}ʔi^{2} ᏚᏕᏲᏅᎢ

da^{21}de^{22}hyo^{23}hv^{3}sgo^{33}ʔi^{2} ᏓᏕᏲᎲᏍᎪᎢ

ta^{2}de^{22}hyo^{22}hv^{11}ga^{2} ᏔᏕᏲᎲᎦ

tsu^{22}de^{22}hyo^{3}hdi^{2} (contracted form) ᏧᏕᏲᏗ

or di^{22}ʔu^{22}de^{22}hyo^{3}hdi^{2} ᏗᎤᏕᏲᏗ

weeping

da^{21}dlo^{22}hyi^{23}ha^{2} ᏓᏠᏱᎯᎭ one is weeping (crying from both eyes)

de^{33}ga^{2}dlo^{11}yi^{23}ha^{2} ᏕᎦᏠᏱᎯᎭ

du^{21}dlo^{22}hyi^{2}lv^{33}ʔi^{2} ᏚᏠᏱᎯᏢᎢ

da^{21}dlo^{22}hyi^{2}ho^{33}ʔi^{2} ᏓᏠᏱᎯᎰᎢ

ta^{2}dlo^{22}hyi^{0}ga^{2} ᏔᏠᏱᎯᎦ

tsu^{22}dlo^{22}hyi^{0}sdi^{2} (contracted form) ᏧᏠᏱᎯᏍᏗ

or di^{22}ʔu^{22}dlo^{22}hyi^{0}sdi^{2} ᏗᎤᏠᏱᎯᏍᏗ

being married

d**a**^{21}**g**a^{2}tsv^{33}sdi^{23}ha^{2} ᏓᎦᏨᏍᏗᎭ one is being married

(pronoun meaning, 'one to another')

d**v**^{21}**gw**a^{2}tsv^{33}sdi^{23}ha^{2} ᏛᏆᏨᏍᏗᎭ

(pronoun meaning, 'another to me')

d**a**^{21}**g**a^{2}tsv^{33}sta^{2}nv^{23}ʔi^{2} ᏓᎦᏨᏍᏔᏅᎢ

(pronoun meaning, 'one to another')

d**a**^{21}**g**a^{2}tsv^{33}sdi^{22}sgo^{33}ʔi^{2} ᏓᎦᏨᏍᏗᏍᎪᎢ

(pronoun meaning, 'one to another')

wi^{2}d(i)**e**^{22}**ts**a^{2}tsv^{11}sda^{2} ᏫᏗᎡᏣᏨᏍᏓ

(pronoun meaning, 'another to you')

ts**a**^{22}**g**a^{2}tsv^{11}sdo^{2}hdi^{2} ᏣᎦᏨᏍᏙᏗ

(pronoun meaning, 'one to another')

setting a price/pricing

da^{21}gv^{22}wa^{2}hlo^{0}hdi^{23}ha^{2} ᏓᎬᏩᎶᏗᎭ one is setting a price

de^{33}tsi^{2}gv^{22}wa^{2}lo^{0}hdi^{23}ha^{2} ᏕᏥᎬᏩᎶᏗᎭ

du^{21}gv^{22}wa^{2}hlo^{0}hta^{3}nv^{33}ʔi^{2} ᏚᎬᏩᎶᏔᏅᎢ

da^{21}gv^{22}wa^{2}hlo^{0}hdi^{22}sgo^{33}ʔi^{2} ᏓᎬᏩᎶᏗᏍᎪᎢ

ti^{2}gv^{22}wa^{2}hlo^{0}hda^{2} ᏘᎬᏩᎶᏓ or ᏗᎯᎬᏩᎶᏓ

tsu^{22}gv^{22}wa^{2}hlo^{0}hdo^{2}hdi^{2} ᏧᎬᏩᎶᏙᏗ

rocking

da^{21}hli^{2}hge^{23}ha^{2} ᏓᏟᎨᎭ one is rocking

de^{33}ga^{2}ʔli^{2}hge^{23}ha^{2} ᏕᎦᎵᎨᎭ

du^{21}hli^{2}hge^{22}hv^{23}ʔi^{2} ᏚᏟᎨᎲᎢ

da^{21}hli^{2}hge^{22}sgo^{33}ʔi^{2} ᏓᏟᎨᏍᎪᎢ

ta^{2}hli^{2}hgv^{22}la^{2} ᏔᏟᎬᎳ

tsu^{22}hli^{2}hge^{2}hdi^{2} ᏧᏟᎨᏗ

drawing/taking a picture

da^{21}hli^{22}lo^{33}sdi^{23}ha^{2} ᏓᏟᎶᏍᏗᎭ one is drawing a picture of another or it
one is taking a picture of another or it

de^{22}tsi^{33}ya^{2}dli^{11}lo^{33}sdi^{23}ha^{2} (animate) ᏕᏥᏯᏟᎶᏍᏗᎭ
de^{33}ga^{2}dli^{11}lo^{33}sdi^{23}ha^{2} (inanimate) ᏕᎦᏟᎶᏍᏗᎭ
du^{21}hli^{22}lo^{33}sta^{2}nv^{23}ʔi^{2} ᏚᏟᎶᏍᏔᏅᎢ
da^{21}hli^{22}lo^{33}sdi^{22}sgo^{33}ʔi^{2} ᏓᏟᎶᏍᏗᏍᎪᎢ
ti^{22}ya^{2}dli^{22}lo^{23}sda^{2} (animate) ᏘᏯᏟᎶᏍᏓ
ta^{2}hli^{22}lo^{23}sda^{2} (inanimate) ᏔᏟᎶᏍᏓ
tsu^{22}hli^{22}lo^{11}sdo^{2}hdi^{2} ᏧᏟᎶᏍᏙᏗ

conversing

da^{21}hli^{2}no^{22}he^{3}ha^{2} ᏓᏟᏃᎮᎭ one is conversing

de^{33}ga^{2}li^{11}no^{22}he^{3}ha^{2} ᏕᎦᎵᏃᎮᎭ
du^{21}hli^{2}no^{22}he^{22}hlv^{23}ʔi^{2} ᏚᏟᏃᎮᏢᎢ
da^{21}hli^{2}no^{22}he^{22}sgo^{33}ʔi^{2} ᏓᏟᏃᎮᏍᎪᎢ
ta^{2}hli^{2}no^{22}hv^{22}la^{2} ᏔᏟᏃᎲᎳ
tsu^{22}hli^{2}no^{22}he^{2}hdi^{2} ᏧᏟᏃᎮᏗ

jumping

da^{21}hli^{0}ta^{2}de^{33}ga^{2} ᏓᎵᏔᏕᎦ one is jumping
'going' conditional suffix

de^{33}ga^{2}li^{11}ta^{2}de^{33}ga^{2} ᏕᎦᎵᏔᏕᎦ
du^{21}hli^{0}ta^{2}di^{23}nv^{32}sv^{23}ʔi^{2} ᏚᏟᏔᏗᏅᏍᏒᎢ
da^{21}hli^{0}ta^{2}de^{33}go^{33}ʔi^{2} ᏓᏟᏔᏕᎪᎢ
ta^{22}hli^{0}ta^{2}du^{11}ga^{2} ᏔᏟᏔᏚᎦ
tsu^{22}hli^{0}ta^{2}di^{23}nv^{32}di^{2} ᏧᏟᏔᏗᏅᏗ

changing clothes

da^{21}**hnu**^{2}wa^{3}ʔi^{22}yv^{33}ʔa^{2}	ᏓᏄᏩᎢᏴᎠ	one is changing one's clothes
de^{33}ga^{2}**nu**^{11}wa^{3}ʔi^{22}yv^{33}ʔa^{2}	ᏕᎦᏄᏩᎢᏴᎠ	
du^{21}hnu^{2}wa^{3}ʔi^{22}yv^{33}sv^{23}ʔi^{2}	ᏚᏄᏩᎢᏴᏍᏒᎢ	
da^{21}hnu^{2}wa^{3}ʔi^{22}yv^{33}sgo^{33}ʔi^{2}	ᏓᏄᏩᎢᏴᏍᎪᎢ	
ta^{2}hnu^{2}wa^{2}ʔi^{22}yv^{23}na^{2}	ᏔᏄᏩᎢᏴᎾ	
tsu^{22}hnu^{2}wa^{2}ʔi^{23}yv^{32}sdi^{2}	ᏧᏄᏩᎢᏴᏍᏗ	

There seems to be some documented phonological problems with this verb. The CED lists the first person form as de^{33}ga^{2}**ni**^{11}wa^{3}ʔi^{22}yv^{33}ʔa^{2}. Firstly, this is a verb that reflects /h/ & /ʔ/ alternation, where the /h/ of /hnu/ is deleted in the first person form. The older way of saying cloth is 'a^{22}hnu^{2}wo$^{3'}$, and many now say 'a^{22}hna^{2}wo$^{3'}$, as it is listed in this particular verb above as an incorporated noun for the verb 'one is changing one's clothes'. Secondly, with regards to first person forms, the syllable that undergoes /h/ deletion also becomes lowered in tone. This is a tonal feature that occurs after the /h/ is deleted. It helps to set the first person form apart from the second person form.

The CED lists the above verb with the syllable /hna/ instead of /hnu/. This is simply because over time many speakers began to simplify some vowel sounds because they are 'faster' to say. The problem with this type of phonological shift is that it causes additional forms that are not easily anticipated by learners (if at all). Due to the fact that the CED entry uses the syllable /hna/ instead of /hnu/ creates the need for vowel shift in the first person form. One may expect to see the third person syllable /hna^{2}/ just simply change to /na^{11}/ for the first person form, where the /h/ was deleted and the /a/ vowel was lowered and lengthened to reflect the /h/ deletion. However, /h/ was deleted and the tone was lowered and lengthened, but the vowel switched to /i/ instead of the expected /a/ vowel. This is because the /a/ vowel is more strenuous to pronounce in this environment so, several speakers just altered the vowel to one that resulted in easier pronunciation and didn't corrupt the meaning of the verb.

Ultimately, these types of changes arise from widespread illiteracy amongst our people. Our Elders had a much greater understanding of our language and how it transitions back and forth between vocal and written forms. This knowledge is what allowed them to maintain morphemic integrity with their speech patterns. Finally, by using the original syllable for this part of the word i.e. /hnu/, there are not any pronunciation problems because the /u/ vowel does not cause any vocal constraints between first and third person forms.

taking clothes off

da^{21}hnu^{2}we^{33}ʔa^{2} ᏓᏄᏪᎠ one is taking one's clothes off

de^{33}ga^{2}nu^{11}we^{33}ʔa^{2} ᏕᎦᏄᏪᎠ
du^{21}hnu^{2}we^{33}sv^{23}ʔi^{2} ᏚᏄᏪᏍᏒᎢ
da^{21}hnu^{2}we^{33}sgo^{33}ʔi^{2} ᏓᏄᏪᏍᎪᎢ
ta^{2}hnu^{2}we^{2}gi^{2} ᏔᏄᏪᎩ
tsu^{22}hnu^{2}we^{11}sdi^{2} ᏧᏄᏪᏍᏗ

putting clothes on

da^{21}hnu^{2}wo^{33}ʔa^{2} ᏓᏄᏬᎠ one is putting clothes on

de^{33}ga^{2}nu^{11}wo^{33}ʔa^{2} ᏕᎦᏄᏬᎠ
du^{21}hnu^{2}wo^{33}ʔv^{23}ʔi^{2} ᏚᏄᏬᎥᎢ
da^{21}hnu^{2}wo^{33}sgo^{33}ʔi^{2} ᏓᏄᏬᏍᎪᎢ
ta^{2}hnu^{2}wo^{23}tsa^{2} ᏔᏄᏬᏣ
tsu^{22}hnu^{2}wo^{11}sdi^{2} ᏧᏄᏬᏍᏗ

putting it into a fire (a solid object)

da^{21}hv^{22}tv^{3}sga^{2} ᏓᎲᏛᏍᎦ one is putting it (a solid object) on a fire

de^{33}tsi^{2}ʔv^{22}tv^{3}sga^{2} ᏕᏥᎥᏛᏍᎦ
du^{21}hv^{22}ta^{3}nv^{33}ʔi^{2} ᏚᎲᏔᏅᎢ
da^{21}hv^{22}tv^{3}sgo^{3}ʔi^{2} ᏓᎲᏛᏍᎪᎢ
ti^{2}hv^{22}tv^{11}ga^{2} ᏘᎲᏛᎦ
tsu^{22}hv^{22}dv^{0}hdi^{2} ᏧᎲᏛᏗ

tickling/spurring

da^{21}hyv^{22}gi^{33}ʔa^{2} ᏓᏴᎩᎠ

one is tickling another or spurring another (i.e. a horse)

de^{22}tsi^{33}yv^{22}gi^{33}ʔa^{2} ᏕᏥᏴᎩᎠ
du^{21}hyv^{33}gv^{23}ʔi^{2} ᏚᏴᎬᎢ
da^{21}hyv^{22}gi^{33}sgo^{33}ʔi^{2} ᏓᏴᎩᏍᎪᎢ
ti^{22}yv^{23}ga^{2} or di^{22}hi^{22}yv^{23}ga^{2} ᏘᏴᎦ or ᏗᎯᏴᎦ
tsu^{22}hyv^{23}gi^{32}sdi^{2} ᏧᏴᎩᏍᏗ

squatting

da^{33}tsi^{2}hlu^{3}sga^{2} ᏓᏥᏢᏍᎦ one is squatting

de^{22}ga^{33}tsi^{2}hlu^{3}sga^{2} ᏕᎦᏥᏢᏍᎦ

du^{33}tsi^{2}hlu^{3}nv^{33}ʔi^{2} ᏚᏥᏢᏅᎢ

da^{33}tsi^{2}hlu^{3}sgo^{3}ʔi^{2} ᏓᏥᏢᏍᎪᎢ

ta^{11}tsi^{2}hlu^{11}ga^{2} (command) ᏔᏣᏢᎦ

tsi^{2}ta^{33}tsi^{2}hlu^{32}ga^{2} (immediate past) ᏥᏔᏥᏢᎦ

tsu^{11}tsi^{2}hlu^{3}sdi^{2} ᏧᏥᏢᏍᏗ

tying

da^{21}ka^{2}n**e**^{23}**hi**^{3}**h**a^{2} ᏓᎧᏁᎯᎭ one is tying it

or da^{21}ka^{2}ne^{22}yi^{33}ga^{2} ᏓᎧᏁᏱᎦ

('with purpose' conditional suffix i.e. /ihih/)

de^{33}tsi^{2}ga^{11}n**e**^{23}**hi**^{3}**h**a^{2} ᏕᏥᎦᏁᎯᎭ

du^{21}ka^{2}n**e**^{23}**hl**v^{23}ʔi^{2} ᏚᎧᏁᏢᎢ

da^{21}ka^{2}n**e**^{23}**hi**^{3}**h**o^{33}ʔi^{2} ᏓᎧᏁᎯᎰᎢ

ti^{2}ka^{2}n**e**^{22}**g**a^{2} ᏘᎧᏁᎦ

tsu^{22}ka^{2}n**e**^{22}**sdi**^{2} ᏧᎧᏁᏍᏗ

The present tense form of this verb is not consistent with the 'purpose' conditional suffix. For it to be consistent, it would have to be said da^{21}ka^{2}ne^{33}ga^{2} however, this would be confused with the 'going' conditional suffix /-e^{33}ga/. I believe it is because over time some speakers have begun to forget how to attach the present tense 'with purpose' conditional suffix /-i^{33}ga^{2}/ to a stem that ends in a vowel. It appears that instead of using the true present tense form of this conditional suffix i.e. /-i^{33}ga^{2}/, they chose to just alter the incompletive form by simply adding the present tense suffix /-a^{2}/ directly to it. This is what could be considered "a work around", but ultimately, this will lead to confusion for second language learners that are trying to learn the true forms of the conditional suffixes–in a clear and concise way.

In order to attach the present tense form of the 'with purpose' conditional suffix to a stem that ends in a vowel, you must first look and see what pronoun classification set it belongs to. This can be done by knowing the classification system or by looking at the present tense form of (any) verb. The present tense form will tell you what the default pronoun class is for that verb. Since this verb i.e. 'tying' is what we are connecting the 'with purpose' conditional suffix with is a Set A verb, we know that we need to use the Set A vowel-vowel connector, which is /-y-/. The final form is da^{21}ka^{2}ne^{22}**y**i^{33}ga^{2}, 'one is tying it'.

untying

da^{21}ka^{2}ne^{23}hyi^{3}ha^{2} ᏓᎧᏁᎯᎭ one is untying it

de^{33}tsi^{2}ga^{11}ne^{23}hyi^{3}ha^{2} ᏕᏥᎦᏁᎯᎭ

du^{21}ka^{2}ne^{23}hyv^{32}hv^{23}ʔi^{2} ᏚᎧᏁᏂᏂᎢ

da^{21}ka^{2}ne^{23}hyi^{32}sgo^{33}ʔi^{2} ᏓᎧᏁᎯᏍᎪᎢ

ti^{2}ka^{2}ne^{22}hya^{2} ᏘᎧᏁᎭ

tsu^{22}ka^{2}ne^{23}hyv^{3}hdi^{2} ᏧᎧᏁᏂᏗ

looking after/watching over

da^{21}ka^{2}no^{22}wa^{2}di^{23}do^{32}ha^{2} ᏓᎧᏃᏩᏗᏙᎭ

one is looking after another (watching over, etc.)

'about (in different places)' conditional suffix

de^{22}tsi^{33}ga^{11}no^{22}wa^{2}di^{23}do^{32}ha^{2} ᏕᏥᎦᏃᏩᏗᏙᎭ

du^{21}ka^{2}no^{22}wa^{2}di^{23}do^{32}lv^{23}ʔi^{2} ᏚᎧᏃᏩᏗᏙᎸᎢ

da^{21}ka^{2}no^{22}wa^{2}di^{23}do^{32}ho^{33}ʔi^{2} ᏓᎧᏃᏩᏗᏙᎰᎢ

ti^{22}ka^{2}no^{22}wa^{2}di^{23}da^{2} ᏘᎧᏃᏩᏗᏓ

or di^{22}hi^{22}ka^{2}no^{22}wa^{2}di^{23}da^{2} ᏗᎯᎧᏃᏩᏗᏓ

tsu^{22}ka^{2}no^{22}wa^{2}di^{23}da^{32}sdi^{2} ᏧᎧᏃᏩᏗᏓᏍᏗ

becoming blind

da^{21}ke^{23}w**a**^{32}**g**a^{2} ᏓᎨᏩᎦ one is becoming blind

(transformative conditional suffix)

de^{33}tsi^{2}ʔge^{23}wa^{32}ga^{2} ᏕᏥᎨᏩᎦ

du^{21}ke^{23}wa^{32}tsv^{23}ʔi^{2} ᏚᎨᏩᏨᎢ

da^{21}ke^{23}wa^{32}go^{33}ʔi^{2} ᏓᎨᏩᎪᎢ

ti^{22}ke^{22}wa^{11}gi^{2} ᏘᎨᏩᎩ

tsu^{22}ke^{23}wa^{3}ʔi^{2}sdi^{2} ᏧᎨᏩᎢᏍᏗ

making smoke/it is smoking

da^{21}ga^{0}sv^{33}sdi^{23}ha^{2} ᏓᎦᏍᎥᏍᏗᎭ one is making smoke or it is smoking

de^{33}tsi^{2}ga^{11}sv^{33}sdi^{23}ha^{2} ᏕᏥᎦᏍᎥᏍᏗᎭ

du^{21}ga^{0}sv^{33}sta^{2}nv^{23}ʔi^{2} ᏚᎦᏍᎥᏍᏔᏅᎢ

da^{21}ga^{0}sv^{33}sdi^{22}sgo^{33}ʔi^{2} ᏓᎦᏍᎥᏍᏗᏍᎪᎢ

ti^{2}ga^{0}sv^{11}sda^{2} ᏘᎦᏍᎥᏍᏓ

tsu^{22}ga^{0}sv^{11}sdo^{2}hdi^{2} ᏧᎦᏍᎥᏍᏙᏗ

blinking

da^{21}ga^{0}ta^{2}na^{32}wa^{0}sga^{2} ᏓᎦᏔᎾᏩᏍᎦ one is blinking

de^{33}ga^{2}ga^{11}ta^{2}na^{32}wa^{0}sga^{2} ᏕᎦᎦᏔᎾᏩᏍᎦ

du^{21}ga^{0}ta^{2}na^{32}wa^{0}sv^{23}ʔi^{2} ᏚᎦᏔᎾᏩᏍᎥᎢ

da^{21}ga^{0}ta^{2}na^{32}wa^{0}sgo^{33}ʔi^{2} ᏓᎦᏔᎾᏩᏍᎪᎢ

ta^{2}ga^{0}ta^{2}na^{11}wa^{2} ᏔᎦᏔᎾᏩ

tsu^{22}ga^{0}ta^{2}na^{11}wa^{0}sdi^{2} ᏧᎦᏔᎾᏩᏍᏗ

closing one's eyes

da^{21}ga^{0}ta^{32}sdi^{23}ha^{2} ᏓᎦᏔᏍᏗᎭ one is closing one's eyes

de^{33}ga^{2}ga^{11}ta^{32}sdi^{23}ha^{2} ᏕᎦᎦᏔᏍᏗᎭ

du^{21}ga^{0}ta^{32}sta^{2}nv^{2}ʔi^{2} ᏚᎦᏔᏍᏔᏅᎢ

da^{21}ga^{0}ta^{32}sdi^{22}sgo^{33}ʔi^{2} ᏓᎦᏔᏍᏗᏍᎪᎢ

ta^{2}ga^{0}ta^{11}sda^{2} ᏔᎦᏔᏍᏓ

tsu^{22}ga^{0}ta^{11}sdo^{2}hdi^{2} ᏧᎦᏔᏍᏙᏗ

attacking

da^{21}ga^{0}ti^{23}le^{32}ga^{2} ᏓᎦᏘᎴᎦ one is attacking another or it

de^{22}tsi^{33}ga^{11}ti^{23}le^{32}ga^{2} (animate) ᏕᏥᎦᏘᎴᎦ

de^{33}tsi^{2}ga^{11}ti^{23}le^{32}ga^{2} (inanimate) ᏕᏥᎦᏘᎴᎦ

du^{21}ga^{0}ti^{23}lv^{32}sv^{23}ʔi^{2} ᏚᎦᏘᎸᏍᏒᎢ

da^{21}ga^{0}ti^{23}le^{32}go^{33}ʔi^{2} ᏓᎦᏘᎴᎪᎢ

ti^{22}ga^{0}ti^{23}lu^{32}ga^{2} (animate) ᏘᎦᏘᎷᎦ

ti^{2}ga^{0}ti^{23}lu^{32}ga^{2} (inanimate) ᏘᎦᏘᎷᎦ

tsu^{22}ga^{0}ti^{23}lv^{32}sdi^{2} ᏧᎦᏘᎸᏍᏗ

taking off glasses

da^{21}ga^{0}ti^{2}nv^{22}de^{33}ʔa^{2} ᏓᎦᏘᏅᏕᎠ one is taking one's glasses off

de^{33}ga^{2}ga^{11}ti^{2}nv^{22}de^{33}ʔa^{2} ᏕᎦᎦᏘᏅᏕᎠ

du^{21}ga^{0}ti^{2}nv^{22}de^{33}sv^{23}ʔi^{2} ᏚᎦᏘᏅᏕᏍᏒᎢ

da^{21}ga^{0}ti^{2}nv^{22}de^{33}sgo^{33}ʔi^{2} ᏓᎦᏘᏅᏕᏍᎪᎢ

ta^{2}ga^{0}ti^{2}nv^{22}de^{2}gi^{2} ᏔᎦᏘᏅᏕᎩ

The CED list's the reversive suffix /-e^{33}-/ as being /-a-/ (i.e. ta^{2}ga^{0}ti^{2}nv^{22}d**a^{2}**gi^{2} 'Take your glasses off!') in the immediate stem forms however, this is just another example of where speakers have switched some vowels out for others in order to make it quicker or easier to say, or both.

It is my belief that this practice came about due to English interference and once Keetoowah speakers were able to speak English fluently, they began to convert some of their Native sounds to those of English. It is up to you which form you choose to use. My only objective is making you aware of original sounds and morphemes in order to make learning the patterns of our grammar more clear.

tsu^{22}ga^{0}ti^{2}nv^{22}de^{11}sdi^{2} ᏧᎦᏘᏅᏕᏍᏗ

putting on glasses

da^{21}ga^{0}ti^{2}nv^{22}tv^{3}sga^{2} ᏓᎦᏘᏅᏛᏍᎦ one is putting one's glasses on

de^{33}ga^{2}ga^{11}ti^{2}nv^{22}tv^{3}sga^{2} ᏕᎦᎦᏘᏅᏛᏍᎦ
du^{21}ga^{0}ti^{2}nv^{23}ta^{3}nv^{23}ʔi^{2} ᏚᎦᏘᏅᏔᏅᎢ
da^{21}ga^{0}ti^{2}nv^{23}tv^{3}sgo^{33}ʔi^{2} ᏓᎦᏘᏅᏛᏍᎪᎢ
ta^{2}ga^{0}ti^{2}nv^{22}tv^{11}ga^{2} ᏔᎦᏘᏅᏛᎦ
tsu^{22}ga^{0}ti^{2}nv^{22}dv^{0}hdi^{2} ᏧᎦᏘᏅᏛᏗ

shelling corn

da^{21}ga^{0}tli^{23}ha^{2} ᏓᎦᏟᎭ one is shelling corn

de^{33}tsi^{2}ga^{11}tli^{23}ha^{2} ᏕᏥᎦᏟᎭ
du^{21}ga^{0}tlv^{22}hv^{23}ʔi^{2} ᏚᎦᏢᎲᎢ
da^{21}ga^{0}tli^{22}sgo^{33}ʔi^{2} ᏓᎦᏟᏍᎪᎢ
ti^{2}ga^{0}tla^{2} ᏘᎦᏝ
tsu^{22}ga^{0}tlv^{2}hdi^{2} ᏧᎦᏢᏗ

snoring

da^{22}kwa^{2}la^{22}gi^{33}ʔa^{2} ᏓᏆᎳᎩᎠ one is snoring

de^{22}tsi^{33}kwa^{2}la^{22}gi^{33}ʔa^{2} ᏕᏥᏆᎳᎩᎠ
du^{22}kwa^{2}la^{22}gi^{33}sv^{23}ʔi^{2} ᏚᏆᎳᎩᏒᎢ
ti^{2}kwa^{2}la^{22}gi^{2} ᏘᏆᎳᎩ
tsu^{22}kwa^{2}la^{22}gi^{11}sdi^{2} ᏧᏆᎳᎩᏍᏗ

sprinkling (a liquid or something granular)

da^{21}kwa^{2}yo^{33}ʔv^{2}sga^{2} ᏓᏆᏲᎥᏍᎦ one is sprinkling it (a liquid or anything granular)

de^{22}tsi^{33}kwa^{2}yo^{33}ʔv^{2}sga^{2} ᏕᏥᏆᏲᎥᏍᎦ
du^{21}kwa^{2}yo^{33}nv^{23}ʔi^{2} ᏚᏆᏲᏅᎢ
da^{21}kwa^{2}yo^{33}ʔv^{2}sgo^{33}ʔi^{2} ᏓᏆᏲᎥᏍᎪᎢ
ti^{2}kwa^{2}yo^{22}ʔv^{11}ga^{2} ᏘᏆᏲᎥᎦ
tsu^{22}kwa^{2}yo^{11}di^{2} ᏧᏆᏲᏗ cf. di^{22}kwa^{2}yo^{33}di^{2} 'pepper' (lit. it is sprinkled)

putting shoes on

da^{21}la^{32}su^{22}hlv^{3}sga^{2} ᏓᎳᏍᏑᎵᏍᎦ one is putting one's shoes on

de^{33}ga^{2}la^{32}su^{22}hlv^{3}sga^{2} ᏕᎦᎳᏍᏑᎵᏍᎦ

du^{21}la^{32}su^{22}hlv^{3}nv^{33}ʔi^{2} ᏚᎳᏑᎵᏅᎢ

da^{21}la^{22}su^{23}hlv^{3}sgo^{33}ʔi^{2} ᏓᎳᏍᏑᎵᏍᎪᎢ

ta^{2}la^{11}su^{22}hlv^{11}ga^{2} ᏔᎳᏍᏑᎵᎦ

tsu^{22}la^{11}su^{23}hlv^{0}hdi^{2} ᏧᎳᏍᏑᎵᏗ

changing shoes

da^{21}la^{32}su^{22}la^{3}ʔi^{22}yv^{33}ʔa^{2} ᏓᎳᏍᏑᎳᎢᏴᎠ one is changing one's shoes

de^{33}ga^{2}la^{32}su^{22}la^{3}ʔi^{22}yv^{33}ʔa^{2} ᏕᎦᎳᏍᏑᎳᎢᏴᎠ

du^{21}la^{32}su^{22}la^{3}ʔi^{22}yv^{33}sv^{23}ʔi^{2} ᏚᎳᏍᏑᎳᎢᏴᏍᏒᎢ

da^{21}la^{32}su^{22}la^{3}ʔi^{22}yv^{33}sgo^{33}ʔi^{2} ᏓᎳᏍᏑᎳᎢᏴᏍᎪᎢ

ta^{2}la^{11}su^{22}la^{2}ʔi^{22}yv^{23}na^{2} ᏔᎳᏍᏑᎳᎢᏴᎾ

tsu^{22}la^{11}su^{22}la^{2}ʔi^{22}yv^{11}sdi^{2} ᏧᎳᏍᏑᎳᎢᏴᏍᏗ

taking shoes off

da^{21}la^{32}su^{22}le^{33}ʔa^{2} ᏓᎳᏍᏑᎴᎠ one is taking one's shoes off

de^{33}ga^{2}la^{32}su^{22}le^{33}ʔa^{2} ᏕᎦᎳᏍᏑᎴᎠ

du^{21}la^{32}su^{22}le^{33}sv^{23}ʔi^{2} ᏚᎳᏍᏑᎴᏍᏒᎢ

da^{21}la^{32}su^{22}le^{33}sgo^{33}ʔi^{2} ᏓᎳᏍᏑᎴᏍᎪᎢ

ta^{2}la^{11}su^{22}le^{2}gi^{2} ᏔᎳᏍᏑᎴᎩ

tsu^{22}la^{11}su^{23}le^{32}sdi ᏧᎳᏍᏑᎴᏍᏗ

standing it/another up

da^{21}le^{2}hdi^{23}ha^{2} ᏓᎴᏗᎭ one is helping another stand up

one is standing up

de^{22}tsi^{33}ya^{2}le^{2}hdi^{23}ha^{2} ᏕᏥᏯᎴᏗᎭ

du^{21}le^{2}hta^{2}nv^{23}ʔi^{2} ᏚᎴᏔᏅᎢ

da^{21}le^{2}hdi^{22}sgo^{33}ʔi^{2} ᏓᎴᏗᏍᎪᎢ

ti^{22}ya^{2}le^{2}hda^{2} (animate) ᏘᏯᎴᏓ

ta^{2}le^{2}hda^{2} (inanimate) ᏔᎴᏓ

tsu^{22}le^{2}hdo^{2}hdi^{2} ᏧᎴᏙᏗ

getting back up/recuperating

da^{21}le^{22}hi^{23}si^{3}ha^{2} ᏓᎴᎯᏍᏏᎭ one is getting back up again (literal)
one is recuperating (figurative)
'customarily again' conditional suffix

de^{33}ga^{2}le^{2}ʔi^{23}si^{3}ha^{2} ᏕᎦᎴᎢᏍᏏᎭ
du^{21}le^{22}hi^{23}sa^{3}hnv^{23}ʔi^{2} ᏚᎴᎯᏌᏅᎢ
da^{21}le^{22}hi^{23}si^{32}sgo^{33}ʔi^{2} ᏓᎴᎯᏍᏏᏍᎪᎢ
ta^{2}le^{22}hi^{23}sa^{2} ᏔᎴᎯᏍᏌ
tsu^{22}le^{22}hi^{23}so^{3}hdi^{2} ᏧᎴᎯᏍᏐᏗ

getting up/rising

da^{21}le^{22}hv^{3}sga^{2} ᏓᎴᎲᏍᎦ one is getting up or rising
de^{33}ga^{2}le^{2}ʔv^{3}sga^{2} ᏕᎦᎴᎥᏍᎦ
du^{21}le^{22}hnv^{23}ʔi^{2} ᏚᎴᏅᎢ
da^{21}le^{22}hv^{3}sgo^{33}i^{2} ᏓᎴᎲᏍᎪᎢ
ta^{2}le^{22}hv^{11}ga^{2} ᏔᎴᎲᎦ
tsu^{22}le^{2}hdi^{2} ᏧᎴᎲᏗ

taking gloves off

da^{21}li^{3}ye^{32}su^{22}le^{33}ʔa^{2} ᏓᎵᏰᏍᏑᎴᎠ one is taking off one's gloves
de^{33}ga^{2}li^{23}ye^{32}su^{22}le^{33}ʔa^{2} ᏕᎦᎵᏰᏍᏑᎴᎠ
da^{21}li^{3}ye^{32}su^{22}le^{33}sv^{23}ʔi^{2} ᏓᎵᏰᏍᏑᎴᏍᏒᎢ
da^{21}li^{2}ye^{32}su^{22}le^{33}sgo^{33}ʔi^{2} ᏓᎵᏰᏍᏑᎴᏍᎪᎢ
ta^{2}li^{2}ye^{11}su^{22}le^{2}gi^{2} ᏔᎵᏰᏍᏑᎴᎩ
tsu^{22}li^{2}ye^{11}su^{23}le^{32}sdi^{2} ᏧᎵᏰᏍᏑᎴᏍᏗ

putting gloves on

da^{21}li^{3}ye^{32}su^{22}li^{3}ʔa^{2} ᏓᎵᏰᏍᏑᎵᎠ one is putting one's gloves on
de^{33}ga^{2}li^{3}ye^{32}su^{22}li^{3}ʔa^{2} ᏕᎦᎵᏰᏍᏑᎵᎠ
du^{21}li^{3}ye^{32}su^{23}**la^{32}n**v^{23}ʔi^{2} ᏚᎵᏰᏍᏑᎳᏅᎢ **(populative suffix)**
da^{21}li^{3}ye^{32}su^{23}li^{32}sgo^{33}ʔi^{2} ᏓᎵᏰᏍᏑᎵᏍᎪᎢ
ta^{2}li^{2}ye^{11}su^{22}lv^{11}ga^{2} ᏔᎵᏰᏍᏑᎸᎦ

tsu^{22}li^{2}ye^{11}su^{23}lo^{32}di^{2} ᏧᎵᏰᏑᎶᏗ

taking socks off

da^{21}li^{23}yo^{32}gi^{33}ʔa^{2} ᏓᎵᏲᎩᎠ one is taking off one's socks

de^{22}ga^{33}li^{23}yo^{32}gi^{33}ʔa^{2} ᏕᎦᎵᏲᎩᎠ

du^{21}li^{23}yo^{32}gi^{33}sv^{23}ʔi^{2} ᏚᎵᏲᎩᏍᏒᎢ

da^{21}li^{23}yo^{32}gi^{33}sgo^{33}ʔi^{2} ᏓᎵᏲᎩᏍᎪᎢ

ta^{22}li^{23}yo^{32}gi^{2} ᏔᎵᏲᎩ

tsu^{22}li^{23}yo^{32}gi^{11}sdi^{2} ᏧᎵᏲᎩᏍᏗ

putting on socks

da^{21}li^{23}yo^{32}hi^{2}ha^{2} ᏓᎵᏲᎯᎭ one is putting on one's socks

de^{22}ga^{33}li^{23}yo^{32}ʔi^{2}ha^{2} ᏕᎦᎵᏲᎢᎭ

du^{21}li^{23}yo^{32}hlv^{23}ʔi^{2} ᏚᎵᏲᏢᎢ

da^{21}li^{23}yo^{32}hi^{2}ho^{33}ʔi^{2} ᏓᎵᏲᎯᎰᎢ

ta^{2}li^{22}yo^{11}ga^{2} ᏔᎵᏲᎦ

tsu^{22}li^{23}yo^{32}sdi^{2} ᏧᎵᏲᏍᏗ

changing socks

da^{21}li^{23}yo^{32}si^{23}ha^{2} ᏓᎵᏲᏍᏏᎭ one is changing one's socks

de^{22}ga^{33}li^{23}yo^{32}si^{23}ha^{2} ᏕᎦᎵᏲᏍᏏᎭ

du^{21}li^{23}yo^{32}sv^{22}hv^{23}ʔi^{2} ᏚᎵᏲᏍᏒᎲᎢ

da^{21}li^{23}yo^{32}si^{22}ho^{33}ʔi^{2} ᏓᎵᏲᏍᏏᎰᎢ

ta^{22}li^{22}yo^{23}sa^{2} ᏔᎵᏲᏍᏌ

tsu^{22}li^{23}yo^{32}sv^{2}hdi^{2} ᏧᎵᏲᏍᏒᏗ

aiming

da^{21}li^{0}so^{23}sdi^{3}ha^{2} ᏓᎵᏍᏐᏍᏗᎭ one is aiming at another or it

de^{22}tsi^{33}ya^{2}li^{11}so^{23}sdi^{3}ha^{2} (animate) ᏕᏥᏯᎵᏍᏐᏍᏗᎭ

de^{33}ga^{2}li^{11}so^{23}sdi^{3}ha^{2} (inanimate) ᏕᎦᎵᏍᏐᏍᏗᎭ

du^{21}li^{0}so^{23}sta^{3}nv^{23}ʔi^{2} ᏚᎵᏍᏐᏍᏔᏅᎢ

da^{21}li^{0}so^{23}sdi^{32}sgo^{33}ʔi^{2} ᏓᎵᏍᏐᏍᏗᏍᎪᎢ

ti^{22}ya^{2}li^{11}so^{23}sda^{2} (animate) ᏘᏯᎵᏍᏐᏍᏓ

ta^{2}li^{0}so^{23}sda^{2} (inanimate) ᏔᎵᏍᏐᏍᏓ

tsu^{22}li^{0}so^{23}sdo^{3}hdi^{2} ᏧᎵᏐᏍᏙᏗ

having trial

da^{21}na^{2}da^{22}hi^{3}ʔli^{23}do^{32}ha^{2} ᏓᎾᏓᎯᏟᏙᎭ they are having trial

do^{21}tsa^{2}da^{22}hi^{3}ʔli^{23}do^{32}ha^{2} ᏙᏣᏓᎯᏟᏙᎭ we are having a trial (not you)

du^{21}na^{2}da^{22}hi^{3}ʔli^{23}do^{32}lv^{23}ʔi^{2} ᏚᎾᏓᎯᏟᏙᎸᎢ

da^{21}na^{2}da^{22}hi^{3}ʔli^{23}do^{32}ho^{33}ʔi^{2} ᏓᎾᏓᎯᏟᏙᎰᎢ

di^{22}tsa^{2}da^{22}hi^{2}ʔli^{22}da^{2} ᏗᏣᏓᎯᏟᏓ

tsu^{22}na^{2}da^{22}hi^{2}ʔli^{23}da^{32}sdi^{2} ᏧᎾᏓᎯᏟᏓᏍᏗ

meeting

da^{21}na^{0}dlo^{22}sga^{2} ᏓᎾᏠᏍᎦ

they are meeting or they are meeting someone

do^{21}tsa^{2}dlo^{22}sga^{2} ᏙᏣᏠᏍᎦ we are meeting

du^{21}na^{2}dlo^{22}sv^{23}ʔi^{2} ᏚᎾᏠᏍᎡᎢ

da^{21}na^{2}dlo^{22}sgo^{33}ʔi^{2} ᏓᎾᏠᏍᎪᎢ

di^{22}tsa^{2}dlo^{23}hi^{2} ᏗᏣᏠᎯ

tsu^{22}na^{2}dlo^{22}hi^{2}sdi^{2} ᏧᎾᏠᎯᏍᏗ

separating

da^{21}na^{0}ga^{2}le^{23}ni^{3}ha^{2} ᏓᎾᎦᎴᏂᎭ they are separating

do^{21}sda^{2}ga^{2}le^{23}ni^{2}ha^{2} ᏙᏍᏓᎦᎴᏂᎭ we two are separating (not you)

du^{21}na^{0}ga^{2}le^{22}nv^{22}hv^{23}ʔi^{2} ᏚᎾᎦᎴᏅᎲᎢ

da^{21}na^{0}ga^{2}le^{22}ni^{23}sgo^{3}ʔi^{2} ᏓᎾᎦᎴᏂᏍᎪᎢ

di^{22}sda^{2}ga^{2}le^{22}na^{2} ᏗᏍᏓᎦᎴᎾ

tsu^{22}na^{0}ga^{2}le^{2}hnv^{0}hdi^{2} ᏧᎾᎦᎴᏅᏗ

playing with another

da^{33}ne^{22}hlo^{0}hdi^{23}ha^{2} ᏓᏁᎶᏗᎭ one is playing with another or it

de^{22}tsi^{33}ya^{22}ne^{22}hlo^{0}hdi^{23}ha^{2} (animate) ᏕᏥᏯᏁᎶᏗᎭ

de^{22}ga^{33}ne^{22}hlo^{0}hdi^{23}ha^{2} (inanimate) ᏕᎦᏁᎶᏗᎭ

du^{33}ne^{22}hlo^{0}hta^{2}nv^{23}ʔi^{2} ᏚᏁᎶᏔᏅᎢ

da^{33}ne^{22}hlo^{0}hdi^{22}sgo^{33}ʔi^{2} ᏓᏁᎶᏗᏍᎪᎢ

ti^{22}ya^{33}ne^{22}hlo^{0}hda^{2} (animate) ᏘᏯᏁᎶᏓ

ta^{33}ne^{22}hlo^{0}hda^{2} (inanimate) ᏔᏁᎶᏓ

tsu^{11}ne^{23}hlo^{0}hdo^{2}hdi^{2} ᏧᏁᎶᏙᏗ

playing

da^{33}ne^{22}lo^{23}hv^{3}sga^{2} ᏓᏁᎶᎲᏍᎦ one is playing

de^{22}ga^{33}ne^{22}lo^{23}hv^{3}sga^{2} ᏕᎦᏁᎶᎲᏍᎦ

du^{33}ne^{23}lo^{3}hnv^{23}ʔi^{2} ᏚᏁᎶᏅᎢ

da^{33}ne^{22}lo^{23}hv^{3}sgo^{33}ʔi^{2} ᏓᏁᎶᎲᏍᎪᎢ

ta^{33}ne^{22}lo^{22}hv^{11}ga^{2} ᏔᏁᎶᎲᎦ

tsu^{11}ne^{23}hlo^{0}hdi^{2} ᏧᏁᎶᏗ

adjourning

da^{21}ni^{22}ye^{22}li^{22}sga^{2} ᏓᏂᏰᎵᏍᎦ they are adjourning

do^{21}tsi^{22}ye^{22}li^{22}sga^{2} ᏙᏥᏰᎵᏍᎦ we are adjourning (not you)

du^{22}ni^{22}ye^{22}li^{22}sv^{23}ʔi^{2} ᏚᏂᏰᎵᏍᎡᎢ

da^{21}ni^{22}ye^{22}li^{22}so^{33}ʔi^{2} ᏓᏂᏰᎵᏍᏐᎢ

di^{22}tsi^{22}ye^{22}li^{22}hi^{2} ᏗᏥᏰᎵᎯ

tsu^{22}ni^{22}ye^{22}li^{23}hi^{3}sdi^{2} ᏧᏂᏰᎵᎯᏍᏗ

shooting

da^{21}sda^{2}yo^{22}hi^{3}ha^{2} ᏓᏍᏓᏲᎯᎭ one is shooting at him
one is shooting

de^{22}tsi^{33}sda^{2}yo^{22}hi^{3}ha^{2} ᏕᏥᏍᏓᏲᎯᎭ

du^{21}sda^{2}yo^{22}hlv^{23}ʔi^{2} ᏚᏍᏓᏲᎸᎢ

da^{21}sda^{2}yo^{22}hi^{2}ho^{33}ʔi^{2} ᏓᏍᏓᏲᎯᎰᎢ

ti^{22}sda^{2}yo^{23}ha^{2} (animate) ᏘᏍᏓᏲᎭ

ti^{2}sda^{2}yo^{23}ha^{2} (inanimate) ᏗᏍᏓᏲᎭ

tsu^{22}sda^{2}yo^{22}sdi^{2} ᏧᏍᏓᏲᏍᏗ

splitting

da^{21}sdlu^{32}y(a)sga^{2} ᏓᏍᏡᏯᏍᎦ one is splitting it

de^{22}tsi^{33}sdlu^{32}y(a)sga^{2} ᏕᏥᏍᏡᏯᏍᎦ

du^{21}sdlu^{32}hyv^{23}ʔi^{2} ᏚᏍᏡᏴᎢ

da^{21}sdlu^{32}y(a)sgo^{33}ʔi^{2} ᏓᏍᏡᏯᏍᎪᎢ

ti^{22}sdlu^{11}hya^{2} ᏗᏍᏡᏯ

tsu^{22}sdlu^{11}y(a)sdi^{2} ᏧᏍᏡᏯᏍᏗ

sprinkling (a liquid)

da^{21}sdu^{22}dli^{23}ʔa^{2} ᏓᏍᏚᏟᎠ one is sprinkling it (a liquid)

de^{22}tsi^{33}sdu^{22}dli^{23}ʔa^{2} ᏕᏥᏍᏚᏟᎠ

du^{21}sdu^{33}dlv^{23}ʔi^{2} ᏚᏍᏚᏢᎢ

da^{21}sdu^{22}dli^{22}sgo^{33}ʔi^{2} ᏓᏍᏚᏟᏍᎪᎢ

ti^{2}sdu^{22}dla^{2} ᏗᏍᏚᏜ

tsu^{22}sdu^{22}dli^{11}sdi^{2} ᏧᏍᏚᏟᏍᏗ

counting

da^{21}se^{2}hi^{3}ha^{2} ᏓᏍᏎᎯᎭ one is counting it or them

de^{22}ga^{33}se^{2}hi^{3}ha^{2} ᏕᎦᏍᏎᎯᎭ

du^{21}se^{2}hlv^{23}ʔi^{2} ᏚᏍᏎᏢᎢ

da^{21}se^{2}hi^{3}ho^{33}ʔi^{2} ᏓᏍᏎᎯᎰᎢ

ta^{2}se^{2}hga^{2} ᏔᏍᏎᎦ

tsu^{22}se^{2}sdi^{2} ᏧᏍᏎᏍᏗ

clapping

da^{21}si^{2}htv^{33}ni^{23}ha^{2} ᏓᏍᏏᏛᏂᎭ one is clapping one's hands

de^{22}ga^{33}si^{2}htv^{33}ni^{23}ha^{2} ᏕᎦᏍᏏᏛᏂᎭ

du^{21}si^{2}htv^{23}ni^{32}lv^{23}ʔi^{2} ᏚᏍᏏᏛᏂᎸᎢ

da^{21}si^{2}htv^{33}ni^{2}ho^{33}ʔi^{2} ᏓᏍᏏᏛᏂᎰᎢ

ta^{2}si^{2}htv^{22}ni^{11}ga^{2} ᏔᏍᏏᏛᏂᎦ

tsu^{22}si^{2}htv^{23}ni^{32}sdi^{2} ᏧᏍᏏᏛᏂᏍᏗ

getting exhausted

da^{33}sta^{2}ye^{22}sga^{2} ᏓᏍᏔᏰᏍᎦ one is getting exhausted

de^{22}ga^{33}sta^{2}ye^{22}sga^{2} ᏕᎦᏍᏔᏰᏍᎦ

du^{33}sta^{2}ye^{22}sv^{23}ʔi^{2} ᏚᏍᏔᏰᏍᎡᎢ

da^{33}sta^{2}ye^{22}sgo^{33}ʔi^{2} ᏓᏍᏔᏰᏍᎪᎢ

ta^{33}sta^{2}ye^{23}hi^{2} ᏔᏍᏔᏰᎯ

tsu^{11}sta^{2}ye^{23}hi^{3}sdi^{2} ᏧᏍᏔᏰᎯᏍᏗ

barking

da^{21}si^{2}hwi^{3}sga^{2} ᏓᏍᏏᏫᏍᎦ one is barking

de^{22}ga^{33}si^{2}hwi^{3}sga^{2} ᏕᎦᏍᏏᏫᏍᎦ

du^{21}si^{2}hwi^{2}sv^{23}ʔi^{2} ᏚᏍᏏᏫᏍᎡᎢ

da^{21}si^{2}hwi^{2}sgo^{33}ʔi^{2} ᏓᏍᏏᏫᏍᎪᎢ

ta^{2}si^{2}hwa^{2} ᏔᏍᏏᏩ

tsu^{22}si^{2}hwi^{2}sdi^{2} ᏧᏍᏏᏫᏍᏗ

scheduling

da^{21}sv^{22}sdi^{23}ha^{2} ᏓᏍᎡᏍᏗᎭ one is scheduling time

de^{22}tsi^{33}sv^{22}sdi^{23}ha^{2} ᏕᏥᏍᎡᏍᏗᎭ

du^{21}sv^{22}sta^{2}nv^{23}ʔi^{2} ᏚᏍᎡᏍᏔᏅᎢ

da^{21}sv^{22}sdi^{22}sgo^{33}ʔi^{2} ᏓᏍᎡᏍᏗᏍᎪᎢ

ti^{2}sv^{22}sda^{2} ᏘᏍᎡᏍᏓ

tsu^{22}sv^{22}sdo^{3}hdi^{2} ᏧᏍᎡᏍᏙᏗ

ironing

da^{21}te^{23}sga^{2} ᏓᏖᏍᎦ one is ironing

de^{22}tsi^{33}te^{23}sga^{2} ᏕᏥᏖᏍᎦ

du^{22}te^{23}sv^{33}ʔi^{2} ᏚᏖᏍᎡᎢ

da^{21}te^{22}sgo^{33}ʔi^{2} ᏓᏖᏍᎪᎢ

ti^{2}tv^{23}la^{2} ᏘᏛᎳ

tsu^{22}te^{23}sdi^{2} ᏧᏖᏍᏗ

releasing another

da^{21}yo^{3}sga^{2} ᏓᏲᏍᎦ one is releasing another

de^{22}tsi^{33}yo^{3}sga^{2} ᏕᏥᏲᏍᎦ

du^{21}yo^{3}sv^{23}ʔi^{2} ᏚᏲᏍᎡᎢ

da^{21}yo^{3}sgo^{33}ʔi^{2} ᏓᏲᏍᎪᎢ

ti^{22}yo^{2}hi^{2} ᏘᏲᎯ

tsu^{22}yo^{3}hi^{3}sdi^{2} ᏧᏲᎯᏍᏗ

slamming

de^{33}ga^{2}lv^{22}dv^{23}ni^{32}sdi^{23}ha^{2} ᏕᎦᎸᏛᏂᏍᏗᎭ one is slamming another or it

de^{22}tsi^{33}lv^{22}dv^{23}ni^{32}sdi^{23}ha^{2} ᏕᏥᎸᏛᏂᏍᏗᎭ

du^{21}lv^{22}dv^{23}ni^{32}sta^{2}nv^{23}ʔi^{2} ᏚᎸᏛᏂᏍᏔᏅᎢ

de^{33}ga^{2}lv^{22}dv^{23}ni^{32}sdi^{22}sgo^{33}ʔi^{2} ᏕᎦᎸᏛᏂᏍᏗᏍᎪᎢ

ti^{22}lv^{22}dv^{22}ni^{11}sda^{2} (animate) ᏘᎸᏛᏂᏍᏓ

ti^{2}lv^{22}dv^{22}ni^{11}sda^{2} (inanimate) ᏘᎸᏛᏂᏍᏓ

tsu^{22}lv^{22}dv^{23}ni^{32}sdo^{2}hdi^{2} ᏧᎸᏛᏂᏍᏙᏗ

crossing (a bridge or road)

de^{33}ga^{2}na^{0}di^{33}hwi^{0}sga^{2} ᏕᎦᎾᏗᏫᏍᎦ one is crossing it (bridge, road, etc.)

de^{33}tsi^{2}na^{2}di^{33}hwi^{0}sga^{2} ᏕᏥᎾᏗᏫᏍᎦ

du^{21}na^{2}di^{33}hwi^{0}sv^{23}ʔi^{2} ᏚᎾᏗᏫᏍᎡᎢ

de^{33}ga^{2}na^{0}di^{33}hwi^{0}sgo^{33}ʔi^{2} ᏕᎦᎾᏗᏫᏍᎪᎢ

tsu^{22}na^{2}di^{11}hwi^{0}sdi^{2} ᏧᎾᏗᏫᏍᏗ

advertising/announcing

de^{33}ga^{2}no^{22}tsa^{2}hlv^{3}sga^{2} ᏕᎦᏃᏣᎸᏍᎦ one is advertising or announcing it

de^{33}tsi^{2}no^{22}tsa^{2}ʔlv^{3}sga^{2} ᏕᏥᏃᏣᎸᏍᎦ

du^{21}no^{22}tsa^{2}hla^{3}nv^{33}ʔi^{2} ᏚᏃᏣᎳᏅᎢ

de^{33}ga^{2}no^{22}tsa^{2}hlv^{3}sgo^{33}ʔi^{2} ᏕᎦᏃᏣᎸᏍᎪᎢ

ti^{2}no^{22}tsa^{2}hlv^{11}ga^{2} ᏘᏃᏣᎸᎦ

tsu^{22}no^{22}tsa^{2}hlv^{0}hdi^{2} ᏧᏃᏣᎸᏗ

crossing it (water)

de^{33}ga^{22}so^{3}hga^{2} ᏕᎦᏍᏐᎦ one is crossing it (water)

de^{22}tsi^{33}so^{3}hga^{2} ᏕᏥᏍᏐᎦ

du^{21}wa^{22}so^{3}htsv^{23}ʔi^{2} ᏚᏩᏍᏐᏨᎢ

de^{22}ga^{33}so^{3}hgo^{33}ʔi ᏕᎦᏍᏐᎪᎢ

ti^{22}so^{2}hgi^{2} ᏗᏍᏐᎩ

tsu^{22}wa^{22}so^{3}hi^{3}sdi^{2} ᏧᏩᏍᏐᎯᏍᏘ

enduring

de^{22}ge^{33}tv^{2}sga^{2} ᏕᎨᏛᏍᎦ one is fence posting (literal)
one is enduring it (figurative)

de^{22}ge^{3}ʔdv^{2}sga^{2} ᏕᎨᏛᏍᎦ

du^{21}we^{22}ti^{2}nv^{23}ʔi^{2} ᏚᏪᏗᏅᎢ

de^{22}ge^{33}tv^{2}sgo^{33}ʔi^{2} ᏕᎨᏛᏍᎪᎢ

te^{22}tv^{11}ga^{2} ᏕᏛᎦ

tsu^{22}we^{22}dv^{0}hdi^{2} ᏧᏪᏛᏘ

explaining

da^{21}go^{33}**si^{23}si^{3}h**a^{2} ᏓᎪᏍᏏᏍᏏᎭ one is explaining it to another
'customarily again' conditional suffix

de^{22}tsi^{33}yo^{33}s**i^{23}si^{3}h**a^{2} ᏕᏥᏲᏍᏏᏍᏏᎭ

da^{21}go^{33}s**i^{23}sa^{3}hn**v^{23}ʔi^{2} ᏓᎪᏍᏏᏍᏌᏅᎢ

da^{21}go^{33}s**i^{23}si^{32}sg**o^{33}ʔi^{2} ᏓᎪᏍᏏᏍᏏᏍᎪᎢ

ti^{22}yo^{11}s**i^{23}sa^{2}** ᏗᏲᏍᏏᏍᏌ

tsu^{22}wo^{11}s**i^{23}so^{3}hdi^{2}** ᏧᏬᏍᏏᏍᏐᏘ

deciding

de^{22}gu^{33}go^{0}di^{23}ha^{2} ᏕᎫᎪᏘᎭ one is deciding

de^{22}gu^{33}go^{11}di^{23}ha^{2} ᏕᎫᎪᏘᎭ

du^{21}wu^{22}go^{0}ta^{2}nv^{23}ʔi^{2} ᏚᏭᎪᏔᏅᎢ

de^{22}gu^{33}go^{0}di^{22}sgo^{33}ʔi^{2} ᏕᎫᎪᏘᏍᎪᎢ

di^{22}hu^{23}go^{0}da^{2} or tu^{23}go^{0}da^{2} ᏘᎱᎪᏓ or ᏚᎪᏓ tsu^{22}wu^{22}go^{0}do^{3}hdi^{2} ᏧᏭᎪᏙᏗ

washing dishes

de^{33}gv^{0}di^{23}ye^{3}ʔa^{2} ᏕᎬᏗᏰᎠ one is washing the dishes

de^{22}gv^{33}di^{23}ye^{3}ʔa^{2} ᏕᎬᏗᏰᎠ

du^{21}wa^{22}di^{23}ye^{3}ʔv^{23}ʔi^{2} ᏚᏩᏗᏰᎥᎢ

de^{22}gv^{33}di^{23}ye^{32}sgo^{33}ʔi^{2} ᏕᎬᏗᏰᏍᎪᎢ

tv^{22}di^{23}ya^{2} ᏛᏗᏯ

tsu^{22}wa^{22}di^{23}ye^{32}di^{2} ᏧᏩᏗᏰᏗ

shelling/hulling

de^{33}gv^{0}to^{2}hi^{33}ʔa^{2} ᏕᎬᏙᎯᎠ one is shelling it or picking it out (i.e. pea pods)

de^{22}gv^{33}to^{2}hi^{33}ʔa^{2} ᏕᎬᏙᎯᎠ

du^{21}wv^{22}to^{2}hi^{33}sv^{23}ʔi^{2} ᏚᏮᏙᎯᏍᏒᎢ

de^{22}gv^{33}to^{2}hi^{33}sgo^{33}ʔi^{2} ᏕᎬᏙᎯᏍᎪᎢ

tv^{22}to^{2}hi^{2} ᏛᏙᎯ

tsu^{22}wv^{22}to^{2}hi^{11}sdi^{2} ᏧᏮᏙᎯᏍᏗ

turning over

de^{33}ka^{2}li^{2}hgwa^{2}d**e**^{33}**g**a^{2} ᏕᎧᎵᏆᏕᎦ one is turning over another or it **('going' conditional suffix)**

de^{22}tsi^{33}li^{2}hgwa^{2}d**e**^{33}**g**a^{2} ᏕᏥᎵᏆᏕᎦ

du^{21}hli^{2}hgwa^{2}di^{23}n**v**^{32}**s**v^{23}ʔi^{2} ᏚᏟᏆᏗᏅᏍᏒᎢ

de^{33}ka^{2}li^{2}hgwa^{2}d**e**^{33}**g**o^{33}ʔi^{2} ᏕᎧᎵᏆᏕᎪᎢ

ti^{22}hli^{2}hgwa^{2}d**u**^{11}**ga**^{2} (animate) ᏘᏟᏆᏚᎦ

ti^{2}hli^{2}hgwa^{2}d**u**^{11}**ga**^{2} (inanimate) ᏘᏟᏆᏚᎦ

tsu^{22}hli^{2}hgwa^{2}di^{23}n**v**^{32}**di**^{2} ᏧᏟᏆᏗᏅᏗ

singing

de^{33}ka^{2}no^{22}gi^{33}ʔa^{2} ᏕᎧᏃᎩᎠ one is singing

de^{22}tsi^{33}no^{22}gi^{33}ʔa^{2} ᏕᏥᏃᎩᎠ

du^{21}hno^{22}gi^{33}sv^{23}ʔi^{2} ᏚᏃᎩᏍᏒᎢ

de^{33}ka^{2}no^{22}gi^{33}sgo^{33}ʔi^{2} ᏕᎧᏃᎩᏍᎪᎢ

ti^{2}hno^{22}gi^{2} ᏘᏃᎩ

tsu^{22}hno^{22}gi^{11}sdi^{2} ᏧᏃᎩᏍᏗ

clawing

de^{33}ka^{2}nu^{22}go^{23}sga^{2} ᏕᎧᏄᎪᏍᎦ one is clawing another

de^{22}tsi^{33}nu^{22}go^{23}sga^{2} ᏕᏥᏄᎪᏍᎦ

du^{21}hnu^{22}go^{23}sv^{33}ʔi^{2} ᏚᏄᎪᏒᎢ

de^{33}ka^{2}nu^{22}go^{23}sgo^{33}ʔi^{2} ᏕᎧᏄᎪᏍᎪᎢ

ti^{22}nu^{22}go^{23}la^{2} ᏘᏄᎪᎳ

tsu^{22}hnu^{22}go^{23}sdi^{2} ᏧᏄᎪᏍᏗ

washing (flexible items)

de^{33}gv^{0}gi^{22}lo^{33}ʔa^{2} ᏕᎬᎩᎶᎠ one is washing them (flexible objects)

de^{22}gv^{33}gi^{22}lo^{33}ʔa^{2} ᏕᎬᎩᎶᎠ

du^{21}gi^{22}lo^{33}ʔv^{23}ʔi^{2} ᏚᎩᎶᎥᎢ

de^{33}gv^{0}gi^{22}lo^{33}sgo^{33}ʔi^{2} ᏕᎬᎩᎶᏍᎪᎢ

tv^{2}hgi^{22}lo^{23}tsa^{2} ᏛᎩᎶᏣ

tsu^{22}hgi^{22}lo^{11}sdi^{2} ᏧᎩᎶᏍᏗ

confronting

du^{21}dlo^{22}sga^{2} ᏚᏠᏍᎦ one is confronting it

da^{21}gwa^{2}dlo^{22}sga^{2} ᏓᏆᏠᏍᎦ

du^{21}dlo^{22}sv^{23}ʔi^{2} ᏚᏠᏒᎢ

du^{21}dlo^{22}sgo^{33}ʔi^{2} ᏚᏠᏍᎪᎢ

di^{22}tsa^{2}dlo^{22}hi^{2} ᏗᏣᏠᎯ

tsu^{22}dlo^{22}hi^{2}sdi^{2} ᏧᏠᎯᏍᏗ

called/named

du^{21}do^{33}ʔa^{2} ᏚᏙᎠ one is called or named

da^{21}gwa^{2}do^{33}ʔa^{2} ᏓᏆᏙᎠ

du^{21}do^{33}ʔv^{23}ʔi^{2} ᏚᏙᎥᎢ

du^{21}do^{33}ʔo^{33}ʔi^{2} ᏚᏙᎣᎢ

de^{33}tsa^{2}do^{33}ʔe^{33}sdi^{2} ᏕᏣᏙᎡᏍᏗ

tsu^{22}do^{11}sdi^{2} ᏧᏙᏍᏗ

staggering

du^{21}do^{32}ga^{0}di^{23}ha^{2} ᏚᏙᎦᏗᎭ one is staggering

da^{21}gwa^{2}do^{32}ga^{0}di^{23}ha^{2} ᏓᏆᏙᎦᏗᎭ

du^{21}do^{32}ga^{0}ta^{2}nv^{23}ʔi^{2} ᏚᏙᎦᏔᏅᎢ

du^{21}do^{32}ga^{0}di^{22}sgo^{33}ʔi^{2} ᏚᏙᎦᏗᏍᎪᎢ

di^{22}tsa^{2}do^{11}ga^{0}da^{2} ᏗᏣᏙᎦᏓ

tsu^{22}do^{11}ga^{0}do^{3}hdi^{2} ᏧᏙᎦᏙᏗ

getting a rash

du^{21}gwe^{22}no^{33}ti^{2}sga^{2} ᏚᏇᏃᏘᏍᎦ one is getting a rash

da^{21}gi^{2}gwe^{22}no^{33}ti^{2}sga^{2} ᏓᎩᏇᏃᏘᏍᎦ

du^{21}gwe^{22}no^{33}ti^{2}sv^{23}ʔi^{2} ᏚᏇᏃᏘᏒᎢ

du^{21}gwe^{22}no^{33}ti^{2}sgo^{33}ʔi^{2} ᏚᏇᏃᏘᏍᎪᎢ

di^{22}tsa^{2}gwe^{22}no^{11}ti^{2}hi^{2} ᏗᏣᏇᏃᏘᎯ

tsu^{22}gwe^{22}no^{11}ti^{2}sdi^{2} ᏧᏇᏃᏘᏍᏗ

has horns

du^{21}hlu^{0}hga^{2} ᏚᏡᎦ one has horns

da^{21}gi^{22}hlu^{0}hga^{2} ᏓᎩᏡᎦ

du^{21}hlu^{0}hgv^{23}ʔi^{2} ᏚᏡᎬᎢ

du^{21}hlu^{0}hgo^{33}ʔi^{2} ᏚᏡᎪᎢ

tsu^{22}hlu^{0}hgo^{11}di^{2} ᏧᏡᎪᏗ

sneezing

da^{21}hyv^{23}sdo^{32}ya^{0}sga^{2} ᏚᏴᏍᏙᏯᏍᎦ one is sneezing

da^{21}ki^{2}yv^{23}sdo^{32}ya^{0}sga^{2} ᏓᎩᏴᏍᏙᏯᏍᎦ

du^{21}hyv^{23}sdo^{32}hyv^{23}ʔi^{2} ᏚᏴᏍᏙᏴᎢ

du^{21}hyv^{23}sdo^{32}ya^{0}sgo^{33}ʔi^{2} ᏚᏴᏍᏙᏯᏍᎪᎢ

di^{22}cha^{2}yv^{22}sdo^{11}hya^{2} ᏗᏣᏴᏍᏙᏯ

tsu^{22}hyv^{23}sdo^{32}ya^{0}sdi^{2} ᏧᏴᏍᏙᏯᏍᏗ

vomiting

du^{21}ga^{0}sdi^{23}ha^{2} ᏚᎦᏍᏗᎭ one is vomiting

da^{21}gi^{2}ga^{0}sdi^{23}ha^{2} ᏓᎩᎦᏍᏗᎭ

du^{21}ga^{0}sta^{2}nv^{23}ʔi^{2} ᏚᎦᏍᏔᏅᎢ

du^{21}ga^{0}sdi^{22}sgo^{33}ʔi^{2} ᏚᎦᏍᏗᏍᎪᎢ

di^{22}tsa^{2}ga^{0}sda^{2} ᏗᏣᎦᏍᏓ

tsu^{22}ga^{0}sdo^{3}hdi^{2} ᏧᎦᏍᏙᏗ

wearing glasses

du^{21}ga^{0}ti^{2}nv^{22}ta^{2} ᏚᎦᏘᏅᏔ one is wearing glasses

da^{21}gwa^{2}ga^{0}ti^{2}nv^{22}ta^{2} ᏓᏆᎦᏘᏅᏔ

du^{21}ga^{0}ti^{2}nv^{22}tv^{23}ʔi^{2} ᏚᎦᏘᏅᏛᎢ

du^{21}ga^{0}ti^{2}nv^{22}to^{33}ʔi^{2} ᏚᎦᏘᏅᏙᎢ

de^{33}tsa^{2}ga^{0}ti^{2}nv^{22}tv^{11}ga^{2} ᏕᏣᎦᏘᏅᏛᎦ

tsu^{22}ga^{0}ti^{2}nv^{22}tv^{0}hdi^{2}ᏧᎦᏘᏅᏛᏗ

wearing shoes

du^{21}la^{32}su^{22}hla^{2} ᏚᎳᏍᏑᏝ one is wearing shoes

da^{21}gwa^{2}la^{32}su^{22}hla^{2} ᏓᏆᎳᏍᏑᎳ

du^{21}la^{32}su^{22}hlv^{23}ʔi^{2} ᏚᎳᏍᏑᎸᎢ

du^{21}la^{32}su^{22}hlo^{33}ʔi^{2} ᏚᎳᏍᏑᎶᎢ

de^{33}tsa^{2}la^{32}su^{22}hlo^{0}hgi^{2} ᏕᏣᎳᏍᏑᎶᎩ

tsu^{22}la^{11}su^{22}hlo^{0}hdi^{23}ʔi^{2} ᏧᎳᏍᏑᎶᏗᎢ

wearing gloves

du^{21}li^{2}ye^{32}su^{22}la^{2} ᏚᎵᏰᏍᏑᎳ one is wearing gloves

da^{21}gwa^{2}li^{2}ye^{32}su^{22}la^{2} ᏓᏆᎵᏰᏍᏑᎳ

du^{21}li^{2}ye^{32}su^{22}lv^{23}ʔi ᏚᎵᏰᏍᏑᎸᎢ

du^{21}li^{2}ye^{32}su^{22}lo^{33}ʔi^{2} ᏚᎵᏰᏍᏑᎶᎢ

ta^{2}li^{2}ye^{11}su^{22}lv^{11}ga^{2} ᏔᎵᏰᏍᏑᎸᎦ

tsu^{22}li^{2}ye^{11}su^{23}lo^{32}di^{3} ᏧᎵᏰᏍᏑᎶᏗ

wearing socks

du^{21}li^{23}yo^{3}ha^{2}	ᏚᎵᏲᎭ	one is wearing socks
da^{21}gwa^{22}li^{23}yo^{3}ha^{2}	ᏓᏆᎵᏲᎭ	
du^{21}li^{23}yo^{32}hv^{23}ʔi^{2}	ᏚᎵᏲᎲᎢ	
du^{21}li^{23}yo^{32}ho^{33}ʔi^{2}	ᏚᎵᏲᎰᎢ	
di^{2}tsa^{33}li^{23}yo^{32}hv^{23}li^{0}	ᏗᏣᎵᏲᎲᎵ	
de^{22}tsa^{33}li^{23}yo^{32}di^{23}ʔi^{2}	ᏕᏣᎵᏲᏗᎢ	

working

du^{21}lv^{23}hwi^{0}sda^{11}ne^{23}ha^{2}	ᏚᎸᏫᏍᏓᏁᎭ	one is working
da^{21}gi^{2}lv^{23}hwi^{0}sda^{11}ne^{23}ha^{2}	ᏓᎩᎸᏫᏍᏓᏁᎭ	
du^{21}lv^{23}hwi^{0}sda^{11}ne^{22}lv^{23}ʔi^{2}	ᏚᎸᏫᏍᏓᏁᎸᎢ	
du^{21}lv^{23}hwi^{0}sda^{11}ne^{22}ho^{33}ʔi^{2}	ᏚᎸᏫᏍᏓᏁᎸᎢ	
di^{22}tsa^{2}lv^{22}hwi^{0}sda^{11}si^{2}	ᏗᏣᎸᏫᏍᏓᏏ	
tsu^{22}lv^{23}hwi^{0}sda^{11}ne^{2}hdi^{2}	ᏧᎸᏫᏍᏓᏁᏗ	

making footsteps

du^{33}sda^{2}no^{22}hyv^{2}hga^{2}	ᏚᏍᏓᏃᏴᎦ	one is making footsteps
da^{21}gwa^{33}sda^{2}no^{22}hyv^{2}h^{2}ga^{2}	ᏓᏆᏍᏓᏃᏴᎦ	
du^{33}sda^{2}no^{22}hyv^{2}hgv^{23}ʔi^{2}	ᏚᏍᏓᏃᏴᎬᎢ	
du^{33}sda^{2}no^{22}hyv^{2}hgo^{33}ʔi^{2}	ᏚᏍᏓᏃᏴᎪᎢ	
di^{2}tsa^{33}sda^{2}no^{22}hyv^{23}la^{2}	ᏗᏣᏍᏓᏃᏴᎳ	
tsu^{22}sda^{2}no^{22}hyv^{22}hli^{2}sdi^{2}	ᏧᏍᏓᏃᏴᎵᏍᏗ	

releasing it (accidentally)

du^{33}sga^{2}le^{33}sdi^{23}ha^{2}	ᏚᏍᎦᎴᏍᏗᎭ	one is releasing it (accidentally)
da^{21}gwa^{33}sga^{2}le^{33}sdi^{23}ha^{2}	ᏓᏆᏍᎦᎴᏍᏗᎭ	
du^{33}sga^{2}le^{33}sta^{2}nv^{23}ʔi^{2}	ᏚᏍᎦᎴᏍᏔᏅᎢ	
du^{33}sga^{2}le^{33}sdi^{22}sgo^{33}ʔi^{2}	ᏚᏍᎦᎴᏍᏗᏍᎪᎢ	
di^{2}tsa^{11}sga^{2}le^{11}sda^{2}	ᏗᏣᏍᎦᎴᏍᏓ	
tsu^{11}sga^{2}le^{11}sdo^{3}hdi^{2}	ᏧᏍᎦᎴᏍᏙᏗ	

tired

du^{21}ya^{2}we^{33}ga^{2} ᏚᏯᏪᎦ one is tired

This is an example of a compound verb. See its individual morphemes below.

d(e^{33}),	verbal pluralizer
u^{21},	third person, Set B pronoun
ya^{2},	inside
w,	Set B morpheme connector
e^{33}g,	'going' incompletive conditional suffix
a	present tense suffix

da^{21}gi^{22}ya^{2}we^{33}ga^{2} ᏓᎩᏯᏪᎦ
du^{21}ya^{2}we^{33}tsv^{23}ʔi^{2} ᏚᏯᏪᏨᎢ
du^{21}ya^{2}we^{33}go^{33}ʔi^{2} ᏚᏯᏪᎪᎢ
di^{2}tsa^{2}ya^{2}we^{11}gi^{2} ᏗᏣᏯᏪᎩ
tsu^{22}ya^{2}we^{11}sdi^{2} ᏧᏯᏪᏍᏗ

releasing (on purpose)

du^{21}**yo**^{3}sga^{2} ᏚᏲᏍᎦ one is releasing it (on purpose)

This is another form of /h/ & /ʔ/ alternation, where the right-most long vowel retains the higher tone to signal third person and the lower tone denotes first person.

da^{21}gi^{3}**yo^{2}**sga^{2} ᏓᎩᏲᏍᎦ
du^{21}yo^{3}sv^{23}ʔi^{2} ᏚᏲᏍᎡᎢ
du^{21}yo^{3}sgo^{33}ʔi^{2} ᏚᏲᏍᎪᎢ
di^{2}tsa^{2}yo^{2}hi^{2} ᏗᏣᏲᎯ
tsu^{22}yo^{3}hi^{3}sdi^{2} ᏧᏲᎯᏍᏗ

going about/at a location

e^{21}**do**^{33}ha^{2} ᎡᏙᎭ one is walking about or on is at a location

In this example of tone alternation, the third person form receives the full long (^{33}) tone and the first person form spreads the (^{33}) tone by allowing one of the (^{3})'s to spread leftward onto the previous syllable. This is what creates the rising (^{23}) and falling (^{32}) sequence.

ge^{23}**do**^{32}ha^{2} ᎨᏙᎭ
u^{21}we^{23}do^{32}lv^{23}ʔi^{2} ᎤᏪᏙᎸᎢ
e^{23}do^{32}ho^{33}ʔi^{2} ᎡᏙᎰᎢ
or e^{21}do^{33}ho^{33}ʔi^{2}
he^{23}da^{2} ᎮᏓ
u^{22}we^{22}da^{11}sdi^{2} ᎤᏪᏓᏍᏗ

going

e^{33}ga^{2} ᎡᎦ one is going

This is a stand alone verb that can be conjugated, and it is also used as a conditional suffix meaning, 'going'. The use of this as a conditional suffix allows you to add the idea of 'going' while the subject is performing the action.

ge^{33}ga^{2} ᎨᎦ
u^{21}we^{33}nv^{23}ʔi^{2} ᎤᏪᏅᎢ

The completive form of this verb according to the CED, I believe is a typo because I have heard several speakers in my lifetime say this verb without the conditional suffix. Rather than keeping the verb consistent–the completive conditional suffix of 'going' was added to the completive stem of going which isn't necessary for his verb.

e^{33}go^{33}ʔi^{2} ᎡᎪᎢ
he^{11}na^{2} ᎮᎾ
u^{22}we^{11}nv^{11}sdi^{2} ᎤᏪᏅᏍᏗ

exists/living

e^{23}ha^{2} ᎡᎭ one exists or one is living

ge^{33}ʔa^{2} ᎡᎠ

u^{22}we^{33}hnv^{23}ʔ^{2} ᎤᏪᏅᎢ

This is a minimal pair. Compare this verb with the completive past verb 'one went' above. The only difference between them is the root suffix.

u^{21}we^{33}**n**v^{23}ʔi^{2} 'one went' n: the action is complete

u^{21}we^{33}**hn**v^{23}ʔi^{2} 'one existed' hn: the action had movement

The /n/ root suffix doesn't not give focal information regarding the subject of the verb. It merely states that the action is completed. The /hn/ root suffix does give focal information about the subject; firstly, that the subject had movement, and secondly, the action is complete.

e^{21}ho^{33}ʔi or e^{23}ho^{3}ʔi^{2} ᎡᎰᎢ

he^{23}hi^{2} ᎮᎯ Exist! or Be living!

u^{22}we^{11}hi^{0}sdi^{23}ʔi^{2} ᎤᏪᎯᏍᏗᎢ

thinks so

e^{23}li^{3}ʔa^{2} ᎡᎵᎠ one thinks it so

ge^{23}li^{3}ʔa^{2} ᎨᎵᎠ

u^{21}we^{23}li^{32}sv^{23}ʔi^{2} ᎤᏪᎵᏍᎡᎢ

e^{23}li^{32}sgo^{33}ʔi ᎡᎵᏍᎪᎢ

he^{23}la^{2} ᎮᎳ

u^{22}we^{22}li^{11}sdi^{2} ᎤᏪᎵᏍᏗ

straightening

ga^{21}chi^{2}n**o^{23}si^{3}h**a^{2} ᎦᏥᏃᏍᏏᎭ one is straightening it

'customarily again' conditional suffix

tsi^{21}chi^{2}n**o^{23}si^{3}h**a^{2} ᏥᏥᏃᏍᏏᎭ

u^{21}wa^{22}chi^{2}n**o^{23}sa^{3}hn**v^{23}ʔi^{2} ᎤᏩᏥᏃᏍᏌᏅᎢ

ga^{22}chi^{2}n**o^{23}si^{32}sg**o^{33}ʔi^{2} ᎦᏥᏃᏍᏏᏍᎪᎢ

hi^{22}chi^{2}n**o^{23}sa^{2}** ᎯᏥᏃᏍᏌ

u^{22}wa^{22}chi^{2}n**o^{23}so^{3}hdi^{2}** ᎤᏩᏥᏃᏍᏐᏗ

hanging (a flexible object)

ga^{2}da^{3}ʔa^{2} ᎦᏓᎠ it or one is hanging (a flexible object)

tsi^{23}da^{3}ʔa^{2} ᏥᏓᎠ I am hanging

Living and flexible objects are sometimes viewed as the same characteristically.

ga^{2}da^{3}ʔo^{33}ʔi^{2} ᎦᏓᎣᎢ

ha^{2}dv^{32}gi^{2} ᎭᏛᎩ Be hanging!

u^{22}da^{3}ʔi^{3}sdi^{23}ʔi^{2} ᎤᏓᎢᏍᏗᎢ for one or it to be hanging

plowing

ga^{22}da^{2}lu^{22}gi^{33}ʔa^{2} ᎦᏓᎷᎩᎠ one is plowing it

tsi^{22}da^{2}lu^{22}gi^{33}ʔa^{2} ᏥᏓᎷᎩᎠ

u^{21}wa^{22}da^{2}lu^{23}g**a^{32}n**v^{23}ʔi^{2} ᎤᏩᏓᎷᎦᏅᎢ (^{3}a^{32}n, the populative infix)

ga^{22}da^{2}lu^{23}gi^{32}sgo^{33}ʔi^{2} ᎦᏓᎷᎩᏍᎪᎢ

hi^{22}da^{2}lu^{22}gv^{11}ga^{2} ᎯᏓᎷᎬᎦ

u^{22}wa^{22}da^{2}lu^{23}go^{32}di^{2} ᎤᏩᏓᎷᎪᏗ

unhanging (a flexible object)

ga^{0}d**e**^{33}ʔa^{2} ᎦᏕᎠ one is unhanging it (a flexible object)

'reversive infix'

ga^{21}d**e**^{33}ʔa^{2} ᎦᏕᎠ
u^{21}d**e**^{33}**s**v^{23}ʔi^{2} ᎤᏕᏍᏒᎢ
ga^{21}d**e**^{33}**sg**o^{33}ʔi^{2} ᎦᏕᏍᎪᎢ
ha^{2}de^{2}**gi**^{2} ᎭᏕᎩ
u^{22}d**e**^{11}**sdi**^{2} ᎤᏕᏍᏗ

turning

ga^{22}de^{23}y**a(**^{32}**)**sdi^{23}ha^{2} ᎦᏕᏯᏍᏗᎭ one is turning it

tsi^{22}de^{23}y**a**^{32}sdi^{23}ha^{2} ᏥᏕᏯᏍᏗᎭ

Here is another form of alternation, where the third person form deletes its final stem vowel, while the first person form retains the stem final vowel.

u^{21}wa^{22}de^{23}y(a^{32})sta^{2}nv^{23}ʔi^{2} ᎤᏩᏕᏯᏍᏔᏅᎢ
ga^{22}de^{23}y(a^{32})sdi^{22}sgo^{33}ʔi^{2} ᎦᏕᏯᏍᏗᏍᎪᎢ
hi^{22}de^{23}y(a)sda^{2} ᎯᏕᏯᏍᏓ
u^{22}wa^{22}de^{23}y(a)sdo^{2}hdi^{2} ᎤᏩᏕᏯᏍᏙᏗ

spinning

ga^{22}di^{33}gwa^{2}lv^{22}de^{23}ya(^{32})sdi^{23}ha^{2} ᎦᏗᏆᎸᏕᏯᏍᏗᎭ one is spinning it

tsi^{22}di^{33}gwa^{2}lv^{22}de^{23}ya^{32}sdi^{23}ha^{2} ᏥᏗᏆᎸᏕᏯᏍᏗᎭ
u^{21}wa^{22}di^{33}gwa^{2}lv^{22}de^{23}ya^{0}sta^{2}nv^{23}ʔi^{2} ᎤᏩᏗᏆᎸᏕᏯᏍᏔᏅᎢ
ga^{22}di^{33}gwa^{2}lv^{22}de^{23}ya^{0}sdi^{22}sgo^{33}ʔi^{2} ᎦᏗᏆᎸᏕᏯᏍᏗᏍᎪᎢ
hi^{22}di^{11}gwa^{2}lv^{22}de^{23}ya^{0}sda^{2} ᎯᏗᏆᎸᏕᏯᏍᏓ
u^{22}wa^{22}di^{11}gwa^{2}lv^{22}de^{23}ya^{0}sdo^{2}hdi^{2} ᎤᏩᏗᏆᎸᏕᏯᏍᏙᏗ

strapping/belting it down

ga^{33}dlo^{22}hi^{3}ha^{2} ᎦᏢᎯᎭ one is strapping it or belting it down

'with a purpose' conditional suffix

tsi^{33}dlo^{22}hi^{3}ha^{2} ᏥᏢᎯᎭ

u^{21}wa^{33}dlo^{22}hlv^{23}ʔi^{2} ᎤᏩᏢᏈᎢ

ga^{33}dlo^{22}hi^{2}ho^{33}ʔi^{2} ᎦᏢᎯᎰᎢ

hi^{11}dlo^{23}ga^{2} ᎯᏢᎦ

u^{22}wa^{11}dlo^{23}sdi^{2} ᎤᏩᏢᏍᏗ

pitying

ga^{22}do^{23}li^{32}ga^{2} ᎦᏙᎵᎦ one is pitying another

tsi^{22}ya^{22}do^{23}li^{32}ga^{2} ᏥᏯᏙᎵᎦ

u^{21}wa^{22}do^{23}li^{32}tsv^{23}ʔi^{2} ᎤᏩᏙᎵᏨᎢ

ga^{22}do^{23}li^{32}go^{33}ʔi^{2} ᎦᏙᎵᎪᎢ

hi^{22}ya^{22}do^{22}li^{11}gi^{2} ᎯᏯᏙᎵᎩ

u^{22}wa^{22}do^{22}li^{3}sdi^{2} ᎤᏩᏙᎵᏍᏗ

dropping (flexible)

ga^{2}do^{3}hnv^{0}hdi^{3}ha^{2} ᎦᏙᏅᏗᎭ one is dropping another or it (flexible)

tsi^{22}ya^{2}do^{3}hnv^{0}hdi^{3}ha^{2} (animate) ᏥᏯᏙᏅᏗᎭ

ga^{2}do^{3}hnv^{0}hdi^{3}ha^{2} (inanimate) ᎦᏙᏅᏗᎭ

u^{21}do^{3}hnv^{0}hta^{3}nv^{23}ʔi^{2} ᎤᏙᏅᏔᏅᎢ

ga^{2}do^{3}hnv^{0}hdi^{32}sgo^{33}ʔi^{2} ᎦᏙᏅᏗᏍᎪᎢ

hi^{22}ya^{2}do^{1}hnv^{0}hda^{2} (animate) ᎯᏯᏙᏅᏓ

ha^{2}do^{1}hnv^{0}hda^{2} (inanimate) ᎭᏙᏅᏓ

u^{22}do^{1}hnv^{0}hdo^{3}hdi^{2} ᎤᏙᏅᏙᏗ

falling from hanging (flexible)

ga^{0}do^{3}sga^{2} ᎦᏙᏍᎦ it is falling from a hanging position (flexible)

- ga^{2}do^{3}sga^{2} ᎦᏙᏍᎦ
- u^{21}do^{3}sv^{23}ʔi^{2} ᎤᏙᏍᏛᎢ
- ga^{2}do^{3}sgo^{33}ʔi^{2} ᎦᏙᏍᎪᎢ
- ha^{2}do^{11}hi^{2} ᎭᏙᎯ
- u^{22}do^{11}hi^{3}sdi^{2} ᎤᏙᎯᏍᏗ

baking

ga^{33}du^{22}hv^{3}sga^{2} ᎦᏚᏴᏍᎦ one is baking it

- tsi^{33}du^{22}hv^{3}sga^{2} ᏥᏚᏴᏍᎦ
- u^{21}wa^{33}du^{22}hnv^{23}ʔi^{2} ᎤᏩᏚᏅᎢ
- ga^{33}du^{22}hv^{3}sgo^{33}ʔi^{2} ᎦᏚᏴᏍᎪᎢ
- hi^{11}du^{22}hv^{11}ga^{2} ᎯᏚᏴᎦ
- u^{22}wa^{11}du^{0}hdi^{2} ᎤᏩᏚᏴᏗ

hanging up (a flexible object)

ga^{0}dv^{33}ʔv^{2}sga^{2} ᎦᏛᎢᏍᎦ one is hanging up another or it (a flexible object)

- tsi^{22}ya^{2}dv^{33}ʔv^{2}sga^{2} (animate) ᏥᏯᏛᎢᏍᎦ
- ga^{2}dv^{33}ʔv^{2}sga^{2} (inanimate) ᎦᏛᎢᏍᎦ
- u^{21}dv^{33}nv^{23}ʔi^{2} ᎤᏛᏅᎢ
- ga^{0}dv^{33}ʔv^{2}sgo^{33}ʔi^{2} ᎦᏛᎢᏍᎪᎢ
- ha^{2}dv^{2}ʔv^{11}ga^{2} ᎭᏛᎢᎦ
- u^{22}dv^{11}di^{2} ᎤᏛᏗ

rowing/paddling

ga^{22}ga^{2}we^{33}sga^{2} ᎦᎦᏪᏍᎦ one is rowing or paddling

- tsi^{22}ga^{2}we^{33}sga^{2} ᏥᎦᏪᏍᎦ
- u^{21}wa^{22}ga^{2}we^{33}sv^{23}ʔi^{2} ᎤᏩᎦᏪᏍᏛᎢ
- ga^{22}ga^{2}we^{33}sgo^{33}ʔi^{2} ᎦᎦᏪᏍᎪᎢ
- hi^{22}ga^{2}we^{11}hi^{2} ᎯᎦᏪᎯ

u^{22}wa^{22}ga^{2}we^{11}sdi^{2} ᎤᏩᎦᏪᏍᏗ

pecking

ga^{22}gwa^{2}yo^{23}hi^{3}ha^{2} ᎦᏆᏲᎯᎭ one is pecking another or it

tsi^{22}ya^{22}gwa^{2}yo^{2}ʔi^{3}ha^{2} (animate) ᏥᏯᏆᏲᎢᎭ

tsi^{22}gwa^{2}yo^{2}ʔi^{3}ha^{2} (inanimate) ᏥᏆᏲᎢᎭ

u^{21}wa^{22}gwa^{2}yo^{22}hlv^{23}ʔi^{2} ᎤᏩᏆᏲᏢᎢ

ga^{22}gwa^{2}yo^{22}hi^{2}ho^{33}ʔi^{2} ᎦᏆᏲᎯᎰᎢ

hi^{22}ya^{22}gwa^{2}yo^{23}ha^{2} (animate) ᎯᏯᏆᏲᎭ

hi^{22}gwa^{2}yo^{23}ha^{2} (inanimate) ᎯᏆᏲᎭ

putting it into a container

ga^{2}hlo^{0}hdi^{23}ha^{2} ᎦᏰᏗᎭ one is putting it into a container

tsi^{2}lo^{11}di^{2}ha^{2} ᏥᏰᏗᎭ

u^{22}hlo^{0}hta^{2}nv^{23}ʔi^{2} ᎤᏰᏔᏅᎢ

ga^{2}hlo^{0}hdi^{22}sgo^{33}ʔi^{2} ᎦᏰᏗᏍᎪᎢ

hi^{22}hlo^{0}hda^{2} ᎯᏰᏓ

u^{22}hlo^{0}hdo^{2}hdi^{2} ᎤᏰᏙᏗ

sleeping

ga^{2}hli^{3}ha^{2} ᎦᏟᎭ one is sleeping

tsi^{2}ʔli^{3}ha^{2} ᏥᎵᎭ

u^{21}hlv^{22}nv^{23}ʔi^{2} ᎤᏢᏅᎢ

ga^{2}hli^{2}ho^{33}ʔi^{2} ᎦᏟᎰᎢ

hi^{2}hlv^{23}na^{2} ᎯᏢᎾ

u^{22}hlv^{22}nv^{0}hdi^{2} ᎤᏢᏅᏗ

gathering

ga^{33}hl**i^{23}si^{3}h**a^{2} ᎦᏟᏍᏏᎭ one is gathering it

'customary' conditional suffix

tsi^{33}hl**i^{23}si^{3}h**a^{2} ᏥᏟᏍᏏᎭ

u^{21}wa^{33}hl**i^{23}sa^{3}hn**v^{2}ʔi^{2} ᎤᏩᏟᏍᏌᏅᎢ

ga^{33}hli^{23}s**i^{32}sg**o^{33}ʔi^{2} ᎦᏟᏍᏏᏍᎪᎢ

hi^{11}hl**i^{23}sa^{2}** ᎯᏟᏍᏌ

u^{22}wa^{11}hl**i^{23}so^{3}hdi^{2}** ᎤᏩᏟᏍᏐᏗ

piling

ga^{33}hlu^{2}sga^{2} ᎦᏡᏍᎦ one is piling it up

tsi^{33}hlu^{2}sga^{2} ᏥᏡᏍᎦ

u^{21}wa^{33}hlu^{2}nv^{23}ʔi^{2} ᎤᏩᏡᏅᎢ

ga^{33}hlu^{2}sgo^{33}ʔi^{2} ᎦᏡᏍᎪᎢ

hi^{11}hlu^{11}ga^{2} ᎯᎷᎦ

u^{22}wa^{11}hlu^{3}sdi^{2} ᎤᏩᏡᏍᏗ

tying up

ga^{2}hlv^{33}ʔi^{2}ha^{2} ᎦᏢᎢᎭ one is tying up another or it

tsi^{22}ya^{2}ʔlv^{33}ʔi^{2}ha^{2} (animate) ᏥᏯᎸᎢᎭ

ga^{2}ʔlv^{33}ʔi^{2}ha^{2} (inanimate) ᎦᎸᎢᎭ

u^{21}hlv^{33}lv^{23}ʔi^{2} ᎤᏢᎸᎢ

ga^{2}hlv^{33}ʔi^{2}ho^{33}ʔi^{2} ᎦᏢᎢᎰᎢ

hi^{2}ya^{2}hlv^{23}tsa^{2} ᎯᏯᏢᏣ

u^{22}hlv^{11}sdi^{2} ᎤᏢᏍᏗ

putting it in a hole or container

ga^{2}hlv^{3}sga^{2} ᎦᏢᏍᎦ one is putting in a hole or container

tsi^{2}ʔlv^{3}sga^{2} ᏥᎸᏍᎦ

u^{22}hla^{3}nv^{33}ʔi^{2} ᎤᏝᏅᎢ

ga^{2}hlv^{3}sgo^{3}ʔi^{2} ᎦᏢᏍᎪᎢ

hi^{2}hlv^{11}ga^{2} ᎯᏢᎦ

u^{22}hli^{0}hdi^{2} ᎤᏢᏗ

sleepy

ga^{2}hlv^{22}sga^{2} ᎦᏢᏍᎦ one is sleepy

tsi^{2}ʔlv^{22}sga^{2} ᏥᎸᏍᎦ

u^{21}hlv^{22}hnv^{23}ʔi^{2} ᎤᏢᏅᎢ

ga^{2}hlv^{22}sgo^{33}ʔi^{2} ᎦᏢᏍᎪᎢ

hi^{2}hlv^{23}na^{2} ᎯᏢᎾ

u^{22}hlv^{22}nv^{0}hdi^{2} ᎤᏢᏅᏗ

taking it somewhere by hand (a flexible object)

ga^{2}hn**e^{33}g**a^{2} ᎦᏁᎦ one is taking it somewhere by hand (a flexible object)

'going' conditional suffix

- tsi^{2}ʔn**e^{33}ga**^{2} ᏥᏁᎦ
- u^{21}hn**v^{33}s**v^{23}ʔi^{2} ᎤᏅᏒᎢ
- ga^{2}hn**e^{33}go**^{33}ʔi^{2} ᎦᏁᎪᎢ
- hi^{2}hn**u^{11}ga^{2}** ᎯᏄᎦ
- u^{22}hn**v^{11}sdi^{2}** ᎤᏅᏍᏗ

holding in one's hand (a flexible object)

ga^{2}hne^{33}ha^{2} ᎦᏁᎭ one is holding it or one has it in hand (a flexible object)

- tsi^{2}ʔne^{33}ha^{2} ᏥᏁᎭ
- u^{21}hne^{33}hv^{23}ʔi^{2} ᎤᏁᎲᎢ
- ga^{2}hne^{33}ho^{33}ʔi^{2} ᎦᏁᎰᎢ
- hi^{2}hnv^{11}ga^{2} ᎯᏅᎦ
- u^{22}hni^{23}da^{32}sdi^{23}ʔi^{2} ᎤᏂᏓᏍᏗᎢ

carrying around by hand (a flexible object)

ga^{2}hni^{23}do^{32}ha^{2} ᎦᏂᏙᎭ one is carrying it around by hand (a flexible object)

- tsi^{2}ʔni^{23}do^{32}ha^{2} ᏥᏂᏙᎭ
- u^{21}hni^{23}do^{32}lv^{23}ʔi^{2} ᎤᏂᏙᎸᎢ
- ga^{2}hni^{23}do^{32}ho^{33}ʔi^{2} ᎦᏂᏙᎰᎢ
- hi^{2}hni^{23}da^{2} ᎯᏂᏓ
- u^{22}hni^{23}da^{32}sdi^{2} ᎤᏂᏓᏍᏗ

eating (a flexible object)

ga^{22}hye^{33}ʔa^{2} ᎦᏰᎠ one is eating it (a flexible object)

tsi^{22}ya^{11}ye^{33}ʔa^{2} (animate) ᏥᏯᏰᎠ

tsi^{22}ye^{33}ʔa^{2} (inanimate) ᏥᏰᎠ

u^{21}wa^{22}hye^{33}ʔv^{23}ʔi^{2} ᎤᏩᏰᎥᎢ

ga^{22}hye^{33}sgo^{33}ʔi^{2} ᎦᏰᏍᎪᎢ

hi^{22}ya^{11}hye^{2}ga^{2} (animate) ᎯᏯᏰᎦ

hi^{22}hye^{2}ga^{2} (inanimate) ᎯᏰᎦ

u^{22}wa^{22}hye^{11}sdi^{2} ᎤᏩᏰᏍᏗ

ripping

ga^{22}tsa^{2}ga^{2}li^{23}ha^{2} ᎦᏣᎦᎵᎭ one is ripping it

tsi^{22}tsa^{2}ga^{2}li^{23}ʔa^{2} ᏥᏣᎦᎵᎠ

u^{21}wa^{22}tsa^{2}ga^{2}lv^{22}hv^{23}ʔi^{2} ᎤᏩᏣᎦᎸᎲᎢ

ga^{22}tsa^{2}ga^{2}li^{22}sgo^{33}ʔi^{2} ᎦᏣᎦᎵᏍᎪᎢ

hi^{22}tsa^{2}ga^{2}la^{2} ᎯᏣᎦᎳ

u^{22}wa^{22}tsa^{2}ga^{2}hlv^{0}hdi^{2} ᎤᏩᏣᎦᎸᏗ

scratching another

ga^{22}tsa^{2}li^{0}go^{33}sga^{2} ᎦᏣᎵᎪᏍᎦ one is scratching another or it

tsi^{22}ya^{22}tsa^{2}li^{0}go^{33}sga^{2} (animate) ᏥᏯᏣᎵᎪᏍᎦ

tsi^{22}tsa^{2}li^{0}go^{33}sga^{2} (inanimate) ᏥᏣᎵᎪᏍᎦ

u^{21}wa^{22}tsa^{2}li^{0}go^{33}sv^{23}ʔi^{2} ᎤᏩᏣᎵᎪᏒᎢ

ga^{22}tsa^{2}li^{0}go^{33}sgo^{33}ʔi^{2} ᎦᏣᎵᎪᏍᎪᎢ

hi^{22}ya^{22}tsa^{2}li^{0}go^{23}la^{2} (animate) ᎯᏯᏣᎵᎪᎳ

hi^{22}tsa^{2}li^{0}go^{23}la^{2} (inanimate) ᎯᏣᎵᎪᎳ

u^{22}wa^{22}tsa^{2}li^{0}go^{11}sdi^{2} ᎤᏩᏣᎵᎪᏍᏗ

pricking/injecting

ga^{22}tsa^{2}y**o**^{23}**hi**^{3}**h**a^{2}	ᎦᏣᏲᎯᎭ	one is pricking or injecting another or it
		'for a purpose' conditional suffix
tsi^{22}ya^{22}tsa^{2}y**o**^{2}**ʔi**^{3}**h**a^{2} (animate)	ᏥᏯᏣᏲᎢᎭ	
tsi^{22}tsa^{2}y**o**^{2}**ʔi**^{3}**h**a^{2} (inanimate)	ᏥᏣᏲᎢᎭ	
u^{21}wa^{22}tsa^{2}y**o**^{23}**hl**v^{3}ʔi^{2}	ᎤᏩᏣᏲᏢᎢ	
ga^{22}tsa^{2}y**o**^{23}**hi**^{3}**h**o^{33}ʔi^{2}	ᎦᏣᏲᎯᎰᎢ	
hi^{22}ya^{22}tsa^{2}y**o**^{23}**h**a^{2} (animate)	ᎯᏯᏣᏲᎭ	
hi^{22}tsa^{2}y**o**^{23}**h**a^{2} (inanimate)	ᎯᏣᏲᎭ	
u^{22}wa^{22}tsa^{2}y**o**^{22}**sdi**^{2}	ᎤᏩᏣᏲᏍᏗ	

wringing out

ga^{33}tsv^{23}wa^{32}sdi^{23}ha^{2}	ᎦᏨᏩᏍᏗᎭ	one is wringing it out
tsi^{33}tsv^{23}wa^{32}sdi^{23}ha^{2}	ᏥᏨᏩᏍᏗᎭ	
u^{21}wa^{33}tsv^{23}wa^{32}sta^{2}nv^{23}ʔi	ᎤᏩᏨᏩᏍᏔᏅᎢ	
ga^{33}tsv^{23}wa^{32}sdi^{22}sgo^{33}ʔi^{2}	ᎦᏨᏩᏍᏗᏍᎪᎢ	
hi^{11}tsv^{22}wa^{11}sda^{2}	ᎯᏨᏩᏍᏓ	
u^{22}wa^{11}tsv^{23}wa^{32}sdo^{2}hdi^{2}	ᎤᏩᏨᏩᏍᏙᏗ	

stinging

ga^{22}tsv^{23}y(a^{32})sga^{2}	ᎦᏨᏯᏍᎦ	one is stinging another
tsi^{22}ya^{22}tsv^{23}y(a^{32})sga^{2}	ᏥᏯᏨᏯᏍᎦ	
u^{21}wa^{22}tsv^{33}hyv^{23}ʔi^{2}	ᎤᏩᏨᏴᎢ	
ga^{22}tsv^{23}y(a^{32})sgo^{33}ʔi	ᎦᏨᏯᏍᎪᎢ	
hi^{22}ya^{22}tsv^{11}hya^{2}	ᎯᏯᏨᏯ	
u^{22}wa^{22}tsv^{11}ya^{0}sdi^{2}	ᎤᏩᏨᏯᏍᏗ	

leaving behind (a living being)

ga^{22}ka^{2}hi^{23}ya^{3}ʔa^{2} ᎦᎧᎯᏯᎠ one is leaving another behind (living being)

tsi^{22}ya^{11}ka^{2}hi^{23}ya^{3}ʔa^{2} ᏥᏯᎧᎯᏯᎠ

u^{21}wa^{22}ka^{2}hi^{33}yv^{23}ʔi^{2} ᎤᏩᎧᎯᏴᎢ

ga^{22}ka^{2}hi^{23}ya^{32}sgo^{33}ʔi^{2} ᎦᎧᎯᏯᏍᎪᎢ

hi^{22}ya^{11}ka^{2}hi^{23}ya^{2} ᎯᏯᎧᎯᏯ

u^{22}wa^{22}ka^{2}hi^{23}ya^{32}sdi^{2} ᎤᏩᎧᎯᏯᏍᏗ

giving it to another (a living being)

ga^{22}ka^{32}ne^{23}ha^{2} ᎦᎧᏁᎭ one is giving it to another (a living being)

tsi^{22}ya^{11}ka^{32}ne^{23}ha^{2} ᏥᏯᎧᏁᎭ

u^{21}wa^{22}ka^{32}ne^{22}lv^{23}ʔi^{2} ᎤᏩᎧᏁᎸᎢ

ga^{22}ka^{32}ne^{22}ho^{33}ʔi^{2} ᎦᎧᏁᎰᎢ

hi^{22}ya^{11}ka^{11}si^{2} ᎯᏯᎧᏏ

u^{22}wa^{22}ka^{11}ne^{3}hdi^{2} ᎤᏩᎧᏁᏗ

wrapping

ga^{22}gwe^{22}nv^{22}sga^{2} ᎦᏇᏅᏍᎦ one is wrapping another or it

tsi^{22}ya^{11}gwe^{22}nv^{22}sga^{2} (animate) ᏥᏯᏇᏅᏍᎦ

tsi^{22}gwe^{22}nv^{22}sga^{2} (inanimate) ᏥᏇᏅᏍᎦ

u^{21}wa^{22}gwe^{22}nv^{22}hnv^{23}ʔi^{2} ᎤᏩᏇᏅᏅᎢ

ga^{22}gwe^{22}nv^{22}sgo^{33}ʔi^{2} ᎦᏇᏅᏍᎪᎢ

hi^{22}ya^{11}gwe^{22}nv^{23}na^{2} (animate) ᎯᏯᏇᏅᎾ

hi^{22}gwe^{22}nv^{23}na^{2} (inanimate) ᎯᏇᏅᎾ

u^{22}wa^{22}gwe^{22}nv^{0}hdi^{2} ᎤᏩᏇᏅᏗ

putting it into a container (a long object)

ga^{2}la^{3}di^{3}ʔa^{2} ᎦᎳᏗᎠ one is putting it in a container (a long object)

tsi^{2}la^{3}di^{3}ʔa^{2} ᏥᎳᏗᎠ

u^{23}la^{3}dv^{23}ʔi^{2} ᎤᎳᏛᎢ

ga^{2}la^{3}di^{32}sgo^{33}ʔi ᎦᎳᏗᏍᎪᎢ

hi^{2}la^{2}da^{2} ᎯᎳᏓ

u^{22}la^{2}di^{11}sdi^{2} ᎤᎳᏗᏍᏗ

taking it out of a container (a flexible object)

ga^{2}l**e**^{33}ʔa^{2} ᎦᎴᎠ one is taking it out of a container (a flexible object)

'reversive' infix

tsi^{2}l**e**^{33}ʔa^{2} ᏥᎴᎠ

u^{21}l**e**^{33}sv^{23}ʔi^{2} ᎤᎴᏍᏒᎢ

ga^{2}l**e**^{33}sgo^{33}ʔi^{2} ᎦᎴᏍᎪᎢ

hi^{2}l**e**^{2}gi^{2} ᎯᎴᎩ

u^{22}l**e**^{11}sdi^{2} ᎤᎴᏍᏗ

climbing

ga^{3}ʔle^{32}ga^{2} ᎦᎴᎦ one is climbing it

tsi^{3}ʔle^{32}ga^{2} ᏥᎴᎦ

u^{21}ʔlv^{32}sv^{23}ʔi^{2} ᎤᎸᏍᏒᎢ

ga^{3}ʔle^{32}go^{33}ʔi^{2} ᎦᎴᎪᎢ

hi^{2}ʔlu^{11}ga^{2} ᎯᎷᎦ (**minimal pair**, cf. 'Kill it!', hi^{22}lu^{11}ga^{2})

u^{22}lv^{11}sdi^{2} ᎤᎸᏍᏗ

burning

ga^{2}le^{33}yv^{22}sga^{2} ᎦᎴᏴᏍᎦ one is burning

tsi^{2}le^{33}yv^{22}sga^{2} ᏥᎴᏴᏍᎦ

u^{21}le^{33}yv^{22}sv^{23}ʔi^{2} ᎤᎴᏴᏍᏒᎢ

ga^{2}le^{33}yv^{22}sgo^{33}ʔi^{2} ᎦᎴᏴᏍᎪᎢ

hi^{2}le^{11}yv^{23}hi^{2} ᎯᎴᏴᎯ

u^{22}le^{11}yv^{23}hi^{3}sdi^{2} ᎤᎴᏴᎯᏍᏗ

I'm burning up with sweat.

ᏙᏳ ᎠᏢ ᏥᎴᏴᏍᎦ

do^{23}yu^{3} a^{22}li^{2} tsi^{2}le^{33}yv^{22}sga^{0}

falling from upright (a long object)

ga^{2}le^{22}yv^{23}sga^{2} ᎦᎴᏴᏍᎦ it is falling from an upright position (a long object)

All of these forms are identical to the verb 'burning'. Each are distinguished by tone alone.

tsi^{2}le^{22}yv^{33}sga^{2} ᏥᎴᏴᏍᎦ
u^{22}le^{22}yv^{33}sv^{23}ʔi^{2} ᎤᎴᏴᏍᏒᎢ
ga^{2}le^{22}yv^{33}sgo^{33}ʔi^{2} ᎦᎴᏴᏍᎪᎢ
hi^{2}le^{22}yv^{23}hi^{2} ᎯᎴᏴᎯ
u^{22}le^{22}yv^{23}hi^{3}sdi^{2} ᎤᎴᏴᎯᏍᏗ

climbing around

ga^{3}ʔl**i^{23}do^{32}h**a ᎦᎵᏙᎭ one is climbing around

'going about (different places each time) conditional suffix'

tsi^{3}ʔl**i^{23}do^{32}h**a^{2} ᏥᎵᏙᎭ
ga^{3}ʔl**i^{23}do^{32}h**o^{33}ʔi^{2} ᎦᎵᏙᎰᎢ
hi^{2}ʔl**i^{23}da^{2}** ᎯᎵᏓ
u^{22}l**i^{23}da^{32}sdi^{2}** ᎤᎵᏓᏍᏗ

taking it out of a container (a long object)

ga^{2}li^{33}ha^{2} ᎦᎵᎭ one is taking it out of a container (a long object)

tsi^{2}li^{33}ʔa^{2} ᏥᎵᎠ
u^{21}lv^{33}hv^{23}ʔi^{2} ᎤᎸᎲᎢ
ga^{2}li^{33}sgo^{33}ʔi^{2} ᎦᎵᏍᎪᎢ
hi^{2}la^{2} ᎯᎳ
u^{22}hlv^{0}hdi^{2} ᎤᏢᏗ

dying (an animal or plant)

ga^{2}l**i**^{22}hwo^{33}ga^{2} ᎦᎵᏉᎦ one is dying (an animal or plant)
tsi^{2}l**i**^{11}hwo^{33}ga^{2} ᏥᎵᏉᎦ (as if I am a plant or animal)
u^{22}li^{22}hwo^{33}tsv^{23}ʔi^{2} ᎤᎵᏉᏨᎢ
ga^{2}li^{22}hwo^{33}go^{33}ʔi^{2} ᎦᎵᏉᎪᎢ
hi^{2}li^{22}hwo^{11}gi^{2} ᎯᎵᏉᎩ
u^{22}li^{22}hwo^{11}sdi^{2} ᎤᎵᏉᏍᏗ

spanking

ga^{2}lv^{32}hni^{23}ha^{2} ᎦᎸᏂᎭ one is spanking another
tsi^{22}lv^{32}hni^{23}ha^{2} ᏥᎸᏂᎭ
u^{21}lv^{32}hni^{2}lv^{23}ʔi^{2} ᎤᎸᏂᎸᎢ
ga^{2}lv^{32}hni^{2}ho^{33}ʔi^{2} ᎦᎸᏂᎰᎢ
hi^{22}lv^{11}hni^{0}ga^{2} ᎯᎸᏂᎦ
u^{22}lv^{11}hni^{0}sdi^{2} ᎤᎸᏂᏍᏗ

hoeing

ga^{2}lo^{22}gi^{33}ʔa^{2} ᎦᎶᎩᎠ one is hoeing it
tsi^{2}lo^{22}gi^{33}ʔa^{2} ᏥᎶᎩᎠ
u^{21}lo^{23}**ga**^{32}**n**v^{23}ʔi^{2} ᎤᎶᎦᏅᎢ (^{3}a^{32}n, the populative infix)
ga^{2}lo^{22}gi^{33}sgo^{33}ʔi^{2} ᎦᎶᎩᏍᎪᎢ
hi^{2}lo^{22}gv^{11}ga^{2} ᎯᎶᎬᎦ
u^{22}lo^{23}go^{32}di^{2} ᎤᎶᎪᏗ

stopping (on the way)

ga^{2}lo^{22}hi^{2}sdi^{23}ha^{2} ᎦᎶᎯᏍᏗᎭ one is stopping (on one's way somewhere)
tsi^{2}lo^{2}ʔi^{2}sdi^{23}ha^{2} ᏥᎶᎢᏍᏗᎭ
u^{21}lo^{22}hi^{2}ta^{2}nv^{23}ʔi ᎤᎶᎯᏍᏔᏅᎢ
ga^{2}lo^{22}hi^{2}sdi^{22}sgo^{33}ʔi^{2} ᎦᎶᎯᏍᏗᏍᎪᎢ
hi^{2}lo^{22}hi^{2}sda^{2} ᎯᎶᎯᏍᏓ
u^{22}lo^{22}hi^{2}sdo^{3}hdi^{2} ᎤᎶᎯᏍᏙᏗ

overtaking

ga^{2}l**o^{22}h**i^{2}s**e^{23}h**a^{2} ᎦᎶᎯᏍᏎᎭ one is overtaking another or it

'for another or benefactive' conditional suffix

tsi^{22}l**o^{2}ʔ**i^{2}s**e^{23}h**a^{2} ᏥᎶᎢᏍᏎᎭ

u^{21}lo^{22}hi^{2}s**e^{22}lv**^{23}ʔi^{2} ᎤᎶᎯᏍᏎᎸᎢ

ga^{2}lo^{22}hi^{2}s**e^{22}h**o^{33}ʔi^{2} ᎦᎶᎯᏍᏎᎰᎢ

hi^{22}lo^{2}ʔ**i^{2}si^{2}** ᎯᎶᎢᏍᏏ

u^{22}lo^{22}hi^{2}s**e^{2}hdi^{2}** ᎤᎶᎯᏍᏎᏗ

bluffing/tricking/deceiving

ga^{2}lo^{23}na^{32}sdi^{23}ha^{2} ᎦᎶᎾᏍᏗᎭ one is bluffing, tricking, or deceiving another

tsi^{22}lo^{23}na^{32}sdi^{23}ha^{2} ᏥᎶᎾᏍᏗᎭ

u^{21}lo^{23}na^{32}sta^{2}nv^{23}ʔi^{2} ᎤᎶᎾᏍᏔᏅᎢ

ga^{2}lo^{23}na^{32}sdi^{22}sgo^{33}ʔi^{2} ᎦᎶᎾᏍᏗᏍᎪᎢ

hi^{22}lo^{22}na^{11}sda^{2} ᎯᎶᎾᏍᏓ

u^{22}lo^{22}na^{11}sdo^{3}hdi^{2} ᎤᎶᎾᏍᏙᏗ

oiling

ga^{2}lo^{33}ne^{23}ʔa^{2} or ga^{2}lo^{23}ne^{3}ʔa^{2} ᎦᎶᏁᎠ one is oiling it

tsi^{2}lo^{33}ne^{23}ʔ^{2} or tsi^{2}lo^{23}ne^{3}ʔa^{2} ᏥᎶᏁᎠ

u^{21}lo^{23}ne^{3}ʔv^{23}ʔi^{2} ᎤᎶᏁᎥᎢ

ga^{2}lo^{33}ne^{22}sgo^{33}ʔi^{2} or ga^{2}lo^{23}ne^{32}sgo^{33}ʔi^{2} ᎦᎶᏁᏍᎪᎢ

hi^{2}lo^{23}na^{2} ᎯᎶᎾ

u^{22}lo^{23}ne^{32}di^{2} ᎤᎶᏁᏗ

making one fall from above

ga^{2}lo^{32}nv^{0}hdi^{23}ha^{2} ᎦᎶᏅᏗᎭ

one is making another fall from an elevated position

tsi^{22}lo^{32}nv^{0}hdi^{23}ha^{2} ᏥᎶᏅᏗᎭ

u^{21}lo^{32}nv^{0}hta^{2}nv^{23}ʔi^{2} ᎤᎶᏅᏔᏅᎢ

ga^{2}lo^{32}nv^{0}hdi^{22}sgo^{33}ʔi^{2} ᎦᎶᏅᏗᏍᎪᎢ

hi^{22}lo^{11}nv^{0}hda^{2} ᎯᎶᏅᏓ

u^{22}lo^{11}nv^{0}hdo^{3}hdi^{2} ᎤᎶᏅᏙᏗ

cheating

ga^{2}lo^{22}nu^{22}**he**^{23}ha^{2} ᎦᎶᏄᎮᎭ one is cheating

tsi^{2}lo^{22}nu^{2}**ʔe**^{23}ha^{2} ᏥᎶᏄᎡᎭ

u^{21}lo^{22}nu^{22}he^{22}hlv^{23}ʔi^{2} ᎤᎶᏄᎮᏢᎢ

ga^{2}lo^{22}nu^{22}he^{22}sgo^{33}ʔi^{2} ᎦᎶᏄᎮᏍᎪᎢ

hi^{2}lo^{22}nu^{22}hv^{23}la^{2} ᎯᎶᏄᎲᎳ

u^{22}lo^{22}nu^{22}he^{2}hdi^{2} ᎤᎶᏄᎮᏗ

passing by (without stopping)

ga^{2}l**o**^{22}sga^{2} ᎦᎶᏍᎦ one is passing by (without stopping, going right by)
one is passing a test (figurative)

tsi^{2}l**o**^{11}sga^{2} ᏥᎶᏍᎦ

u^{21}lo^{22}sv^{23}ʔi^{2} ᎤᎶᏍᏒᎢ

ga^{2}lo^{22}sgo^{33}ʔi^{2} ᎦᎶᏍᎪᎢ

hi^{2}lo^{23}hi^{2} ᎯᎶᎯ

u^{22}lo^{22}hi^{2}sdi^{2} ᎤᎶᎯᏍᏗ

falling from above

ga^{2}lo^{32}sga^{2} ᎦᎶᏍᎦ one is falling from an elevated position

tsi^{2}lo^{32}sga^{2} ᏥᎶᏍᎦ

u^{21}lo^{32}sv^{23}ʔi ᎤᎶᏍᏒᎢ

ga^{2}lo^{32}sgo^{33}ʔi^{2} ᎦᎶᏍᎪᎢ

hi^{2}lo^{11}hi^{2} ᎯᎶᎯ

u^{22}lo^{11}hi^{2}sdi^{2} ᎤᎶᎯᏍᏗ

arriving

ga^{3}ʔlu^{2}hga^{2} ᎦᎷᎦ one is arriving

tsi^{3}ʔlu^{2}hga^{2} ᏥᎷᎦ

u^{21}lu^{3}htsv^{23}ʔi^{2} ᎤᎷᏨᎢ

ga^{3}ʔlu^{2}hgo^{33}ʔi^{2} ᎦᎷᎪᎢ

hi²ʔlu²hgi² ᎯᎷᎩ
u²²lu³hi³sdi² ᎤᎷᎯᏍᏗ

lacking/missing

ga²lu²³lo³²ga² ᎦᎷᎶᎦ one is lacking it or one is missing it

tsi²lu²³lo³²ga² ᏥᎷᎶᎦ
u²¹lu²³lo³²tsv²³ʔi ᎤᎷᎶᏨᎢ
ga²lu²³lo³²go³³ʔi² ᎦᎷᎶᎪᎢ
hi²lu²²lo¹¹gi² ᎯᎷᎶᎩ
u²²lu²³lo³²sdi² ᎤᎷᎶᏍᏗ

chopping it

ga²lu³²ya⁰sga² ᎦᎷᏯᏍᎦ one is chopping it

tsi²lu³²ya⁰sga² ᏥᎷᏯᏍᎦ
u²¹lu³²hyv²³ʔi² ᎤᎷᏴᎢ
ga²lu³²ya⁰sgo³³ʔi² ᎦᎷᏯᏍᎪᎢ
hi²lu¹¹hya² ᎯᎷᏯ
u²²lu²²ya⁰sdi² ᎤᎷᏯᏍᏗ

beating up another

ga²lv³³hni²³ha² ᎦᎸᏂᎭ one is beating up another

tsi²²lv³³hni²³ha² ᏥᎸᏂᎭ
u²¹lv³³hni²lv²³ʔi² ᎤᎸᏂᎸᎢ
ga²lv³³hni²ho³³ʔi² ᎦᎸᏂᎰᎢ
hi²²lv¹¹hni⁰ga² ᎯᎸᏂᎦ
u²²lv¹¹hni⁰sdi² ᎤᎸᏂᏍᏗ

putting it in a hole or container (a flexible object)

ga²lv³³sga² ᎦᎸᏍᎦ one is putting it in a hole or container (a flexible object)

tsi²lv³³sga² ᏥᎸᏍᎦ
u²²lv³³nv²³ʔi² ᎤᎸᏅᎢ
ga²lv³³sgo³³ʔi² ᎦᎸᏍᎪᎢ
hi²lv²ʔv¹¹ga² ᎯᎸᎥᎦ
u²²lv¹¹di² ᎤᎸᏗ

selling

ga^{2}na^{2}d**e**^{33}**g**a^{2} ᎦᎾᏕᎦ one is selling it

'going' conditional suffix

tsi^{2}na^{2}d**e**^{33}**g**a^{2} ᏥᎾᏕᎦ

u^{21}na^{2}di^{23}n**v**^{32}**s**v^{23}ʔi^{2} ᎤᎾᏗᏅᏍᏒᎢ

ga^{2}na^{2}d**e**^{33}**g**o^{33}ʔi^{2} ᎦᎾᏕᎪᎢ

hi^{22}na^{2}d**u**^{11}**ga**^{2} ᎯᎾᏚᎦ

u^{22}na^{2}di^{23}n**v**^{32}**di**^{2} ᎤᎾᏗᏅᏗ

hiring

ga^{2}na^{32}hlv^{2}sga^{2} ᎦᎾᎵᏍᎦ one is hiring another

tsi^{22}na^{32}hlv^{2}sga^{2} ᏥᎾᎵᏍᎦ

u^{21}na^{32}hlv^{22}nv^{23}ʔi^{2} ᎤᎾᎵᏅᎢ

ga^{2}na^{32}hlv^{2}sgo^{33}ʔi^{2} ᎦᎾᎵᏍᎪᎢ

hi^{22}na^{11}hlv^{2}ʔv^{11}ga^{2} ᎯᎾᎵᎥᎦ

u^{22}na^{11}hlv^{11}di^{2} ᎤᎾᎵᏗ

finding it (a flexible object)

ga^{2}na^{32}hwa^{0}hti^{23}ha^{2} ᎦᎾᏩᏘᎭ one is finding it (a flexible object)

tsi^{22}na^{32}wa^{0}hti^{23}ha^{2} (animate) ᏥᎾᏩᏘᎭ

tsi^{2}na^{32}wa^{0}hti^{23}ha^{2} (inanimate) ᏥᎾᏩᏘᎭ

u^{21}na^{32}hwa^{0}htv^{22}hv^{23}ʔi^{2} ᎤᎾᏩᏛᎲᎢ

ga^{2}na^{32}hwa^{0}hti^{22}sgo^{33}ʔi^{2} ᎦᎾᏩᏘᏍᎪᎢ

hi^{22}na^{11}hwa^{0}hta^{2} (animate) ᎯᎾᏩᏔ

hi^{2}na^{11}hwa^{0}hta^{2} (inanimate) ᎯᎾᏩᏔ

u^{22}na^{11}hwa^{0}htv^{3}hdi^{2} ᎤᎾᏩᏛᏗ

getting/picking it up (a flexible object)

ga^{2}ne^{33}ʔa^{2}	ᎦᏁᎠ	one is getting it or picking it up (a flexible object)
tsi^{22}ne^{33}ʔa^{2}	ᏥᏁᎠ	
u^{21}ne^{33}sv^{23}ʔi^{2}	ᎤᏁᏒᎢ	
ga^{2}ne^{33}sgo^{33}ʔi^{2}	ᎦᏁᏍᎪᎢ	
hi^{22}na^{2}gi^{2} (animate)	ᎯᎾᎩ	
hi^{2}na^{2}gi^{2} (inanimate)	ᎯᎾᎩ	
u^{22}ne^{11}sdi^{2}	ᎤᏁᏍᏗ	

changing it

ga^{2}ne^{23}dli^{32}yv^{23}ʔa^{2}	ᎦᏁᏟᏴᎠ	one is changing it
tsi^{2}ne^{23}dli^{32}yv^{23}ʔa^{2}	ᏥᏁᏟᏴᎠ	
u^{21}ne^{23}dli^{32}yv^{22}sv^{23}ʔi^{2}	ᎤᏁᏟᏴᏒᎢ	
ga^{2}ne^{23}dli^{32}yv^{22}sgo^{33}ʔi^{2}	ᎦᏁᏟᏴᏍᎪᎢ	
hi^{2}ne^{22}dli^{22}yv^{23}na^{2}	ᎯᏁᏟᏴᎾ	
u^{22}ne^{22}dli^{22}yv^{11}sdi^{2}	ᎤᏁᏟᏴᏍᏗ	

taking it somewhere by hand (a long object)

ga^{22}n**e^{33}g**a^{2}	ᎦᏁᎦ	one is taking somewhere by hand (a long object) **'going' conditional suffix**
tsi^{22}n**e^{33}g**a^{2}	ᏥᏁᎦ	
u^{21}wa^{22}n**v^{33}s**v^{23}ʔi^{2}	ᎤᏩᏅᏒᎢ	
ga^{22}n**e^{33}g**o^{33}ʔi^{2}	ᎦᏁᎪᎢ	
hi^{22}n**u^{11}ga^{2}**	ᎯᏄᎦ	
u^{22}wa^{22}n**v^{11}sdi^{2}**	ᎤᏩᏅᏍᏗ	

peeling/skinning

ga^{2}ne^{33}ga^{2}li^{23}ha^{2} ᎦᏁᎦᎵᎭ one is peeling/skinning another or it

tsi^{22}ne^{33}ga^{2}li^{23}ha^{2} (animate) ᏥᏁᎦᎵᎭ

tsi^{2}ne^{33}ga^{2}li^{23}ha^{2} (inanimate) ᏥᏁᎦᎵᎭ

u^{21}ne^{33}ga^{2}lv^{22}hv^{23}ʔi^{2} ᎤᏁᎦᎸᎲᎢ

ga^{2}ne^{33}ga^{2}li^{22}sgo^{33}ʔi^{2} ᎦᏁᎦᎵᏍᎪᎢ

hi^{22}ne^{11}ga^{2}la^{2} (animate) ᎯᏁᎦᎳ

hi^{2}ne^{11}ga^{2}la^{2} (inanimate) ᎯᏁᎦᎳ

u^{22}ne^{11}ga^{2}hlv^{0}hdi^{2} ᎤᏁᎦᎸᏗ

getting/picking it up (a liquid)

ga^{2}ne^{22}gi^{33}ʔa^{2} ᎦᏁᎩᎠ one is getting it or one is picking it up (a liquid)

tsi^{2}ne^{22}gi^{33}ʔa^{2} ᏥᏁᎩᎠ

u^{21}ne^{22}gi^{33}sv^{23}ʔi^{2} ᎤᏁᎩᏍᏒᎢ

ga^{2}ne^{22}gi^{33}sgo^{33}ʔi^{2} ᎦᏁᎩᏍᎪᎢ

hi^{2}ne^{23}gi^{2} ᎯᏁᎩ

u^{22}ne^{22}gi^{11}sdi^{2} ᎤᏁᎩᏍᏗ

take it from another (a liquid)

ga^{2}ne^{22}gi^{3}ʔe^{23}ha^{2} ᎦᏁᎩᎡᎭ

one is taking a liquid from another

one is milking it (when one is saying 'taking milk from another)

tsi^{22}ne^{22}gi^{3}ʔe^{23}ha^{2} ᏥᏁᎩᎡᎭ

u^{21}ne^{22}gi^{3}ʔe^{22}lv^{23}ʔi^{2} ᎤᏁᎩᎡᎸᎢ

ga^{2}ne^{22}gi^{3}ʔe^{22}ho^{33}ʔi^{2} ᎦᏁᎩᎡᎰᎢ

hi^{22}ne^{22}gi^{11}si^{2} ᎯᏁᎩᏍᏏ

u^{22}ne^{22}gi^{2}ʔe^{3}hdi^{2} ᎤᏁᎩᎡᏗ

leaving it behind (a liquid)

ga^{2}ne^{22}hi^{23}ya^{3}ʔa^{2} ᎦᏁᎯᏯᎠ one is leaving it (a liquid)

tsi^{2}ne^{2}ʔi^{23}ya^{3}ʔa^{2} ᏥᏁᎢᏯᎠ

u^{21}ne^{22}hi^{33}yv^{23}ʔi^{2} ᎤᏁᎯᏴᎢ

ga^{2}ne^{22}hi^{23}ya^{32}sgo^{33}ʔi^{2} ᎦᏁᎯᏯᏍᎪᎢ hi^{2}ne^{22}hi^{23}ya^{2} ᎯᏁᎯᏯ

u^{22}ne^{22}hi^{23}ya^{32}sdi^{2} ᎤᏁᎯᏯᏍᏗ

giving it to another (a liquid)

ga^{2}ne^{22}hne^{23}ha^{2} ᎦᏁᏁᎭ one is giving it to another (a liquid)

tsi^{22}ne^{11}hne^{23}ha^{2} ᏥᏁᏁᎭ

u^{21}ne^{22}hne^{22}hlv^{23}ʔi^{2} ᎤᏁᏁᎸᎢ

ga^{2}ne^{22}hne^{23}ho^{3}ʔi^{2} ᎦᏁᏁᎰᎢ

or ga^{2}ne^{22}hne^{22}ho^{33}ʔi^{2}

hi^{22}ne^{2}ʔv^{2}ʔsi^{2} ᎯᏁᎥᏍᏏ

u^{22}ne^{22}hne^{3}hdi^{2} ᎤᏁᏁᏗ

finding it (a liquid)

ga^{2}ne^{22}hwa^{0}hti^{23}ha^{2} ᎦᏁᏩᏘᎭ one is finding it (a liquid)

tsi^{2}ne^{11}wa^{0}hti^{23}ha^{2} ᏥᏁᏩᏘᎭ

u^{21}ne^{22}hwa^{2}htv^{22}hv^{23}ʔi^{2} ᎤᏁᏩᏛᏅᎢ

ga^{2}ne^{22}hwa^{0}hti^{22}sgo^{33}ʔi^{2} ᎦᏁᏩᏘᏍᎪᎢ

hi^{2}ne^{22}hwa^{2}hta^{2} ᎯᏁᏩᏔ

u^{22}ne^{22}hwa^{2}htv^{2}hdi^{2} ᎤᏁᏩᏛᏗ

taking it somewhere (a liquid)

ga^{2}ne^{22}hwi^{22}di^{23}ha^{2} ᎦᏁᏫᏗᎭ one is taking it somewhere (a liquid)

tsi^{2}ne^{11}wi^{22}di^{23}ha^{2} ᏥᏁᏫᏗᎭ

u^{21}ne^{22}hwi^{22}dv^{22}hv^{23}ʔi^{2} ᎤᏁᏫᏛᏅᎢ

ga^{2}ne^{22}hwi^{22}di^{22}sgo^{33}ʔi^{2} ᎦᏁᏫᏗᏍᎪᎢ

hi^{2}ne^{22}hwi^{23}da^{2} ᎯᏁᏫᏓ

u^{22}ne^{22}hwi^{22}tv^{0}hdi^{2} ᎤᏁᏫᏛᏗ

lives/resides

ga^{2}ne^{23}la^{2} ᎦᏁᎳ one lives or resides

tsi^{2}ne^{23}la^{2} ᏥᏁᎳ

u^{21}wa^{22}ne^{23}la^{3}dv^{23}ʔi^{2} ᎤᏩᏁᎳᏛᎢ

ga^{2}ne^{23}lo^{3}ʔi^{2} ᎦᏁᎶᎢ

hi^{2}ne^{23}li^{2} ᎯᏁᎵ Be living! or Be residing!

u^{21}ne^{23}la^{3}di^{11}sdi^{23}ʔi^{2} ᎤᏁᎳᏗᏍᏗᎢ

freezing

ga^{2}ne^{23}sda^{3}la^{2}di^{23}ʔa^{2} ᎦᏁᏍᏓᎳᏗᎠ it is freezing

tsi^{2}ne^{23}sda^{3}la^{2}di^{23}ʔa^{2} ᏥᏁᏍᏓᎳᏗᎠ

u^{21}ne^{23}sda^{3}la^{2}dv^{23}ʔi^{2} ᎤᏁᏍᏓᎳᏛᎢ

ga^{2}ne^{23}sda^{3}la^{2}di^{22}sgo^{33}ʔi^{2} ᎦᏁᏍᏓᎳᏗᏍᎪᎢ

hi^{2}ne^{22}sda^{2}la^{2}da^{2} ᎯᏁᏍᏓᎳᏓ

u^{22}ne^{23}sda^{3}la^{2}di^{11}sdi^{23}ʔi^{2} ᎤᏁᏍᏓᎳᏗᏍᏗ

hailing

ga^{2}ne^{22}so^{32}ya^{0}sga^{2} ᎦᏁᏐᏯᏍᎦ it is hailing

tsi^{2}ne^{22}so^{23}ya^{32}sga^{2} ᏥᏁᏯᏍᎦ I'm hailing (as if I am the hail)

u^{21}ne^{22}so^{32}ya^{0}sv^{23}ʔi^{2} ᎤᏁᏐᏯᏍᎥᎢ

ga^{2}ne^{22}so^{32}ya^{0}sgo^{33}ʔi^{2} ᎦᏁᏐᏯᏍᎪᎢ

hi^{2}ne^{22}so^{11}hya^{2} ᎯᏁᏐᏯ Hail!

u^{22}ne^{22}so^{11}ya^{0}sdi^{2} ᎤᏁᏐᏯᏍᏗ

lying down

ga^{2}nv^{0}hga^{2} ᎦᏅᎦ one is lying down

tsi^{2}nv^{11}ga^{2} ᏥᏅᎦ

u^{21}wa^{22}nv^{0}hsi^{3}nv^{23}ʔi^{2} ᎤᏩᏅᏍᏏᏅᎢ

ga^{2}nv^{0}hgo^{33}ʔi^{2} ᎦᏅᎪᎢ

hi^{22}nv^{0}hsv^{32}ga^{2} ᎯᏅᏍᎥᎦ

u^{22}wa^{22}nv^{0}hsi^{2}hdi^{23}ʔi^{2} ᎤᏩᏅᏍᏏᏗᎢ

agitating it (a liquid)

ga^{2}hne^{0}gwa^{3}ʔe^{23}ha^{2} ᎦᏁᏆᎡᎭ one is agitating it (a liquid)

tsi^{22}hne^{0}gwa^{3}ʔe^{23}ha^{2} ᏥᏁᏆᎡᎭ

u^{21}hne^{0}gwa^{3}ʔe^{22}lv^{23}ʔi^{2} ᎤᏁᏆᎡᎸᎢ

ga^{2}hne^{0}gwa^{3}ʔe^{22}sgo^{33}ʔi^{2} ᎦᏁᏆᎡᏍᎪᎢ

hi^{2}hne^{0}gwa^{2}ʔv^{23}la^{2} ᎯᏁᏆᎥᎳ

u^{22}hne^{0}gwa^{2}ʔe^{3}hdi^{2}` ᎤᏁᏆᎡᏗ

taking it by hand somewhere (a liquid)

ga^{2}hne^{0}ts**e**^{33}**g**a^{2} ᎦᏁᏤᎦ one is taking it by hand somewhere (a liquid)

'going' conditional suffix

tsi^{2}ne^{11}ts**e**^{33}**g**a^{2} ᏥᏁᏤᎦ
u^{21}hne^{0}ts**v**^{33}**s**v^{23}ʔi^{2} ᎤᏁᏨᏒᎢ
ga^{2}hne^{0}ts**e**^{33}**g**o^{33}ʔi^{2} ᎦᏁᏤᎪᎢ
hi^{2}hne^{0}ts**u**^{11}**ga**^{2} ᎯᏁᏧᎦ
u^{22}hne^{0}ts**v**^{11}**sdi**^{2} ᎤᏁᏨᏍᏗ

holding it (a liquid)

ga^{2}hne^{0}tse^{23}ha^{2} ᎦᏁᏤᎭ one is holding it (a liquid)

tsi^{2}nv^{11}tse^{23}ha^{2} ᏥᏅᏤᎭ
u^{21}hne^{0}tse^{22}lv^{23}ʔi^{2} ᎤᏁᏤᎸᎢ
ga^{2}hne^{0}tse^{22}ho^{33}ʔi^{2} ᎦᏁᏤᎰᎢ
hi^{2}hne^{0}tsv^{11}ga^{2} ᎯᏁᏨᎦ
u^{22}hne^{0}tse^{3}hdi^{2} ᎤᏁᏤᏗ

carrying it around by hand (a liquid)

ga^{2}hne^{0}tsi^{23}do^{32}ha^{2} ᎦᏁᏥᏙᎭ one is carrying it around by hand (a liquid)

tsi^{2}ne^{11}tsi^{23}do^{32}ha^{2} ᏥᏁᏥᏙᎭ
u^{22}hne^{0}tsi^{23}do^{32}lv^{23}ʔi^{2} ᎤᏁᏥᏙᎸᎢ
ga^{2}hne^{0}tsi^{23}do^{32}ho^{33}ʔi^{2} ᎦᏁᏥᏙᎰᎢ
hi^{2}hne^{0}tsi^{23}da^{2} ᎯᏁᏥᏓ
u^{22}hne^{0}tsi^{23}da^{32}sdi^{2} ᎤᏁᏥᏓᏍᏗ

carrying it around by hand (a long object)

ga^{22}ni^{23}do^{32}ha^{2} ᎦᏂᏙᎭ one is carrying it around by hand (a long object)

tsi^{22}ni^{23}do^{32}ha^{2} ᏥᏂᏙᎭ
u^{21}wa^{22}ni^{23}do^{32}lv^{23}ʔi^{2} ᎤᏩᏂᏙᎸᎢ
ga^{22}ni^{23}do^{32}ho^{33}ʔi^{2} ᎦᏂᏙᎰᎢ
hi^{22}ni^{23}da^{2} ᎯᏂᏓ
u^{22}wa^{22}ni^{23}da^{32}sdi^{2} ᎤᏩᏂᏓᏍᏗ

hating another

ga^{2}ni^{0}gwa^{32}ti^{23}ha^{2} ᎦᏂᏆᏘᎭ one hates another

tsi^{22}ni^{0}gwa^{32}ti^{23}ha^{2} ᏥᏂᏆᏘᎭ

u^{21}ni^{0}gwa^{32}ti^{2}hlv^{23}ʔi^{2} ᎤᏂᏆᏘᏢᎢ

ga^{2}ni^{0}gwa^{32}ti^{2}ho^{33}ʔi^{2} ᎦᏂᏆᏘᎰᎢ

hi^{22}ni^{0}gwa^{11}ti^{2}ga^{2} ᎯᏂᏆᏘᎦ

u^{22}ni^{0}gwa^{11}ti^{3}sdi^{2} ᎤᏂᏆᏘᏍᏗ

setting up a bed

ga^{2}ni^{22}hla^{2}di^{23}ʔa^{2} ᎦᏂᏝᏗᎠ one is setting up a bed

tsi^{2}ni^{11}hla^{2}di^{23}ʔa^{2} ᏥᏂᏝᏗᎠ

u^{22}ni^{22}hla^{2}dv^{23}ʔi^{2} ᎤᏂᏝᏛᎢ

ga^{2}ni^{22}hla^{2}di^{22}sgo^{33}ʔi^{2} ᎦᏂᏝᏗᏍᎪᎢ

hi^{2}ni^{22}hla^{2}da^{2} ᎯᏂᏝᏓ

u^{22}ni^{22}hla^{2}di^{11}sdi^{2} ᎤᏂᏝᏗᏍᏗ

burying

ga^{3}ʔn**i^{23}si^{3}h**a^{2} ᎦᏂᏍᏏᎭ one is burying another

'customary' conditional suffix

tsi^{33}n**i^{23}si^{3}h**a^{2} ᏥᏂᏍᏏᎭ

u^{21}n**i^{33}sa^{3}hn**v^{3}ʔi^{2} ᎤᏂᏍᏌᏅᎢ

ga^{3}ʔn**i^{23}si^{32}sg**o^{33}ʔi^{2} ᎦᏂᏍᏏᏍᎪᎢ

hi^{22}n**i^{23}sa^{2}** ᎯᏂᏍᏌ

u^{22}n**i^{23}so^{3}hdi^{2}** ᎤᏂᏍᏐᏗ

catching/arresting

ga^{3}ʔni^{23}ya^{3}ʔa^{2} ᎦᏂᏯᎠ one is catching or arresting another

one is playing catcher (i.e. baseball)

tsi^{33}ni^{23}yi^{3}ha^{2} (animate) ᏥᏂᏱᎭ

tsi^{3}ʔni^{23}yi^{3}ha^{2} (inanimate) ᏥᏂᏱᎭ

u^{21}ni^{33}yv^{22}hv^{23}ʔi^{2} ᎤᏂᏴᎲᎢ

ga^{3}ʔni^{22}yi^{23}sgo^{3}ʔi^{2} ᎦᏂᏱᏍᎪᎢ

hi^{22}ni^{23}ya^{2} (animate) ᎯᏂᏯ

hi^{2}ʔni^{23}ya^{2} (inanimate) ᎯᏂᏯ

u^{22}ni^{23}yv^{0}hdi^{2} ᎤᏂᏴᏗ

hunting

ga^{2}no^{22}ha^{2}li^{23}do^{32}ha^{2} ᎦᏃᎭᎵᏙᎭ one is going about hunting

tsi^{2}no^{2}ʔa^{2}li^{23}do^{32}ha^{2} ᏥᏃᎠᎵᏙᎭ

u^{21}no^{22}ha^{2}li^{23}do^{32}lv^{23}ʔi^{2} ᎤᏃᎭᎵᏙᎸᎢ

ga^{2}no^{22}ha^{2}li^{23}do^{32}ho^{33}ʔi^{2} ᎦᏃᎭᎵᏙᎰᎢ

hi^{2}no^{22}ha^{2}li^{23}da^{2} ᎯᏃᎭᎵᏓ

u^{22}no^{22}ha^{2}li^{23}da^{32}sdi^{2} ᎤᏃᎭᎵᏓᏍᏗ

flying

ga^{2}no^{22}hi^{23}li^{3}ha^{2} ᎦᏃᎯᎵᎭ one is flying

tsi^{2}no^{2}ʔi^{23}li^{3}ha^{2} ᏥᏃᎢᎵᎭ

u^{22}no^{22}hi^{23}lv^{32}sv^{23}ʔi^{2} ᎤᏃᎯᎸᏍᎡᎢ

ga^{2}no^{22}hi^{23}li^{32}so^{33}ʔi^{2} ᎦᏃᎯᎵᏍᏐᎢ

hi^{2}no^{22}hv^{23}la^{2} ᎯᏃᎲᎳ Be flying!

u^{22}no^{22}hi^{22}li^{23}da^{32}sdi^{2} ᎤᏃᎯᎵᏓᏍᏗ

flooding

ga^{2}no^{22}hu^{23}gi^{3}ʔa^{2} ᎦᏃᎱᎩᎠ it is flooding

tsi^{2}no^{22}hu^{23}gi^{3}ʔa^{2} ᏥᏃᎱᎩᎠ I am flooding (as if I was a liquid)

u^{21}no^{22}hu^{23}g**a**^{32}**n**v^{23}ʔi^{2} ᎤᏃᎱᎦᏅᎢ (^{3}a^{32}n, populative infix)

ga^{2}no^{22}hu^{23}gi^{32}sgo^{33}ʔi^{2} ᎦᏃᎱᎩᏍᎪᎢ

hi^{2}no^{22}hu^{23}gv^{32}ga^{2} ᎯᏃᎱᎬᎦ

Flood! (as if you are speaking to a lake or pond, etc.)

tsi^{2}ga^{2}no^{22}hu^{23}gv^{32}ga^{2} ᏥᎦᏃᎱᎬᎦ He, She or It just now flooded

u^{22}no^{22}hu^{23}go^{32}di^{2} ᎤᏃᎱᎪᏗ

causing it to make sound

ga^{2}no^{22}hyv^{22}hli^{0}sdi^{23}ha^{2} ᎦᏃᏴᎵᏍᏗᎭ one is causing it to make sound

tsi^{2}no^{22}yv^{11}li^{0}sdi^{23}ha^{2} ᏥᏃᏴᎵᏍᏗᎭ

u^{21}no^{22}hyv^{22}hli^{0}sta^{2}nv^{23}ʔi^{2} ᎤᏃᏴᎵᏍᏔᏅᎢ

ga^{2}no^{22}hyv^{22}hli^{0}sdi^{22}sgo^{33}ʔi^{2} ᎦᏃᏴᎵᏍᏗᏍᎪᎢ

hi^{2}no^{22}hyv^{22}hli^{0}sda^{2} ᎯᏃᏴᎵᏍᏓ

u^{22}no^{22}hyv^{22}hli^{0}sdo^{3}hdi^{2} ᎤᏃᏴᎵᏍᏙᏗ

blowing

ga^{2}no^{22}lv^{33}ʔv^{2}sga^{2} ᎦᏃᎸᎥᏍᎦ it is blowing (the wind)

tsi^{2}no^{22}lv^{33}ʔv^{2}sga^{2} ᏥᏃᎸᎥᏍᎦ I am blowing (as if I am the wind)

u^{21}no^{22}lv^{33}nv^{23}ʔi^{2} ᎤᏃᎸᏅᎢ

ga^{2}no^{22}lv^{33}ʔv^{2}sgo^{33}ʔi^{2} ᎦᏃᎸᎥᏍᎪᎢ

hi^{2}no^{22}lv^{11}ga^{2} ᎯᏃᎸᎦ

Blow! (This would be used when speaking to the wind directly, but we would not say something like this so as to not offend the Wind.)

u^{22}no^{22}lv^{11}di^{2} ᎤᏃᎸᏗ

stealing

ga^{2}no^{22}sgi^{33}ʔa^{2} ᎦᏃᏍᎩᎠ one is stealing it

tsi^{2}no^{11}sgi^{33}ʔa^{2} ᏥᏃᏍᎩᎠ

u^{21}no^{22}sgi^{33}sv^{23}ʔi^{2} ᎤᏃᏍᎩᏍᎡᎢ

ga^{2}no^{22}sgi^{33}sgo^{33}ʔi^{2} ᎦᏃᏍᎩᏍᎪᎢ

hi^{2}no^{23}sgi^{3} ᎯᏃᏍᎩ

u^{22}no^{22}sgi^{11}sdi^{2} ᎤᏃᏍᎩᏍᏗ

sinking

ga^{2}no^{23}yv^{32}ga^{2} ᎦᏃᏴᎦ one is sinking

tsi^{2}no^{23}yv^{32}ga^{2} ᏥᏃᏴᎦ

u^{21}no^{23}yv^{32}tsv^{23}ʔi^{2} ᎤᏃᏴᏨᎢ

ga^{2}no^{23}yv^{32}go^{33}ʔi^{2} ᎦᏃᏴᎪᎢ

hi^{2}no^{22}yv^{11}gi^{2} ᎯᏃᏴᎩ

u^{22}no^{23}yv^{3}ʔi^{2}sdi^{2} ᎤᏃᏴᎢᏍᏗ

pulling

ga^{2}hna^{0}sa^{2}ne^{33}ʔa^{2} ᎦᏏᏌᏁᎠ one is pulling another or it

tsi^{22}na^{11}sa^{2}ne^{33}ʔa^{2} (animate) ᏥᎶᏍᏌᏁᎠ

tsi^{2}na^{11}sa^{2}ne^{33}ʔa^{2} (inanimate) ᏥᎶᏍᏌᏁᎠ

u^{21}hna^{0}sa^{2}ne^{33}sv^{23}ʔi^{2} ᎤᏏᏍᏌᏁᏍᎡᎢ

ga^{2}hna^{0}sa^{2}ne^{33}sgo^{33}ʔi^{2} ᎦᏏᏍᏌᏁᏍᎪᎢ

hi^{22}na^{11}sa^{2}ne^{2}gi^{2} (animate) ᎯᏏᏍᏌᏁᎩ

hi^{2}hna^{0}sa^{2}ne^{2}gi^{2} (inanimate) ᎯᏏᏍᏌᏁᎩ

u^{22}hna^{0}sa^{2}ne^{11}sdi^{2} ᎤᏏᏍᏌᏁᏍᏗ

dragging/towing

ga^{22}na^{0}si^{23}n**e**^{32}**g**a^{2} ᎦᎾᏍᏏᏁᎦ one is dragging or towing another or it

'going' conditional suffix

tsi^{22}na^{11}si^{23}n**e**^{32}**g**a^{2} (animate) ᏥᎾᏍᏏᏁᎦ

tsi^{2}na^{11}si^{23}ne^{32}ga^{2} (inanimate) ᏥᎾᏍᏏᏁᎦ

u^{21}na^{0}si^{23}n**v**^{32}**s**v^{23}ʔi^{2} ᎤᎾᏍᏏᏅᏍᎡᎢ

ga^{22}na^{0}si^{23}n**e**^{32}**g**o^{33}ʔi^{2} ᎦᎾᏍᏏᏁᎪᎢ

hi^{22}na^{11}si^{22}n**u**^{11}**ga**^{2} (animate) ᎯᎾᏍᏏᏄᎦ

hi^{2}na^{0}si^{22}n**u**^{11}**ga**^{2} (inanimate) ᎯᎾᏍᏏᏄᎦ

u^{22}na^{0}si^{23}n**v**^{32}**sdi**^{2} ᎤᎾᏍᏏᏅᏍᏗ

exiting

ga^{2}nu^{22}go^{33}ga^{2} ᎦᏄᎪᎦ one is exiting

tsi^{2}nu^{22}go^{33}ga^{2} ᏥᏄᎪᎦ

u^{21}nu^{22}go^{33}tsv^{23}ʔi^{2} ᎤᏄᎪᏨᎢ

ga^{2}nu^{22}go^{33}go^{33}ʔi^{2} ᎦᏄᎪᎪᎢ

hi^{2}nu^{22}go^{2}ʔi^{2} ᎯᏄᎪᎢ

u^{22}nu^{22}go^{11}sdi^{2} ᎤᏄᎪᏍᏗ

twisting

ga^{2}nu^{33}te^{23}yo^{3}ha^{2} ᎦᏄᏖᏲᎭ one is twisting another or it

tsi^{22}nu^{33}te^{23}yo^{3}ha^{2} (animate) ᏥᏄᏖᏲᎭ

tsi^{2}nu^{33}te^{23}yo^{3}ha^{2} (inanimate) ᏥᏄᏖᏲᎭ

u^{21}nu^{33}te^{23}yo^{32}lv^{23}ʔi^{2} ᎤᏄᏖᏲᎸᎢ

ga^{2}nu^{33}te^{23}yo^{3}ho^{33}ʔi^{2} ᎦᏄᏖᏲᎰᎢ

hi^{22}nu^{11}te^{22}ya^{2}ga^{2} (animate) ᎯᏄᏖᏯᎦ

hi^{2}nu^{11}te^{22}ya^{2}ga^{2} (inanimate) ᎯᏄᏖᏯᎦ

u^{22}nu^{11}te^{23}ya^{32}sdi^{23}ʔi^{2} ᎤᏄᏖᏯᏍᏗᎢ

missing someone

ga^{2}nv^{33}di^{23}ʔa^{2}	ᎦᏅᏗᎠ	one is missing another or it
tsi^{22}nv^{33}di^{23}ʔa^{2} (animate)	ᏥᏅᏗᎠ	
tsi^{2}nv^{33}di^{23}ʔa^{2} (inanimate)	ᏥᏅᏗᎠ	
u^{21}nv^{33}dv^{23}ʔi^{2}	ᎤᏅᏛᎢ	
ga^{2}nv^{33}di^{22}sgo^{33}ʔi^{2}	ᎦᏅᏗᏍᎪᎢ	
hi^{22}nv^{23}da^{2} (animate)	ᎯᏅᏓ	
hi^{2}nv^{23}da^{2} (inanimate)	ᎯᏅᏓ	
u^{22}nv^{23}di^{32}sdi^{2}	ᎤᏅᏗᏍᏗ	

falling from an upright/standing position

ga^{2}nv^{33}ga^{2}	ᎦᏅᎦ	one is falling from an upright or standing position
tsi^{2}nv^{33}ga^{2}	ᏥᏅᎦ	
u^{21}nv^{33}tsv^{23}ʔi^{2}	ᎤᏅᏨᎢ	
ga^{2}nv^{33}go^{33}ʔi^{2}	ᎦᏅᎪᎢ	
hi^{2}nv^{11}gi^{2}	ᎯᏅᎩ	
u^{22}nv^{2}ʔi^{3}sdi^{2}	ᎤᏅᎢᏍᏗ	

cleaning

ga^{2}nv^{22}ga^{2}li^{23}ha^{2}	ᎦᏅᎦᎵᎭ	one is cleaning another or it
tsi^{22}nv^{22}ga^{2}li^{23}ʔa^{2} (animate)	ᏥᏅᎦᎵᎠ	
tsi^{2}nv^{22}ga^{2}li^{23}ʔa^{2} (inanimate)	ᏥᏅᎦᎵᎠ	
u^{21}nv^{22}ga^{2}lv^{22}hv^{23}ʔi^{2}	ᎤᏅᎦᎸᎲᎢ	
ga^{2}nv^{22}ga^{2}li^{22}sgo^{33}ʔi^{2}	ᎦᏅᎦᎵᏍᎪᎢ	
hi^{22}nv^{22}ga^{2}la^{2} (animate)	ᎯᏅᎦᎳ	
hi^{2}nv^{22}ga^{2}la^{2} (inanimate)	ᎯᏅᎦᎳ	
u^{22}nv^{22}ga^{2}hlv^{0}hdi^{2}	ᎤᏅᎦᎸᏗ	

hammering

ga^{2}nv^{22}gwa^{2}lo^{33}ʔa^{2} ᎦᏅᏆᎶᎠ one is hammering it

tsi^{2}nv^{22}gwa^{2}lo^{33}ʔa^{2} ᏥᏅᏆᎶᎠ

u^{21}nv^{22}gwa^{2}lo^{33}ʔv^{23}ʔi^{2} ᎤᏅᏆᎶᎥᎢ

ga^{2}nv^{22}gwa^{2}lo^{33}sgo^{33}ʔi^{2} ᎦᏅᏆᎶᏍᎪᎢ

hi^{2}nv^{22}gwa^{2}lo^{23}tsa^{2} ᎯᏅᎦᎶᏣ

u^{22}nv^{22}gwa^{2}lo^{11}sdi^{2} ᎤᏅᎦᎶᏍᏗ

hobbling/applying a brake

ga^{2}nv^{33}hlo^{23}hi^{3}ha^{2} ᎦᏅᏠᎯᎭ one is hobbling or tying up another's leg (literal)
one is applying a brake (figurative)

tsi^{22}nv^{33}hlo^{23}hi^{3}ha^{2} (animate) ᏥᏅᏠᎯᎭ

tsi^{2}nv^{33}hlo^{23}hi^{3}ha^{2} (inanimate) ᏥᏅᏠᎯᎭ

u^{21}nv^{33}hlo^{22}hlv^{23}ʔi^{2} ᎤᏅᏠᏢᎢ

ga^{2}nv^{33}hlo^{23}hi^{3}ho^{33}ʔi^{2} ᎦᏅᏠᎯᎰᎢ

hi^{22}nv^{11}hlo^{23}ga^{2} (animate) ᎯᏅᏠᎦ

hi^{2}nv^{11}hlo^{23}ga^{2} (inanimate) ᎯᏅᏠᎦ

u^{22}nv^{11}hlo^{23}sdi^{2} ᎤᏅᏠᏍᏗ

tossing about

ga^{2}nv^{33}ts**i^{23}do^{32}h**a^{2} ᎦᏅᏥᏙᎭ

one is tossing about (as when one is one a boat)

'going about (in different places)' conditional suffix

tsi^{2}nv^{33}ts**i^{23}do^{32}h**a^{2} ᏥᏅᏥᏙᎭ

[tsinvts, 'I fall'] + [idoh, about (incompletive)] + [a, now]

u^{21}nv^{33}ts**i^{23}do^{32}**lv^{23}ʔi^{2} ᎤᏅᏥᏙᎸᎢ

ga^{2}nv^{33}ts**i^{23}do^{32}h**o^{23}ʔi^{2} ᎦᏅᏥᏙᎰᎢ

hi^{2}nv^{11}ts**i^{23}da^{2}** ᎯᏅᏥᏓ

u^{22}nv^{11}ts**i^{23}da^{32}sdi^{2}** ᎤᏅᏥᏓᏍᏗ

giving it to another (a flexible object)

ga^{2}nv^{33}ne^{23}ha^{2} ᎦᏅᏁᎭ one is giving it to another (a flexible object)

tsi^{22}nv^{33}ne^{23}ha^{2} ᏥᏅᏁᎭ

u^{21}nv^{33}ne^{22}lv^{23}ʔi^{2} ᎤᏅᏁᎸᎢ

ga^{2}nv^{33}ne^{22}ho^{33}ʔi^{2} ᎦᏅᏁᎰᎢ

hi^{22}nv^{11}si^{2} ᎯᏅᏏ

u^{22}nv^{11}ne^{3}hdi^{2} ᎤᏅᏁᏗ

pushing

ga^{22}sa^{2}do^{32}y(a)sga^{2} ᎦᏍᏌᏙᏯᏍᎦ one is pushing another or it

tsi^{22}ya^{11}sa^{2}do^{32}y(a)sga^{2} (animate) ᏥᏯᏍᏌᏙᏯᏍᎦ

tsi^{22}sa^{2}do^{32}y(a)sga^{2} (inanimate) ᏥᏍᏌᏙᏯᏍᎦ

u^{21}wa^{22}sa^{2}do^{32}hyv^{23}ʔi^{2} ᎤᏩᏍᏌᏙᏴᎢ

ga^{22}sa^{2}do^{32}y(a)sgo^{33}ʔi^{2} ᎦᏍᏌᏙᏯᏍᎪᎢ

hi^{22}ya^{11}sa^{2}do^{11}hya^{2} (animate) ᎯᏯᏍᏌᏙᏯ

hi^{22}sa^{2}do^{11}hya^{2} (inanimate) ᎯᏍᏌᏙᏯ

u^{22}wa^{22}sa^{2}do^{11}y(a)sdi^{2} ᎤᏩᏍᏌᏙᏯᏍᏗ

rolling

ga^{22}sa^{2}gwa^{2}l**e^{23}hi^{3}h**a^{2} ᎦᏍᏌᏆᎴᎯᎭ one is rolling another or it

'with a purpose' conditional suffix

tsi^{22}ya^{11}sa^{2}gwa^{2}l**e^{23}hi^{3}h**a^{2} (animate) ᏥᏯᏍᏌᏆᎴᎯᎭ

tsi^{22}sa^{2}gwa^{2}le^{23}hi^{3}ha^{2} (inanimate) ᏥᏍᏌᏆᎴᎯᎭ

u^{21}wa^{22}sa^{2}gwa^{2}l**e^{23}hl**v^{3}ʔi^{2} ᎤᏩᏍᏌᏆᎴᎸᎢ

ga^{22}sa^{2}gwa^{2}l**e^{23}hi^{3}h**o^{33}ʔi^{2} ᎦᏍᏌᏆᎴᎯᎰᎢ

hi^{22}ya^{11}sa^{2}gwa^{2}l**e^{23}ga^{2}** (animate) ᎯᏯᏍᏌᏆᎴᎦ

hi^{22}sa^{2}gwa^{2}l**e^{23}ga^{2}** (inanimate) ᎯᏍᏌᏆᎴᎦ

u^{22}wa^{22}sa^{2}gwa^{2}l**e^{23}sdi^{2}** ᎤᏩᏍᏌᏆᎴᏍᏗ

attaching it behind it (a flexible object)

ga^{33}sa^{2}ne^{23}na^{3}dv^{2}sga^{2} ᎦᏍᏌᏁᎾᏛᏍᎦ one is attaching it behind it (a flexible object)

tsi^{33}sa^{2}ne^{23}na^{3}dv^{2}sga^{2} ᏥᏍᏌᏁᎾᏛᏍᎦ

u^{21}wa^{33}sa^{2}ne^{23}na^{3}dv^{22}nv^{23}ʔi^{2} ᎤᏩᏍᏌᏁᎾᏛᏅᎢ

ga^{33}sa^{2}ne^{23}na^{3}dv^{2}sgo^{33}ʔi^{2} ᎦᏍᏌᏁᎾᏛᏍᎪᎢ

hi^{11}sa^{2}ne^{22}na^{2}dv^{11}ga^{2} ᎯᏍᏌᏁᎾᏛᎦ

u^{22}wa^{11}sa^{2}ne^{22}na^{2}dv^{11}di^{2} ᎤᏩᏍᏌᏁᎾᏛᏗ

dripping

ga^{33}sgwo^{2}ʔ**i^{2}h**a^{2} ᎦᏍᏉᎢᎭ it is dripping (literal)
one is dripping (figurative)
'with a purpose' conditional suffix

tsi^{33}sgwo^{2}ʔ**i^{2}h**a^{2} ᏥᏍᏉᎢᎭ I'm dripping

u^{21}wa^{33}sgwo^{2}ʔ**(i^{23})hl**v^{23}ʔi^{2} ᎤᏩᏍᏉᎢᏢᎢ

ha^{33}sgwo^{2}ʔ**i^{23}ga^{2}** ᎭᏍᏉᎢᎦ Be dripping!

u^{21}wa^{11}sgwo^{2}ʔ**i^{2}sdi^{2}** ᎤᏩᏍᏉᎢᏍᏗ

whistling

ga^{22}sv^{22}hni^{0}ga^{2} ᎦᏍᏒᏂᎦ one is whistling

tsi^{11}sv^{22}hni^{0}ga^{2} ᏥᏍᏒᏂᎦ

u^{21}wa^{22}sv^{22}hni^{0}tsv^{23}ʔi^{2} ᎤᏩᏍᏒᏂᏨᎢ

ga^{22}sv^{22}hni^{0}go^{33}ʔi^{2} ᎦᏍᏒᏂᎪᎢ

hi^{22}sv^{22}hni^{0}gi^{2} ᎯᏍᏒᏂᎩ

u^{22}wa^{22}sv^{22}hni^{0}sdi^{2} ᎤᏩᏍᏒᏂᏍᏗ

pilling it up

ga^{33}sv^{22}tv^{3}sga^{2} ᎦᏍᏒᏛᏍᎦ one is piling it up

tsi^{33}sv^{22}tv^{3}sga^{2} ᏥᏍᏒᏛᏍᎦ

u^{21}wa^{33}sv^{22}ta^{3}nv^{33}ʔi^{2} ᎤᏩᏍᏒᏔᏅᎢ

ga^{33}sv^{22}tv^{3}sgo^{3}ʔi^{2} ᎦᏍᏒᏛᏍᎪᎢ

hi^{11}sv^{22}tv^{11}ga^{2} ᎯᏍᏒᏛᎦ

u^{22}wa^{11}sv^{23}tv^{0}hdi^{2} ᎤᏩᏍᏒᏛᏗ

stabbing

ga^{22}ti^{23}ha^{2} ᎦᏘᎭ one is stabbing another or it

tsi^{22}ya^{11}ti^{23}ha^{2} (animate) ᏥᏯᏘᎭ

tsi^{22}ti^{23}ha^{2} (inanimate) ᏥᏘᎭ

u^{21}wa^{22}ti^{2}hlv^{23}ʔi^{2} ᎤᏩᏘᎵᎢ

ga^{22}ti^{22}ho^{33}ʔi^{2} ᎦᏘᎰᎢ

hi^{22}ya^{11}ti^{2}ga^{2} (animate) ᎯᏯᏘᎦ

hi^{22}ti^{2}ga^{2} (inanimate) ᎯᏘᎦ

u^{22}wa^{22}ti^{2}sdi^{2} ᎤᏩᏘᏍᏗ

hanging it up

g**a**^{2}**t**v^{3}sga^{2} ᎦᏛᏍᎦ one is hanging it up

/h/ & /ʔ/ alternation

g**a**^{2}**ʔ**dv^{3}sga^{2} ᎦᏛᏍᎦ

u^{21}ta^{3}nv^{33}ʔi^{2} ᎤᏔᏅᎢ

ga^{2}tv^{3}sgo^{33}ʔi^{2} ᎦᏛᏍᎪᎢ

ha^{2}tv^{11}ga^{2} ᎭᏛᎦ

u^{22}tv^{0}hdi^{2} ᎤᏛᏝᏗ

joking/teasing

ga^{2}we^{33}hli^{23}ha^{2} ᎦᏪᏟᎭ one is joking or teasing

tsi^{2}we^{33}hli^{23}ha^{2} ᏥᏪᏟᎭ

u^{21}we^{33}hlv^{22}hnv^{23}ʔi^{2} ᎤᏪᎵᏅᎢ

ga^{2}we^{33}hli^{22}sgo^{33}ʔi^{2} ᎦᏪᏟᏍᎪᎢ

hi^{2}we^{11}hlv^{23}na^{2} ᎯᏪᎵᎾ

u^{22}we^{11}hlv^{3}hdi^{2} ᎤᏪᎵᏗ

resting

ga^{2}we^{33}so^{22}lv^{33}sdi^{23}ha^{2} ᎦᏪᏍᏐᎸᏍᏗᎭ one is resting another

tsi^{22}ya^{2}we^{33}so^{22}lv^{33}sdi^{23}ha^{2} ᏥᏯᏪᏍᏐᎸᏍᏗᎭ

u^{21}ya^{2}we^{33}so^{22}lv^{33}sta^{2}nv^{23}ʔi^{2} ᎤᏯᏪᏍᏐᎸᏍᏔᏅᎢ

ga^{2}we^{33}so^{22}lv^{33}sdi^{22}sgo^{33}ʔi^{2} ᎦᏪᏍᏐᎸᏍᏗᏍᎪᎢ

hi^{22}ya^{2}we^{11}so^{22}lv^{11}sda^{2} ᎯᏯᏪᏐᎸᏍᏓ
u^{22}ya^{2}we^{11}so^{22}lv^{11}sdo^{2}hdi^{2} ᎤᏯᏪᏐᎸᏍᏙᏗ

bathing

a^{21}ga^{2}wo^{33}ʔa^{2} ᎠᎦᏬᎠ one is bathing another
tsi^{22}ya^{2}wo^{33}ʔa^{2} ᏥᏯᏬᎠ
u^{21}wo^{33}ʔv^{23}ʔi^{2} ᎤᏬᎥᎢ
a^{21}ga^{2}wo^{33}sgo^{33}ʔi^{2} ᎠᎦᏬᏍᎪᎢ
hi^{22}ya^{2}wo^{23}tsa^{2} ᎯᏯᏬᏣ
u^{22}wo^{11}sdi^{2} ᎤᏬᏍᏗ

replying

ga^{2}wo^{33}**hi^{2}**li^{23}yv^{3}ʔa^{2} ᎦᏬᎯᎵᏴᎠ one is replying
/h/ & /ʔ/ alternation
ga^{2}wo^{33}**ʔi^{2}**li^{23}yv^{3}ʔa^{2} ᎦᏬᎢᎵᏴᎠ
u^{21}wo^{33}hi^{2}li^{22}yv^{11}sv^{23}ʔi^{2} ᎤᏬᎯᎵᏴᏍᏒᎢ
ga^{2}wo^{33}hi^{2}li^{22}yv^{11}sgo^{33}ʔi^{2} ᎦᏬᎯᎵᏴᏍᎪᎢ
ha^{2}wo^{11}hi^{2}li^{22}yv^{23}na^{2} ᎭᏬᎯᎵᏴᎾ
u^{22}wo^{11}hi^{2}li^{22}yv^{11}sdi^{2} ᎤᏬᎯᎵᏴᏍᏗ

lecturing

ga^{2}wo^{33}nv^{0}hdi^{23}ha^{2} ᎦᏬᏅᏗᎭ one is lecturing another
tsi^{22}wo^{33}nv^{0}hdi^{2}ha^{2} ᏥᏬᏅᏗᎭ
u^{21}wo^{33}nv^{0}hta^{2}nv^{23}ʔi^{2} ᎤᏬᏅᏔᏅᎢ
ga^{2}wo^{33}nv^{0}hdi^{22}sgo^{33}ʔi^{2} ᎦᏬᏅᏗᏍᎪᎢ
hi^{22}wo^{11}nv^{0}hda^{2} ᎭᏬᏅᏓ
u^{22}wo^{11}nv^{0}hdo^{3}hdi^{2} ᎤᏬᏅᏙᏗ

speaking

ga^{2}wo^{33}ni^{23}ha^{2} ᎦᏬᏂᎭ one is speaking
tsi^{2}wo^{33}ni^{23}ha^{2} ᏥᏬᏂᎭ
u^{21}wo^{33}ni^{22}sv^{23}ʔi^{2} ᎤᏬᏂᏍᏒᎢ
ga^{2}wo^{33}ni^{22}sgo^{33}ʔi^{2} ᎦᏬᏂᏍᎪᎢ
hi^{2}wo^{11}ni^{23}hi^{2} ᎯᏬᏂᎯ
u^{21}wo^{11}ni^{23}hi^{3}sdi^{2} ᎤᏬᏂᎯᏍᏗ

sewing

ga²ye²²wa⁰sga² ᎦᏰᏩᏍᎦ one is sewing it

- tsi²²ye²²wa⁰sga² ᏥᏰᏩᏍᎦ
- u²¹wa²²ye²²wa⁰sv²³ʔi² ᎤᏩᏰᏩᏍᏒᎢ
- ga²²ye²²wa⁰sgo³³ʔi² ᎦᏰᏩᏍᎪᎢ
- hi²²ye²³wa² ᎯᏰᏩ
- u²²wa²²ye²²wa⁰sdi² ᎤᏩᏰᏩᏍᏗ

feeding

ge²²hlo³ha² ᎨᏠᎭ one is feeding another or it

- tsi²²ye²²hlo³ha² ᏥᏰᎶᎯᎭ
- u²¹we²²hla²lv²³ʔi² ᎤᏪᎳᎸᎢ
- ge²²hlo²ho³³ʔi² ᎨᏠᎰᎢ
- hi²²ye²²lo¹¹ga² ᎯᏰᎶᎦ
- u²²we²²lo⁰sdi² ᎤᏪᎶᏍᏗ

yelling/screaming

ge²²**hlu**²hv³sga² ᎨᏡᎲᏍᎦ one is yelling or screaming

/h/ & /ʔ/ alternation

- ge²²**lu**²hv³sga² ᎨᎷᎲᏍᎦ
- u²¹we²²hlu²hnv²³ʔi² ᎤᏪᏡᏅᎢ
- ge²²hlu²hv²sgo³³ʔi² ᎨᏡᎲᏍᎪᎢ
- he²²hlu²hv¹¹ga² ᎮᏡᎲᎦ
- u²²we²²hlu²hv³sdi² ᎤᏪᏡᎲᏍᏗ

leading by a leash

ge²²li²²si³³ne²³ha² ᎨᎵᏍᏏᏁᎭ one is leading another by a leash

- tsi²²ye²²li²²si³³ne²³ha² ᏥᏰᎵᏍᏏᏁᎭ
- u²¹we²²li²²si³³ne²²lv²³ʔi² ᎤᏪᎵᏍᏏᏁᎸᎢ
- ge²²li²²si³³ne²²ho³³ʔi² ᎨᎵᏍᏏᏁᎰᎢ
- hi²²ye²²li²²si¹¹ni²³da² ᎯᏰᎵᏍᏏᏂᏓ

u^{22}we^{22}li^{22}si^{11}ne^{3}hdi^{2} ᎤᏪᎵᏍᏏᏁᏗ

sticking it into the ground (a long object)

ge^{22}tv^{3}(ʔv^{3})sga^{2} ᎨᏛᎥᏍᎦ one is sticking it into the ground (a long object)

ge^{2}ʔdv^{3}(ʔv^{3})sga^{2} ᎨᏛᎥᏍᎦ
u^{21}we^{23}ti^{3}nv^{23}ʔi^{2} ᎤᏪᏘᏅᎢ
ge^{22}tv^{3}(ʔv^{3})sgo^{33}ʔi^{2} ᎨᏛᎥᏍᎪᎢ
he^{22}tv^{11}ga^{2} ᎮᏛᎦ
u^{22}we^{22}t(vhv)hdi^{2} ᎤᏪᏛᏗ

leading by the hand

go^{22}hi^{23}n**e**^{32}**g**a^{2} ᎪᎯᏁᎦ one is leading another by the hand

'going' conditional suffix

The rising tone of the morpheme /i^{23}n/, meaning 'through' causes the (^{33}) tone of the 'going' conditional suffix to spread one syllable mora leftward in order to evenly distribute the (^{33}) tone amongst the two vowels.

tsi^{22}yo^{2}ʔi^{23}n**e**^{32}**g**a^{0} ᏥᏲᎢᏁᎦ
u^{21}wo^{22}hi^{23}n**v**^{32}**s**v^{23}ʔi^{2} ᎤᏬᎯᏅᏒᎢ
go^{22}hi^{23}n**e**^{32}**g**o^{33}ʔi^{2} ᎪᎯᏁᎪᎢ
hi^{22}yo^{2}ʔi^{22}n**u**^{11}**ga**^{2} ᎯᏲᎢᏄᎦ
u^{2}wo^{22}hi^{23}n**v**^{32}**sdi**^{2} ᎤᏬᎯᏅᏍᏗ

believes in another

go^{22}hi^{22}hyu^{0}da^{32}ne^{23}ha^{2} ᎪᎯᏳᏓᏁᎭ one believes in another

tsi^{22}yo^{2}ʔi^{2}hyu^{0}da^{32}ne^{23}ha^{2} ᏥᏲᎢᏳᏓᏁᎭ
u^{21}wo^{22}hi^{22}hyu^{0}da^{32}ne^{23}ha^{2} ᎤᏬᎯᏳᏓᏁᎭ
go^{22}hi^{2}hyu^{0}hda^{32}ne^{22}ho^{33}ʔi^{2} ᎪᎯᏳᏓᏁᎰᎢ
hi^{22}yo^{2}ʔhi^{2}hyu^{0}da^{11}si^{2} ᎯᏲᎯᏳᏓᏍᏏ
u^{22}wo^{22}hi^{2}hyu^{0}da^{11}ne^{3}hdi^{2} ᎤᏬᎯᏳᏓᏁᏗ

recognizes another

a^{21}go^{22}hli^{0}ga^{2} ᎠᎪᎵᎦ one recognizes another

- tsi^{22}yo^{22}li^{11}ga^{2} ᏥᏲᎵᎦ
- u^{21}wo^{22}hli^{0}tsv^{23}ʔi^{2} ᎤᏬᎵᏨᎢ
- a^{21}go^{22}hli^{0}go^{33}ʔi^{2} ᎠᎪᎵᎪᎢ
- hi^{22}yo^{22}li^{11}gi^{2} ᎯᏲᎵᎩ
- u^{22}wo^{22}hli^{3}sdi^{2} ᎤᏬᏟᏍᏗ

understands

go^{22}hli^{0}ga^{2} ᎪᎵᎦ one understands it

- go^{22}li^{11}ga^{2} ᎪᎵᎦ
- u^{21}wo^{22}hli^{0}tsv^{23}ʔi^{2} ᎤᏬᎵᏨᎢ
- go^{22}hli^{0}go^{33}ʔi^{2} ᎪᎵᎪᎢ
- ho^{22}hli^{0}gi^{2} ᎰᎵᎩ
- u^{22}wo^{22}hli^{3}sdi^{2} ᎤᏬᏟᏍᏗ

getting full

g**o**^{22}**h**lv^{3}sga^{2} ᎪᏢᏍᎦ one is getting full

/h/ & /ʔ/ alternation

- g**o**^{11}lv^{3}sga^{2} ᎪᎸᏍᎦ
- u^{21}wo^{22}hlv^{3}sv^{33}ʔi^{2} ᎤᏬᏢᏍᏒᎢ
- go^{22}hlv^{3}sgo^{33}ʔi^{2} ᎪᏢᏍᎪᎢ
- ho^{22}hlv^{2}hi^{2} ᎰᏢᎯ
- u^{22}wo^{22}hlv^{3}hi^{3}sdi^{2} ᎤᏬᏢᎯᏍᏗ

making

g**o**^{22}**h**lv^{22}sga^{2} ᎪᏢᏍᎦ one is making it

/h/ & /ʔ/ alternation

- g**o**^{11}lv^{22}sga^{2} ᎪᎸᏍᎦ
- u^{21}wo^{22}hlv^{22}hnv^{23}ʔi^{2} ᎤᏬᏢᏅᎢ
- go^{22}hlv^{22}sgo^{33}ʔi^{2} ᎪᏢᏍᎪᎢ

ho^{22}hlv^{23}na^{2} ᎰᏢᎾ
u^{22}wo^{22}hlv^{22}nv^{0}hdi^{2} ᎤᏬᏢᏅᏗ

making it fall (a round or long object)

g**o**^{22}**h**o^{22}hnv^{0}di^{23}ha^{2} ᎪᎰᏅᏗᎭ one is making it fall (a round or long object)
/h/ & /ʔ/ alternation

go^{2}ʔo^{22}hnv^{0}di^{23}ha^{2} ᎪᎣᏅᏗᎭ
u^{21}wo^{22}ho^{22}hnv^{0}ta^{2}nv^{23}ʔi^{2} ᎤᏬᎰᏅᏔᏅᎢ
go^{22}ho^{22}hnv^{0}di^{22}sgo^{33}ʔi^{2} ᎪᎰᏅᏗᏍᎪᎢ
ho^{22}ho^{22}hnv^{0}da^{2} ᎰᎰᏅᏓ
u^{22}wo^{22}ho^{22}hnv^{0}do^{3}hdi^{2} ᎤᏬᎰᏅᏙᏗ

falling (a long or round object)

g**o**^{22}**h**o^{2}sga^{2} ᎪᎰᏍᎦ it is falling (a long or round object)
/h/ & /ʔ/ alternation

g**o**^{2}**ʔ**o^{2}sga^{2} ᎪᎣᏍᎦ
u^{21}wo^{22}ho^{2}sv^{23}ʔi^{2} ᎤᏬᎰᏍᎡᎢ
go^{22}ho^{2}sgo^{33}ʔi^{2} ᎪᎰᏍᎪᎢ
ho^{22}ho^{2}hi^{2} ᎰᎰᎯ
u^{22}wo^{22}ho^{2}hi^{2}sdi^{2} ᎤᏬᎰᎯᏍᏗ

writing

g**o**^{22}**h**we^{22}li^{23}ʔa^{2} ᎪᏪᎵᎠ one is writing it
/h/ & /ʔ/ alternation

g**o**^{11}we^{22}li^{23}ʔa^{2} ᎪᏪᎵᎠ
u^{21}wo^{22}hwe^{23}la^{32}nv^{23}ʔi^{2} ᎤᏬᏪᎳᏅᎢ
go^{22}hwe^{23}li^{32}sgo^{33}ʔi^{2} ᎪᏪᎵᏍᎪᎢ
ho^{22}hwe^{22}lv^{11}ga^{2} ᎰᏪᎸᎦ
u^{22}wo^{22}hwe^{23}lo^{32}di^{2} ᎤᏬᏪᎶᏗ

pulling a trigger

go^{32}tsa^{2}ne^{33}ha^{2} ᎪᏣᏁᎭ one is pulling a trigger

go^{32}tsa^{2}ne^{33}ʔa^{2} ᎪᏣᏁᎠ

u^{21}wo^{32}tsa^{2}ne^{33}sv^{23}ʔi^{2} ᎤᏬᏣᏁᏍᏒᎢ

go^{32}tsa^{2}ne^{33}sgo^{33}ʔi^{2} ᎪᏣᏁᏍᎪᎢ

ho^{11}tsa^{2}ne^{2}gi^{2} ᎰᏣᏁᎩ

u^{22}wo^{11}tsa^{2}ne^{11}sdi^{2} ᎤᏬᏣᏁᏍᏗ

smoking it

go^{22}gi^{0}sga^{2} ᎪᎩᏍᎦ one is smoking it

go^{22}gi^{11}sga^{2} ᎪᎩᏍᎦ

u^{21}wo^{22}gi^{0}sv^{23}ʔi^{2} ᎤᏬᎩᏍᏒᎢ

go^{22}gi^{0}sgo^{33}ʔi^{2} ᎪᎩᏍᎪᎢ

ho^{23}gi^{2} ᎰᎩ

u^{22}wo^{22}gi^{0}sdi^{2} ᎤᏬᎩᏍᏗ

batting

go^{22}sdv^{33}ni^{2}ha^{2} ᎪᏍᏛᏂᎭ one is batting it

go^{11}sdv^{33}ni^{2}ha^{2} ᎪᏍᏛᏂᎭ

u^{21}wo^{22}sdv^{23}ni^{32}lv^{23}ʔi^{2} ᎤᏬᏍᏛᏂᎸᎢ

go^{22}sdv^{33}ni^{2}ho^{33}ʔi^{2} ᎪᏍᏛᏂᎰᎢ

ho^{22}sdv^{22}ni^{11}ga^{2} ᎰᏍᏛᏂᎦ

u^{22}wo^{22}sdv^{23}ni^{32}sdi^{2} ᎤᏬᏍᏛᏂᏍᏗ

saying to another

go^{11}se^{3}ha^{2} ᎪᏍᏎᎭ one is saying it to another

tsi^{22}yo^{11}se^{3}ha^{2} ᏥᏲᏍᏎᎭ

u^{21}wo^{11}se^{22}lv^{23}ʔi^{2} ᎤᏬᏍᏎᎸᎢ

go^{11}se^{22}ho^{33}ʔi^{2} ᎪᏍᏎᎰᎢ

hi^{22}yo^{11}si^{2} ᎯᏲᏍᏏ

u^{22}wo^{11}se^{3}hdi^{2} ᎤᏬᏍᏎᏗ

swelling

go^{22}ti^{2}sga^{2}	ᎪᏘᏍᎦ	one or it is swelling
go^{11}ti^{2}sga^{2}	ᎪᏘᏍᎦ	
u^{21}wo^{22}ti^{2}sv^{23}ʔi^{2}	ᎤᏬᏘᏍᎡᎢ	
go^{22}ti^{2}sgo^{33}ʔi^{2}	ᎪᏘᏍᎪᎢ	
ho^{22}ti^{2}hi^{2}	ᎰᏘᎯ	
u^{22}wo^{22}ti^{2}hi^{2}sdi^{2}	ᎤᏬᏘᎯᏍᏗ	

building a fire

g**o^{23}t**v^{3}sga^{2}	ᎪᏛᏍᎦ	one is building a fire **/h/ & /ʔ/ alternation**
g**o^{23}d**v^{3}sga^{2}	ᎪᏛᏍᎦ	
u^{21}wo^{23}ta^{3}nv^{23}ʔi^{2}	ᎤᏬᏔᏅᎢ	
go^{23}tv^{3}sgo^{33}ʔi^{2}	ᎪᏛᏍᎪᎢ	
ho^{22}tv^{11}ga^{2}	ᎰᏛᎦ	
u^{22}wo^{23}tv^{0}hdi^{2}	ᎤᏬᏛᏗ	

unhitching/unhooking/unplugging

gu^{22}da^{2}l**e^{33}**ʔa^{2}	ᎫᏓᎴᎠ	one is unhitching another one is unhooking or unplugging it **'reversive' infix**
tsi^{22}yu^{22}da^{2}l**e^{33}**ʔa^{2} (animate)	ᏥᏳᏓᎴᎠ	
gu^{22}da^{2}le^{33}ʔa^{2} (inanimate)	ᎫᏓᎴᎠ	
u^{21}wu^{22}da^{2}l**e^{33}**sv^{23}ʔi^{2}	ᎤᏭᏓᎴᏍᎡᎢ	
gu^{22}da^{2}l**e^{33}**sgo^{33}ʔi^{2}	ᎫᏓᎴᏍᎪᎢ	
hi^{22}yu^{22}da^{2}l**e^{2}**gi^{2} (animate)	ᎯᏳᏓᎴᎩ	
hu^{22}da^{2}l**e^{2}**gi^{2} (inanimate)	ᎱᏓᎴᎩ	
u^{22}wu^{22}da^{2}l**e^{11}**sdi^{2}	ᎤᏭᏓᎴᏍᏗ	

hitching/hooking up/plugging in

gu^{22}da^{2}lv^{3}(ʔv)^{2}sga^{2} ᎫᏓᎸᎥᏍᎦ one is hitching another
one is hooking it up or plugging it in

tsi^{22}yu^{22}da^{2}lv^{3}(ʔv)^{2}sga^{2} (animate) ᏥᏳᏓᎸᎥᏍᎦ
gu^{22}da^{2}lv^{3}(ʔv)^{2}sga^{2} (inanimate) ᎫᏓᎸᎥᏍᎦ
u^{21}wu^{22}da^{2}lv^{3}(ʔv)^{2}nv^{23}ʔi^{2} ᎤᏭᏓᎸᏅᎢ
gu^{22}da^{2}lv^{3}(ʔv)^{2}sgo^{33}ʔi^{2} ᎫᏓᎸᎥᏍᎪᎢ
hi^{22}yu^{22}da^{2}lv^{2}ʔv^{11}ga^{2} (animate) ᎯᏳᏓᎸᎥᎦ
hu^{22}da^{2}lv^{2}ʔv^{11}ga^{2} (inanimate) ᎱᏓᎸᎥᎦ
u^{22}wu^{22}da^{2}lv^{11}di^{2} ᎤᏭᏓᎸᏗ

affixing a handle to something

g**u^{22}h**a^{2}hlv^{3}sga^{2} ᎫᎭᏢᏍᎦ one is affixing a handle to a something (i.e. a tool)
/h/ & /ʔ/ alternation

g**u^{2}ʔ**a^{2}hlv^{3}sga^{2} ᎫᎠᏢᏍᎦ
u^{21}wu^{22}ha^{2}hla^{3}nv^{33}ʔi^{2} ᎤᏭᎭᏝᏅᎢ
gu^{22}ha^{2}hlv^{3}sgo^{3}ʔi^{2} ᎫᎭᏢᏍᎪᎢ
hu^{22}ha^{2}hlv^{11}ga^{2} ᎱᎭᏢᎦ
u^{22}wu^{22}ha^{2}hlv^{0}di^{2} ᎤᏭᎭᏢᏗ

washing

g**u^{22}h**i^{22}lo^{33}ʔa^{2} ᎫᎯᎶᎠ one is washing it
/h/ & /ʔ/ alternation

g**u^{2}ʔ**i^{22}lo^{33}ʔa^{2} ᎫᎢᎶᎠ
u^{21}wu^{22}hi^{22}lo^{33}ʔv^{23}ʔi^{2} ᎤᏭᎯᎶᎥᎢ
gu^{22}hi^{22}lo^{33}sgo^{33}ʔi^{2} ᎫᎯᎶᏍᎪᎢ
hu^{22}hi^{22}lo^{23}tsa^{2} ᎱᎯᎶᏣ
u^{22}wu^{22}hi^{22}lo^{11}sdi^{2} ᎤᏭᎯᎶᏍᏗ

accusing

gu^{22}hi^{23}sdi^{3}ha^{2}	ᎫᎯᏍᏗᎠ	one is accusing another
tsi^{22}yu^{2}ʔi^{23}sdi^{3}ha^{2}	ᏥᏳᎢᏍᏗᎭ	
u^{21}wu^{22}hi^{23}sta^{3}nv^{23}ʔi^{2}	ᎤᏫᎯᏍᏔᏅᎢ	
gu^{22}hi^{23}sdi^{32}sgo^{33}ʔi^{2}	ᎫᎯᏍᏗᏍᎪᎢ	
hi^{22}yu^{2}ʔi^{23}sda^{2}	ᎯᏳᎢᏍᏓ	
u^{22}wu^{22}hi^{23}sdo^{3}hdi^{2}	ᎤᏫᎯᏍᏙᏗ	

covering/putting a lid on

gu^{33}hlv(^{3}ʔv)^{2}sga^{2}	ᎫᏟᎥᏍᎦ	one is covering it one is putting a lid on it
gu^{33}ʔlv(^{3}ʔv)^{2}sga^{2}	ᎫᎸᎥᏍᎦ	
u^{21}wu^{33}hlv(^{3}ʔv)^{2}nv^{23}ʔi^{2}	ᎤᏫᏟᏅᎢ	
gu^{33}hlv(^{3}ʔv)^{2}sgo^{33}ʔi^{2}	ᎫᏟᎥᏍᎪᎢ	
hu^{11}hlv^{2}ʔv^{11}ga^{2}	ᎱᏟᎥᎦ	
u^{22}wu^{11}hlv^{11}di^{2}	ᎤᏫᏟᏗ	

putting in water

g**u^{22}h**v^{3}sga^{2}	ᎫᎲᏍᎦ	one is putting it in water **/h/ & /ʔ/ alternation**
g**u^{2}ʔ**v^{3}sga^{2}	ᎫᎥᏍᎦ	
u^{21}wu^{22}hnv^{23}ʔi^{2}	ᎤᏫᏅᎢ	
gu^{22}hv^{2}sgo^{33}ʔi^{2}	ᎫᎲᏍᎪᎢ	
hu^{22}hv^{11}ga^{2}	ᎱᎲᎦ	
u^{22}wu^{2}hdi^{2}	ᎤᏫᏗ	

picking up

gu^{22}te^{33}ʔa^{2} ᎫᏖᎠ one is picking another or it up

tsi^{22}yu^{22}te^{33}ʔa^{2} (animate) ᏥᏳᏖᎠ

gu^{11}te^{33}ʔa^{2} (inanimate) ᎫᏖᎠ

u^{21}wu^{22}te^{33}sv^{23}ʔi^{2} ᎤᏭᏖᏍᎥᎢ

gu^{22}te^{33}sgo^{33}ʔi^{2} ᎫᏖᏍᎪᎢ

hi^{22}yu^{22}te^{2}gi^{2} (animate) ᎯᏳᏖᎩ

hu^{22}te^{2}gi^{2} (inanimate) ᎱᏖᎩ

u^{22}wu^{22}te^{11}sdi^{2} ᎤᏭᏖᏍᏗ

snowing

gu^{22}ti^{23}ha^{2} ᎫᏘᎭ it is snowing

tsi^{2}ʔu^{22}ti^{23}ha^{2} ᏥᎤᏘᎭ I'm snowing (as if I am the snow itself)

u^{21}wu^{22}ta^{2}hnv^{23}ʔi^{2} ᎤᏭᏔᏅᎢ

gu^{22}ti^{22}sgo^{33}ʔi^{2} ᎫᏘᏍᎪᎢ

hu^{22}ta^{2} ᎱᏔ Be snowing!

u^{22}wu^{22}to^{2}hdi^{2} ᎤᏭᏙᏗ

sifting

gv^{22}gu^{33}sdi^{23}ha^{2} ᎬᎫᏍᏗᎭ one is sifting it

gv^{22}gu^{11}sdi^{23}ha^{2} ᎬᎫᏍᏗᎭ

u^{21}wa^{22}gu^{33}sta^{2}nv^{23}ʔi^{2} ᎤᏩᎫᏍᏔᏅᎢ

gv^{22}gu^{33}sdi^{22}sgo^{33}ʔi^{2} ᎬᎫᏍᏗᏍᎪᎢ

hv^{22}gu^{23}sda^{2} ᎲᎫᏍᏓ

u^{22}wa^{22}gu^{23}sdo^{3}hdi^{2} ᎤᏩᎫᏍᏙᏗ

leaking

gv^{22}gu^{23}sga^{2} ᎬᎫᏍᎦ it is leaking

tsi^{2}ʔv^{22}gu^{22}sga^{2} ᏥᎥᎫᏍᎦ I'm leaking

u^{21}wa^{22}gu^{22}sv^{23}ʔi^{2} ᎤᏩᎫᏍᎥᎢ

gv^{22}gu^{22}sgo^{33}ʔi^{2} ᎬᎫᏍᎪᎢ

hv^{22}gu^{23}hi^{2} — ᎲᎫᎯ — Be leaking!

u^{22}wa^{22}gu^{23}sdi^{2} — ᎤᏩᎫᏍᏗ

hitting another/knocking

g**v**^{22}**h**ni^{23}ha^{2} — ᎬᏂᎭ — one is hitting another

one is knocking (i.e. on the door)

/h/ & /ʔ/ alternation

tsi^{22}y**v**^{22}**n**i^{23}ha^{2} (animate) — ᏥᏴᏂᎭ

g**v**^{22}**n**i^{23}ha^{2} (inanimate) — ᎬᏂᎭ

u^{21}wa^{22}hni^{2}lv^{23}ʔi^{2} — ᎤᏩᏂᎸᎢ

gv^{22}hni^{2}ho^{33}ʔi^{2} — ᎬᏂᎰᎢ

hi^{22}yv^{22}ni^{11}ga^{2} (animate) — ᎯᏴᏂᎦ

hv^{22}hni^{0}ga^{2} (inanimate) — ᎲᏂᎦ

u^{22}wa^{22}hni^{0}sdi^{2} — ᎤᏩᏂᏍᏗ

fixing (a specific meal)

g**v**^{22}**hn**i^{2}sdi^{23}ha^{2} — ᎬᏂᏍᏗᎭ — one is fixing or cooking it (a specific meal)

/h/ & /ʔ/ alternation

g**v**^{22}**n**i^{2}sdi^{23}ha^{2} — ᎬᏂᏍᏗᎭ

u^{21}wa^{22}hni^{0}sta^{2}nv^{23}ʔi^{2} — ᎤᏩᏂᏍᏔᏅᎢ

gv^{22}hni^{0}sdi^{22}sgo^{33}ʔi^{2} — ᎬᏂᏍᏗᏍᎪᎢ

hv^{22}hni^{0}sda^{2} — ᎲᏂᏍᏓ

u^{22}wa^{22}hni^{0}sdo^{3}hdi^{2} — ᎤᏩᏂᏍᏙᏗ

frying

g**v**^{22}tsa^{2}hlv^{3}sga^{2} — ᎬᏣᏢᏍᎦ — one is frying it

/h/ & /ʔ/ alternation

g**v**^{11}tsa^{2}hlv^{3}sga^{2} — ᎬᏣᏢᏍᎦ

u^{21}wv^{22}tsa^{2}hla^{2}nv^{23}ʔi^{2} — ᎤᏮᏣᏝᏅᎢ

gv^{22}tsa^{2}hlv^{2}sgo^{33}ʔi^{2} — ᎬᏣᏢᏍᎪᎢ

hv^{22}tsa^{2}hlv^{11}ga^{2} — ᎲᏣᏢᎦ

u^{22}wv^{22}tsa^{2}hlv^{0}hdi^{2} — ᎤᏮᏣᏢᏗ

melting it

gv^{22}na^{2}hwo^{0}di^{23}ha^{2} ᎬᎾᏬᏗᎭ one is melting it

gv^{22}na^{2}wo^{11}di^{23}ha^{2} ᎬᎾᏬᏗᎭ

u^{21}wv^{22}na^{2}hwo^{0}ta^{2}nv^{23}ʔi^{2} ᎤᏮᎾᏬᏔᏅᎢ

gv^{22}na^{2}hwo^{0}di^{22}sgo^{33}ʔi^{2} ᎬᎾᏬᏗᏍᎪᎢ

hv^{22}na^{2}hwo^{0}da^{2} ᎲᎾᏬᏓ

u^{22}wv^{22}na^{2}hwo^{0}do^{3}hdi^{2} ᎤᏮᎾᏬᏙᏗ

it is melting

gv^{22}na^{2}wo^{22}sga^{2} ᎬᎾᏬᏍᎦ it is melting

gv^{22}na^{2}wo^{11}sga^{2} ᎬᎾᏬᏍᎦ

u^{21}wa^{22}na^{2}wo^{22}sv^{23}ʔi^{2} ᎤᏩᎾᏬᏍᏒᎢ

gv^{22}na^{2}wo^{22}sgo^{33}ʔi^{2} ᎬᎾᏬᏍᎪᎢ

hv^{22}na^{2}wo^{23}hi^{2} ᎲᎾᏬᎯ

u^{22}wv^{22}na^{2}wo^{22}hi^{2}sdi^{2} ᎤᏮᎾᏬᎯᏍᏗ

sweeping

gv^{22}no^{22}sa^{3}sga^{2} ᎬᏃᏍᏌᏍᎦ one is sweeping it

gv^{22}no^{11}sa^{3}sga^{2} ᎬᏃᏍᏌᏍᎦ

u^{21}wv^{22}no^{22}sa^{2}hv^{23}ʔi^{2} ᎤᏮᏃᏍᏌᎲᎢ

gv^{22}no^{22}sa^{2}sgo^{33}ʔi^{2} ᎬᏃᏍᏌᏍᎪᎢ

hv^{22}no^{23}sa^{2} ᎲᏃᏍᏌ

u^{22}wv^{22}no^{22}sa^{2}sdi^{2} ᎤᏮᏃᏍᏌᏍᏗ

becoming done/ripening

gv^{22}hni^{0}sga^{2} ᎬᏂᏍᎦ it is becoming done (something that is cooking
it is ripening (i.e. a fruit)

gv^{22}ni^{11}sga^{2} ᎬᏂᏍᎦ

u^{21}wa^{22}hni^{0}sv^{23}ʔi^{2} ᎤᏩᏂᏍᏒᎢ

gv^{22}hni^{0}sgo^{33}ʔi^{2} ᎬᏂᏍᎪᎢ

hv^{23}hni^{2} ᎲᏂ

u^{22}wa^{22}hni^{0}sdi^{2} ᎤᏩᏂᏍᏗ

hiding it (neutral)

gv^{22}sg**a^{2}h**lv^{3}sga^{2} ᎬᏍᎦᏢᏍᎦ one is hiding it

/h/ & /ʔ/ alternation

gv^{22}sg**a^{2}ʔ**lv^{3}sga^{2} ᎬᏍᎦᎸᏍᎦ

u^{21}wa^{22}sga^{2}hla^{2}nv^{23}ʔi^{2} ᎤᏩᏍᎦᏝᏅᎢ

gv^{22}sga^{2}hlv^{2}sgo^{33}ʔi^{2} ᎬᏍᎦᏢᏍᎪᎢ

hv^{22}sga^{2}hlv^{11}ga^{2} ᎲᏍᎦᏢᎦ

u^{22}wa^{22}sga^{2}hlv^{0}hdi^{2} ᎤᏩᏍᎦᏢᏗ

hiding it (a long object)

gv^{0}sga^{2}la^{2}di^{23}ʔa^{2} ᎬᏍᎦᎳᏗᎠ one is hiding it (a long object)

gv^{11}sga^{2}la^{2}di^{23}ʔa^{2} ᎬᏍᎦᎳᏗᎠ

u^{21}wa^{22}sga^{2}la^{2}dv^{23}ʔi^{2} ᎤᏩᏍᎦᎳᏛᎢ

gv^{22}sga^{2}la^{2}di^{22}sgo^{33}ʔi^{2} ᎬᏍᎦᎳᏗᏍᎪᎢ

hv^{22}sga^{2}la^{2}da^{2} ᎲᏍᎦᎳᏓ

u^{22}wa^{22}sga^{2}la^{2}di^{11}sdi^{2} ᎤᏩᏍᎦᎳᏗᏍᏗ

hiding it (a flexible object)

gv^{22}sga^{3}l**v^{3}hv^{2}sg**a^{2} ᎬᏍᎦᎸᎲᏍᎦ

one is hiding another or it (a flexible object)

'taking time'/'reduplicative' conditional suffix

tsi^{22}yv^{22}sga^{3}l**v^{3}ʔv^{2}sg**a^{2} (animate) ᏥᏴᏍᎦᎸᎥᏍᎦ

gv^{22}sga^{3}l**v^{3}ʔv^{2}sg**a^{2} (inanimate) ᎬᏍᎦᎸᎥᏍᎦ

u^{21}wa^{22}sga^{3}l**v^{3}hv^{2}n**v^{23}ʔi^{2} ᎤᏩᏍᎦᎸᎲᏅᎢ

gv^{22}sga^{3}l**v^{3}hv^{2}sg**o^{33}ʔi^{2} ᎬᏍᎦᎸᎲᏍᎪᎢ

hi^{22}yv^{22}sga^{2}l**v^{2}ʔv^{11}ga^{2}** (animate) ᎯᏴᏍᎦᎸᎥᎦ

hv^{22}sga^{2}l**v^{2}ʔv^{11}ga^{2}** (inanimate) ᎲᏍᎦᎸᎥᎦ

u^{22}wa^{22}sga^{2}l**v^{11}di^{2}** ᎤᏩᏍᎦᎸᏗ

cracking it

g**v**^{22}sgwa^{2}lo^{33}ʔa^{2} ᎬᏍᏆᎶᎠ one is cracking it

/h/ & /ʔ/ alternation

g**v**^{11}sgwa^{2}lo^{33}ʔa^{2} ᎬᏍᏆᎶᎠ
u^{21}wa^{22}sgwa^{2}lo^{33}ʔv^{23}ʔi^{2} ᎤᏩᏍᏆᎶᎥᎢ
gv^{22}sgwa^{2}lo^{33}sgo^{33}ʔi^{2} ᎬᏍᏆᎶᏍᎪᎢ
hv^{22}sgwa^{2}lo^{23}tsa^{2} ᎲᏍᏆᎶᏣ
u^{22}wa^{22}sgwa^{2}lo^{11}sdi^{2} ᎤᏩᏍᏆᎶᏍᏗ

putting it into a fire (neutral)

gv^{22}**t**v^{3}sga^{2} ᎬᏛᏍᎦ one is putting it into a fire

/h/ & /ʔ/ alternation

gv^{22}**d**v^{3}sga^{2} ᎬᏛᏍᎦ
u^{21}wv^{22}ta^{2}nv^{23}ʔi^{2} ᎤᏮᏔᏅᎢ
gv^{22}tv^{2}sgo^{33}ʔi^{2} ᎬᏛᏍᎪᎢ
hv^{22}tv^{11}ga^{2} ᎲᏛᎦ
u^{22}wv^{22}tv^{0}hdi^{2} ᎤᏮᏛᏗ

soaking it (a flexible object)

gv^{33}wa^{2}hl**v^{3}hv**^{2}sga^{2} one is soaking it (a flexible object)

/h/ & /ʔ/ alternation

gv^{33}wa^{2}hl**v^{3}ʔv**^{2}sga^{2}
u^{21}wv^{33}wa^{2}hlv^{3}ʔv^{2}nv^{23}ʔi^{2}
gv^{33}wa^{2}hlv^{3}ʔv^{2}sgo^{33}ʔi^{2}
hv^{11}wa^{2}hlv^{2}ʔv^{11}ga^{2} or hv^{11}wa^{2}hlv^{11}ga^{2}
u^{22}wv^{11}wa^{2}hlv^{0}hdi^{2}

going uphill/incline

ka^{2}na^{2}lu^{22}sga^{2} ᎧᎾᎷᏍᎦ one is going uphill

tsi^{22}na^{2}lu^{22}sga^{2} ᏥᎾᎷᏍᎦ
u^{21}hna^{2}lu^{22}sv^{23}ʔi^{2} ᎤᎿᎷᏍᏒᎢ

ka^{2}na^{2}lu^{22}sgo^{33}ʔi^{2} ᎧᎾᎷᏍᎪᎢ

hi^{2}hna^{2}lu^{23}hi^{2} ᎯᏁᎷᎯ

u^{22}hna^{2}lu^{22}hi^{2}sdi^{2} ᎤᏁᎷᎯᏍᏗ

making another angry

ka^{2}na^{23}lv^{32}sdi^{23}ha^{2} ᎧᎾᎸᏍᏗᎭ one is making another angry

tsi^{22}na^{23}lv^{32}sdi^{23}ha^{2} ᏥᎾᎸᏍᏗᎭ

u^{21}hna^{23}lv^{32}sta^{2}nv^{23}ʔi^{2} ᎤᏁᎸᏍᏔᏅᎢ

ka^{2}na^{23}lv^{32}sdi^{22}sgo^{33}ʔi^{2} ᎧᎾᎸᏍᏗᏍᎪᎢ

hi^{22}na^{22}lv^{22}sda^{2} ᎯᎾᎸᏍᏓ

u^{22}hna^{22}lv^{22}sdo^{2}hdi^{2} ᎤᏁᎸᏍᏙᏗ

uprooting it

ka^{2}na^{32}sde^{22}dli^{23}ha^{2} ᎧᎾᏍᏕᏟᎭ one is uprooting it

tsi^{22}na^{32}sde^{22}dli^{23}ha^{2} ᏥᎾᏍᏕᏟᎭ

u^{21}hna^{32}sde^{22}dlv^{22}hv^{23}ʔi^{2} ᎤᏁᏍᏕᏢᎲᎢ

ka^{2}na^{32}sde^{22}dli^{22}sgo^{33}ʔi^{2} ᎧᎾᏍᏕᏟᏍᎪᎢ

hi^{2}hna^{11}sde^{23}dla^{2} ᎯᏁᏍᏕᏜ

u^{22}hna^{11}sde^{23}dlv^{0}hdi^{2} ᎤᏁᏍᏕᏢᏗ

getting cold

ka^{2}na^{3}w**o**^{32}**g**a^{2} ᎧᎾᏬᎦ one is getting cold

'transformative' conditional suffix

tsi^{22}na^{3}w**o**^{32}**g**a^{2} ᏥᎾᏬᎦ

u^{21}hna^{3}w**o**^{32}**ts**v^{23}ʔi^{2} ᎤᏁᏬᏨᎢ

ka^{2}na^{3}w**o**^{32}**g**o^{33}ʔi^{2} ᎧᎾᏬᎪᎢ

hi^{2}hna^{2}w**o**^{11}**gi**^{2} ᎯᏁᏬᎩ

u^{22}hna^{2}w**o**^{11}**sdi**^{2} ᎤᏁᏬᏍᏗ

prying it up

ka^{2}ne^{33}gwa^{2}di^{23}ha^{2} ᎧᏁᏆᏗᎭ one is prying it up

tsi^{22}ne^{33}gwa^{2}di^{23}ha^{2} ᏥᏁᏆᏗᎭ

u^{21}hne^{33}gwa^{2}dv^{22}hv^{23}ʔi^{2} ᎤᏁᏆᏛᎲᎢ

ka^{2}ne^{33}gwa^{2}di^{22}sgo^{33}ʔi^{2} ᎧᏁᏆᏗᏍᎪᎢ

hi^{22}hne^{11}gwa^{2}da^{2} ᎯᏁᏆᏓ

u^{22}hne^{11}gwa^{3}tv^{0}hdi^{2} ᎤᏂᏁᏆᏛᏗ

accumulating/gaining/increasing

ka^{2}ne^{2}hgwo^{33}ʔa^{2} ᎧᏁᏉᎠ one is accumulating, gaining, or increasing it

tsi^{22}ne^{2}hgwo^{33}ʔa^{2} ᏥᏁᏉᎠ

u^{21}hne^{2}hgwo^{33}ʔv^{23}ʔi^{2} ᎤᏁᏉᎥᎢ

ka^{2}ne^{2}hgwo^{33}sgo^{33}ʔi^{2} ᎧᏁᏉᏍᎪᎢ

hi^{2}hne^{2}hgwo^{23}tsa^{2} ᎯᏁᏉᏣ

u^{22}hne^{2}hgwo^{11}sdi^{2} ᎤᏁᏉᏍᏗ

ka^{2}ne^{2}hgw**o^{33}g**a^{2} ᎧᏁᏉᎦ

one or it is accumulating, gaining, or increasing

'transformative' conditional suffix

tsi^{22}ne^{2}hgw**o^{33}g**a^{2} ᏥᏁᏉᎦ

u^{21}hne^{2}hgw**o^{33}ts**v^{23}ʔi^{2} ᎤᏁᏉᏨᎢ

ka^{2}ne^{2}hgw**o^{33}g**o^{33}ʔi^{2} ᎧᏁᏉᎪᎢ

hi^{2}hne^{2}hgw**o^{11}gi^{2}** ᎯᏁᏉᎩ

u^{22}hne^{2}hgw**o^{11}sdi^{2}** ᎤᏁᏉᏍᏗ

mentioning/stating

ka^{2}ne^{33}ʔi^{2}sdi^{23}ha^{2} ᎧᏁᎢᏍᏗᎭ one is mentioning or stating it

tsi^{22}hne^{33}ʔi^{2}sdi^{23}ha^{2} ᏥᏁᎢᏍᏗᎭ

u^{21}hne^{33}ʔi^{2}sta^{2}nv^{23}ʔi^{2} ᎤᏁᎢᏍᏔᏅᎢ

ka^{2}ne^{33}ʔi^{2}sdi^{22}sgo^{33}ʔi^{2} ᎧᏁᎢᏍᏗᏍᎪᎢ

hi^{2}hne^{2}ʔi^{2}sda^{2} ᎯᏁᎢᏍᏓ

u^{22}hne^{2}ʔi^{2}sdo^{3}hdi^{2} ᎤᏁᎢᏍᏙᏗ

contaminated

ka^{2}ne^{33}sa^{2}hla^{2} ᎧᏁᏍᏌᏝ one or it is contaminated

a^{21}ki^{2}ne^{33}sa^{2}hla^{2} ᎠᎩᏁᏍᏌᏝ

u^{21}hne^{33}sa^{2}hlv^{23}ʔi^{2} ᎤᏁᏍᏌᏢᎢ

ka^{2}ne^{33}sa^{2}hlo^{33}ʔi^{2} ᎧᏁᏍᏌᏠᎢ

tsa^{2}hne^{33}sa^{2}hlv^{11}ga^{2} ᏣᏁᏍᏌᏢᎦ

Be contaminated! (this can be said but it not common)

u^{22}hne^{33}sa^{2}hlv^{0}hdi^{2} ᎤᏁᏍᏌᏢᏗ

contaminating it

ka^{2}ne^{33}sa^{2}hlv^{3}sga^{2} ᎧᏁᏍᏌᏢᏍᎦ one is contaminating it

tsi^{22}hne^{33}sa^{2}hlv^{3}sga^{2} ᏥᏁᏍᏌᏢᏍᎦ

u^{21}hne^{33}sa^{2}hla^{3}nv^{3}ʔi^{2} ᎤᏁᏍᏌᏢᏅᎢ

ka^{2}ne^{33}sa^{2}hlv^{3}ʔv^{2}sgo^{33}ʔi^{2} ᎧᏁᏍᏌᏢᎥᏍᎪᎢ

hi^{2}hne^{11}sa^{2}hlv^{11}ga^{2} ᎯᏁᏍᏌᏢᎦ

u^{22}hne^{11}sa^{3}hlv^{0}hdi^{2} ᎤᏁᏍᏌᏢᏗ

being conjured

gv^{22}wa^{2}hne^{33}sa^{2}hlv^{3}sga^{2} ᎬᏩᏁᏍᏌᏢᏍᎦ one is being conjured by another

gv^{22}ki^{2}ne^{33}sa^{2}hlv^{3}sga^{2} ᎬᎩᏁᏍᏌᏢᏍᎦ

gv^{22}wa^{2}hne^{33}sa^{2}hla^{3}nv^{3}ʔi^{2} ᎬᏩᏁᏍᏌᏢᏅᎢ

gv^{22}wa^{2}hne^{33}sa^{2}hlv^{3}sgo^{3}ʔi^{2} ᎬᏩᏁᏍᏌᏢᏍᎪᎢ

ge^{22}tsa^{2}hne^{11}sa^{2}hlv^{11}ga^{2} ᎨᏣᏁᏍᏌᏢᎦ Be conjured by another!

This can be said but is not commonly said or culturally accepted.

gv^{22}wa^{2}hne^{11}sa^{3}hlv^{0}hdi^{2} ᎬᏩᏁᏍᏌᏢᏗ

telling it

ka^{2}no^{22}he^{3}ha^{2} ᎦᏃᎮᎭ one is telling it

tsi^{22}no^{22}he^{3}ha^{2} ᏥᏃᎮᎭ

u^{21}hno^{22}he^{22}hlv^{23}ʔi^{2} ᎤᏃᎮᏢᎢ

ka^{2}no^{22}he^{22}sgo^{33}ʔi^{2} ᎦᏃᎮᏍᎪᎢ

hi^{2}hno^{22}hv^{23}la^{2} ᎯᏃᎲᎳ

u^{22}hno^{22}he^{2}hdi^{2} ᎤᏃᎮᏗ

omitting/leaving out

ka^{2}no^{22}hi^{23}ya^{3}ʔa^{2} ᎦᏃᎯᏯᎠ one is omitting or leaving out another

tsi^{22}no^{22}hi^{23}ya^{3}ʔa^{2} ᏥᏃᎯᏯᎠ

u^{21}hno^{23}hi^{32}yv^{23}ʔi^{2} ᎤᏃᎯᏴᎢ

ka^{2}no^{22}hi^{23}ya^{32}sgo^{33}ʔi^{2} ᎦᏃᎯᏯᏍᎪᎢ

hi^{22}hno^{22}hi^{23}ya^{2} (animate) ᎯᏃᎯᏯ

hi^{2}hno^{22}hi^{23}ya^{2} (inanimate) ᎯᏃᎯᏯ

u^{22}hno^{22}hi^{23}ya^{32}sdi^{2} ᎤᏃᎯᏯᏍᏗ

fanning

ka^{2}no^{33}ye^{23}ha^{2} ᎦᏃᏰᎭ one is fanning another or it

tsi^{22}no^{33}ye^{23}ha^{2} ᏥᏃᏰᎭ

u^{21}hno^{33}ye^{22}hv^{23}ʔi^{2} ᎤᏃᏰᎲᎢ

ka^{2}no^{33}ye^{22}sgo^{33}ʔi^{2} ᎦᏃᏰᏍᎪᎢ

hi^{22}hno^{22}yv^{23}la^{2} (animate) ᎯᏃᏴᎳ

hi^{2}hno^{22}yv^{23}la^{2} (inanimate) ᎯᏃᏴᎳ

u^{22}hno^{22}ye^{3}hdi^{2} ᎤᏃᏰᏗ

misting

ka^{2}nu^{33}yo^{22}la^{2}di^{23}ʔa^{2} ᎦᏄᏲᎳᏗᎠ it is misting

tsi^{22}nu^{33}yo^{22}la^{2}di^{23}ʔa^{2} ᏥᏄᏲᎳᏗᎠ I'm misting

u^{21}hnu^{33}yo^{22}la^{2}dv^{23}ʔi^{2} ᎤᏄᏲᎳᏛᎢ

ka^{2}nu^{33}yo^{22}la^{2}di^{22}sgo^{33}ʔi^{2} ᎧᏄᏲᎳᏗᏍᎪᎢ
ha^{2}hnu^{33}yo^{22}la^{2}dv^{11}ga^{2} ᎭᏄᏲᎳᏛᎦ Be misting!
u^{22}hnu^{11}yo^{23}la^{0}di^{32}sdi^{2} ᎤᏄᏲᎳᏗᏍᏗ

straining

ka^{2}nv^{33}so^{22}lv^{23}sdi^{3}ha^{2} ᎧᏅᏐᎸᏍᏗᎭ one is straining it
tsi^{22}nv^{33}so^{22}lv^{23}sdi^{3}ha^{2} ᏥᏅᏐᎸᏍᏗᎭ
u^{21}hnv^{33}so^{22}lv^{23}sta^{3}nv^{23}ʔi^{2} ᎤᏅᏐᎸᏍᏔᏅᎢ
ka^{2}nv^{33}so^{22}lv^{23}sdi^{32}sgo^{33}ʔi^{2} ᎧᏅᏐᎸᏍᏗᏍᎪᎢ
hi^{2}hnv^{11}so^{22}lv^{23}sda^{2} ᎯᏅᏐᎸᏍᏓ
u^{22}hnv^{11}so^{23}lv^{32}sdo^{2}hdi^{2} ᎤᏅᏐᎸᏍᏙᏗ

curing/doctoring/welding

ka^{2}nv^{23}wi^{3}ʔa^{2} ᎧᏅᏫᎠ one is curing or doctoring another
one is welding it
tsi^{22}nv^{23}wi^{3}ʔa^{2} ᏥᏅᏫᎠ
u^{21}hnv^{23}wa^{32}nv^{23}ʔi^{2} ᎤᏅᏩᏅᎢ
ka^{2}nv^{23}wi^{32}sgo^{33}ʔi^{2} ᎧᏅᏫᏍᎪᎢ
hi^{22}nv^{22}wv^{11}ga^{2} (animate) ᎯᏅᏮᎦ
hi^{2}hnv^{22}wv^{11}ga^{2} (inanimate) ᎯᏅᏮᎦ
u^{22}hnv^{23}wo^{32}di^{2} ᎤᏅᏬᏗ

breathing

ka^{2}wo^{22}la^{0}de^{33}ʔa^{2} ᎧᏬᎳᏕᎠ one is breathing
ga^{2}ʔwo^{22}la^{2}de^{33}ʔa^{2} ᎦᏬᎳᏕᎠ
u^{21}hwo^{22}la^{0}de^{33}sv^{23}ʔi^{2} ᎤᏬᎳᏕᏍᏒᎢ
ka^{2}wo^{22}la^{0}de^{33}sgo^{33}ʔi^{2} ᎧᏬᎳᏕᏍᎪᎢ
ha^{2}hwo^{22}la^{0}de^{2}gi^{2} ᎭᏬᎳᏕᎩ
u^{22}hwo^{22}la^{0}de^{11}sdi^{22} ᎤᏬᎳᏕᏍᏗ

parting (in death)

a^{21}ga^{2}de^{33}ga^{2} ᎠᎦᏕᎦ one is parting from another (in death
tsi^{22}yv^{11}de^{33}ga^{2} ᏥᏴᏕᎦ
u^{21}wa^{2}de^{33}tsv^{23}ʔi^{2} ᎤᏩᏕᏨᎢ
a^{21}ga^{2}de^{33}go^{33}ʔi^{2} ᎠᎦᏕᎪᎢ

hi^{22}yv^{22}de^{11}gi^{2} ᎯᏴᏕᎩ

u^{22}hwv^{0}de^{11}sdi^{2} ᎤᏮᏕᏍᏗ

using

gv^{0}di^{3}ha^{2} ᎬᏗᎭ one is using it

gv^{11}di^{3}ha^{2} ᎬᏗᎭ

u^{21}hwv^{0}ta^{2}nv^{23}ʔi^{2} ᎤᏮᏔᏅᎢ

gv^{0}di^{23}sgo^{3}ʔi^{2} ᎬᏗᏍᎪᎢ

hv^{2}hda^{2} ᎲᏓ

u^{22}hwv^{0}do^{3}hdi^{2} ᎤᏮᏙᏗ

putting a fire out/extinguishing a fire

gv^{0}dla^{2}di^{23}ʔa^{2} ᎬᏜᏗᎠ one is putting a fire out

gv^{11}dla^{2}di^{23}ʔa^{2} ᎬᏜᏗᎠ

u^{21}hwv^{0}dla^{2}dv^{23}ʔi^{2} ᎤᏮᏜᏛᎢ

gv^{0}dla^{2}di^{22}sgo^{33}ʔi^{2} ᎬᏜᏗᏍᎪᎢ

hv^{2}hdla^{2}da^{2} ᎲᏜᏓ

u^{22}hwv^{0}dla^{2}di^{11}sdi^{2} ᎤᏮᏜᏗᏍᏗ

sharpening

gv^{0}dli^{23}ha^{2} ᎬᏟᎭ one is sharpening it

gv^{11}dli^{23}ha^{2} ᎬᏟᎭ

u^{21}hwv^{0}dlv^{22}hv^{23}ʔi^{2} ᎤᏮᏢᎲᎢ

gv^{0}dli^{22}sgo^{33}ʔi^{2} ᎬᏟᏍᎪᎢ

hv^{2}hdla^{2} ᎲᏜ

u^{22}hwv^{0}dlv^{2}hdi^{2} ᎤᏮᏢᏗ

fire or light is going out

gv^{0}dlo^{22}sga^{2} ᎬᏠᏍᎦ a fire or light is going out

gv^{22}dlo^{22}sga^{2} ᎬᏠᏍᎦ I am going out (as I am a fire or light)

u^{21}hwv^{0}dlo^{22}sv^{23}ʔi^{2} ᎤᏮᏠᏍᏒᎢ

gv^{0}dlo^{22}sgo^{33}ʔi^{2} ᎬᏠᏍᎪᎢ

hv^{2}hdlo^{23}hi^{2} ᎲᏠᎯ

u^{22}hwv^{0}dlo^{22}hi^{2}sdi^{2} ᎤᏮᏠᎯᏍᏗ

putting it into a fire (a flexible object)

gv^{0}dv^{3}ʔv^{2}sga^{2} ᎬᏫᎥᏍᎦ — one is putting it into a fire (a flexible object)

gv^{11}dv^{3}ʔv^{2}sga^{2} ᎬᏫᎥᏍᎦ

u^{21}hwv^{0}dv^{33}nv^{23}ʔi^{2} ᎤᏮᏫᏅᎢ

gv^{0}dv^{3}ʔv^{2}sgo^{33}ʔi^{2} ᎬᏫᎥᏍᎪᎢ

hv^{2}hdv^{2}ʔv^{11}ga^{2} ᏂᏫᎥᎦ

u^{22}hwv^{0}dv^{11}di^{2} ᎤᏮᏫᏗ

membering/mingling

ke^{2}la^{3}hd**i^{23}do^{32}h**a^{2} ᎨᏓᏗᏙᎭ

one is membering around (literally)

one is mingling amongst others (English equivalent meaning)

'going about (in different places)' conditional suffix

ge^{2}ʔla^{3}hd**i^{23}do^{32}h**a^{2} ᎨᏓᏗᏙᎭ

u^{21}hwe^{2}la^{3}hd**i^{23}do^{32}l**v^{23}ʔi^{2} ᎤᏪᏓᏗᏙᏢᎢ

ke^{2}la^{3}hd**i^{23}do^{32}h**o^{33}ʔi^{2} ᎨᏓᏗᏙᎰᎢ

he^{2}la^{2}hd**i^{23}da^{2}** ᎮᏓᏗᏓ

u^{22}hwe^{2}la^{2}hd**i^{23}da^{32}sdi^{2}** ᎤᏪᏓᏗᏓᏍᏗ

linking/putting together/connecting

gv^{22}**h**i^{2}hlv^{3}sga^{2} ᎬᎯᏢᏍᎦ — one is linking it (i.e. putting it together)

/h/ & /ʔ/ alternation

gv^{2}**ʔi^{2}**hlv^{3}sga^{2} ᎬᎢᏢᏍᎦ

u^{21}hwi^{2}hlv^{32}nv^{23}ʔi^{2} ᎤᏫᏢᏅᎢ

gv^{22}hi^{2}hlv^{3}ʔv^{2}sgo^{33}ʔi^{2} ᎬᎯᏫᎥᏍᎪᎢ

hv^{22}hi^{2}hlv^{11}ga^{2} ᏂᎯᏢᎦ

u^{22}hwi^{2}hlv^{0}hdi^{2} ᎤᏫᏢᏗ — cf. u^{22}hwi^{2}tlv^{44}hi^{2}, 'his or her joint'

shaking (a flexible object)

gv^{22}tsa^{2}g**v^{3}hv^{2}sg**a^{2} ᎬᏣᎬᎲᏍᎦ one is shaking it (a flexible object)

'taking time' conditional suffix

gv^{22}tsa^{2}g**v^{3}ʔv^{2}sg**a^{2} ᎬᏣᎬᎥᏍᎦ

tsi^{22}yv^{11}tsa^{2}g**v^{3}ʔv^{2}sg**a^{2} (animate) ᏥᏴᏣᎬᎥᏍᎦ

tsi^{22}tsa^{2}g**v^{3}ʔv^{2}sg**a^{2} (inanimate) ᏥᏣᎬᎥᏍᎦ

u^{21}hwv^{0}tsa^{2}g**v^{32}n**v^{23}ʔi^{2} ᎤᏮᏣᎥᏅᎢ

gv^{22}tsa^{2}g**v^{3}hv^{2}sg**o^{33}ʔi^{2} ᎬᏣᎬᎲᏍᎪᎢ

hi^{22}yv^{22}tsa^{2}gv^{2}ʔv^{11}ga^{2} (animate) ᎯᏴᏣᎬᎥᎦ

hi^{22}tsa^{2}gv^{2}ʔv^{11}ga^{2} (inanimate) ᎯᏣᎬᎥᎦ

u^{22}hwv^{0}tsa^{2}g**v^{11}di^{2}** ᎤᏮᏣᎬᏗ

hanging it up (a long object)

gv^{0}to^{33}sa^{2}di^{23}ʔa^{2} ᎬᏙᏌᏗᎠ one is hanging it up (a long object)

gv^{22}to^{33}sa^{2}di^{23}ʔa^{2} ᎬᏙᏌᏗᎠ

u^{21}hwv^{0}to^{33}sa^{2}dv^{23}ʔi^{2} ᎤᏮᏙᏌᏛᎢ

gv^{0}to^{33}sa^{2}di^{22}sgo^{33}ʔi^{2} ᎬᏙᏌᏗᏍᎪᎢ

hv^{22}to^{11}sa^{2}da^{2} ᎲᏙᏌᏓ

u^{22}hwv^{0}to^{11}sa^{2}di^{11}sdi^{2} ᎤᏮᏙᏌᏗᏍᏗ

number of them

na^{22}ni^{33}ʔa^{2} ᎾᏂᎠ there are a specific number of them

no^{22}tsi^{33}ʔa^{2} ᏃᏥᎠ there are specific number of us

nu^{22}ni^{33}ʔv^{23}ʔi^{2} ᏄᏂᎥᎢ there were a specific number of them

na^{22}ni^{33}ʔo^{33}ʔi^{2} ᎾᏂᎣᎢ there are usually a specific number of them

wi^{2}na^{22}ni^{33}ʔe^{33}sdi^{2} ᏫᎾᏂᎡᏍᏗ let there be a specific number of them

nu^{22}ni^{33}ʔi^{2}sdi^{2} ᏄᏂᎢᏍᏗ for there to be a specific number of them

saying

ni^{2}ga^{2}we^{23}ʔa^{2} ᏂᎦᏪᎠ one is saying

ni^{2}tsi^{2}we^{23}ʔa^{2} ᏂᏥᏪᎠ

nu^{22}we^{11}sv^{23}ʔi^{2} ᏄᏪᏍᏒᎢ

ni^{2}ga^{2}we^{11}sgo^{33}ʔi^{2} ᏂᎦᏪᏍᎪᎢ

ni^{0}hi^{2}wi^{2} ᏂᎯᏫ

i^{2}yu^{33}we^{11}sdi^{2} ᎢᏳᏪᏍᏗ

taking it off

ni^{2}gv^{33}ne^{0}hde^{33}ha^{2} ᏂᎬᏁᏕᎭ one is taking it off

ni^{2}gv^{33}ne^{0}hde^{33}ʔa^{2} ᏂᎬᏁᏕᎠ

nu^{21}wa^{33}ne^{0}hde^{33}sv^{23}ʔi^{2} ᏄᏩᏁᏕᏍᏒᎢ

ni^{2}gv^{33}ne^{0}hde^{33}sgo^{33}ʔi^{2} ᏂᎬᏁᏕᏍᎪᎢ

ni^{0}hv^{11}ne^{0}hde^{2}gi^{2} ᏂᎲᏁᏕᎩ

i^{2}yu^{33}wa^{11}ne^{0}hde^{11}sdi^{2} ᎢᏳᏩᏁᏕᏍᏗ

putting it on

ni^{2}gv^{33}ne^{0}hdi^{23}ha^{2} ᏂᎬᏁᏗᎭ one is putting it on

ni^{2}gv^{33}ne^{0}hdi^{23}ʔa^{2} ᏂᎬᏁᏗᎠ

nu^{21}wa^{33}ne^{0}hta^{2}nv^{23}ʔi^{2} ᏄᏩᏁᏔᏅᎢ

ni^{2}gv^{33}ne^{0}hdi^{22}sgo^{33}ʔi^{2} ᏂᎬᏁᏗᏍᎪᎢ

ni^{0}hv^{11}ne^{0}hda^{2} ᏂᎲᏁᏓ

i^{2}yu^{33}wa^{11}ne^{0}hdo^{3}hdi^{2} ᎢᏳᏩᏁᏙᏗ

having something on (an object)

nu^{21}wa^{33}ne^{0}hdi^{23}ha^{2} ᏄᏩᏁᏗᎭ one has something on (an object)

na^{21}gwv^{33}ne^{0}hdi^{23}ha ᎾᏋᏁᏗᎭ

nu^{21}wa^{33}ne^{3}hdv^{23}ʔi^{2} ᏄᏩᏁᏛᎢ

nu^{21}wa^{33}ne^{0}hdo^{33}ʔi^{2} ᏄᏩᏁᏙᎢ

ni^{2}tsv^{11}ne^{0}hda^{2} ᏂᏨᏁᏓ

ni^{2}tsv^{11}ne^{0}hdi^{2} ᏂᏨᏁᏗ

praying

u^{21}da^{22}do^{23}li^{32}sdi^{23}ha^{2} ᎤᏓᏙᎵᏍᏗᎭ one is praying

a^{21}gwa^{2}da^{22}do^{23}li^{32}sdi^{23}ha^{2} ᎠᏆᏓᏙᎵᏍᏗᎭ

u^{21}da^{22}do^{23}li^{32}sta^{2}nv^{23}ʔi^{2} ᎤᏓᏙᎵᏍᏔᏅᎢ

u^{21}da^{22}do^{23}li^{32}sdi^{22}sgo^{33}ʔi^{2} ᎤᏓᏙᎵᏍᏗᏍᎪᎢ

tsa^{2}da^{22}do^{22}li^{11}sda^{2} ᏣᏓᏙᎵᏍᏓ

u^{22}da^{22}do^{22}li^{11}sdo^{3}hdi^{2} ᎤᏓᏙᎵᏍᏙᏗ

loves it

u^{21}da^{22}ge^{22}yu^{33}ha^{2} ᎤᏓᎨᏳᎭ one loves it

a^{21}gwa^{2}da^{22}ge^{22}yu^{33}ha^{2} ᎠᏆᏓᎨᏳᎭ

u^{21}da^{22}ge^{22}yu^{33}sv^{23}ʔi^{2} ᎤᏓᎨᏳᏍᎡᎢ

u^{21}da^{22}ge^{22}yu^{33}so^{33}ʔi^{2} ᎤᏓᎨᏳᏍᏐᎢ

tsa^{2}da^{22}ge^{22}yu^{23}hi^{2} ᏣᏓᎨᏳᎯ

u^{22}da^{22}ge^{22}yu^{0}hdi^{2} ᎤᏓᎨᏳᏗ

wrinkled

u^{21}da^{2}ne^{33}go^{23}yu^{3}ha^{2} ᎤᏓᏁᎪᏳᎭ it is wrinkled

a^{21}gwa^{2}da^{22}ne^{33}go^{23}yu^{3}ha^{2} ᎠᏆᏓᏁᎪᏳᎭ

u^{21}da^{2}ne^{33}go^{22}yu^{33}sv^{23}ʔi^{2} ᎤᏓᏁᎪᏳᏍᎡᎢ

u^{21}da^{2}ne^{33}go^{22}yu^{33}so^{33}ʔi^{2} ᎤᏓᏁᎪᏳᏍᏐᎢ

tsa^{2}da^{2}ne^{11}go^{22}yu^{23}hi^{2} ᏣᏓᏁᎪᏳᎯ

u^{22}da^{2}ne^{11}go^{22}yu^{3}hdi^{2} ᎤᏓᏁᎪᏳᏗ

feels

u^{21}da^{22}hnv^{0}ta^{2} ᎤᏓᏅᏔ one feels

a^{21}gwa^{2}da^{22}hnv^{0}ta^{2} ᎠᏆᏓᏅᏔ

u^{21}da^{22}hnv^{0}tv^{23}ʔi^{2} ᎤᏓᏅᏛᎢ

u^{21}da^{22}hnv^{0}to^{33}ʔi^{2} ᎤᏓᏅᏙᎢ

tsa^{2}da^{22}hnv^{0}ta^{2}dv^{11}ga^{2} ᏣᏓᏅᏔᏛᎦ
u^{22}da^{22}hnv^{0}ta^{2}di^{11}sdi^{2} ᎤᏓᏅᏔᏗᏍᏗ

being in view

u^{21}da^{2}yv^{23}la^{3}ta^{2} ᎤᏓᏴᎳᏔ one or it is in view

a^{21}gwa^{2}da^{2}yv^{23}la^{3}ta^{2} ᎠᏆᏓᏴᎳᏔ
u^{21}da^{2}yv^{22}la^{2}tv^{23}ʔi^{2} ᎤᏓᏴᎳᏛᎢ
u^{21}da^{2}yv^{22}la^{2}to^{33}ʔi^{2} ᎤᏓᏴᎳᏙᎢ
tsa^{2}da^{2}yv^{22}la^{2}tv^{11}ga^{2} ᏣᏓᏴᎳᏛᎦ
u^{22}da^{2}yv^{22}la^{2}tv^{0}hdi^{2} ᎤᏓᏴᎳᏛᏗ

throwing/pitching

u^{21}d**e**^{33}**g**a^{2} ᎤᏕᎦ one is throwing it or one is pitching (i.e. baseball)
'going' conditional suffix

a^{21}gwa^{2}d**e**^{33}**g**a^{2} ᎠᏆᏕᎦ
u^{21}di^{23}n**v**^{32}**s**v^{23}ʔi^{2} ᎤᏗᏅᏒᎢ
u^{21}d**e**^{33}**g**o^{33}ʔi^{2} ᎤᏕᎪᎢ
tsa^{2}d**u**^{11}**ga**^{2} ᏣᏚᎦ
u^{22}di^{23}n**v**^{32}**di**^{2} ᎤᏗᏅᏗ

having a birthday

u^{21}de^{22}ti^{2}yi^{23}ha^{2} ᎤᏕᏘᏱᎭ it is one's birthday

a^{21}gwa^{2}de^{22}ti^{2}yi^{23}ha^{2} ᎠᏆᏕᏘᏱᎭ
u^{21}de^{22}ti^{2}yv^{22}hv^{23}ʔi^{2} ᎤᏕᏘᏴᎲᎢ
u^{21}de^{22}ti^{2}yi^{22}sgo^{33}ʔi^{2} ᎤᏕᏘᏱᏍᎪᎢ
tsa^{2}de^{22}ti^{2}ya^{2} ᏣᏕᏘᏯ
u^{22}de^{22}ti^{2}yv^{2}hdi^{23}ʔi^{2} ᎤᏕᏘᏴᏗᎢ

fevering

u^{21}di^{22}hle^{3}hv^{3}sga^{2} ᎤᏕᏞᎲᏍᎦ one is fevering

a^{21}gwa^{2}di^{22}hle^{3}hv^{3}sgv^{23}ʔi^{2} ᎠᏆᏗᏞᎲᏍᎬᎢ
u^{21}di^{22}hle^{3}hv^{3}sgv^{23}ʔi^{2} ᎤᏗᏞᎲᏍᎬᎢ

u^{21}di^{22}hle^{3}hv^{3}sgo^{33}ʔi^{2} ᎤᏗᏞᎲᏍᎪᎢ
tsa^{2}di^{22}hle^{2}hv^{2}hi^{2} ᏣᏗᏞᎲᎯ
u^{22}di^{22}hle^{3}hv^{3}sdi^{2} ᎤᏗᏞᎲᏍᏗ

one is hiding

u^{21}di^{23}sga^{3}hla^{2} ᎤᏗᏍᎦᏝ one is hiding
a^{21}gwa^{2}di^{23}sga^{3}hla^{2} ᎠᏆᏗᏍᎦᏝ
u^{21}di^{22}sga^{2}hlv^{23}ʔi^{2} ᎤᏗᏍᎦᏢᎢ
u^{21}di^{22}sga^{2}hlo^{33}ʔi^{2} ᎤᏗᏍᎦᏠᎢ
tsa^{2}di^{22}sga^{2}hli^{2} ᏣᏗᏍᎦᏟ
u^{22}di^{22}sga^{2}hlv^{0}hdi^{2} ᎤᏗᏍᎦᏢᏗ

getting well/recovering

u^{21}di^{32}wa^{0}sga^{2} ᎤᏗᏩᏍᎦ one is getting well or recovering
a^{21}gwa^{2}di^{32}wa^{0}sga^{2} ᎠᏆᏗᏩᏍᎦ
u^{21}di^{32}wa^{0}sv^{23}ʔi^{2} ᎤᏗᏩᏍᏒᎢ
u^{21}di^{32}wa^{0}sgo^{33}ʔi^{2} ᎤᏗᏩᏍᎪᎢ
tsa^{2}di^{11}hwa^{2} ᏣᏗᏩ
u^{22}di^{11}wa^{0}sdi^{2} ᎤᏗᏩᏍᏗ

being an opening

u^{21}dla^{2}nv^{22}da^{2} ᎤᏜᏅᏓ one or it is an opening
a^{21}gwa^{2}dla^{2}nv^{22}da^{2} ᎠᏆᏜᏅᏓ
u^{21}dla^{2}nv^{22}dv^{23}ʔi^{2} ᎤᏜᏅᏛᎢ
u^{21}dla^{2}nv^{22}do^{33}ʔi^{2} ᎤᏜᏅᏙᎢ
tsa^{2}dla^{2}nv^{22}de^{33}sdi^{2} ᏣᏜᏅᏕᏍᏗ
u^{22}dla^{2}nv^{22}da^{2}di^{11}sdi^{23}ʔi^{2} ᎤᏜᏅᏓᏗᏍᏗᎢ

having time

u^{21}dla^{2}nv^{22}da^{3}ʔd**e**^{23}**h**a^{2} ᎤᏜᏅᏓᏕᎭ one has time
'applicative' conditional suffix
a^{21}gwa^{2}dla^{2}nv^{22}da^{3}ʔd**e**^{23}**h**a^{2} ᎠᏆᏜᏅᏓᏕᎭ

u^{21}dla^{2}nv^{22}da^{3}ʔd**e**^{22}**lv**^{23}ʔi^{2} ᎤᏝᏅᏓᏕᎸᎢ
u^{21}dla^{2}nv^{22}da^{3}ʔd**e**^{22}**ho**^{33}ʔi^{2} ᎤᏝᏅᏓᏕᎰᎢ
tsa^{2}dla^{2}nv^{22}da^{2}d**i**^{11}**si**^{2} ᏣᏝᏅᏓᏗᏍᏏ
u^{22}dla^{2}nv^{22}da^{2}ʔd**e**^{3}**hdi**^{2} ᎤᏝᏅᏓᏕᏗ

taking revenge

u^{21}dle^{33}ga^{2} ᎤᏞᎦ one is taking revenge
a^{21}gwa^{2}dle^{33}ga^{2} ᎠᏆᏞᎦ
u^{21}dle^{33}tsv^{23}ʔi^{2} ᎤᏞᏨᎢ
u^{21}dle^{33}go^{33}ʔi^{2} ᎤᏞᎪᎢ
tsa^{2}dle^{11}gi^{2} ᏣᏞᎩ
u^{22}dle^{2}ʔi^{3}sdi^{2} ᎤᏞᎢᏍᏗ

wearing earrings

du^{21}dli^{33}ʔa^{2}da^{2} ᏚᏟᎠᏓ one is wearing earrings
da^{21}gwa^{2}dli^{33}ʔa^{2}da^{2} ᏓᏆᏟᎠᏓ
du^{21}dli^{33}ʔa^{2}dv^{23}ʔi^{2} ᏚᏟᎠᏛᎢ
du^{21}dli^{33}ʔa^{2}do^{33}ʔi^{2} ᏚᏟᎠᏙᎢ
di^{22}tsa^{2}dli^{33}ʔa^{2}dv^{11}ga^{2} ᏗᏣᏟᎠᏛᎦ
du^{22}dli^{33}ʔa^{2}dv^{11}di^{23}ʔi^{2} ᏚᏟᎠᏛᏗᎢ

being sick

u^{21}dlv^{33}ga^{2} ᎤᏢᎦ one is sick
a^{21}gi^{0}dlv^{33}ga^{2} ᎠᎩᏢᎦ
u^{21}dlv^{33}tsv^{23}ʔi^{2} ᎤᏢᏨᎢ
u^{21}dlv^{33}go^{33}ʔi^{2} ᎤᏢᎪᎢ
tsa^{0}dlv^{11}gi^{2} ᏣᏢᎩ
u^{22}dlv^{2}ʔi^{3}sdi^{2} ᎤᏢᎢᏍᏗ

standing (in a liquid)

u^{21}du^{33}ha^{2} ᎤᏚᎭ one is standing in a liquid

a^{21}gwa^{2}du^{33}ha^{2} ᎠᏆᏚᎭ

u^{21}du^{33}sv^{23}ʔi^{2} ᎤᏚᏒᎢ

u^{21}du^{33}so^{33}ʔi^{2} ᎤᏚᏐᎢ

tsa^{2}du^{11}hi^{2} ᏣᏚᎯ

u^{22}du^{2}hdi^{2} ᎤᏚᏗ

wants it

u^{21}du^{22}li^{23}ha^{2} ᎤᏚᎵᎭ one wants it

a^{21}gwa^{2}du^{22}li^{23}ha^{2} ᎠᏆᏚᎵᎭ

u^{21}du^{22}lv^{22}hv^{23}ʔi^{2} ᎤᏚᎸᎲᎢ

u^{21}du^{22}li^{22}sgo^{33}ʔi^{2} ᎤᏚᎵᏍᎪᎢ

tsa^{2}du^{23}la^{2} ᏣᏚᎳ

u^{22}du^{22}hlv^{0}hdi^{2} ᎤᏚᎸᏗ

willing

u^{21}dv^{22}nv^{33}ʔi^{2}sdi^{23}ha^{2} ᎤᏛᏅᎢᏍᏗᎭ one is willing

a^{21}gwa^{2}dv^{22}nv^{33}ʔi^{2}sdi^{23}ha^{2} ᎠᏆᏛᏅᎢᏍᏗᎭ

u^{21}dv^{22}nv^{33}ʔi^{2}sdv^{23}ʔi^{2} ᎤᏛᏅᎢᏍᏛᎢ

u^{21}dv^{22}nv^{33}ʔi^{2}sdo^{33}ʔi^{2} ᎤᏛᏅᎢᏍᏙᎢ

tsa^{2}dv^{22}nv^{33}ʔi^{2}sda^{2} ᏣᏛᏅᎢᏍᏓ

u^{22}dv^{22}nv^{33}ʔi^{2}sdo^{3}hdi^{2} ᎤᏛᏅᎢᏍᏙᏗ

getting warm

u^{21}ga^{22}na^{2}wo^{22}sga^{2} ᎤᎦᎾᏬᏍᎦ one is getting warm

a^{21}gi^{2}ga^{22}na^{2}wo^{22}sga^{2} ᎠᎩᎦᎾᏬᏍᎦ

u^{21}ga^{22}na^{2}wo^{22}sv^{23}ʔi^{2} ᎤᎦᎾᏬᏒᎢ

u^{21}ga^{22}na^{2}wo^{22}sgo^{33}ʔi^{2} ᎤᎦᎾᏬᏍᎪᎢ

tsa^{2}ga^{22}na^{2}wo^{23}hi^{2} ᏣᎦᎾᏬᎯ
u^{22}ga^{22}na^{2}wo^{22}hi^{2}sdi^{2} ᎤᎦᎾᏬᎯᏍᏗ

being late

u^{21}go^{22}hni^{23}yo^{32}ga^{2} ᎤᎪᏂᏲᎦ one is late
a^{21}gi^{2}go^{22}hni^{23}yo^{32}ga^{2} ᎠᎩᎪᏂᏲᎦ
u^{21}go^{22}hni^{23}yo^{32}tsv^{23}ʔi^{2} ᎤᎪᏂᏲᏨᎢ
u^{21}go^{22}hni^{23}yo^{32}go^{33}ʔi^{2} ᎤᎪᏂᏲᎪᎢ
tsa^{2}go^{22}hni^{22}yo^{11}gi^{2} ᏣᎪᏂᏲᎩ
u^{22}go^{22}hni^{23}yo^{32}sdi^{2} ᎤᎪᏂᏲᏍᏗ

decaying/spoiling

u^{21}go^{22}sga^{2} ᎤᎪᏍᎦ one or it is decaying or spoiling
a^{21}gi^{2}go^{22}sga^{2} ᎠᎩᎪᏍᎦ
u^{21}go^{22}sv^{23}ʔi^{2} ᎤᎪᏍᏒᎢ
u^{21}go^{22}sgo^{33}ʔi^{2} ᎤᎪᏍᎪᎢ
tsa^{2}go^{23}hi^{2} ᏣᎪᎯ
u^{22}go^{22}hi^{2}sdi^{2} ᎤᎪᎯᏍᏗ

having it (a solid object)

u^{23}ha^{2} ᎤᎭ one has it (a solid object)
a^{21}gi^{2}ha^{2} ᎠᎩᎭ
u^{21}hv^{23}ʔi^{2} ᎤᎲᎢ
u^{21}ho^{33}ʔi^{2} ᎤᎰᎢ
tsa^{2}ha^{2} ᏣᎭ
u^{22}hv^{0}hdi^{23}ʔi^{2} ᎤᎲᏗᎢ

yawning

u^{21}ha^{2}hlo^{33}ge^{23}ha^{2} ᎤᎭᏠᎨᎭ one is yawning
a^{21}ki^{0}(h)a^{2}hlo^{33}ge^{23}ha^{2} ᎠᎩᎭᏠᎨᎭ
u^{21}ha^{2}hlo^{33}ge^{22}hv^{23}ʔi^{2} ᎤᎭᏠᎨᎲᎢ
u^{21}ha^{2}hlo^{33}ge^{22}sgo^{33}ʔi^{2} ᎤᎭᏠᎨᏍᎪᎢ

tsa^{2}ha^{2}hlo^{11}gv^{23}la^{2} ᏣᎭᎶᎬᎳ
u^{22}ha^{2}hlo^{11}ge^{3}hdi^{2} ᎤᎭᎶᎨᏗ

smothering or suffocating

u^{21}ha^{2}wo^{33}sdi^{23}ha^{2} ᎤᎭᏬᏍᏗᎭ one is smothering or suffocating

a^{21}ki^{0}(h)a^{2}wo^{33}sdi^{23}ha^{2} ᎠᎩᎭᏬᏍᏗᎭ
u^{21}ha^{2}wo^{33}sta^{2}nv^{23}ʔi^{2} ᎤᎭᏬᏍᏔᏅᎢ
u^{21}ha^{2}wo^{33}sdi^{22}sgo^{33}ʔi^{2} ᎤᎭᏬᏍᏗᏍᎪᎢ
tsa^{2}ha^{2}wo^{11}sda^{2} ᏣᎭᏬᏍᏓ
u^{22}ha^{2}wo^{11}sdo^{3}hdi^{2} ᎤᎭᏬᏍᏙᏗ

there is dew

u^{21}hi^{33}sa^{2}ta^{2} ᎤᎯᏍᏌᏔ one is dew or there is dew

a^{21}gi^{2}hi^{33}sa^{2}ta^{2} ᎠᎩᎯᏍᏌᏔ
u^{21}hi^{33}sa^{2}tv^{23}ʔi^{2} ᎤᎯᏍᏌᏛᎢ
u^{21}hi^{33}sa^{2}to^{33}ʔi^{2} ᎤᎯᏍᏌᏙᎢ
tsa^{2}hi^{33}sa^{2}tv^{11}ga^{2} ᏣᎯᏍᏌᏛᎦ
u^{22}hi^{33}sa^{2}tv^{0}hdi^{23}ʔi^{2} ᎤᎯᏍᏌᏛᏗᎢ

being lonesome

u^{21}hi^{22}so^{2}hda^{32}ne^{23}ha^{2} ᎤᎯᏍᏐᏓᏁᎭ one is lonesome

a^{21}ki^{22}hi^{0}so^{2}hda^{32}ne^{23}ha^{2} ᎠᎩᎯᏍᏐᏓᏁᎭ
u^{21}hi^{22}so^{2}hda^{32}ne^{22}lv^{23}ʔi^{2} ᎤᎯᏍᏐᏓᏁᎸᎢ
u^{21}hi^{22}so^{2}hda^{32}ne^{22}ho^{33}ʔi^{2} ᎤᎯᏍᏐᏓᏁᎰᎢ
tsa^{2}hi^{22}so^{2}hda^{11}si^{2} ᏣᎯᏍᏐᏓᏍᏏ
u^{22}hi^{22}so^{2}hda^{11}ne^{3}hdi^{2} ᎤᎯᏍᏐᏓᏁᏗ

becoming angry

u^{21}hna^{23}lv^{32}ga^{2} ᎤᏏᎸᎦ one is becoming angry

a^{21}ki^{2}na^{23}lv^{32}ga^{2} ᎠᎩᎾᎸᎦ
u^{21}hna^{23}lv^{32}tsv^{23}ʔi^{2} ᎤᏏᎸᏨᎢ
u^{21}hna^{23}lv^{32}go^{33}ʔi^{2} ᎤᏏᎸᎪᎢ

cha^{2}na^{22}lv^{11}gi^{2} ᏣᎾᎸᎩ
u^{22}hna^{23}lv^{3}ʔi^{2}sdi^{2} ᎤᎿᎸᎢᏍᏗ

being angry

u^{21}hna^{23}lv^{32}ha^{2} ᎤᎿᎸᎭ one is angry
a^{21}ki^{2}na^{23}lv^{32}ha^{2} ᎠᎩᎾᎸᎭ
u^{21}hna^{23}lv^{32}sv^{23}ʔi^{2} ᎤᎿᎸᏍᏒᎢ
u^{21}hna^{23}lv^{32}so^{33}ʔi^{2} ᎤᎿᎸᏍᏐᎢ
cha^{2}na^{22}lv^{23}hi^{2} ᏣᎾᎸᎯ
u^{22}hna^{22}lv^{11}di^{23}ʔi^{2} ᎤᎿᎸᏗᎢ

stubbing a toe

u^{21}hna^{32}sgwa^{2}lo^{33}ʔa^{2} ᎤᎿᏍᏆᎶᎠ one is stubbing one's toe
a^{21}ki^{2}na^{32}sgwa^{2}lo^{33}ʔa^{2} ᎠᎩᎾᏍᏆᎶᎠ
u^{21}hna^{32}sgwa^{2}lo^{33}ʔv^{23}ʔi^{2} ᎤᎿᏍᏆᎶᎥᎢ
u^{21}hna^{32}sgwa^{2}lo^{33}sgo^{33}ʔi^{2} ᎤᎿᏍᏆᎶᏍᎪᎢ
cha^{2}na^{11}sgwa^{2}lo^{23}tsa^{2} ᏣᎾᏍᏆᎶᏣ
u^{22}hna^{11}sgwa^{2}lo^{11}sdi^{2} ᎤᎿᏍᏆᎶᏍᏗ

having a chill

u^{21}hna^{2}wa^{32}sdi^{23}ha^{2} ᎤᎿᏩᏍᏗᎭ one has a chill
a^{21}ki^{2}na^{2}wa^{32}sdi^{23}ha^{2} ᎠᎩᎾᏩᏍᏗᎭ
u^{21}hna^{2}wa^{32}sta^{2}nv^{23}ʔi^{2} ᎤᎿᏩᏍᏔᏅᎢ
u^{21}hna^{2}wa^{32}sdi^{22}sgo^{33}ʔi^{2} ᎤᎿᏩᏍᏗᏍᎪᎢ
cha^{2}na^{2}wa^{11}sda^{2} ᏣᎾᏩᏍᏓ
u^{22}hna^{2}wa^{11}sdo^{3}hdi^{2} ᎤᎿᏩᏍᏙᏗ

being in bed

u^{23}hni^{3}ha^{2} ᎤᏂᎭ one is in bed
a^{21}gwa^{23}hni^{3}ha^{2} ᎠᏆᏂᎭ
u^{23}hni^{3}hv^{23}ʔi^{2} ᎤᏂᎲᎢ
u^{23}hni^{3}ho^{33}ʔi^{2} ᎤᏂᎰᎢ

tsa^{23}hni^{3}he^{33}sdi^{2} ᏣᏂᎮᏍᏗ

u^{23}hni^{3}hdi^{2} ᎤᏂᏗ

wearing a shirt/coat

u^{21}hnu^{3}ʔwa^{2} ᎤᏄᏩ one is wearing a shirt or coat

a^{21}gwa^{2}hnu^{3}ʔwa^{2} ᎠᏆᏄᏩ

u^{21}hnu^{3}ʔwv^{23}ʔi^{2} ᎤᏄᏮᎢ

u^{21}hnu^{3}ʔwo^{3}ʔi^{2} ᎤᏄᏬᎢ

tsa^{2}hnu^{32}we^{33}sdi^{2} ᏣᏄᏪᏍᏗ

u^{22}hnu^{3}ʔwa^{2}dv^{11}di^{23}ʔi^{2} ᎤᏄᏩᏛᏗᎢ

buying

u^{21}hwa^{3}sga^{2} ᎤᏩᏍᎦ one is buying it

a^{21}ki^{2}wa^{3}sga^{2} ᎠᎩᏩᏍᎦ

u^{21}hwa^{2}sv^{23}ʔi^{2} ᎤᏩᏍᎬᎢ

u^{21}hwa^{2}sgo^{33}ʔi^{2} ᎤᏩᏍᎪᎢ

cha^{2}wa^{2}hi^{2} ᏣᏩᎯ

u^{22}hwa^{3}hi^{3}sdi^{2} ᎤᏩᎯᏍᏗ

looking for (animate)

u^{21}hyo^{3}ha^{2} ᎤᏲᎭ one is looking for it (inanimate)

a^{21}ki^{2}yo^{3}ha^{2} ᎠᎩᏲᎭ

u^{21}hya^{2}lv^{23}ʔi^{2} ᎤᏯᎸᎢ

u^{21}hyo^{2}ho^{33}ʔi^{2} ᎤᏲᎰᎢ

tsa^{22}hya^{0}ga^{2} ᏣᏯᎦ

u^{22}ya^{0}sdi^{23}ʔi^{2} ᎤᏯᏍᏗᎢ

it is floating

u^{21}hyo^{22}lu^{33}ha^{2} ᎤᏲᎷᎭ one or it is floating

a^{21}ki^{2}yo^{22}lu^{33}ha^{2} ᎠᎩᏲᎷᎭ

u^{21}hyo^{22}lu^{33}sv^{23}ʔi^{2} ᎤᏲᎷᏍᎬᎢ

u^{21}hyo^{22}lu^{33}so^{33}ʔi^{2} ᎤᏲᎷᏍᏐᎢ

hi^{22}hyo^{22}lu^{22}hv^{11}ga^{2} ᎯᏲᎷᎲᎦ

u^{22}hyo^{22}lu^{3}h(i)sdi^{2} ᎤᏲᎷᎯᏍᏗ

having a cold

u^{22}hyv^{22}dla^{0} u^{21}ni^{33}yi^{23}ha^{2} ᎤᏴᏝ ᎤᏂᏱᎭ one has a cold

u^{22}hyv^{22}dla^{0} a^{21}gi^{3}ʔni^{22}yi^{23}ha^{2} ᎤᏴᏝ ᎠᎩᏂᏱᎭ

u^{22}hyv^{22}dla^{0} u^{21}ni^{33}yv^{22}hv^{23}ʔi^{2} ᎤᏴᏝ ᎤᏂᏴᎲᎢ

u^{22}hyv^{22}dla^{0} u^{21}ni^{33}yi^{22}sgo^{33}ʔi^{2} ᎤᏴᏝ ᎤᏂᏱᏍᎪᎢ

u^{22}hyv^{22}dla^{0} wi^{2}tsa^{3}ʔni^{22}ya^{2} ᎤᏴᏝ ᏫᏣᏂᏯ

u^{22}hyv^{22}dla^{0} u^{22}ni^{23}yv^{0}hdi^{2} ᎤᏴᏝ ᎤᏂᏴᏗ

choking

u^{21}hyv^{2}htsi^{22}nv^{22}di^{0}ga^{2} ᎤᏴᏥᏅᏗᎦ one is choking on it

a^{21}ki^{2}yv^{2}htsi^{22}nv^{22}di^{0}ga^{2} ᎠᎩᏴᏥᏅᏗᎦ

u^{21}hyv^{2}htsi^{22}nv^{22}di^{0}tsv^{23}ʔi^{2} ᎤᏴᏥᏅᏗᏨᎢ

u^{21}hyv^{2}htsi^{22}nv^{22}di^{0}go^{33}ʔi^{2} ᎤᏴᏥᏅᏗᎪᎢ

cha^{2}yv^{2}htsi^{22}nv^{22}di^{0}gi^{2} ᏣᏴᏥᏅᏗᎩ

u^{22}hyv^{2}htsi^{22}nv^{22}di^{0}hdi^{2} ᎤᏴᏥᏅᏗᏗ

getting drunk

u^{21}hyv^{2}sde^{33}ʔa^{2} ᎤᏴᏍᏕᎠ one is getting drunk

a^{21}ki^{2}yv^{2}sde^{22}ʔa^{2} ᎠᎩᏴᏍᏕᎠ

u^{21}hyv^{2}sda^{3}ʔv^{23}ʔi^{2} ᎤᏴᏍᏓᎥᎢ

u^{21}hyv^{2}sde^{33}sgo^{33}ʔi^{2} ᎤᏴᏍᏕᏍᎪᎢ

cha^{2}yv^{22}sda^{2}ga^{2} ᏣᏴᏍᏓᎦ

u^{22}hyv^{2}de^{11}sdi^{2} ᎤᏴᏍᏕᏍᏗ

being inside (a close or confined space)

u^{21}tsa^{3}ʔa^{2} ᎤᏣᎠ one is inside it (a close or confined space)

a^{21}gwa^{2}tsa^{3}ʔa^{2} ᎠᏆᏣᎠ

u^{21}tsa^{3}ʔv^{23}ʔi^{2} ᎤᏣᎥᎢ

u^{21}tsa^{3}ʔo^{33}ʔi^{2} ᎤᏣᎣᎢ

tsa^{2}tsa^{3}ʔv^{11}ga^{2} ᏣᏣᎥᎦ

u^{22}tso^{32}di^{23}ʔi^{2} ᎤᏦᏗᎢ

grinning

u^{21}tse^{22}ti^{0}sdi^{23}ha^{2} ᎤᏤᏘᏍᏗᎭ one is grinning

a^{21}gwa^{2}tse^{22}ti^{0}sdi^{23}ha^{2} ᎠᏆᏤᏘᏍᏗᎭ

u^{21}tse^{22}ti^{0}sdv^{23}ʔi^{2} ᎤᏤᏘᏍᏛᎢ

u^{21}tse^{22}ti^{0}sdo^{33}ʔi^{2} ᎤᏤᏘᏍᏙᎢ

ha^{2}tse^{22}ti^{0}sda^{2} ᎭᏤᏘᏍᏓ

u^{22}tse^{22}ti^{0}sdo^{3}hdi^{2} ᎤᏤᏘᏍᏙᏗ

rattling

u^{21}tso^{23}na^{3}ta^{2} ᎤᏦᎾᏔ one or it is rattling

a^{21}gwa^{2}tso^{23}na^{3}ta^{2} ᎠᏆᏦᎾᏔ

u^{21}tso^{22}na^{2}tv^{23}ʔi^{2} ᎤᏦᎾᏛᎢ

u^{21}tso^{22}na^{2}to^{33}ʔi^{2} ᎤᏦᎾᏙᎢ

tsa^{2}tso^{22}na^{2}tv^{11}ga^{2} ᏣᏦᎾᏛᎦ

u^{22}tso^{22}na^{2}tv^{0}hdi^{23}ʔi^{2} ᎤᏦᎾᏛᏘᎢ

sticking out

u^{23}ga^{0}sa^{3}ta^{2} ᎤᎦᏍᏌᏔ one or it is sticking out

a^{21}gwa^{23}ga^{0}sa^{3}ta^{2} ᎠᏆᎦᏍᏌᏔ

u^{21}ga^{0}sa^{2}tv^{23}ʔi^{2} ᎤᎦᏍᏌᏛᎢ

u^{21}ga^{0}sa^{2}to^{33}ʔi^{2} ᎤᎦᏍᏌᏙᎢ

tsa^{2}ga^{0}sa^{2}tv^{11}ga^{2} ᏣᎦᏍᏌᏛᎦ

u^{22}ga^{0}sa^{2}tv^{0}hdi^{23}ʔi^{2} ᎤᎦᏍᏌᏛᏘᎢ

watching/being careful or watchful

u^{21}ga^{0}se^{2}sdi^{23}ha^{2}	ᎤᎦᏍᏎᏍᏗᎭ	one is watching another one is being careful or watchful
tsi^{22}ya^{2}ga^{11}se^{2}sdi^{23}ha^{2} (animate)	ᏥᏯᎦᏍᏎᏍᏗᎭ	
a^{21}gwa^{2}ga^{0}se^{2}sdi^{23}ha^{2} (inanimate)	ᎠᏆᎦᏍᏎᏍᏗᎭ	
u^{21}ga^{0}se^{2}sdv^{23}ʔi^{2}	ᎤᎦᏍᏎᏍᏛᎢ	
u^{21}ga^{0}se^{2}sdo^{33}ʔi^{2}	ᎤᎦᏍᏎᏍᏙᎢ	
hi^{22}ya^{2}ga^{0}se^{2}sda^{2} (animate)	ᎯᏯᎦᏍᏎᏍᏓ	
tsa^{2}ga^{0}se^{2}sda^{2} (inanimate)	ᏣᎦᏍᏎᏍᏓ	
u^{22}ga^{0}se^{2}sdo^{3}hdi^{2}	ᎤᎦᏍᏎᏍᏙᏗ	

losing the way

u^{21}le^{22}na^{23}hi^{3}ha^{2}	ᎤᎴᎾᎯᎭ	one is losing one's way
a^{21}gwa^{2}le^{22}na^{23}hi^{3}ha^{2}	ᎠᏆᎴᎾᎯᎭ	
u^{21}le^{22}na^{23}hlv^{3}ʔi^{2}	ᎤᎴᎾᏢᎢ	
u^{21}le^{22}na^{23}hi^{3}ho^{33}ʔi^{2}	ᎤᎴᎾᎯᎰᎢ	
tsa^{2}le^{22}na^{23}ga^{2}	ᏣᎴᎾᎦ	
u^{22}le^{22}na^{23}sdi^{2}	ᎤᎴᎾᏍᏗ	

making a mistake

u^{21}li^{23}da^{32}sdi^{23}ha^{2}	ᎤᎵᏓᏍᏗᎭ	one is making a mistake
a^{21}gi^{2}li^{23}da^{32}sdi^{23}ha^{2}	ᎠᎩᎵᏓᏍᏗᎭ	
u^{21}li^{23}da^{32}sta^{2}nv^{23}ʔi^{2}	ᎤᎵᏓᏍᏔᏅᎢ	
u^{21}li^{23}da^{32}sdi^{22}sgo^{33}ʔi	ᎤᎵᏓᏍᏗᏍᎪᎢ	
tsa^{2}li^{22}da^{11}sda^{2}	ᏣᎵᏓᏍᏓ	
u^{22}li^{23}da^{32}sdo^{2}hdi^{2}	ᎤᎵᏓᏍᏙᏗ	

moaning

u^{21}li^{23}ye^{32}di^{23}ha^{2}	ᎤᎵᏰᏗᎭ	one is moaning

a^{21}gi^{2}li^{23}ye^{32}di^{23}ha^{2} ᎠᎩᎵᏰᏗᎭ
u^{21}li^{23}ye^{32}ta^{2}nv^{23}ʔi^{2} ᎤᎵᏰᏔᏅᎢ
u^{21}li^{23}ye^{32}di^{22}sgo^{33}ʔi^{2} ᎤᎵᏰᏗᏍᎪᎢ
tsa^{2}li^{22}ye^{11}da^{2} ᏣᎵᏰᏓ
u^{22}li^{23}ye^{32}do^{2}hdi^{2} ᎤᎵᏰᏙᏗ

happening

u^{21}li^{0}sda^{32}hne^{23}ha^{2} ᎤᎵᏍᏓᏁᎭ it is happening to someone
a^{21}gwa^{2}li^{0}sda^{32}hne^{23}ha^{2} ᎠᏆᎵᏍᏓᏁᎭ
u^{21}li^{0}sda^{32}hne^{22}lv^{23}ʔi^{2} ᎤᎵᏍᏓᏁᎸᎢ
u^{21}li^{0}sda^{32}hne^{22}ho^{33}ʔi^{2} ᎤᎵᏍᏓᏁᎰᎢ
tsa^{22}li^{0}sda^{11}si^{2} ᏣᎵᏍᏓᏏ
u^{22}li^{0}sda^{11}hne^{3}hdi^{2} ᎤᎵᏍᏓᏁᏗ

wearing a cap

u^{21}li^{0}sdu^{33}la^{2} ᎤᎵᏍᏚᎳ one is wearing a cap
a^{21}gwa^{2}li^{0}sdu^{33}la^{2} ᎠᏆᎵᏍᏚᎳ
u^{21}li^{0}sdu^{33}lv^{23}ʔi^{2} ᎤᎵᏍᏚᎸᎢ
u^{21}li^{0}sdu^{33}lo^{33}ʔi^{2} ᎤᎵᏍᏚᎶᎢ
tsa^{22}li^{0}sdu^{11}la^{2} ᏣᎵᏍᏚᎳ
u^{22}li^{0}sdu^{11}hlo^{0}hdi^{23}ʔi^{2} ᎤᎵᏍᏚᎶᏗᎢ

sticking one's head out

u^{21}li^{0}sgwa^{2}lu^{33}da^{2} ᎤᎵᏍᏆᎷᏓ one is sticking one's head out
a^{21}gwa^{2}li^{0}sgwa^{2}lu^{33}da^{2} ᎠᏆᎵᏍᏆᎷᏓ
u^{21}li^{0}sgwa^{2}lu^{33}dv^{23}ʔi^{2} ᎤᎵᏍᏆᎷᏛᎢ
u^{21}li^{0}sgwa^{2}lu^{33}do^{33}ʔi^{2} ᎤᎵᏍᏆᎷᏙᎢ
tsa^{22}li^{0}sgwa^{2}lu^{11}da^{2} ᏣᎵᏍᏆᎷᏓ
u^{22}li^{0}sgwa^{2}lu^{11}di^{23}ʔi^{2} ᎤᎵᏍᏆᎷᏗᎢ

wearing a hat

u^{21}li^{0}sgwe^{33}tu^{2}hga^{2} ᎤᎵᏍᏇᏚᎦ one is wearing a hat
a^{21}gwa^{2}li^{0}sgwe^{33}tu^{2}hga^{2} ᎠᏆᎵᏍᏇᏚᎦ
u^{21}li^{0}sgwe^{33}tu^{2}hgv^{23}ʔi^{2} ᎤᎵᏍᏇᏚᎬᎢ

u^{21}li^{0}sgwe^{33}tu^{2}hgo^{33}ʔi^{2}	ᎤᎵᏍᏇᏚᎪᎢ
tsa^{22}li^{0}sgwe^{33}tu^{2}hga^{2}	ᏣᎵᏍᏇᏚᎦ
u^{22}li^{0}sgwe^{33}tu^{2}hgo^{11}di^{23}ʔi^{2}	ᎤᎵᏍᏇᏚᎪᏗᎢ

likes

u^{21}lv^{23}gwo^{0}di^{23}ha^{2}	ᎤᎸᏉᏗᎭ	one likes another or it
tsi^{22}lv^{23}gwo^{0}di^{23}ha^{2} (animate)	ᏥᎸᏉᏗᎭ	
a^{21}gi^{2}lv^{23}gwo^{0}di^{23}ha^{2} (inanimate)	ᎠᎩᎸᏉᏗᎭ	
u^{21}lv^{23}gwo^{0}dv^{23}ʔi^{3}	ᎤᎸᏉᏛᎢ	
u^{21}lv^{23}gwo^{0}do^{33}ʔi^{2}	ᎤᎸᏉᏙᎢ	
hi^{22}lv^{22}gwo^{11}da^{2} (animate)	ᎯᎸᏉᏓ	
hi^{2}lv^{22}gwo^{0}da^{2} (inanimate)	ᎯᎸᏉᏓ	
u^{22}lv^{23}gwo^{0}do^{2}hdi^{23}ʔi^{2}	ᎤᎸᏉᏙᏗᎢ	

having it (a flexible object)

u^{21}na^{3}ʔa^{2}	ᎤᎾᎠ	one has it (a flexible object)
a^{21}gi^{2}na^{3}ʔa^{2}	ᎠᎩᎾᎠ	
u^{21}na^{3}ʔv^{23}ʔi^{2}	ᎤᎾᎥᎢ	
u^{21}na^{3}ʔo^{33}ʔi^{2}	ᎤᎾᎣᎢ	
tsa^{2}na^{3}ʔe^{33}sdi^{2}	ᏣᎾᎡᏍᏗ	
u^{22}na^{3}hdi^{23}ʔi^{2}	ᎤᎾᏗᎢ	

being together

u^{21}na^{2}li^{33}go^{23}ha^{2}	ᎤᎾᎵᎪᎭ	they are together
o^{21}ga^{2}li^{33}go^{23}ha^{2}	ᎣᎦᎵᎪᎭ	we are together
u^{21}na^{2}li^{33}go^{22}sv^{23}ʔi^{2}	ᎤᎾᎵᎪᏒᎢ	they were together
u^{21}na^{2}li^{33}go^{22}so^{33}ʔi^{2}	ᎤᎾᎵᎪᏐᎢ	they are usually together
wi^{22}tsa^{2}li^{11}go^{23}hi^{2}	ᏫᏣᎵᎪᎯ	you all be together
u^{22}na^{2}li^{11}go^{0}hdi^{23}ʔi^{2}	ᎤᎾᎵᎪᏗᎢ	for them to be together

being mean

u^{21}ne^{23}gu^{32}tsa^{2}	ᎤᏁᎫᏣ	one is being mean

a^{21}gi^{2}ne^{23}gu^{32}tsa^{2}	ᎠᎩᏁᎫᏣ	
u^{21}ne^{23}gu^{32}tsv^{23}ʔi^{2}	ᎤᏁᎫᏨᎢ	
u^{21}ne^{23}gu^{32}tso^{33}ʔi^{2}	ᎤᏁᎫᏦᎢ	
tsa^{2}ne^{23}gu^{32}tse^{33}sdi^{2}	ᏣᏁᎫᏤᏍᏗ	
u^{22}ne^{23}gu^{32}ʔi^{2}sdi^{23}ʔi^{2}	ᎤᏁᎫᎢᏍᏗᎢ	

having it (a liquid)

u^{21}ne^{23}ha^{2}	ᎤᏁᎭ	one has it (a liquid)
a^{21}gi^{2}ne^{23}ha^{2}	ᎠᎩᏁᎭ	
u^{21}ne^{22}hv^{23}ʔi^{2}	ᎤᏁᎲᎢ	
u^{21}ne^{22}ho^{33}ʔi^{2}	ᎤᏁᎰᎢ	
tsa^{2}ne^{22}he^{33}sdi^{2}	ᏣᏁᎮᏍᏗ	
u^{22}ne^{2}hdi^{23}ʔi^{2}	ᎤᏁᏗᎢ	

knows it

u^{21}nv^{0}ta^{2}	ᎤᏅᏔ	one knows it
a^{21}gwa^{22}nv^{0}ta^{2}	ᎠᏆᏅᏔ	
u^{21}nv^{0}tv^{23}ʔi^{2}	ᎤᏅᏛᎢ	
u^{21}nv^{0}to^{33}ʔi^{2}	ᎤᏅᏙᎢ	
tsa^{22}nv^{0}te^{33}sdi^{2}	ᏣᏅᏖᏍᏗ	
u^{22}nv^{0}ta^{2}di^{11}di^{23}ʔi^{2}	ᎤᏅᏔᏗᏍᏗᎢ	

sounding

u^{21}no^{22}hyv^{3}hga^{2}	ᎤᏃᏴᎦ	one or it is sounding
a^{21}gi^{2}no^{22}hyv^{3}hga^{2}	ᎠᎩᏃᏴᎦ	
u^{21}no^{22}hyv^{22}hli^{0}sv^{23}ʔi^{2}	ᎤᏃᏴᎵᏍᏒᎢ	
u^{21}no^{22}hyv^{2}hgo^{33}ʔi^{2}	ᎤᏃᏴᎪᎢ	
tsa^{2}no^{22}hyv^{23}la^{2}	ᏣᏃᏴᎳ	
u^{22}no^{22}hyv^{22}hli^{2}sdi^{23}ʔi^{2}	ᎤᏃᏴᎵᏍᏗᎢ	

being punished

u^{21}sdv^{22}di^{23}ʔa^{2}	ᎤᏍᏛᏗᎠ	one is being punished
a^{21}gi^{0}sdv^{22}di^{23}ʔa^{2}	ᎠᎩᏍᏛᏗᎠ	
u^{21}sdv^{33}dv^{23}ʔi^{2}	ᎤᏍᏛᏛᎢ	

u^{21}sdv^{23}di^{32}sgo^{33}ʔi^{2} ᎤᏍᏛᏗᏍᎪᎢ
tsa^{0}sdv^{23}da^{2} ᏣᏍᏛᏓ
u^{22}sdv^{23}di^{32}sdi^{23}ʔi^{2} ᎤᏍᏛᏗᏍᏗᎢ

coughing

u^{21}si^{2}hwa^{3}sga^{2} ᎤᏍᏏᏩᏍᎦ one is coughing

a^{21}gi^{0}si^{2}hwa^{3}sga^{2} ᎠᎩᏍᏏᏩᏍᎦ
u^{21}si^{2}hwa^{2}sgv^{23}ʔi^{2} ᎤᏍᏏᏩᏍᎨᎢ
u^{21}si^{2}hwa^{2}sgo^{33}ʔi^{2} ᎤᏍᏏᏩᏍᎪᎢ
tsa^{22}si^{2}hwa^{2}hi^{2} ᏣᏍᏏᏩᎯ
u^{22}si^{2}hwa^{2}hi^{2}sdi^{23}ʔi^{2} ᎤᏍᏏᏩᎯᏍᏗᎢ

wearing pants

u^{33}su^{22}la^{2} ᎤᏍᏑᎳ one is wearing pants

a^{21}gwa^{33}su^{22}la^{2} ᎠᏆᏍᏑᎳ
u^{33}su^{22}lv^{23}ʔi^{2} ᎤᏍᏑᎸᎢ
u^{33}su^{22}lo^{33}ʔi^{2} ᎤᏍᏑᎶᎢ
tsa^{33}su^{22}le^{33}sdi^{2} ᏣᏍᏑᎴᏍᏗ
u^{33}su^{22}lo^{0}hdi^{23}ʔi^{2} ᎤᏍᏑᎶᏗᎢ

going to bed

u^{21}sv^{23}hi^{3}ha^{2} ᎤᏍᏒᎯᎭ one is going to bed

a^{21}gi^{0}sv^{23}hi^{3}ha^{2} ᎠᎩᏍᏒᎯᎭ
u^{21}sv^{22}hlv^{23}ʔi^{2} ᎤᏍᏒᏢᎢ
u^{21}sv^{23}hi^{3}ho^{33}ʔi^{2} ᎤᏍᏒᎯᎰᎢ
tsa^{0}sv^{23}ha^{2} ᏣᏍᏒᎭ
u^{22}sv^{22}sdi^{23}ʔi^{2} ᎤᏍᏒᏍᏗᎢ

ha^{22}dlv^{4} tsa^{0}sv^{23}hi^{3}ho^{33}ʔi^{2}
ᎭᏢ ᏣᏍᏒᎯᎰᎢ
Where are you staying the night?

being thirsty

u^{21}ta^{2}de^{22}gi^{23}ʔa^{2} ᎤᏔᏕᎩᎠ one is thirsty

a^{21}gi^{0}ta^{2}de^{22}gi^{23}ʔa^{2} ᎠᎩᏔᏕᎩᎠ

u^{21}ta^{2}de^{23}ga^{32}nv^{23}ʔi^{2} ᎤᏔᏕᎦᏅᎢ

u^{21}ta^{2}de^{23}gi^{32}sgo^{33}ʔi^{2} ᎤᏔᏕᎩᏍᎪᎢ

tsa^{0}ta^{2}de^{22}gv^{11}ga^{2} ᏣᏔᏕᎬᎦ

u^{22}ta^{2}de^{23}go^{32}di^{23}ʔi^{2} ᎤᏔᏕᎪᏗᎢ

becoming enraged/irate

u^{21}ta^{2}hla^{2}wo^{22}sga^{2} ᎤᏔᏝᏬᏍᎦ one is becoming enraged, irate, etc.

a^{21}gi^{0}ta^{2}hla^{2}wo^{22}sga^{2} ᎠᎩᏔᏝᏬᏍᎦ

u^{21}ta^{2}hla^{2}wo^{22}sv^{23}ʔi^{2} ᎤᏔᏝᏬᏒᎢ

u^{21}ta^{2}hla^{2}wo^{22}sgo^{33}ʔi^{2} ᎤᏔᏝᏍᎪᎢ

tsa^{0}ta^{2}hla^{2}wo^{23}hi^{2} ᏣᏔᏝᏬᎯ

u^{22}ta^{2}hla^{2}wo^{22}hi^{2}sdi^{23}ʔi^{2} ᎤᏔᏝᏬᎯᏍᏗᎢ

listening

u^{21}tv^{23}da^{32}sdi^{23}ha^{2} ᎤᏛᏓᏍᏗᎭ one is listening to another or it

tsi^{22}ya^{11}tv^{23}da^{32}sdi^{23}ha^{2} (animate) ᏥᏯᏛᏓᏍᏗᎭ

a^{21}gwa^{0}tv^{23}da^{32}sdi^{23}ha^{2} (inanimate) ᎠᏆᏛᏓᏍᏗᎭ

u^{21}tv^{23}da^{32}sdv^{23}ʔi^{2} ᎤᏛᏓᏍᏛᎢ

u^{21}tv^{23}da^{32}sdo^{33}ʔi^{2} ᎤᏛᏓᏍᏙᎢ

hi^{22}ya^{22}tv^{23}da^{32}sda^{2} (animate) ᎯᏯᏛᏓᏍᏓ

tsa^{2}tv^{23}da^{32}sda^{2} (inanimate) ᏣᏛᏓᏍᏓ

u^{22}tv^{23}da^{32}sdo^{3}hdi^{2} ᎤᏛᏓᏍᏙᏗ

forgetting

u^{21}wa^{22}ke^{22}wa^{0}sga^{2} ᎤᏩᎨᏩᏍᎦ one is forgetting

a^{21}gwv^{22}ke^{22}wa^{0}sga^{2} ᎠᏋᎨᏩᏍᎦ

u^{21}wa^{22}ke^{22}wa^{0}sv^{23}ʔi^{2} ᎤᏩᎨᏩᏍᏒᎢ
u^{21}wa^{22}ke^{22}wa^{0}sgo^{33}ʔi^{2} ᎤᏩᎨᏩᏍᎪᎢ
wi^{2}tsv^{22}ke^{23}wa^{2} ᏫᏨᎨᏩ
u^{22}wa^{22}ke^{23}hwa^{32}sdi^{23}ʔi^{2} ᎤᏩᎨᏩᏍᏗᎢ

belching/burping

u^{21}wa^{22}ku^{23}le^{32}ga^{2} ᎤᏩᎫᎴᎦ one is belching
a^{21}gi^{22}ku^{23}le^{32}ga^{2} ᎠᎩᎫᎴᎦ
u^{21}wa^{22}ku^{23}le^{32}tsv^{23}ʔi^{2} ᎤᏩᎫᎴᏨᎢ
u^{21}wa^{22}ku^{23}le^{32}go^{33}ʔi^{2} ᎤᏩᎫᎴᎪᎢ
tsa^{22}ku^{22}le^{11}gi^{2} ᏣᎫᎴᎩ
u^{22}wa^{22}ku^{23}le^{32}ʔi^{2}sdi^{23}ʔi^{2} ᎤᏩᎫᎴᎢᏍᏗᎢ

shivering

u^{21}wa^{33}na^{22}wi^{23}ʔa^{2} ᎤᏩᎾᏫᎠ one is shivering
tone initial vowel stem
a^{21}gi^{33}na^{22}wi^{23}ʔa^{2} ᎠᎩᎾᏫᎠ
u^{21}wa^{33}na^{22}wv^{23}ʔi^{2} ᎤᏩᎾᏮᎢ
u^{21}wa^{33}na^{22}wi^{22}sgo^{33}ʔi^{2} ᎤᏩᎾᏫᏍᎪᎢ
tsa^{11}na^{23}wa^{2} ᏣᎾᏩ
u^{22}wa^{11}na^{23}wi^{32}sdi^{23}ʔi^{2} ᎤᏩᎾᏫᏍᏗᎢ

being in a hurry

u^{21}wa^{22}nv^{33}ga^{2} ᎤᏩᏅᎦ one is in a hurry
a^{21}gwv^{22}nv^{33}ga^{2} ᎠᏋᏅᎦ
u^{21}wa^{22}nv^{33}gv^{23}ʔi^{2} ᎤᏩᏅᎬᎢ
u^{21}wa^{22}nv^{33}go^{33}ʔi^{2} ᎤᏩᏅᎪᎢ
tsv^{22}nv^{11}gi^{2} ᏨᏅᎩ
u^{22}wa^{22}nv^{11}sdi^{23}ʔi^{2} ᎤᏩᏅᏍᏗᎢ

smells it

u^{21}wa^{22}wa^{0}sv^{32}ga^{2} ᎤᏩᏩᏍᏒᎦ one smells it
a^{21}gi^{22}wa^{0}sv^{32}ga^{2} ᎠᎩᏩᏍᏒᎦ
u^{21}wa^{22}wa^{0}sv^{32}tsv^{23}ʔi^{2} ᎤᏩᏩᏒᏨᎢ

u^{21}wa^{22}wa^{0}sv^{32}go^{33}ʔi^{2} ᎤᏩᏩᏍᏒᎪᎢ

tsa^{22}wa^{0}sv^{11}gi^{2} ᏣᏩᏒᎩ

u^{22}wa^{22}wa^{0}sv^{11}sdi^{23}ʔi^{2} ᎤᏩᏩᏍᏒᏍᏗᎢ

having it (a long object)

u^{21}wa^{23}ya^{2} ᎤᏩᏯ one has it (a long object)

a^{21}gwv^{23}ya^{2} ᎠᏋᏯ

u^{21}wa^{33}yv^{23}ʔi^{2} ᎤᏩᏴᎢ

u^{21}wa^{33}yo^{33}ʔi^{2} ᎤᏩᏲᎢ

tsv^{33}ye^{33}sdi^{2} ᏨᏰᏍᏗ

u^{22}wa^{23}yv^{0}hdi^{23}ʔi^{2} ᎤᏩᏴᏗᎢ

being in pain/hurting

u^{21}we^{22}hi^{2}sda^{32}ne^{23}ha^{2} ᎤᏪᎯᏍᏓᏁᎭone is in pain or hurting

a^{21}gwe^{22}ʔi^{2}sda^{32}ne^{23}ha^{2} ᎠᏇᎢᏍᏓᏁᎭ

u^{21}we^{22}hi^{2}sda^{32}ne^{22}lv^{23}ʔi^{2} ᎤᏪᎯᏍᏓᏁᎸᎢ

u^{21}we^{22}hi^{2}sda^{32}ne^{22}ho^{33}ʔi^{2} ᎤᏪᎯᏍᏓᏁᎰᎢ

tse^{22}hi^{2}sda^{11}si^{2} ᏤᎯᏍᏓᏏ

u^{22}we^{22}hi^{2}sda^{11}ne^{3}hdi^{2} ᎤᏪᎯᏍᏓᏁᏗ

yelling/screaming

u^{21}we^{22}hlu^{3}hga^{2} ᎤᏪᏡᎦ one is yelling, screaming, etc.

a^{21}gwe^{22}hlu^{3}hga^{2} ᎠᏇᏡᎦ

u^{21}we^{22}hlu^{2}hnv^{23}ʔi^{2} ᎤᏪᏡᏅᎢ

u^{21}we^{22}hlu^{2}hgo^{33}ʔi^{2} ᎤᏪᏡᎪᎢ

he^{22}hlu^{2}hv^{11}ga^{2} ᎮᏡᎲᎦ

u^{22}we^{22}hlu^{2}hv^{3}sdi^{23}ʔi^{2} ᎤᏪᏡᎲᏍᏗᎢ

having it (a living being)

u^{21}wa^{22}ka^{3}ha^{2} ᎤᏩᎧᎭ one has it (a living being)

a^{21}gi^{22}ka^{3}ha^{2} ᎠᎩᎧᎭ

u^{21}wa^{22}ka^{2}hv^{23}ʔi^{2} ᎤᏩᎧᎲᎢ

u^{21}wa^{22}ka^{2}ho^{33}ʔi^{2} ᎤᏩᎧᎰᎢ

tsa^{22}ka^{2}he^{33}sdi^{2} ᏣᎧᎮᏍᏗ

u^{22}wa^{22}ka^{0}sdi^{23}ʔi^{2} or u^{22}we^{22}ka^{0}sdi^{23}ʔi^{2} ᎤᏩᎧᏍᏗᎢ

being worried/anxious

u^{21}we^{22}li^{23}hi^{3}ʔa^{2} ᎤᏪᎵᎯᎠ one is worried or anxious

a^{21}gwe^{22}li^{23}hi^{3}ʔa^{2} ᎠᏇᎵᎯᎠ

u^{21}we^{22}li^{23}hi^{32}sgv^{23}ʔi^{2} ᎤᏪᎵᎯᏍᎬᎢ

u^{21}we^{22}li^{23}hi^{32}sgo^{33}ʔi^{2} ᎤᏪᎵᎯᏍᎪᎢ

wi^{2}tse^{22}li^{23}hi^{2} ᏫᏤᎵᎯ

u^{22}we^{22}li^{23}hi^{3}sdi^{23}ʔi^{2} ᎤᏪᎵᎯᏍᏗᎢ

confident/believing

u^{21}wo^{22}hi^{2}yu^{33}ha^{2} ᎤᏬᎯᏳᎭ one is confident or one believes so

a^{21}gwo^{22}hi^{2}yu^{33}ha^{2} ᎠᏉᎯᏳᎭ

u^{21}wo^{22}hi^{2}yu^{33}sv^{23}ʔi^{2} ᎤᏬᎯᏳᏒᎢ

u^{21}wo^{22}hi^{2}yu^{33}so^{33}ʔi^{2} ᎤᏬᎯᏳᏐᎢ

tso^{2}hi^{2}yu^{33}se^{33}sdi^{2} ᏦᎯᏳᏎᏍᏗ

u^{22}wo^{22}hi^{2}yu^{0}hdi^{23}ʔi^{2} ᎤᏬᎯᏳᏗᎢ

sitting

u^{21}wo^{23}hla^{2} ᎤᏬᎳ one is sitting

a^{21}gwo^{23}hla^{2} ᎠᏉᎳ

u^{21}wo^{22}hlv^{23}ʔi^{2} ᎤᏬᎸᎢ

u^{21}wo^{22}hlo^{33}ʔi^{2} ᎤᏬᎶᎢ

tso^{23}hla^{2} ᏦᏝ

u^{22}wo^{22}hlv^{0}hdi^{23}ʔi^{2} ᎤᏬᎸᏗᎢ

laughing

u^{21}ye^{22}ti^{0}sga^{2} ᎤᏰᏘᏍᎦ one is laughing

a^{21}gi^{2}ye^{22}ti^{0}sga^{2} ᎠᎩᏰᏘᏍᎦ

u^{21}ye^{22}ti^{0}sgv^{23}ʔi^{2} ᎤᏰᏘᏍᎬᎢ

u^{21}ye^{22}ti^{0}sgo^{33}ʔi^{2} ᎤᏰᏘᏍᎪᎢ

tsa^{2}ye^{23}ti^{0}sa^{2} ᏣᏰᏘᏍᏌ

u^{22}ye^{22}ti^{0}sdi^{23}ʔi^{2} ᎤᏰᏘᏍᏗᎢ

itching

u^{21}yo^{22}de^{33}ʔa^{2} ᎤᏲᏕᎠ one is itching

a^{21}gi^{2}yo^{22}de^{33}ʔa^{2} ᎠᎩᏲᏕᎠ

u^{21}yo^{22}de^{33}sgv^{23}ʔi^{2} ᎤᏲᏕᏍᎬᎢ

u^{21}yo^{22}de^{33}sgo^{33}ʔi^{2} ᎤᏲᏕᏍᎪᎢ

tsa^{2}yo^{22}de^{2}gi^{2} ᏣᏲᏕᎩ

u^{22}yo^{22}de^{11}sdi^{23}ʔi^{2} ᎤᏲᏕᏍᏗᎢ

losing it

u^{21}yo^{22}hu^{33}se^{23}ha^{2} ᎤᏲᎱᏍᏎᎭ one is losing it

a^{21}gi^{2}yo^{22}hu^{33}se^{23}ha^{2} ᎠᎩᏲᎱᏍᏎᎭ

u^{21}yo^{22}hu^{33}se^{22}lv^{23}ʔi^{2} ᎤᏲᎱᏍᏎᎸᎢ

u^{21}yo^{22}hu^{33}se^{22}ho^{33}ʔi^{2} ᎤᏲᎱᏍᏎᎰᎢ

tsa^{2}yo^{22}hu^{23}si^{2} ᏣᏲᎱᏍᏏ

u^{22}yo^{22}hu^{23}se^{3}hdi^{23}ʔi^{2} ᎤᏲᎱᏍᏎᏗᎢ

being hungry

u^{22}yo^{33}si^{23}ha^{2} ᎤᏲᏍᏏᎭ one is hungry

'customarily again' conditional suffix

a^{21}gi^{2}yo^{33}si^{23}ha^{2} ᎠᎩᏲᏍᏏᎭ

u^{21}yo^{33}si^{23}sa^{3}hnv^{23}ʔi^{2} ᎤᏲᏍᏏᏍᏌᏅᎢ

u^{21}yo^{33}si^{22}sgo^{33}ʔi^{2} ᎤᏲᏍᏏᏍᎪᎢ

tsa^{2}yo^{11}si^{23}sa^{2} ᏣᏲᏍᏏᏍᏌ

u^{22}yo^{11}si^{23}so^{3}hdi^{23}ʔi^{2} ᎤᏲᏍᏏᏍᏐᏗᎢ

sending it (a long object)

wa^{2}di^{3}ʔa^{2} ᏩᏗᎠ one is sending it (a long object)

wi^{2}tsi^{2}di^{3}ʔa^{2} ᏫᏥᏗᎠ

wu^{21}dv^{23}ʔi^{2} ᏭᏛᎢ

wa^{2}di^{32}sgo^{33}ʔi^{2} ᏩᏗᏍᎪᎢ

wi^{2}hi^{2}da^{2} or hwi^{2}da^{2} ᏫᎯᏓ

wu^{22}di^{11}sdi^{23}ʔi^{2} ᏭᏗᏍᏗᎢ

sending it (neutral)

wa^{2}hv^{3}sga^{2} ᏩᏫᏍᎦ one is sending it

wi^{2}tsi^{2}ʔv^{3}sga^{2} ᏫᏥᎥᏍᎦ

wu^{21}hnv^{23}ʔi^{2} ᏭᏅᎢ

wa^{2}hv^{3}sgo^{33}ʔi^{2} ᏩᏫᏍᎪᎢ

wi^{2}hi^{2}hv^{32}ga^{2} ᏫᎯᏫᎦ

or hwi^{2}hv^{32}ga^{2}

wu^{2}hdi^{23}ʔi^{2} ᏭᏗᎢ

heading there

wa^{21}ga^{0}ti^{23}ha^{2} ᏩᎦᏘᎭ one is heading there

wi^{2}tsi^{2}ga^{11}ti^{23}ha^{2} ᏫᏥᎦᏘᎭ

wa^{21}ga^{0}tv^{23}ʔi^{2} ᏩᎦᏛᎢ

wa^{21}ga^{0}to^{33}ʔi^{2} ᏩᎦᏙᎢ

wi^{2}hi^{2}ga^{0}te^{33}sdi^{2} ᏫᎯᎦᏖᏍᏗ

wu^{22}wa^{22}ga^{0}tv^{0}hdi^{23}ʔi^{2} ᏭᏩᎦᏛᏘᎢ

sending/taking (a living being)

wi^{2}ga^{21}ka^{2}hv^{3}sga^{2} ᏫᎦᎧᏫᏍᎦ

one is sending another or taking another (a living being)

wi^{2}tsi^{22}ya^{11}ka^{2}hv^{3}sga^{2} ᏫᏥᏯᎧᏫᏍᎦ

wu^{21}wa^{22}ka^{2}nv^{23}ʔi^{2} ᏭᏩᎧᏅᎢ

wi^{2}ga^{22}ka^{2}hv^{2}sgo^{33}ʔi^{2} ᏫᎦᎧᏫᏍᎪᎢ

wi^{2}hi^{22}ya^{22}ka^{2}hv^{11}ga^{2} ᏫᎯᏯᎧᏫᎦ

wu^{22}wa^{22}ka^{2}ho^{2}hdi^{23}ʔi^{2} ᏭᏩᎧᎰᏘᎢ

sending/taking (a liquid)

wi^{2}ga^{2}ne^{33}hv^{2}sga^{2} ᏫᎦᏁᏫᏍᎦ one is sending or taking it (a liquid)

wi^{2}tsi^{2}ne^{33}ʔv^{2}sga^{2} ᏫᏥᏁᎥᏍᎦ

wu^{21}ne^{22}hnv^{23}ʔi^{2} ᏭᏁᏅᎢ

wi^{2}ga^{2}ne^{33}hv^{2}sgo^{33}ʔi^{2} ᏫᎦᏁᎲᏍᎪᎢ

wi^{2}hi^{2}ne^{33}hv^{11}ga^{2} ᏫᎯᏁᎲᎦ

wu^{22}ne^{2}hdi^{23}ʔi^{2} ᏭᏁᏗᎢ

sending/taking (a flexible object)

wi^{2}ga^{2}nv^{33}ʔv^{2}sga^{2} ᏫᎦᏅᎥᏍᎦ one is sending or taking it (a flexible object)

wi^{2}tsi^{2}nv^{33}ʔv^{2}sga^{2} ᏫᏥᏅᎥᏍᎦ

wu^{21}nv^{33}nv^{23}ʔi^{2} ᏭᏅᏅᎢ

wi^{2}ga^{2}nv^{33}ʔv^{2}sgo^{33}ʔi^{2} ᏫᎦᏅᎥᏍᎪᎢ

wi^{2}hi^{2}nv^{3}ʔv^{11}ga^{2} ᏫᎯᏅᎥᎦ

wu^{22}nv^{11}di^{23}ʔi^{2} ᏭᏅᏗᎢ

going out of sight

wu^{21}de^{23}li^{32}ga^{2} ᏭᏕᎵᎦ one or it is going out of sight

wa^{21}gwa^{2}de^{23}li^{32}ga^{2} ᏩᏆᏕᎵᎦ

wu^{21}de^{23}li^{32}tsv^{23}ʔi^{2} ᏭᏕᎵᏨᎢ

wu^{21}de^{23}li^{32}go^{33}ʔi^{2} ᏭᏕᎵᎪᎢ

wi^{2}tsa^{2}de^{22}li^{11}gi^{2} ᏫᏣᏕᎵᎩ

wu^{22}de^{23}li^{32}sdi^{23}ʔi^{2} ᏭᏕᎵᏍᏗᎢ

VERB TABLE. INCOMPLETIVE

Prefix	Pronoun A	Pronoun B	Infix	Root	Root Suffix	Condition	Time	Suffix
y(i^{2}), i^{22}	g, tsi^{22}	a^{21}gw, a^{21}gi^{2},	a^{22}d, a^{22}da^{22}, a^{22}da^{22}d		ʔ	-i^{23}si^{3}(^{2})ha^{2}, -i^{23}si^{32}sg- AGAIN	-a^{2}, -i^{2} PRESENT, IMPER., IMMED.	s, x^{23}tsu^{3}, x^{3}ke^{3}, sgo^{21} QUESTION
ts(i^{2})	i^{21}n, i^{21}ni^{22}	gi^{2}n, gi^{2}ni^{22}	a^{22}l(i^{2}), a^{2}li^{11}		h	-i^{23}lo^{3}(^{2})ʔa^{2}, -i^{23}lo^{32}sg - REPEAT	-v^{23}ʔi^{2} PAST	sgo^{21}hv^{2} BUT IS
w(i^{2})	o^{21}sd, o^{21}sdi^{22}	o^{21}gi^{2}n, o^{21}gi^{2}ni^{2} ^{2}			s	-do^{3}hdi^{3}(^{3})ha^{2}, -do^{3}hdi^{32}sg- ACCIDENTAL	-o^{33}ʔi^{2}, -o^{3}ʔi^{2} USUALLY	gwu^{3}(^{3}), wu^{3}(^{3}) JUST/ONLY
n(i^{2})	i^{21}d, i^{21}di^{22},	i^{21}g, i^{21}gi^{22}			ts	-o^{23}hv^{3}sga^{2}, -o^{23}hv^{3}sg- FINISHING	-e^{33}ʔi^{2}, -e^{3}ʔi^{2} RUMOR	le^{2} yi^{2}gi^{2} OR
d(e^{33})/di^{22}	o^{21}ts, o^{21}tsi^{22}	o^{21}g, o^{21}gi^{22}				-i^{23}do^{32}ha^{2}, -i^{23}do^{32}h- PLACE-TO-PLACE	-e^{33}sdi^{2} WILL BE	dv^{33} DEFINITELY
da^{2} (FUT), dv^{2} (FUT), da^{2}y (FUT)	h, hi^{22}	ts, tsa^{2}				-e^{33}ga^{2}, -e^{33}g- GOING		na^{3} HOW ABOUT
d (TOW), da^{2} (TOW), dv^{22} (TOW),	sd, sdi^{22}	sd, sdi^{22}				-i^{33}ga^{2}, -i^{23}hi^{3}h- COME TO DO		hno^{33}, hno^{3} hnv^{3},

da^{2}y (TOW), di^{22} (TOW), ts (TOW)								hnv^{32}, AND/ALSO he^{33}hno^{3}, he^{33}hn(o^{3}), BECAUSE hye^{33}hno^{3}, hye^{33}hn(o^{3}) THEREFORE
di^{2} (AWAY)	i^{21}ts, i^{21}tsi^{22}	i^{21}ts, i^{21}tsi^{22}				-i^{44}di^{2}(ha^{2}), -i^{23}di^{32}sg- ABOUT TO		sgi^{2}ni^{2}, sgi^{2}n(i^{2}) BUT
i^{22}x^{3}/i^{3}ʔ	g, a^{21}, ga^{21}	u^{21}, u^{21}w				-v^{22}hv^{3}sga^{2}, -v^{22}hv^{3}sg- TAKING TIME		do^{23}ka^{3}, ka^{3}, do^{23}hv^{32} AIN'T IT SO?
ga^{22}		u^{21}n, u^{21}ni^{22}				-o^{32}ga^{2}, -o^{32}g- BECOMING		gi^{2} CLARIFIER
e^{22}								di^{44}na^{2} UNTIL THEN
								yo^{21} GUESSING
								di^{23}hv^{32} SO THEN
								e^{33}ga^{2} CERTAINLY

VERB TABLE. COMPLETIVE STEM

Prefix	Pronoun		Infix	Root	Root Suffix	Condition	Time	Suffix
	A	B						
y(i^{2}), i^{22}	g, tsi^{22}	a^{21}gw, a^{21}gi^{2},	a^{22}d, a^{22}da^{22}, a^{22}da^{22}d		ʔ	-i^{23}sa^{3}hn- AGAIN	-a^{2}, -i^{2} PRESENT, IMPER., IMMED.	s, x^{23}tsu^{3}, x^{3}ke^{3}, sgo^{21} QUESTION
ts(i^{2})	i^{21}n, i^{21}ni^{22}	gi^{2}n, gi^{2}ni^{22}	a^{22}l(i^{2}), a^{2}li^{11}		h	-i^{23}lo^{32}ts- REPEAT	-v^{23}ʔi^{2} PAST	sgo^{21}hv^{2} BUT IS
w(i^{2})	o^{21}sd, o^{21}sdi^{22}	o^{21}gi^{2}n, o^{21}gi^{2}ni^{2} ^{2}			s	-do^{3}hta^{2}n- ACCIDENTAL	-o^{33}ʔi^{2}, -o^{3}ʔi^{2} USUALLY	gwu^{3}(^{3}), wu^{3}(^{3}) JUST/ONLY
n(i^{2})	i^{21}d, i^{21}di^{22},	i^{21}g, i^{21}gi^{22}			ts	-o^{3}hn- FINISHING	-e^{33}ʔi^{2}, -e^{3}ʔi^{2} RUMOR	le^{2} yi^{2}gi^{2} OR
d(e^{33})/di^{22}	o^{21}ts, o^{21}tsi^{22}	o^{21}g, o^{21}gi^{22}				-i^{23}da^{32}l- PLACE-TO-PLACE	-e^{33}sdi^{2} WILL BE	dv^{33} DEFINITELY
da^{2} (FUT), dv^{2} (FUT), da^{2}y (FUT)	h, hi^{22}	ts, tsa^{2}				-v^{33}s- GOING		na^{3} HOW ABOUT
d (TOW), da^{2} (TOW), dv^{22} (TOW), da^{2}y (TOW),	sd, sdi^{22}	sd, sdi^{22}				-i^{23}hl- COME TO DO		hno^{33}, hno^{3} hnv^{3}, hnv^{32},

di^{22} (TOW), ts (TOW)								AND/ALSO he^{33}hno^{3}, he^{33}hn(o^{3}), BECAUSE hye^{33}hno^{3}, hye^{33}hn(o^{3}) THEREFORE
di^{2} (AWAY)	i^{21}ts, i^{21}tsi^{22}	i^{21}ts, i^{21}tsi^{22}				-i^{23}di^{32}s- ABOUT TO		sgi^{2}ni^{2}, sgi^{2}n(i^{2}) BUT
i^{22}x^{3}/i^{3}?	g, a^{21}, ga^{21}	u^{21}, u^{21}w				-v^{22}hn- TAKING TIME		do^{23}ka^{3}, ka^{3}, do^{23}hv^{32} AIN'T IT SO?
ga^{22}		u^{21}n, u^{21}ni^{22}				-o^{22}ts- BECOMING		gi^{2} CLARIFIER
e^{22}								di^{44}na^{2} UNTIL THEN
								yo^{21} GUESSING
								di^{23}hv^{32} SO THEN
								e^{33}ga^{2} CERTAINLY

VERB TABLE. IMMEDIATE STEM

Prefix	Pronoun		Infix	Root	Root Suffix	Condition	Time	Suffix
	A	B						
$y(i^{2})$, i^{22}	g, tsi^{22}	$a^{21}gw$, $a^{21}gi^{2}$,	$a^{22}d$, $a^{22}da^{22}$, $a^{22}da^{22}d$		g	$-i^{23}sa^{2}$- AGAIN	$-a^{2}$, $-i^{2}$ PRESENT, IMPER., IMMED.	s, $x^{23}tsu^{3}$, $x^{3}ke^{3}$, sgo^{21} QUESTION
$ts(i^{2})$	$i^{21}n$, $i^{21}ni^{22}$	$gi^{2}n$, $gi^{2}ni^{22}$	$a^{22}l(i^{2})$, $a^{2}li^{11}$		n	$-i^{22}lo^{23}tsa^{2}$ REPEAT	$-v^{23}ʔi^{2}$ PAST	$sgo^{21}hv^{2}$ BUT IS
$w(i^{2})$	$o^{21}sd$, $o^{21}sdi^{22}$	$o^{21}gi^{2}n$, $o^{21}gi^{2}ni^{22}$			Ø	$-do^{3}hda^{2}$ ACCIDENTAL	$-o^{33}ʔi^{2}$, $-o^{3}ʔi^{2}$ USUALLY	$gwu^{3}(^{3})$, $wu^{3}(^{3})$ JUST/ONLY
$n(i^{2})$	$i^{21}d$, $i^{21}di^{22}$,	$i^{21}g$, $i^{21}gi^{22}$				$-o^{2}hna^{2}$ FINISHING	$-e^{33}ʔi^{2}$, $-e^{3}ʔi^{2}$ RUMOR	le^{2} $yi^{2}gi^{2}$ OR
$d(e^{33})/di^{22}$	$o^{21}ts$, $o^{21}tsi^{22}$	$o^{21}g$, $o^{21}gi^{22}$				$-i^{23}da^{2}$ PLACE-TO-PLACE	$-e^{33}sdi^{2}$ WILL BE	dv^{33} DEFINITELY
da^{2} (FUT), dv^{2} (FUT), $da^{2}y$ (FUT)	h, hi^{22}	ts, tsa^{2}				$-e^{33}na^{2}$, $-u^{11}ga^{2}$ GOING		na^{3} HOW ABOUT
d (TOW), da^{2} (TOW), dv^{22} (TOW), $da^{2}y$ (TOW),	sd, sdi^{22}	sd, sdi^{22}				$-i^{22}ga^{2}$ COME TO DO		hno^{33}, hno^{3} hnv^{3}, hnv^{32},

di^{22} (TOW), ts (TOW)								AND/ALSO $he^{33}hno^{3}$, $he^{33}hn(o^{3})$, BECAUSE $hye^{33}hno^{3}$, $hye^{33}hn(o^{3})$ THEREFORE
di^{2} (AWAY)	$i^{21}ts$, $i^{21}tsi^{22}$	$i^{21}ts$, $i^{21}tsi^{22}$				$-i^{22}de^{44}na^{2}$ ABOUT TO		$sgi^{2}ni^{2}$, $sgi^{2}n(i^{2})$ BUT
$i^{22}x^{3}/i^{3}ʔ$	g, a^{21}, ga^{21}	u^{21}, $u^{21}w$				$-v^{22}hv^{11}ga^{2}$ TAKING TIME		$do^{23}ka^{3}$, ka^{3}, $do^{23}hv^{32}$ AIN'T IT SO?
ga^{22}		$u^{21}n$, $u^{21}ni^{22}$				$-o^{11}gi^{2}$ BECOMING		gi^{2} CLARIFIER
e^{22}								$di^{44}na^{2}$ UNTIL THEN
								yo^{21} GUESSING
								$di^{23}hv^{32}$ SO THEN
								$e^{33}ga^{2}$ CERTAINLY

VERB TABLE. INFINITIVE STEM

Prefix	Pronoun		Infix	Root	Root Suffix	Condition	Time	Suffix
	A	B						
y(i^{2}), i^{22}	g, tsi^{22}	a^{21}gw, a^{21}gi^{2},	a^{22}d, a^{22}da^{22}, a^{22}da^{22}d		h	-i^{23}so^{3}hdi^{2} AGAIN	-a^{2}, -i^{2} PRESENT, IMPER., IMMED.	s, x^{23}tsu^{3}, x^{3}ke^{3}, sgo^{21} QUESTION
ts(i^{2})	i^{21}n, i^{21}ni^{22}	gi^{2}n, gi^{2}ni^{22}	a^{22}l(i^{2}), a^{2}li^{11}		s	-i^{23}lo^{32}sdi^{2} REPEAT	-v^{23}ʔi^{2} PAST	sgo^{21}hv^{2} BUT IS
w(i^{2})	o^{21}sd, o^{21}sdi^{22}	o^{21}gi^{2}n, o^{21}gi^{2}ni^{2} ^{2}				-do^{3}hdi^{2} ACCIDENTAL	-o^{33}ʔi^{2}, -o^{3}ʔi^{2} USUALLY	gwu^{3}(^{3}), wu^{3}(^{3}) JUST/ONLY
n(i^{2})	i^{21}d, i^{21}di^{22},	i^{21}g, i^{21}gi^{22}				-o^{3}hv^{3}sdi^{2} FINISHING	-e^{33}ʔi^{2}, -e^{3}ʔi^{2} RUMOR	le^{2} yi^{2}gi^{2} OR
d(e^{33})/di^{22}	o^{21}ts, o^{21}tsi^{22}	o^{21}g, o^{21}gi^{22}				-i^{23}da^{32}sdi^{2} PLACE-TO-PLACE	-e^{33}sdi^{2} WILL BE	dv^{33} DEFINITELY
da^{2} (FUT), dv^{2} (FUT), da^{2}y (FUT)	h, hi^{22}	ts, tsa^{2}				-v^{33}sdi^{2} GOING		na^{3} HOW ABOUT
d (TOW), da^{2} (TOW), dv^{22} (TOW), da^{2}y (TOW),	sd, sdi^{22}	sd, sdi^{22}				-i^{2}sdi^{2} COME TO DO		hno^{33}, hno^{3} hnv^{3}, hnv^{32},

di^{22} (TOW), ts (TOW)								AND/ALSO he^{33}hno^{3}, he^{33}hn(o^{3}), BECAUSE hye^{33}hno^{3}, hye^{33}hn(o^{3}) THEREFORE
di^{2} (AWAY)	i^{21}ts, i^{21}tsi^{22}	i^{21}ts, i^{21}tsi^{22}				-i^{22}d(vh)di^{2} ABOUT TO		sgi^{2}ni^{2}, sgi^{2}n(i^{2}) BUT
i^{22}x^{3}/i^{3}ʔ	g, a^{21}, ga^{21}	u^{21}, u^{21}w				-(v^{11})hdi TAKING TIME		do^{23}ka^{3}, ka^{3}, do^{23}hv^{32} AIN'T IT SO?
ga^{22}		u^{21}n, u^{21}ni^{22}				-o^{11}sdi BECOMING		gi^{2} CLARIFIER
e^{22}								di^{44}na^{2} UNTIL THEN
								yo^{21} GUESSING
								di^{23}hv^{32} SO THEN
								e^{33}ga^{2} CERTAINLY

Bibliography

Feeling, Durbin. 1975. Cherokee-English Dictionary. Tahlequah; Cherokee Nation of Oklahoma.

Made in the USA
Las Vegas, NV
14 January 2025